ZOOARCHAEOLOGY AND CONSERVATION BIOLOGY

Zooarchaeology and Conservation Biology

EDITED BY

R. LEE LYMAN AND

KENNETH P. CANNON

THE UNIVERSITY OF UTAH PRESS

Salt Lake City

09 08 07 06 05 04
5 4 3 2 1

Index prepared by Andrew L. Christenson

The Defiance House Man colophon is a registered trademark of The University of Utah Press. It is based upon a four-foot-tall, Ancient Puebloan pictograph (late PIII) near Glen Canyon, Utah.

Library of Congress Cataloging-in-Publication Data

Zooarchaeology and conservation biology / edited by R. Lee Lyman and Kenneth P. Cannon.
p. cm.
Includes bibliographical references and index.
ISBN 0-87480-801-4 (alk. paper)
1. Animal remains (Archaeology)—North America. 2. Conservation biology—North America. 3. North America—Antiquities.
I. Lyman, R. Lee. II. Cannon, Kenneth P.
CC79.5.A5Z65 2004
560'.45'097—dc22 2004010719

Contents

LIST OF FIGURES

LIST OF TABLES

Foreword

At last, a collection of essays that provides important examples of how the field of zooarchaeology can be applied to difficult problems in wildlife management and conservation biology. This collection offers the reader substantial insight into a field of science that can be used to incorporate a deep temporal perspective into management plans of, and recovery efforts for, biota that have been negatively influenced by human activities.

The distribution of animals varies across the landscape and changes through time. Although few would dispute this idea, until recently it was commonly ignored in wildlife science and management. Previously, ecosystems were envisioned mechanistically in terms of equilibrium conditions that vary around long-term means. Time frames of management rarely exceeded decades, and disturbances were viewed simply as disruptive events that moved a system away from equilibrium. In most cases restoration to equilibrium would be expected to occur following a relatively brief period of direct management manipulations and subsequent recovery.

The recent development of more contextualistic perspectives for resource management has resulted in efforts to maintain and restore processes and spatial and temporal relationships. Hierarchy theory, landscape ecology, and ecosystem management are rooted in this emerging perspective. In the past several decades there has been substantial progress in the potential to identify complex landscape patterns of animal distribution and the habitats that influence this distribution. For example, technological advances in remote sensing provide the means to view the landscape at a variety of scales, and with concomitant advances in the ability to process vast quantities of information, it is possible to examine features of the landscape from sites to continents. This shift in conceptualization and visualization provides scientists and managers with the ability to truly integrate spatial constraints into resource management.

Unfortunately, efforts to incorporate temporal change into resource management have lagged. Paleontologists were among the first to appreciate the importance of changes in climate and physical habitat to the distribution of animals; however, this information has rarely been used in practical management applications. Findings of recent climatological research underscore the critical need to incorporate a strong temporal perspective, but often the time frame is limited to the period of European influence in North America or, more frequently in the western United States, to the period of settlement that occurred in the later half of the 19th century.

Current crises in the decline of native biota and human attempts to reverse those trends underscore the need for a broader temporal perspective. Knowledge concerning the prehistoric ranges of specific taxa and the environments in which they evolved is critical to management efforts to reintroduce extirpated biota. Fortunately, this book contains specific examples of how zooarchaeological information can be used in these efforts. It is apparent that in some cases the ability for broad inference may be limited, but cases where samples are more numerous and spatially dispersed underscore the potential importance of the zooarchaeological approach. It is difficult to imagine that readers of this collection will not walk away with a new appreciation of the long-term temporal perspective and its utility in modern management and conservation issues. What were the native fauna? How were they distributed across the landscape? How were they influenced by the presence of humans prior to European settlement of North America? Answers to these questions can be found in the zooarchaeological record, and the chapters in this book exemplify the usefulness of this information for solving complicated problems associated with the management and conservation of species of special concern.

Robert E. Gresswell
U.S. Geological Survey
Forest and Rangeland Ecosystem Science Center
Corvallis, Oregon

Preface and Acknowledgments

R. Lee Lyman and Kenneth P. Cannon

Zooarchaeologists are in a unique position to move beyond the important anthropological and archaeological issues on which they focus and to broaden the scope of their inquiries to include issues that are today, and will in the future be, important to humanity. There is a little-explored avenue of zooarchaeological research that has been referred to as *applied zooarchaeology* that involves doing zooarchaeology in order to assist wildlife management and conservation biology. Many modern ecological problems facing humanity concern direct or indirect anthropogenic impacts on biological phenomena—destruction of the rain forest, decreasing harvests of marine fish, and the like. We believe that zooarchaeology has a major role to play in the resolution of these problems. Many zooarchaeologists know this, and so do some ecologists. But many do not, as evidenced by the near-total absence of applied zooarchaeological studies in major journals such as *Biological Conservation, Conservation Biology, Ecology, Ecological Applications, Ecological Monographs, Environmental Management, Oryx: The International Journal of Conservation,* and *Restoration and Management Notes.* A book presenting a series of case studies in applied zooarchaeology is, we think, an appropriate way to introduce the topic and will, we hope, result in similar publications in these and related journals.

Many nations have one or more forms of national park and game preserve. Modern efforts are geared toward managing these spatial units in such a manner as to protect in perpetuity the biota included within their boundaries. Sometimes attempts are made to enhance or modify the included biotas so that they reflect what are variously referred to as pristine ecosystems, wilderness, or native (preindustrial) or natural biotas. Further, most nations have various legal controls on the hunting and trapping of animal species and regarding which species can be harvested and which are to remain unmolested. Managing wildlife sometimes involves supplementing resident populations with individual organisms transplanted from elsewhere or attempting to reestablish species in areas where native populations were extirpated. With its unique perspective on the time depth of ecosystems and biotas, and their evolution and history, zooarchaeological research can be used to help ensure that the best-informed wildlife-management decisions are made and that well-informed efforts in conservation biology are undertaken.

This book comprises the argument that what is today often referred to as conservation biology or wildlife management can ill afford to ignore any data pertinent to making wise decisions regarding biological conservation and management. Some of those data derive from zooarchaeological research—the identification and analysis of faunal remains recovered from archaeological deposits. These data are particularly relevant to those who make decisions and write guidelines and policies for how extant biota will be used today and in the future. The data provided by zooarchaeological research are only obtainable by studying the past, and the past provides many important lessons on long-term human (and nonhuman) influences on biotas and ecosystems. It represents a set of previously undertaken laboratory experiments. As a result, from the perspective of long time spans provided by zooarchaeological research we can begin to understand the biogeographic dynamics of particular taxa and why they are present in some areas and not in others. We can determine past migration and behavioral patterns that are today invisible to the biologist who studies living organisms over the mere span of several years. These and many more reasons to develop an applied zooarchaeology are explored through the series of case studies presented in this collection. Our focus here is unabashedly on the faunal record, though we predict that future efforts at conservation biology, should they be informed by the studies in this book and related research, will eventually also incorporate paleoethnobotanical data as well.

We thank Jeff Grathwohl for his interest in this project, Robert Gresswell for his thoughts, and two anonymous reviewers for their many helpful comments. D. Glover provided advice on the preparation of the figures. M. J. O'Brien helped in several small but significant ways. Elisabeth A. Graves served as copy editor; we thank her for sharp eyes and a sharp pencil. Lyman thanks those who by example in the 20th century have shown the value of applied zooarchaeology. Cannon acknowledges those whose discussions over the years have helped to lead him down this intellectual path—Paul W. Parmalee, Walter E. Klippel, and Paul Schullery. Each in his own way has contributed to this work. Cannon also thanks Ralph Hartley for his support.

1

Applied Zooarchaeology, Because It Matters

R. Lee Lyman and Kenneth P. Cannon

A knowledge of local archeology and history should be a part of the ecologist's equipment.

—G. M. Day, "The Indian as an Ecological Factor in the Northeastern Forest" (1953:343)

At the beginning of the 21st century humanity faces a dilemma of its own creation. Global change wrought by a continuously growing and ever more resource-hungry human population is the most obvious symptom. The dilemma comprises the fact that the world's ecology is being anthropogenically altered, and it is unclear whether humans will be able to survive the alteration (Palumbi 2001; Vitousek et al. 1997). If we survive, what will our "quality of life" be like? Will there still be wild places to visit? Will people still be able to "get back to nature" on a weekend camping trip? Is the loss of biodiversity inevitable, and will such a loss be deleterious to ecosystem structure and function, as well as to humanity? These are pressing and significant questions, and this book is about one of the seldom-noted ways we can go about building answers to some of them. It grew from a discipline known as zooarchaeology—the study of animal remains recovered from archaeological excavations. We use the term *paleozoology* to refer to zooarchaeological and paleontological data.

During the early and middle decades of the 20th century Americanist ecologists and biologists explicitly noted the value of zooarchaeological data for addressing various wildlife-management concerns and conservation issues (Gilmore 1949; Wintemberg 1919). Over the next several decades virtually no one pursued this potential source of data with the explicit intention of addressing such concerns. In the middle of the 20th century a few biologists used zooarchaeological data to measure the influence of First American peoples on wildlife populations (Elder 1965;

Simenstad et al. 1978). At the same time, at least one paleobiologist suggested that Late Quaternary fossils should be consulted in the interests of conservation biology (Martin 1970), but most zooarchaeologists did not address what might be gained from applying their (or paleontological) data to biological conservation issues. Their silence with respect to the latter largely remained in the 1970s and 1980s, even though more zooarchaeologists turned from strictly archaeological and anthropological concerns to questions of prehistoric ecology and biogeography (Graham 1985; Grayson 1976, 1977, 1981; Gustafson 1968; Lyman 1983, 1986; Lyman and Livingston 1983; Parmalee et al. 1980, 1982). This turn spawned a new set of questions at the same time that the apparent crisis presented by an anthropogenically altered global ecology was becoming clear.

By the middle 1980s it had become obvious that paleozoological data, whether derived from archaeological or paleontological contexts, are valuable for the information they represent with respect to ecosystems and how those ecosystems have changed over time (Graham 1988, 1992; Grayson 1987; Livingston 1987; Lyman 1988a, 1988b; Parmalee and Klippel 1984), and these new research avenues came to be more frequently pursued. At the same time, ecologists began to ask paleozoologists to contribute what they knew to overviews of various taxa (Graham and Graham 1994) and of faunal-management problems (Graham 1992). A few years later, paleozoologists began to write explicitly about what their data indicate regarding prehistoric anthropogenic effects on ecosystems (Steadman 1995), and they began to argue with conservation biologists and wildlife managers about the significance of data on prehistoric conditions for making modern wildlife-management decisions (Houston and Schreiner 1995; Lyman 1994a; Scheffer 1993). Sometimes zooarchaeological data have suggested that prehistoric humans were an incredibly significant agent of ecological change in the past (Boesch et al. 2001; Grayson 2001; Kay 1994; Peterson et al. 2001), although this is clearly an empirical matter that must be evaluated on a case-by-case basis (see, e.g., the debate between Lyman [1988b, 1989, 1995c, 2003b] and Hildebrandt and Jones [1992, 2002; Jones and Hildebrandt 1995] and examples in Sarkar 1999).

Perhaps the most significant outgrowth of the new questions asked of faunal remains regarding the nature of prehistoric ecosystems has emerged in the last decade. During that time several zooarchaeologists offered explicit commentary about the value of their data to ecological management decisions, particularly those pertaining to faunas (Amorosi et al. 1996; Barker 1996; Grayson 2001; Livingston 1999; Lyman 1994a, 1996, 1998). It was with this recognition firmly in mind that we developed a plan to produce a book of case studies in which specific zooarchaeological data are brought to bear on particular ecosystem management concerns and conservation issues. Because the concerns and issues are as disparate as the faunal taxa involved, the book could not be authored by a single individual or even by several individuals. Rather, the requirements demanded that multiple authors—each with specific knowledge not only of a particular set of zooarchaeological data but also of a particular wildlife-management or conservation biology issue—be asked to contribute. Many of the following chapters were originally solicited for presentation at the 67th Annual Meeting of the Society for American Archaeology in Denver (March 2002). Additional essays were solicited to increase geographic, taxonomic, and topical coverage.

Authors were instructed to identify a management issue of concern, to describe and analyze relevant zooarchaeological data, and to offer recommendations as to possible resolutions of the management or conservation issue. Authors were to specify how prehistoric data might make for better-informed decisions regarding faunal ecosystem maintenance or restoration. Simply stating in an essay that zooarchaeological data are relevant to a conservation problem was an insufficient warrant for its inclusion here. Similarly, simply documenting that the structure of a prehistoric ecosystem was different from a modern one was insufficient. Some of the following chapters specify a pressing and particularistic management or conservation problem. The authors of these chapters react to those problems by outlining potential management efforts that zooarchaeological data suggest will produce the desired solution. Other chapters are more proactive in the sense that a pressing critical problem is not identified but, rather, one or more management concerns that do not yet require immediate attention are described and possible ways to resolve those concerns are derived from relevant zooarchaeological data. We believe that such reactive and proactive uses, respectively, of paleozoology's unique data are equally pertinent to modern conservation biology. And we contend that it would be a sad state of affairs indeed were all management efforts simply reactions to immediate crises.

We are archaeologists by training, and we have found this chapter equally exciting and challenging to write. This is so because we have had to walk a fine line between offending and patronizing either or both conservation biologists and zooarchaeologists. Despite our efforts, we will probably do a bit of both with respect to both sets of professionals. This is not a book of case studies aimed at archaeologists, although we think that they and other paleoecologists will find some things of interest. Our introduction, for example, is written largely with paleoecologists rather than environmental managers and conservationists in mind. The latter may therefore find it sophomoric or pedantic, but we offer it in the hope that it will provide insight to what at least some paleoecologists think about how paleoecological data can be applied in modern management settings. It can also serve as a primer for paleozoologists who are unfamiliar with the basics of conservation biology and wildlife management. This is a book about past ecosystems, particularly the faunal aspects of them, and how knowledge of those ecosystems is of value to those who contend with global change. The chapters are in no topical order; all of them are equally important and significant, so they are presented in the order of the authors' alphabetized names.

This book is not a set of case studies that can be categorized within the field known among anthropologists, geographers, and environmental historians as historical ecology (Balée 1998; Crumley 1994b). That field focuses on the fact that humans, throughout their history on the planet, have not just adapted to the earth's various environments but, rather, there has been a dialectic, a constant interaction between human cultures as adaptive systems and nature (Crumley 1994a). Each influences and responds to the other. Anthropologists have long recognized that this interaction has been ongoing virtually since our early hominid ancestors used culture (tools and learned behaviors) as a nongenetic means of adaptation (e.g., Heizer 1955), but until recently the basic notion has been that humanity's influence on the environment was minimal until, say, the last several thousand years; we now know that this is simply false (Redman 1999). Culture, no matter how primitive or sophisticated, is modified in response to environmental change, and environments are in turn modified to one degree or another by human-wielded culture. The literature on this topic is increasingly large, but to briefly summarize the underlying epistemology, the historical ecology viewpoint has made explicit the fact that modern environments are historical phenomena; they are a function of historical and evolutionary events and the order in which they have occurred (e.g., Russell 2003; Winterhalder 1994). Applied zooarchaeology explicitly adopts this epistemology and similarly explicitly acknowledges the anthropogenic effects of humans on environments, particularly the faunal portion of the environment. But applied zooarchaeology also goes beyond documenting the history of the dialectic between humans and the environments in which they live and attempts to use that historical knowledge to assist in ensuring the future of both humanity and the environment (Lyman 1996).

All studies included here are based on data from North America because that is the area where we work; we are familiar with the biology and geography, and we know many potential contributors working on the continent. Despite this geographic focus, we believe that we have compiled a number of exemplary contributions to what has been termed "applied zooarchaeology" (Lyman 1996). We agree completely with the implications of the title of Virginia Butler and Michael Delacorte's contribution (chap. 2) but have altered it a bit for the title to this introductory chapter. Not only *might* zooarchaeology matter in arenas other than archaeology, it simply *does* matter in many cases; and this constitutes the short description of applied zooarchaeology as well as the goal of this book—to show that zooarchaeological research *matters*. Later in this chapter we outline what exactly applied zooarchaeology entails by providing an overview of some of the kinds of issues that can be addressed under this rubric. First, however, it is necessary to consider several conceptual issues that are critical to the discussions found in all of the chapters. Some of the following will seem simplistic and superficial to resource managers, but paleoecologists and zooarchaeologists are not always familiar with the nuances of conservation biology. What follows is our take on some of those nuances.

CONCEPTUAL ISSUES

Various concepts must be clearly and explicitly defined if we are to determine what ecological restoration and ecosystem health comprise (Anderson and Dugger 1998; Falk 1990; Higg 1997; Huff 1997; Rees 2001; Scherer 1994; Smith et al. 1993; Stanturf et al. 1998; T. Young 2000). Conservation biologists do not always agree on basic ecological concepts within their own discipline (Angermeier and Karr 1994; Hall et al. 1997; Sarkar 1999). Two fundamental problems therefore attend various key concepts that underpin conservation biology and wildlife management, concepts such as sustainability, conservation, preservation, biodiversity, and integrity (of ecosystems). First, the concepts attending conservation are variously value laden (Callicott and Mumford 1997; Jepson and Canney 2003; Lélé and Norgaard 1996; Ludwig et al. 2001). The source of the value can reside in ecological or biological theory, the economics of resource exploitation, a personal or policy-dictated vision of "nature" or "natural," or some combination of these or other ecological, social, political, and economic variables (Bennett 1994; Doak and Mills 1994; Hull et al. 2003; Lawton 1997; Meffe and Viederman 1995). A recent book refers to these aspects of conservation biology as "political ecology," defined as those instances when ecological data are selected "to support preordained philosophical values or political agendas" (Kay and Simmons 2002a:xiv–xv).

The second problem is intimately related to the first and comprises the fact that there are no generally agreed-on definitions for many key conservation concepts precisely because virtually any definition carries with it some implied value (Angermeier 1992; Callicott et al. 1999; Hull et al. 2003; Margules and Pressey 2000; Noss 1983, 1990). An excellent example of the context-specific nature of the value concept resides in changes in the management goals of national parks in the United States. These changes have tracked shifting sociopolitical climates as well as modifications in ecological theory and resulted in alterations to various policies and management activities over the nearly 100 years the National Park Service has been in existence (McClelland 1998; Sellars 1997; Wagner et al. 1995; Zube 1996). For example, the bison herd of Yellowstone National Park was rescued from near extinction when the park was created in the late 19th century. Management initially involved keeping the local native herd separate from another herd made up of bison procured from private herds. These two herds were eventually allowed to interbreed, and as the total population grew, culling became a common practice. In response to the Leopold Report (Leopold et al. 1963)—one of the founding documents of modern wildlife management—Yellowstone managers shifted policies dramatically and adopted a noninterventionist approach to natural resource management. Park managers and wildlife personnel now rely on natural processes to effect change and control the sizes of bison and other wildlife populations (Keiter 1997; Schullery et al. 1998). This "natural regulation" of wildlife populations has been referred to as the "great experiment" by some Park Service personnel, and over the past decade it has come under critical scrutiny (Wagner et al. 1995).

It is not our intent in this book to resolve slippery and often contentious terminological and conceptual issues, let alone policy issues. The reality of conservation biology simply is that multiple factions have varied interests in the outcome of management efforts. Hunters will want a population with maximum harvest potential—that is, large—and a high proportion of trophy animals. Farmers may want small populations that cause minimal damage to crops and fences and which do not compete for open grazing range with livestock. Avocational naturalists and wildlife photographers may want many animals to observe and photograph closeup in nonurban settings. City dwellers will likely not want wild animals in their backyards or on the highway to the office. These and a plethora of other conflicting values, not to mention the shortages of funding and personnel, make conservation biology a challenge, and we do not envy those who have chosen it as a way to make a living.

Given the geographic focus of this book on North America, there is one concept that warrants detailed consideration. Discussions of what exactly a "natural" or "pristine" ecosystem—sometimes termed "wilderness"—comprises have occupied much space in various publications (Anderson 1991; Angermeier 2000; Callicott 1995; Dobb 1992; Foreman 1995; Guthrie 1971; Hoerr 1993; Hunter 1996; Landres et al. 2001; Lowenthal 1964; Maser 1990; Noss 1995b; Povilitis 2002; Scott 2002; Sloan 2002; Truett 1996; Wagner et al. 1995). Wildlife biologists in particular have grappled with conceptions of pristine/natural (Houston and Schreiner 1995; Meine 1999; see also the essays introduced by Flores and Bolen 1995). Although it was recognized much earlier (Day 1953), over the past two decades or so an increasing number of geographers, historians, and biologists have acknowledged that there is no post-Pleistocene (< 10,000-year-old) ecosystem or landscape in North (or South) America that is natural or pristine in the sense of simultaneously being both immediately pre- or post-Columbian and unmodified by human activities (Bonnicksen 1989; Denevan 1992; Gómez-Pompa and Kaus 1992; Rolston 2001; Schullery 2001; Shrader-Frechette and McCoy 1995; Sprugel 1991; Vale 1998; Wright 1974; see also the chapters in Kay and Simmons 2002b).

The initial goal is to identify an ecosystem that management and conservation efforts then seek to re-create and maintain. It is thus critical to recognize that as time passes, ecosystems change for myriad reasons other than (as well as in addition to) human or anthropogenic influences (Botkin 2001; Dickinson 1995; Lawton 1997; Sprugel 1991; Todd and Elmore 1997). Most of our perceptions of ecosystems come from post-Columbian observations, and much of what has been perceived during the last 500 years is a result of climatic history (Hewitt 2000). Three significant changes in North American ecosystems are known to be the direct result of Euro-American colonization of the continent. One change resulted from the fur trade that decimated some populations of beaver (*Castor canadensis* [Johnson and Chance 1974]), sea otter (*Enhydra lutris* [Ogden 1933]), and other fur-bearing taxa in the late 18th and early 19th centuries. In this case, of course, Euro-Americans often had the help—sometimes willing, sometimes coerced—of First American peoples. The horse *(Equus caballus)* was introduced to North America in the 17th and 18th centuries (Haines 1938a, 1938b); this resulted in significant changes not only to First American cultures but also to ecosystems, as horses competed with native ungulates for forage. The third change involved the introduction of European diseases that abruptly decimated populations of First Americans (for introductory discussions, see Black 1992; Meltzer 1992; Thornton 1997); this altered (human) predator–prey relationships, and in some cases prey populations increased, apparently as a result of decreased human predation (Butler 2000b).

People have been present in North America for more than 10,000 years. Nevertheless, awareness of Euro-American influences on the landscape prompts some to suggest that a pre-Columbian or near-Columbian contact-era ecosystem is desirable (Anderson 1996; Bonnicksen and Stone 1985; Egan and Howell 2001; Jordan 1999; Sprugel 1991). To be accurate, this means that either one must assume that there were no pre-Columbian anthropogenic influences on ecosystems—a notion we find patently absurd—or one must replicate First American influences on ecosystems (Parsons et al. 1986). The latter begs the question of which influences: the ones 10,000 years ago, 5,000 years ago, 1,000 years ago, or 500 years ago? The latter also means that we must be able to sort out anthropogenic influences from climatically driven ones among the various paleoecological records available, for climates have fluctuated considerably during the last 10,000 years or what is known as the Holocene, or Recent, epoch (Bartlein et al. 1998).

One might argue that the ecosystems dating prior to human colonization of the Americas are the ones to use as ecological baselines (Flannery 2001), but this not only ignores the significant differences between terminal Pleistocene environments and modern environments irrespective of human influences; it is also naive with respect to the major social and political changes that would have to attend the adoption of such baseline conditions (Willers 2002). Despite such difficulties, some paleoecologists continue to make this argument (Burney et al. 2002; Martin and Burney 1999). Recognizing such difficulties, some characterize First American peoples as wise, ecologically aware resource users who had minimal, if any, influence on ecosystems (Anderson 1996; Vale 1999).

The notion of an ecologically wise First American colonist—often referred to as an ecologically noble savage—has roots in the 17th and 18th centuries during the period of exploration, discovery, and colonization of new and exotic lands (for discussions of this concept in modern anthropology, see Headland 1997 and Krech 1999; for a detailed history of the concept, see Ellingson 2001). A number of scholars, including natural historians who formulated the bases of what were to become various scientific disciplines, were "attracted by visions of utopian landscapes peopled by noble savages" who, in the view of the natural historians, managed the landscapes and ecosystems they occupied in nondegrading ways (Grove 1992:45). That perception rested on ecological naïveté and the use of anthropogenically modified European landscapes as comparative baselines. At the time, the ecologically noble savage was an icon for European colonists searching for new, untapped (relative to what was observed in Europe) resources in what they took to be recently discovered lands (Bowden 1992; Dods 2002; Wilson 1992). The notion of an ecologically noble savage served as a basis for early conservation efforts on the part of natural historians (Grove 1992; Krech 1999; Yousef 2001). The notion still permeates aspects of modern conservation biology (Buege 1996; Grande 1999; Redford 1990, 1991), but today it is often tinted with various political agendas (Krech 1999; see also various comments in Headland 1997)—a form of value context. An example will help make clear, from a paleoecological perspective, the difficulty of adopting the alternative that First American peoples were ecologically wise.

Ethno-ecologist Kat Anderson's (1996:158) model of how humans in North America altered the trajectory of "ecosystem change" is shown in Figure 1.1. That her focus is on humans as the catalyst for change is evidenced by the lack of "disturbance" over some portion of the Late Pleistocene prior to when humans first arrived in the Americas and a low level of "disturbance" between the time of initial colonization by First Americans and the first Euro-American colonists. Her model fails to explicitly define "disturbance" (Sprugel 1991), though the figure clearly indicates that only humans "disturb" ecosystems and thus are, by implication, unnatural. Others (Guthrie 1971; Murray 1996) indicate that some natural processes such as avalanches, fires, and the behaviors of various nonhuman organisms "disturb" ecosystems: "Traditionally, disturbances have been viewed as uncommon, irregular events that cause abrupt structural changes in natural communities and move them away from static, near equilibrium conditions" (Sousa 1984:355). It has become clear, however, that ecological equilibriums or steady states are analytical constructs rather than reality (see below).

Anderson's figure also lacks any sense of scale on the vertical axis that is meant to measure the magnitude of disruption, and perhaps that is why it conflates "ecosystem change" and "disturbance." Ecosystem change can be climatically (or simply evolutionarily) driven; disturbance could be any nonclimatic process that disrupts or alters the trajectory of change, such as the immigration of a new organism, including but not limited to humans. Anderson's model implies that First American peoples caused

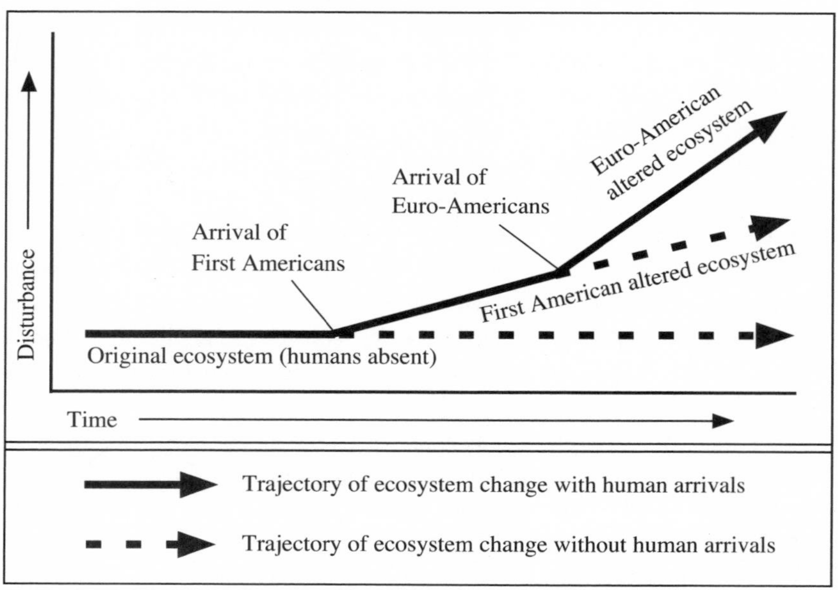

Figure 1.1. Model of how humans in North America altered the trajectory of ecosystem change (redrawn from Anderson 1996).

some degree of disturbance significantly less (or at a slower rate) than that caused by Euro-Americans and that the latter exacerbated the disturbance initiated by the former. Yet Anderson argues that First American peoples "had and continue to have a highly participatory relationship with nature [by] judiciously harvesting, crafting, and using products from nature" (1996:156). Although this may be true in some places at some times among some peoples, zooarchaeological and historical evidence suggests that it is not universally true (Grayson 2001; Low 1996; Martin and Szuter 1999a, 1999b). In fact, ascertaining the degree of influence of First American peoples on ecosystems is presently an extremely controversial issue in both North America (Krech 1999) and South America (Mann 2002). It has been controversial in North America throughout the 20th century (Adler 1969; Callicott 1989; Diamond 1986; Grieder 1970; Heizer 1955; Macleod 1936; Martin 1981; Mitchell 1978; Presnall 1943; Speck 1938; Wilson 1949).

Given the nature of their subject matter, archaeologists have long known that humans throughout time have influenced past ecosystems (Grayson 2001; Stahl 1996), but they have seldom explored this in research or scholastic contexts other than ones of interest to themselves. Many ecologists, too, are not so naive as to believe that humans did not influence ecosystems until the Industrial Age began (Day 1953; Hamel and Buckner 1998; Hunter 1996). What has happened ecologically in the past several decades, however, has made it abundantly clear that humans can be incredibly significant agents of ecosystem modification and change (Palumbi 2001; Vitousek et al. 1997), even with primitive or nonindustrial technology (Krech 1999; Low 1996; Mann 2002). This simple fact has prompted the emergence of numerous paradigms and disciplinary fields—ecosystem restoration, ecosystem health, conservation biology, restoration ecology, and the like—all of which are to some degree crisis oriented.

Ecologists, conservation biologists, and resource planners and managers think in terms of long-term human influences on ecosystems, but they look to the future and seldom into the past (Glick et al. 2001; Joyce and Hansen 2001; Westbrooks 2001). Archaeologists have been taught to think in terms of diachronic processes and long temporal spans, and they study members of the family Hominidae and their interactions with other animals. But archaeologists look into the past and seldom to the future. The pathway to useful synergy is indicated by the blinders of each.

The structure (composition) and function (processes) of an ecosystem can be conceived at various spatial and temporal scales. Given the spatiotemporal limits of what a single biologist can observe in his or her lifetime, it is not surprising that concepts such as the "balance of nature" tend to be modeled as if an ecosystem is in dynamic equilibrium, which allows concepts and analytical methods to be synchronically focused. Changes in ecosystem structure and function that occur with changes in season constitute a sort of stable, cyclical change that can be monitored by one individual. Ecosystem change driven by short-term chaotic events such as a wildfire can also be studied by a single individual. Longer-term directional changes such as shifts in timberline prompted by climatic change might also be monitored by one observer if the rate of change is sufficiently rapid or good historical data for a long time span are available. But change that occurs over long time spans, say, several hundred years, cannot be observed by a single person. As Chris Darwent and John Darwent (chap. 4) demonstrate, long-term data sets such as those represented by zooarchaeological data provide a unique perspective on colonization, extinction, and recolonization that might indicate whether or not we should be concerned about local extirpation events.

Landres (1992) emphasizes that we may only know if a perceived change is directional, chaotic, or cyclical if it is placed in a truly long-term set of observations. He also implies that we may be able to distinguish changes driven by nonhuman catalysts within a specified ecosystem from those driven by anthropogenic causes with data sets spanning long temporal durations. In both cases, paleoecological data would provide the requisite time spans. If archaeological data on prehistoric human behaviors are available for the same time span, then we can determine if any directional, chaotic, or cyclical changes have anthropogenic causes.

Some zoologists concerned with resource management and exploitation have pointed out that choosing wise management policies often depends on long-term experimental data that are variously unavailable or unobtainable (Ludwig et al. 1993). The historic record provides time depth that is to various degrees limited, but the prehistoric record potentially has limitless time depth. The historic record may be incomplete; it may be biased from the view of the author of the historic document; it may be unsystematic; it typically is nonreplicable. The prehistoric record also has potential problems, such as being incomplete or biased with respect to some analytical question (Lyman 1994c), and the temporal resolution of microscale ecological processes may be poor, though macroscale, long-term ecological processes typically are apparent. Further, although it is a historic record, the prehistoric record is often replicable in a very important sense. If one collection of bones and teeth does not answer your questions, then another collection from a similar spatial or temporal context might answer them, given the vagaries of formation and preservation (or taphonomy) of the zooarchaeological record (Lyman 1994c). And often one can find multiple cases of ecological events such as the extirpation of a local population. It is in fact easy to conceive of the prehistoric record as a suite of various sorts of empirical data comprising the results of multiple experiments; it therefore often provides precisely the sorts of data biologists have bemoaned as lacking.

Modifying the model in Figure 1.1 to account for what an archaeologist brings to the table results in the model in Figure 1.2. The latter is quite general owing to the fact that the scales of the two axes will vary considerably depending on the particular spatiotemporal context where it is applied. Note that we have labeled the vertical axis "change," that change can be in either direction, and that we do not mean to imply any particular kind of mechanism of change. Our model underscores two facts. First, a "natural" or "pristine" ecosystem unaltered by human hands is difficult to determine because change is incessant over time, irrespective of the presence of humans. Second, to determine what a "natural" ecosystem (as usually defined) comprised requires that we study the Pleistocene, a time when North (and South) American ecology was quite different from what we are familiar with as a result of (climatically driven) change

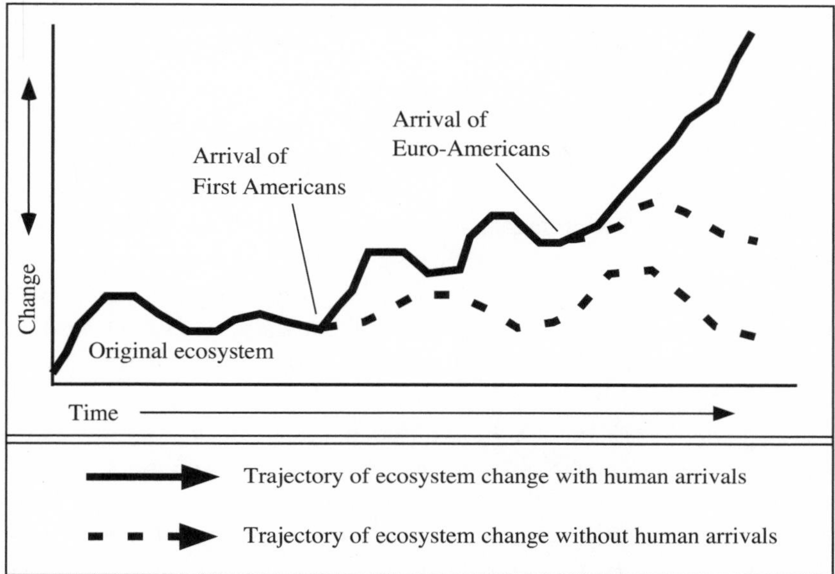

Figure 1.2. Revised model of how humans in North America altered the trajectory of ecosystem change (compare with Figure 1.1). The influence of climatic fluctuation on ecosystem change has been added.

in ecosystems (FAUNMAP Working Group 1996). We thus suggest that whatever reference ecosystem is called on by restorationists and conservationists, the spatiotemporal context of that ecosystem must be explicit. If that context can be identified in the archaeological record, then zooarchaeologists can bring the data they generate to bear on issues of conservation biology and restoration ecology.

As archaeologists we find that the words *natural, pristine,* and *wilderness* are false when defined roughly as "uninfluenced by humans," as they typically are. Instead of these terms, we suggest using the term *historic landscape* (Egan and Howell 2001; Jordan 1999) or *historic ecosystem* for the baseline that one seeks to maintain or restore. These terms are sensitive to spatiotemporal variation in ecosystems if they are accompanied by the identification of the spatiotemporal coordinates of the landscape or ecosystem specified. Given that any specified historic landscape will have existed not at a single point in time and space but, instead, over some period of time and some portion of space (Landres 1992), restoration ecologists note that the "historical range of variability" within the specified spatiotemporal coordinates must be determined (Egan and Howell 2001). Zooarchaeological material can provide just such data, and although the baseline for restorationists and conservationists may be something of a moving target, we find this far superior to the false concept of a pristine or natural ecosystem uninfluenced by humans.

WILDLIFE MANAGEMENT AND CONSERVATION BIOLOGY

About 30 years ago wildlife management could be defined as "the process by which closely related needs of wild animals and of people are evaluated, reconciled, and met" (Scheffer 1976:51). At about the time that this definition was penned, what some characterize as a "new" discipline called "conservation biology" began to emerge (Noss 1999). An early definition, though certainly not the first, is provided by one of the originators of the field, Michael Soulé: "Conservation biology [involves] the application of science to conservation problems [and] addresses the biology of species, communities, and ecosystems that are perturbed, either directly or indirectly, by human activities or other agents. Its goal is to provide principles and tools for preserving biological diversity. [It is a] mission- or crisis-oriented discipline" (1985:727). Discussion and debate over differences between traditional wildlife management and the allegedly new conservation biology appeared shortly after this definition was published (Edwards 1989; Gavin 1989; Jensen and Krausman 1993; Teer 1988; Wagner 1989). What made conservation biology *new*? What ecological and biological variables had wildlife management *not* been considering all along (Knight 1996; Shafer 2001; Temple et al. 1988; J. Young 2000)?

Major differences between the two that we derived from various articles published in major journals of each paradigm are given in Table 1.1 (see also Bunnell and Dupuis 1995; Jensen and Krausman 1993; Noss 1995a). Prior to the middle 1970s many wildlife managers and ecologists attempted to be "objective" in their scientific endeavors and concomitantly to not advocate solutions to "biotic impoverishment" (Noss 1999:114–115). Increasing awareness of potential ecological crises in the middle of the 20th century resulted in the passage of various environmental laws and policies in the United States, but these speak of the "human environment"—what is used and, particularly, exploited and modified—rather than the maintenance of some historic landscape or ecosystem, "native" species, and biodiversity. It is the latter topics that have become the central focus of conservation biology, along with an additional concern for the preservation of ecological and evolutionary processes (Angermeier and Karr 1994; Crandall et al. 2000; Moritz 2002; Murray 1996; Smith et al. 1993; Srivastrava 2002).

TABLE 1.1. Fundamental Differences between Traditional Wildlife Management and Conservation Biology.

Basis for Comparison	Wildlife Management	Conservation Biology
Central goal	Manipulations of population size	Maintenance of biological diversity
Basis for paradigm	Mostly empirical	Mostly theoretical
Taxonomic focus	Higher vertebrates, especially game species	All taxa

Note: Modified from Aplet et al. 1992.

Whether or not conservation biologists *should* be advocates for particular management policies is still hotly debated (see the articles introduced by Noss 1996, Rykiel 2001, and Wagner 1996). But the initial friction between traditional wildlife managers and the Young-Turk conservation biologists has waned considerably because of the recognition of common ground, including not only shared biological and ecological questions but also how to have the most effect on policy decisions (Beissinger 1990; Meefe and Viederman 1995; Temple 1992). Our point is simple. Because the focus of this book is on zooarchaeological data, the term *wildlife management* is sometimes used; but do not be misled—the contributors are concerned with modern issues of conservation biology.

Twenty years ago wildlife management was characterized as a science of "muddling through" (Bailey 1982) and as comprising "scientific experimentation" (McNab 1983) because complete knowledge with respect to the short- and long-term outcomes of a particular management activity was not available. The same characterization applies to conservation biology. Yet decisions must be made, and management and conservation activities must take place, else one is following "a path to inaction" (Wagner et al. 1995:175) and is susceptible to the "paralysis of analysis" (Hutchins 1995:1326) in which no action is undertaken because of inadequate knowledge. Such is neither management nor conservation. And although it is recognized that complete knowledge will never be available, it has become increasingly clear that *more* knowledge is better than less when it comes to making decisions and taking action (Ludwig et al. 2001).

This book is about a particular kind of knowledge—knowledge extractable only from zooarchaeological data, although a growing number of paleontologists are also recognizing how their data might be brought to bear in an applied arena (Barnosky et al. 2003; Burnham 2001; Chure 2002; Flessa 2002; Sepkoski 1997). It is the shared position of the contributors to this book that zooarchaeological data can often help answer questions of management and conservation. Thus, less muddling through will result, although it is also clear that we often have insufficient data to answer the questions we as archaeologists seek to answer and, thus, our data may also be inadequate to answer questions a wildlife manager or conservation biologist might ask. But we can sometimes evaluate empirically in either analytical context whether we have the requisite data or not (e.g., Lyman 1995a), and this can be a contribution in and of itself, as Lyman points out in chapter 8.

APPLIED ZOOARCHAEOLOGY

Zooarchaeologists have long borrowed ecological and behavioral data from the wildlife sciences to help interpret the shells, teeth, and broken bones they study. Seldom have they given back information of use to wildlife scientists. This book reflects the fact that the data zooarchaeologists generate may be quite relevant to various wildlife-management concerns. The kinds of conservation problems that zooarchaeological research might help resolve are typically very specific to a particular geographical place and a particular species or set of ecologically or taxonomically related species. The size of the geographic place can range from an area the size of several counties within a state to one the size of several states. Some of the kinds of problems that might be addressed with zooarchaeological data are noted in the next several paragraphs. The chapters making up the remainder of this book present additional, more fully developed examples.

One way to ensure that populations of organisms isolated by habitat patchiness survive is to "defragment" the patches by constructing habitat corridors among them (Kaiser 2001a). Zooarchaeological data can help determine where corridors once existed and, thus, where new corridors should perhaps be constructed, and such data may also indicate if isolation is the result of natural processes or anthropogenic ones and, thus, how to reverse fragmentation processes. The *cause* of isolation may, depending on the applicable policy, have a bearing on a management decision. Small, genetically isolated populations of species tend to be more prone to extinction than large or nonisolated ones (Korn 1994). Large populations provide sufficient genetic variation to ensure the survival of a species, and large areas more readily allow migration between population nodes because corridors between them tend to be short relative to those between small areas. The isolation of population nodes from one another, or the restriction of those nodes to small geographic areas or both, increases the probability that one or more of those nodes will cease to exist. Some mountaintops in the western United States, for example, contain small isolated populations of alpine mammals (Brown 1971, 1978; see also Brown 1986; MacArthur and Wilson 1967) that zooarchaeological research indicates today cannot be reached by habitat corridors (Grayson 1987). Related examples are provided by Susan Hughes (chap. 7) and Paul Sanders and Mark Miller (chap. 9). Hughes uses zooarchaeological data to show that the modern migration patterns between seasonal ranges followed by bighorn sheep *(Ovis canadensis)* were established about 5,000 years ago and that Euro-American land use has resulted in alteration of those patterns and ranges. Similarly, Sanders and Miller demonstrate that a modern migration corridor used by pronghorn antelope *(Antilocapra americana)* to move between seasonal ranges seems to have been used in like manner 5,000 years ago.

Ensuring that isolated habitat patches (or migration corridors) are not artificially disrupted in the future may be the only way to guarantee the survival of their included populations of small mammals. In such cases, knowledge of the historic and prehistoric causes of habitat patch diminution and destruction would seem to be valuable to management decisions (Beever 2002; Beever et al. 2003). An example will help make this clear. The pygmy rabbit *(Brachylagus idahoensis)* is a diminutive leporid with a modern range restricted to two areas of the western United States. One area is relatively large and encompasses portions of four states: northern Nevada, western Utah, southern Idaho, and southeastern Oregon. The other historically documented area is the central portion of eastern Washington State. Populations in the two areas are presently isolated from one another. Over the past 40 years the eastern Washington population has shrunk to an alarmingly small size, prompting the Washington Wildlife Commission (a) to list this population as "threatened" and to suggest that it be listed as "endangered" (McAllister and Allen 1993) and (b) to develop a management plan with the aim of ensuring the survival of the population (McAllister 1995). The zooarchaeological record for pygmy rabbits indicates that this species occupied a wider range in central Washington during the Holocene than it presently does. Remains of this species have been recovered from 17 archaeological and two paleontological sites in the area (Lyman 1991, 2004b). Some remains have been recovered from extralimital geographic locations where pygmy rabbits have not been historically documented. The botanical and faunal records suggest that when big sagebrush *(Artemisia tridentata)* was more widespread in central Washington—during the middle Holocene climatic interval known as the Altithermal—pygmy rabbits were also more widespread. When the Altithermal ended about 4,000 years ago the range of sagebrush shrank, and so too did the range of pygmy rabbits. Then, during the late 19th and early 20th centuries, land was cleared of sagebrush for agricultural purposes. This produced a second diminution of sagebrush and pygmy rabbit range.

Ecological studies of pygmy rabbits indicate that this leporid is dependent on big sagebrush for food and for shelter from predation (Gabler et al. 2001; Green and Flinders 1980a, 1980b). The zooarchaeological and paleobotanical records indicate that both species responded to climatic change in like manners. The fossil record suggests that the prehistoric source of Washington's pygmy rabbits resides in the area of the larger extant population to the south. Today it would be impractical to develop a migration corridor between the two populations, and it would also be impossible given the climatic and land-use histories of the area. The probable corridor between the two today is characterized by vegetation habitats that are not conducive to the survival of pygmy rabbits, and much of that area is now under cultivation and irrigation. The zooarchaeological record indicates, however, that the extant population might be supplemented by individuals transplanted from southeastern Oregon because the latter seem to be the genetic source of the former. This supposition could be tested by study of the DNA preserved in the prehistoric bones. The prehistoric record also indicates that the maintenance of habitats dominated by big sagebrush is critical to the survival of the species, and the historic record indicates that the maintenance of pertinent habitats must involve changes in human land-use practices.

When local populations have been extirpated, one management alternative is to transplant individuals from other populations to the vacated range in an attempt to reestablish a population. Zooarchaeological research can play several roles in these situations. As Judy Harpole (chap. 6) notes, such research can indicate locations where the species of interest once existed and may be most capable of surviving today, and it might also indicate locations where the transplanted species may not survive given historic modifications to habitats (see also Emslie 1987; D. Gordon 1994; Owen-Smith 1989). Morphometric and biogeographic analysis of zooarchaeological remains may suggest which extant population should be sampled for individuals to transplant (Lyman 1988b). Most conservation biologists agree that taxa should not be transplanted to areas "outside" of their "historical range" (D. Gordon 1994:33), and biogeographic analysis of zooarchaeological remains can help establish a taxon's historical distribution. The International Union for the Conservation of Nature and Natural Resources (IUCN)—renamed the World Conservation Union—has drafted guidelines for reintroductions. These read, in part, as follows:

> An assessment should be made of the taxonomic status of individuals to be reintroduced. They should be of the same taxonomic unit (and ideally closely related genetically) as those which were extirpated. An investigation of historical information about the loss and fate of individuals from the reintroduction area, as well as molecular genetic studies, should be undertaken in case of doubt. . . . Release stock ideally should be closely related genetically to the original native stock. (IUCN Reintroduction Specialist Group 1992:2–3)

Burney et al. (2002) refer to artificial efforts to rebuild diminishing biodiversity and "jump-start" ecological processes by transplanting organisms into areas where their conspecifics or congeners are now extinct as "evolution's second chance." What they mean by *evolution* is the creation of "independent evolutionary track[s] into the future, where there would have been few (if any) otherwise" (Burney et al. 2002:15), but of course this begs again the question of how close genetically is close enough when it comes to, say, restarting evolutionary lineages that have not existed for 10,000 years with a related genus from another continent. Ignoring this slippery (and value-laden) issue, it is clear that a search of not only historic but also prehistoric information may be necessary to determine which extant population would be the most appropriate genetically as a source of transplantable animals. The study of ancient DNA extracted from prehistoric skeletal tissues (Richards et al. 1993; Richards et al. 1995) seems to have great potential for contending with IUCN and similar guidelines, as demonstrated by Michael Etnier (chap. 5). Fortunately, the technique is applicable to curated as well as newly acquired zooarchaeological specimens (Pääbo 1993), and thus new archaeological excavations need not take place so long as appropriate collections are curated and accessible.

Biogeographic evidence in the form of prehistoric remains of a taxon in locations where that taxon no longer occurs can help establish which taxa are recolonizing once-occupied areas. Such a determination is critically important in light of the recently growing interest in "invasion biology" (Vermeij 1996) and "invasive" species, a major threat to indigenous taxa (Wilcove et al. 1998). Invading species are those that come to occupy areas outside their historically documented range as a direct or indirect result of anthropogenic processes. The importance of identifying invasive species resides in two arenas: the invasion process homogenizes community and global ecology, evolution, and biodiversity; and the invading taxa often threaten the survival of native species (Lodge 1993; Mooney and Cleland 2001). Dave Schmitt (chap. 10) presents zooarchaeological data that show how the invasion of a plant species to many areas of the western United States has resulted in the modification of small mammal communities. Many species have invaded new habitats and geographic locations as a (often unintentional) result of human activities. The black rat *(Rattus rattus)*, Norway rat *(R. norvegicus)*, and house mouse *(Mus musculus)* are all native to the Old World but were able to colonize the Americas along with European humans. There are numerous more recent examples, and all of these taxa are generally referred to as "exotic," "nonnative," or "alien."

If a particular taxon (ecotype, subspecies, or species) is exotic to an area meant to be characteristic of a historic landscape, then it may be necessary to remove that taxon from the area in order to re-create the historic ecosystem and biota. Thus, we must have a solid definition of exotic taxa above and beyond the notion that they include recent invasive species. The U.S. National Park Service (NPS) defines an *exotic species* as one "that occurs in a given place as a result of direct or indirect, deliberate or accidental actions by humans (not including deliberate reintroductions)" (Hester 1991:127; see also NPS 1978). *Native species* "are those which presently occur, or once did occur prior to some human influence, in a given place, area, or region as the result of ecological processes that operate and have operated without significant direct or indirect, deliberate or accidental alterations by humans" (NPS 1978). These definitions take a relatively synchronic perspective. From the temporally deep perspective of dynamic biogeographic history, the definitions of native and exotic species are contradictory. Exotic species occur in a given place as a result of actions by humans, whereas native species are those that presently occur or *once did occur* in a place as the sole result of natural ecological processes. The emphasized phrase is where the contradiction resides, for it indicates that if a taxon *ever* occurred at some time in the past in an area, then *by definition* that taxon represents a native species, irrespective of human intervention at a later date. Recognizing this contradiction some years ago, Lyman argued that the NPS "should rethink policy issues" (1988a:22). Some NPS biologists later came to the same conclusion (Houston and Schreiner 1995). The definition of an exotic species as "one whose comparatively short historical residency stems directly or indirectly from human actions" (Povilitis 2002:72) is a step in the right direction, but it begs the question of how little time *short* comprises. Zooarchaeologists can perhaps help clarify and resolve such issues.

If a historic landscape or ecosystem is to be re-created by exclusion of exotic species or reintroduction of artificially extirpated native species, then we must have a baseline list of the original native species. In the United States, such a list is typically derived from the earliest historical documents for the area included within a piece of landscape such as a national park (Houston and Schreiner 1995; Leopold et al. 1963). That people were present in North America more than 10,000 years before the historical period may be acknowledged when compiling a list of "native" species, but it is typically ignored (Houston and Schreiner 1995). The ethnocentricity of such a procedure is unavoidable from a practical standpoint. More important, historical documents are sometimes incomplete and at other times inaccurate. Such documents can be supplemented and tested with zooarchaeological data, as Butler and Delacorte (chap. 2) and Thomas Whyte (chap. 11) demonstrate.

Bison *(Bison bison)* were artificially introduced to a portion of the State of Alaska that was subsequently to become Wrangell–St. Elias National Park and Preserve (Peek et al. 1987). Historic records suggest that bison were not present when the first white men visited the area in the middle and late 19th century. A review of the zooarchaeological and paleontological record indicates that bison were present in Alaska between about 450 years ago and the early 20th century (Stephenson et al. 2001). By definition, the bison introduced to Wrangell–St. Elias National Park should be considered exotic, and the NPS considers them to be so because of the lack of evidence that bison were present when the first white explorers passed through the area (Houston and Schreiner 1995). NPS biologists also note that the introduced form of bison was of a nonnative genetic stock (a distinct subspecies or ecotype), given current beliefs about bison taxonomy, so they argue that the extant bison of Wrangell–St. Elias should be removed. However, because it cannot be demonstrated that native bison were locally extinct prior to the transplanting event, it is possible that extant bison are hybrids of native and introduced genetic stocks. Perhaps DNA testing of extant bison and of prehistoric bison remains would clarify this. In the event that it does not, only more zooarchaeological and paleontological research will establish the timing of the local extirpation of native Alaskan bison populations and whether or not all Alaskan populations were extinct when transplanting occurred in the middle of the 20th century. Once the facts are determined, we will have strong bases for making a decision regarding the ultimate fate of the bison presently extant in Wrangell–St. Elias National Park and Preserve.

The preceding is but one example of many similar situations (Laundré 1991; Lyman 1998; Schullery and Whittlesey 2001; Varley and Varley 1996). All of these underscore several facts. First, the quality and quantity of zooarchaeological research—the sampling effort—may be insufficient to be reliable (Lyman 1995b). No one suspected, for example, that mountain goats *(Oreamnos americanus)* were once present on Vancouver Island off the western coast of British Columbia, but a recent report of paleontological remains of this species recovered from a high-altitude cave on the island proves otherwise (Nagorsen and Keddie 2000). Similarly, as Etnier (chap. 5) notes, until zooarchaeological materials were studied, no one suspected that Guadalupe fur seals *(Arctocephalus townsendi)* used to be found along the Pacific coast of Washington State and seem to have had breeding colonies there during the late prehistoric period. Taphonomic problems—those concerning biased or poor preservation of faunal remains—are also critically important in applied zooarchaeology, and zooarchaeologists can help biologists and ecologists interpret the zooarchaeological data used to inform management decisions (Cannon 2001; Etnier 2002b; see also Church 1997; Sisk and Noon 1995).

Finally, paleozoologist Russell Graham (1988) notes that the boundaries of many parks and preserves are defined on the basis of modern climatic and environmental conditions. Those conditions change over time, however, and the probability of significant change increases as the length of time increases (Landres 1992). Graham argues that much conservation planning operates under the assumption that biotas or communities of organisms tend to respond to environmental change as intact units. The paleobiological record indicates, however, that "individual species respond to environmental changes by migrating in different directions, at different rates, during different times" (Graham 1988:392; see also Hunter et al. 1988). Such taxonomically individualistic responses to environmental change imply that the biological preserves of today are artifacts of the time when they were identified and created. Zooarchaeological research has confirmed this implication time and time again. That research can also provide indications of what might happen to those preserves should climates change (Graham 1992). And as Ken Cannon and Molly Cannon (chap. 3) demonstrate with respect to the world's first national park, zooarchaeological data may prove to be invaluable to the restoration and maintenance of parks in some chosen conditions.

DISCUSSION

Archaeologists are beginning to argue that they must make their discipline relevant to modern concerns, but they are not always clear about why they should do so other than to note that archaeology provides a time depth to anthropogenically created ecologies (van der Leeuw and Redman 2002). We have outlined some much more explicit reasons in this chapter, and they are echoed throughout this book. The manner in which zooarchaeological research can be used in modern biological conservation is specific to a place or to a taxon. This makes "applied zooarchaeology" intellectually challenging. Broadening the scope of zooarchaeology to conservation and management applications will, we believe, be beneficial to our future, not only from the perspective of helping to ensure the preservation of biological diversity for future generations but also from the perspective of paleozoological studies in general, which might otherwise be increasingly perceived as the pursuit of esoteric knowledge of little practical use. Thus, applied zooarchaeology *matters* not only to zooarchaeologists but to all of humanity as well.

From a disciplinary-selfish perspective, we believe that a well-developed applied zooarchaeology will provide a new job market and new sources of funding. Both may become available if we convince wildlife managers and conservation biologists that because their policies are typically aimed at the future, knowing something of the past can result in better-informed decisions. Although we cannot predict exactly when the next ice age or glacial period will begin, we can argue convincingly that climates and environments will change, and knowing this, we can use the prehistoric record to test our predictions about how certain kinds of changes may affect biotas of the future. And confirmed—or even rejected or falsified—predictions would be the strong selling point. Federal land-managing agencies whose charge includes conservation might well pay a zooarchaeologist to help them make wise management decisions. The other selling point is less selfish and comprises the fact that a less desirable kind of price—ecosystem destruction and the loss of biodiversity—might otherwise have to be paid.

Some of the necessary convincing has already transpired. Many of those practicing landscape restoration, for example, are well aware of the value of data concerning historic and prehistoric ecosystems. They use such data "to determine what needs to be restored, why it was lost, and how best to make it live again" (Egan and Howell 2001:1); pertinent data regarding the past reveal "reference conditions" that serve as baselines toward which restoration efforts may be aimed (Egan and Howell 2001:2). Whether or not restoration activities actually attain such baseline conditions depends on a host of social, political, and other value-laden contextual variables. Yet the important point is that those reference conditions must somehow be established. One of the messages of the chapters in this book is that it is through paleozoological research that many of them can be determined.

In the preceding we have said that "many" restoration ecologists are aware of the value of historic and prehistoric data pertaining to ecosystems. In fact, ecologists of various sorts have during the past decade begun to pay much more attention to the deep histories of ecosystems, occasionally calling on zooarchaeological data to increase their knowledge of the history of particular variables (Jackson et al. 2001; Ludwig et al. 2001; Schullery and Whittlesey 2001). Such cases have yet, however, to become commonplace. For example, every one of a recently published set of 13 articles on ecosystem-recovery planning (introduced by Kareiva 2002) fails to mention paleoecological data. The case studies in the following chapters demonstrate the value of zooarchaeological data in particular and paleoecological data in general to conservation biology. This book also makes clear that the opinion recently expressed by conservation biologist Reed Noss is easily characterized as prejudicial. In his introduction to an edited collection on the restoration of large mammals, Noss (2001:13) indicates that only those North American taxa impacted by "Europeans" should be restored. Those impacted or driven to extinction by First American peoples, apparently, should not be the subject of restoration efforts. As we noted earlier, Euro-Americans did not work alone in impacting populations of furbearers across the continent. Given this, and in light of increasing archaeological evidence of the prehistoric impact of First American peoples on animal populations, biologists should find it increasingly difficult to maintain Noss's position without charges of racial and cultural discrimination.

We believe that no one can afford to ignore any potentially relevant data when it comes to planning and working toward an ecological future that is not only pleasant but also safe for humanity and ecosystemically wise. The following studies demonstrate the value of one kind of what we take to be *very* relevant data.

2

Doing Zooarchaeology as if It Mattered: Use of Faunal Data to Address Current Issues in Fish Conservation Biology in Owens Valley, California

Virginia L. Butler and Michael G. Delacorte

Ecologists are increasingly incorporating concepts such as "legacy" into their explanations of current ecosystems (Harding et al. 1998). This approach acknowledges that understanding the structure and function of extant ecosystems (or predicting future responses to climate change) requires knowledge of historical forces that have been operating for decades, centuries, or longer (Foster 2000; Moorhead et al. 1999). Indeed, recognition of the need for such long-term historical records is demonstrated by the level of National Science Foundation funding for the Long-Term Ecological Research (LTER) network (Kaiser 2001b; LTER Network 2001). Over 1,100 researchers funded by the LTER carry out research on 24 designated sites that have been studied from a few years to several decades (Kaiser 2001b). These studies cover a range of topics with the overall goal of "investigating ecological processes over long temporal and broad spatial scales" (LTER Network 2001). This goal is precisely that of zooarchaeology. Yet, to our knowledge, zooarchaeological expertise and data have not been incorporated into the LTER network. Our point is simply that ecological sciences seeking to understand the long-term properties of ecosystems have direct access to such information through zooarchaeology.

Zooarchaeology needs to collaborate with wildlife sciences because of the increasing speed with which habitats and biotas are being lost in the face of human population growth and habitat destruction (Minckley and Deacon 1991; Vitousek et al. 1997). In response to legislation such as the

Endangered Species Act of 1973 (16USC1531–1547, Public Law 93–205), recovery plans are constantly being developed across the United States. Drawing from recent, often limited historical records, decisions are routinely made on which taxa are native, which are exotic, which should be targeted for recovery, and which should be disregarded. In stark terms, these are determinations of which organisms "belong on the ark." Given zooarchaeology's (and paleontology's) access to faunal records dating back hundreds and thousands of years, we can assist with these decisions. To demonstrate this with respect to fisheries management, we here discuss our recent work on the ancient fish fauna of Owens Valley, California.

BACKGROUND

Owens Valley is a deep, 130-km-long block-faulted graben in southeastern California, on the western edge of the hydrographic Great Basin (Figure 2.1). It is a narrow, roughly north–south-trending valley sandwiched between two mountain ranges with 14,000-ft (4,265-m) peaks. The Sierra Nevada Range to the west captures most of the precipitation arriving from the west; the Inyo-White Mountains lie to the east. Whereas only 16 cm of rain fall on the valley floor, a significant winter snowpack in the high Sierra provides meltwater throughout the year. Owens River heads in the Sierra Nevada north of Owens Valley and is fed by numerous tributaries draining the range at various points along the valley. Prior to historic water-diversion projects, the river traveled southward about 130 km before it emptied into Owens Lake. Historically the lake was shallow (2–15 m), was moderately saline (5–15 percent salts [Smith and Bischoff 1997]), and did not support fish populations (Gilbert 1893). The Quaternary record of Owens Lake shows that it has undergone significant changes in water level and chemistry over the last several hundred thousand years (Benson et al. 1996; Benson et al. 1997; Smith and Bischoff 1997). Basically, the lake is a remnant of a vast Pleistocene lake system that once connected basins extending from south of Mono Lake on the north to Death Valley at the southern end of the chain (Hubbs and Miller 1948; Miller 1946; Sada and Vinyard 2002).

Although minor changes to the historic aquatic system began as early as the 1870s, when irrigation projects began to divert Owens River water, the aquatic system was drastically altered beginning in 1913 with the construction of the Los Angeles Aqueduct. Reservoirs were constructed, canals were dug, and most significant, much of the water from Sierran streams and the Owens River itself was siphoned off, seriously reducing the amount

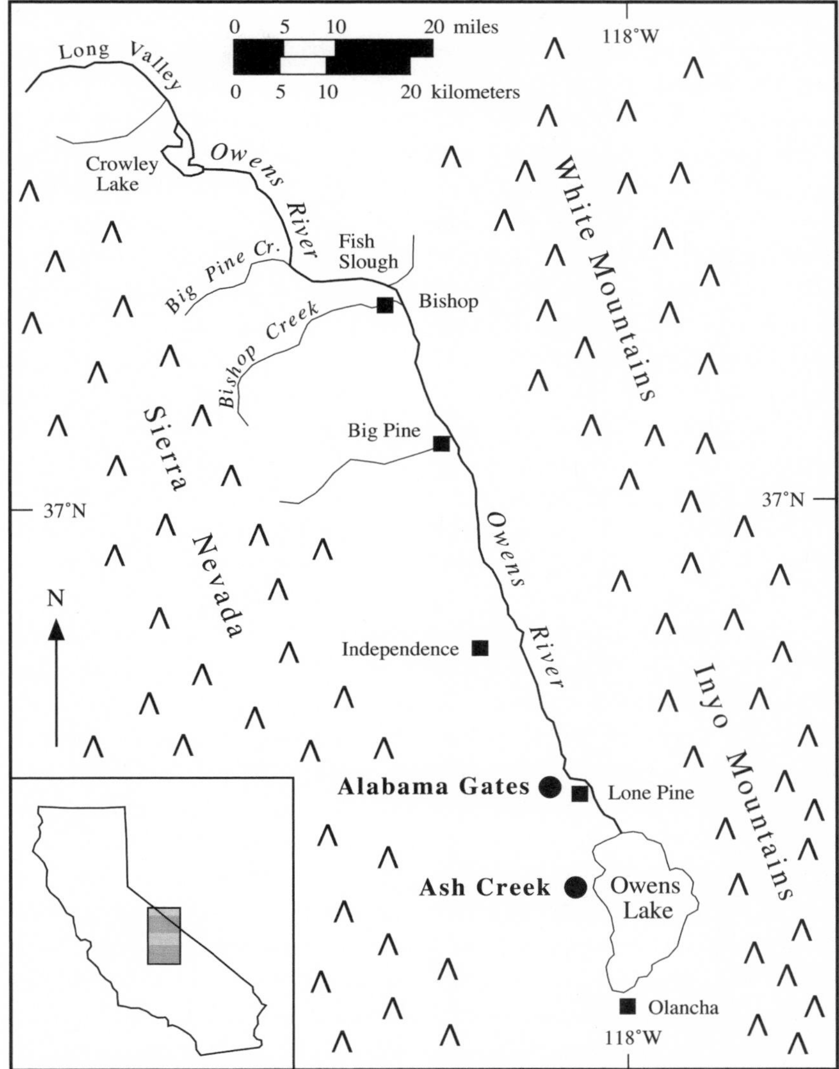

Figure 2.1. Owens Valley, California, showing locations of geographic features and archaeological projects. Circles denote archaeological projects; squares denote towns.

of water that reached the valley bottom (Kahrl 1982). By the 1930s Owens Lake had become a dry playa that accumulates water only in exceptionally wet years. Sometime before 1890 catfish (Ictaluridae), carp *(Cyprinus carpio),* and salmonids were introduced to the basin (Gilbert 1893), and not long after, bass (*Micropterus* sp.), sunfish (*Lepomis* sp.), and other alien fish and amphibians were introduced (U.S. Department of the Interior, Fish and Wildlife Service 1998).

Given the major loss of habitat and the introduction of alien, non-native species, the populations of most native fish in the valley have been in severe decline for the last 75 years. Of the four native species, two are endangered (Owens pupfish *[Cyprinidon radiosus]* and Owens tui chub *[Gila bicolor snyderi]*), and one is a "species of concern" (Owens speckled dace [*Rhinichthys osculus* ssp.]); only one species (Owens sucker *[Catostomus fumeiventris]*) is believed to be doing relatively well (U.S. Department of the Interior, Fish and Wildlife Service 1998). Owens Valley fish show a high level of endemism typical of Great Basin fish in hydrologically isolated basins; two unique species are present (the sucker and pupfish), and two unique subspecies (the chub and dace) occur in the valley (Miller 1973; U.S. Department of the Interior, Fish and Wildlife Service 1998).

In response to the severe declines in these taxa and the Endangered Species Act, recovery plans for Owens Basin wetlands have been developed "to provide a means whereby the ecosystems upon which endangered and threatened species depend may be conserved" (U.S. Department of the Interior, Fish and Wildlife Service 1998:1). This plan calls for the creation of 16 conservation areas that will provide appropriate physical conditions (water level, chemistry, temperature, and plant growth) for fish survival as well as reduce the populations of deleterious alien species—mainly carnivorous fish that prey on native taxa. To identify habitat requirements, the recovery plan uses historic records on fish distribution and abundance as well as information from closely related species in nearby regions. Although recognizing the limitations of historic records, the authors of the plan note that these records "provide the *best* description of Owens Basin plant and animal communities prior to perturbations that caused the decline of many rare species" (U.S. Department of the Interior, Fish and Wildlife Service 1998:17, emphasis added).

Historic accounts are extremely useful for establishing certain baseline information on species distributions and abundances in recent times, but it is arguable whether they provide the "best description." Table 2.1 summarizes the primary historic accounts of Owens Valley fish. The first recorded observation by a natural scientist was in 1891, and the first long-term observations were carried out in the 1910s. Given that several non-native fish (catfish, carp, and salmonids) were already well established in the valley by this time, it is difficult to gage how much the native fish fauna and aquatic communities had changed. The first extensive collections and observations of native fish were in the 1940s and 1950s by University of Michigan ichthyologists, decades after the aquatic conditions had been drastically altered by Los Angeles County water-diversion projects. Moreover, a review of these studies reveals that most observers were working in limited areas and over brief periods of time (Table 2.1).

The zooarchaeological record can greatly expand our knowledge of Owens Valley fish by providing a substantially longer history of fish in the area. Recent archaeological projects in southern Owens Valley provide a faunal record that spans much of the Holocene. Further, extensive data on regional paleoenvironments (Benson et al. 1997; Smith and Bischoff 1997; Stine 1998) indicate that the aquatic system may have undergone significant change over the last several thousand years. These data can be used to suggest how fish have responded to these conditions and why some species are managing better than others under modern circumstances.

METHODS AND MATERIALS

Our study is based on analysis of fish remains from two archaeological projects in southern Owens Valley (Figure 2.1). The Alabama Gates sites are located within 2 km of the current river channel, about 15 km north of Owens Lake (Delacorte 1999). The Ash Creek sites are located west of the lake, near tributary streambeds or ancient embayments of the former lakeshore (Gilreath and Holanda 2000).

Seven sites from these projects provided fish remains, all of which were excavated and analyzed in similar ways (Butler 1999, 2000a). In the field, matrix was screened through 1/8-in (3.2-mm) mesh, except for small volumes during initial testing efforts that were screened through 1/4-in (6.4-mm) mesh. Bulk samples were collected in the field and wet sieved through nested 1/8-in and 1/16-in (1.6-mm) mesh in the lab (Alabama Gates—156 l; Ash Creek—488 l). Except for vertebrae, which were assigned to Catostomidae/Cyprinidae (sucker/minnow) because of morphological similarity, most skeletal elements could be assigned to at least taxonomic family. Maxillae and dentaries were used to identify sucker species, and pharyngeals were used to identify cyprinid species. Specimens were quantified using the number of identified specimens (NISP [Grayson 1984]). Vertebra diameters were measured (for the measurement used, see Casteel 1976) to estimate fish body length and changes in fish size, given the well-established relationship between vertebra size and body size. Because vertebrae from minnows and suckers cannot be distinguished, the measure provides a coarse-grained record of change in body size.

TABLE 2.1. Historic References to Fish in Owens Valley.

Year(s)	Observer	Comments	Source	Time and Duration of Visit
1859	Captain Davidson	"River is filled with a small fish, supposed to be a new species.... about 2 inches in length.... The Indians catch these fish in great quantities in sieve-like baskets.... These fish were confined to the river, I did not see any of them in its tributaries." (based on drawing provided, likely *Cyprinidon radiosus* [Owens pupfish])	Wilke and Lawton 1976:30	July–August
1872–1876	Anonymous	Numerous references to the raising of trout and initial stocking of Owens River tributaries in 1873	*Inyo Independent* (newspaper, various editions)	
1891	C. H. Gilbert	Noted specimens of *Rutilus symmetricus* (or *Gila bicolor snyderi,* the Owens tui chub [Miller 1973]) from Owens Lake. Also noted that carp and catfish are common in the Lower Owens River and were found dead along the Owens Lake shore. Specimens of *Salmo mykiss agua-bonita* (golden trout) were collected in Cottonwood Creek, which drains into Owens Lake; according to Gilbert, these were transplants from Kern River.	Gilbert 1893	Unknown; all collecting localities were in the southern end of the valley, from Lone Pine south to Owens Lake

1910s	C. H. Kennedy	"The fish, *Cyprinidon macularius* (= *C. radiosus,* Owens pupfish) was found in abundance in all the shallower parts of the sloughs and tule swamps at both Lone Pine and Laws. Every pool cut off by a gravel bar along the river contained a few of these little fish. They were apparently entirely comfortable in water not over 4 inches deep."	Snyder 1917:205	Unknown; probably multi-seasonal residence in the valley; most observations were made near Laws, about 5 km north of Bishop
		Noted that *Agosia robusta* (or *Rhinichthys osculus,* the dace) "is not common."	Snyder 1917:205	
		"Suckers (*Catostomus arenarius* = *C. fumeiventris,* Owens sucker) are common everywhere in the main river, usually lying in schools on the inflow side of pools."	Snyder 1917:202	
		Siphateles obesus (or *Gila bicolor snyderi,* the Owens tui chub) was collected, but observations on distribution and abundance were not provided.	Snyder 1917	
1933	J. H. Steward	Noted Paiute names for six fish, including a native minnow, two names for suckers (depending on age), two salmonids, and one type Steward could not match with a Euro-American name. "Fish occurred in Owens river, fresh-water sloughs, and the Sierra Nevada streams."	Steward 1933:250	Six weeks, summers of 1927 and 1928; short time in December 1931
1973	R. R. Miller	First systematic species accounts of Owens sucker and Owens tui chub, based on collections made by Snyder and University of Michigan ichthyologists.	Miller 1973	Unknown; collection localities indicate extensive travel throughout the valley, sampling the river, reservoirs, sloughs, irrigation ditches, etc.

Sites or portions thereof were assigned to one of four time periods based on radiocarbon dates, temporally diagnostic projectile points, and source-specific obsidian hydration ages: pre-7000 B.P., 3500–1350 B.P., 1350–650 B.P., 650–100 B.P. (Delacorte 1999; Gilreath and Holanda 2000). The earliest time period, marked by Great Basin Stemmed and Pinto series projectile points (Basgall and Hall 2001; Tuohy and Layton 1979), encompasses the broadest and least securely dated interval, owing to the lack of directly associated organic residues suitable for radiometric assay. Three radiocarbon dates were obtained from a buried soil just beneath the artifact-bearing stratum at one of the sites (INY-4554); these dates fall between 7780 ± 90 and 6740 ± 90 B.P. Obsidian hydration readings on more than 130 flakes and tools from the same deposit indicate that all of the artifacts are of broadly similar age, as evidenced by the low coefficient of variation in hydration (14 percent). It is reasonable to conclude, therefore, that most of the INY-4554 fish bone and other cultural remains date to the interval around or shortly after the two-sigma calibrated dates for the soil horizon (8960–7477 B.P.), as befits points of the Stemmed and Pinto series. Virtually identical dates are suggested for the other early archaeological components by statistically similar or slightly older obsidian hydration values and projectile point series.

RESULTS

A total of 1,371 fish remains was identified to at least family or sucker/minnow. Figure 2.2 shows the overall frequency of fish taxa with all the site assemblages aggregated. The sucker/minnow category has the most specimens, followed by the family categories—Catostomidae and Cyprinidae—and finally the species—tui chub, Owens sucker, and speckled dace. As Owens sucker was the only species in the family identified, all of the remains identified to the sucker family are presumably from Owens sucker as well. Of the 54 Cyprinidae (minnow) pharyngeals identified to species, 52 are from tui chub, and two are from speckled dace. Given the absolute dominance of tui chub in the deposits, it is reasonable to assume for analytical purposes that most of the specimens identified to Cyprinidae are from tui chub.

Remains of speckled dace are extremely rare, and no remains of Owens pupfish were identified. Because dace and pupfish are very small (maximum lengths = 100–150 mm), their scarcity could be explained by recovery bias, but this is unlikely given that large quantities of sediment were processed through 1/16-in mesh. Further, remains of very small fish were

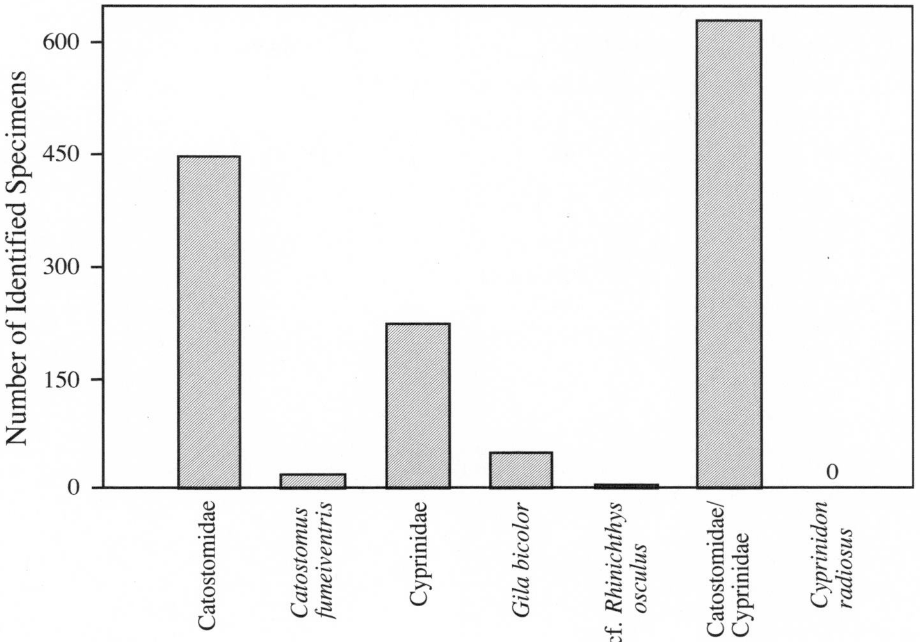

Figure 2.2. Fish taxonomic frequency, all sites combined.

recovered, judging by vertebra sizes (see below), just not those of dace and pupfish. Thus, the scarcity of dace and pupfish reflects something real about taxonomic representation in the archaeological deposits. There are several ways to interpret this pattern. The scarcity might indicate that aboriginal peoples did not target these fish or the habitats they occupied. The low frequency could also mean that one or both species were never abundant in the river system (or the habitats exploited by people). Perhaps both of these explanations are correct in part. Ethnohistoric descriptions emphasize that Native Americans used sieved baskets to catch small fish in the Owens Valley (Davidson, in Wilke and Lawton 1976; Steward 1933, 1941). As we discuss below, fish recovered from late-prehistoric contexts (< 3000 B.P.) are generally very small (< 200 mm long), and it is likely that most of them were caught using mass harvesting gear. If all species were occupying the same habitat, then one would expect that at least some individuals of all taxa would be captured by indiscriminate fishing techniques. As Owens sucker and tui chub absolutely dominate the assemblages, the implication is that dace and pupfish were not occupying the same habitats as the sucker and chub or that these very small fish occurred in negligible quantities in these habitats. The absence of pupfish and near absence of speckled dace suggest that these taxa were never very abundant in the lower river, where the archaeological assemblages were found. Faunal samples from other locations may substantiate this suggestion.

Temporal Patterning

Table 2.2 summarizes the temporal distribution of identified fish remains (NISP) across site components and time periods. Several points can be highlighted. Each time period has multiple components with fish remains, although the sample sizes in many components are extremely small. In our comparisons of taxonomic frequency over time, we include only those components with ≥ 30 NISP. Table 2.2 also shows a 3,500-year gap in faunal records (7000–3500 B.P.) that reflects the lack of dated archaeological deposits for this interval. Whether this gap is an artifact of archaeological sampling or some other phenomenon such as reduced human population density is unclear in Owens Valley and numerous Great Basin localities where middle Holocene occupations are often underrepresented.

To examine variation in sucker and chub abundance over time, we used a simple index (Σ Catostomidae NISP / Σ Cyprinidae NISP + Σ Catostomidae NISP) and calculated values for the five archaeological components with ≥ 30 NISP. All specimens identified to at least the family level were included. The index generates a value between 1.0 and 0, with higher values indicating a greater representation of sucker relative to minnow. Sucker absolutely dominates in the two early-period components (with index values close to 1.0); later components show a more even representation of sucker and minnow (Figure 2.3).

Another striking pattern is the change in vertebra diameter over time (Figure 2.4). Early deposits are dominated by large vertebrae (≥ 6 mm), and given that sucker dominates these early assemblages, the vertebrae indicate relatively large sucker. Later deposits are dominated by small vertebrae (typically 1–4 mm) and hence smaller fish, chub and sucker (Figure 2.4). For reference, fish > 300 mm long have vertebra > 5 mm wide; fish about 60 mm long have vertebra approximately 1 mm wide. Screen size is not responsible for the varying vertebra sizes, as fine-mesh samples from all site components were studied.

Search for Causes: Cultural

These patterns in taxonomic representation and body size could result from both cultural factors (human selection, technology) and environmental

TABLE 2.2. FREQUENCIES (NUMBER OF IDENTIFIED SPECIMENS) OF FISH REMAINS IN OWENS VALLEY ARCHAEOLOGICAL SITES AND COMPONENTS.

	Component						
Project Site	"Early" Pre 7000 B.P.	7000–3500 B.P.[a]	3500–1350 B.P.	1350–650 B.P.	1350–100 B.P.[b]	650–100 B.P.	Total
Alabama Gates							
INY 328H, loc. A	253						253
INY 328H, loc. D	5						5
INY 3767	7						7
INY 2750				1	10	66	77
INY 3778			2		26	4	32
INY 3769			158			602	760
Ash Creek							
INY 4554	134						134
INY 1428				2			2

[a]There are no records for this time period.
[b]These materials are from stratigraphically mixed deposits.

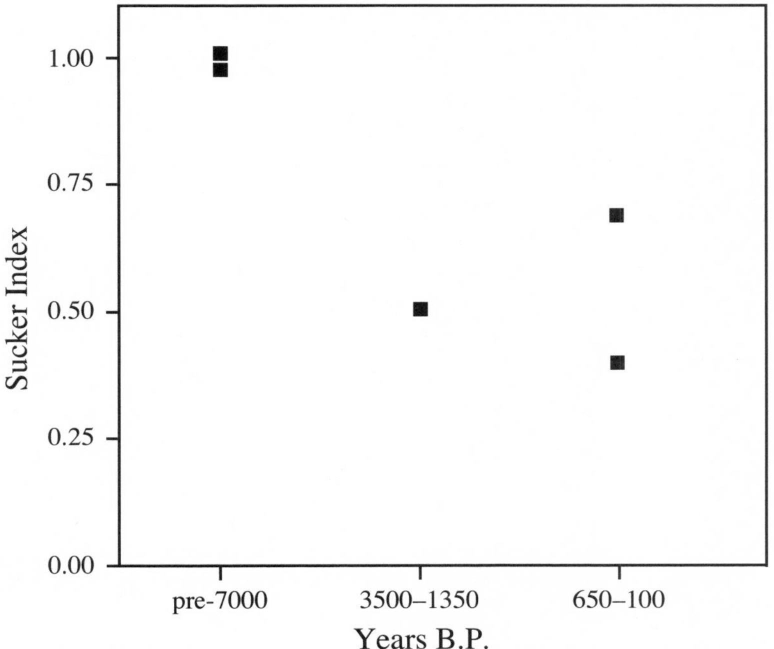

Figure 2.3. Change in relative frequency of sucker remains over time.

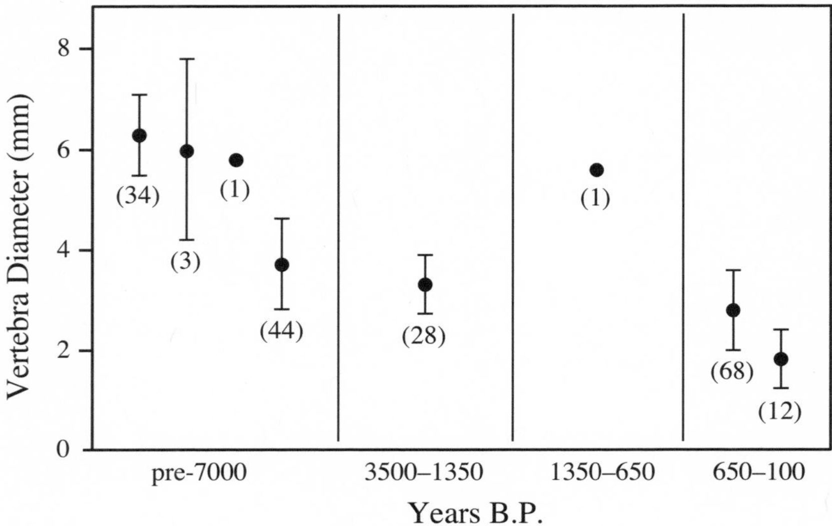

Figure 2.4. Change in vertebra diameter over time. Each error bar represents mean and standard deviation; sample size is in parenthesis.

factors (water conditions). The absence of small fish in the early period must result primarily from cultural practices because small fish were certainly present. This absence would be predicted by a prey-choice model derived from foraging theory, wherein highly ranked resources such as large fish are selectively targeted until their abundance declines to the point that pursuit of lower-ranked foods is of equal or better economic return (Broughton 1994, 1999; Grayson 2001). Given that prey rank is highly and positively correlated with body size, the model predicts that human foragers in Owens Valley would initially target large rather than small fish if the former were available in the river.

The same explanation and other cultural factors might also account for the late-prehistoric presence of small fish. Various zooarchaeological and paleoethnobotanical indicators point to more intensive subsistence practices and an expansion in late-prehistoric diet breadth (Bettinger 1976; Delacorte 1995, 1999). The adoption of mass harvesting technologies such as nets or basketry sieves would likewise result in the capture of primarily small fish, as documented in ethnohistoric accounts (Steward 1933; Wilke and Lawton 1976). Thus, cultural factors (predator–prey relationships, technology) probably account for some of the patterning.

But what is responsible for the absence of large fish late in the sequence? Were large fish common in the river and adjacent streams and marshes but not targeted by human foragers because of scheduling or other cultural constraints? Or were fish in the aquatic system simply smaller later in time? Delacorte (1999) believes that a shift from springtime fishing for mature fish during the spawning season to predominantly summer/fall fishing for juvenile fish and smaller species could have produced the archaeological pattern. Support for this hypothesis is provided by the seasonality of late-prehistoric components. Still, if large fish were present in the aquatic system, they probably should have been taken to some extent, as the prey-choice model predicts. Because the relatively large fish in early archaeological contexts are Owens sucker, the question more specifically relates to body size changes in sucker. Aquatic habitats in the Great Basin in general and Owens Valley in particular have undergone significant change over the last several thousand years, and it is reasonable to think that such changes have affected not only species abundances but fish size as well (Smith 1981).

Search for Causes: Environmental Change

The end of the Pleistocene brought increasingly arid conditions and the disappearance of the huge pluvial lakes that once covered much of the Great Basin. In Owens and nearby valleys, records of change in aquatic habitats come from studies of lake-bed cores and relict tree stumps. Given that most of the water in eastern California lakes comes from Sierran stream runoff, major fluctuations in lake level also monitor changes in the extent and size of riverine and other aquatic habitats throughout the valleys. Benson et al.'s (1997) oxygen isotope analysis of an Owens Lake core establishes periods when the basin was closed (low flow, dry interval) and open (high flow, wet interval—wherein water overflowed the Owens Basin, filling pluvial lakes to the south and east). Owens Lake experienced four extremely dry, closed-basin intervals between 15,800 and 6,700 years ago that were preceded by wetter episodes (all ages are calibrated). Dry intervals centered on dates of 15,100, 13,200, 12,200, and 11,100 years ago. Following the last dry interval, the basin remained closed, with the lake itself desiccating completely about 6,700 years ago. Support for this desiccation period comes from Bischoff et al.'s (1997) work on another Owens Lake core. Both studies suggest that conditions became wetter after the desiccation period. This period of hyperaridity coincides with numerous western Great Basin paleoclimatic records (macrobotanical, pollen, tree line fluctuations, relict stumps) that chronicle a significant dry/warm interval from about 7,500 until 4,500 years ago (Grayson 1993).

Lake level fluctuations over the last 5,000 years have been reconstructed by Stine (1990, 1994a, 1994b, 1998), who has dated relict tree stumps found in growth position on former lakeshores, 10 m or more below historic lake levels. Stine's detailed studies of multiple basins indicate that lakes have undergone dramatic changes in water level—from a Holocene high stand 3,800 years ago to periods of extremely low levels or complete desiccation. The two lowest lake levels occurred between A.D. 900–1100 and A.D. 1200–1350, periods of extreme drought, for which Stine (1998) estimates inflow was less than 68 percent of modern levels (averaged from the years 1937–1979). A stump from Owens Lake located only 3 m above the lowest point on the lake bed dates to A.D. ~1020 and indicates that the lake was extremely shallow at that time (Stine 1998). The second-highest stand of the Holocene was reached about 375 years ago. The close correspondence of the dates for lake level changes across multiple basins (Tahoe, Mono, Owens), the absence of geomorphic explanations for the changes, and the corroborating evidence for paleoclimatic changes from other data such as tree rings (Graumlich 1993; Hughes and Graumlich 1996; LaMarche 1974) strongly argues for a unifying explanation: changes in precipitation, changes in evapotranspiration, or both (Stine 1998).

These records indicate that Owens Basin wetlands (river, tributaries, marshes, lake) have changed dramatically in size, depth, chemistry, and flow conditions over the last 15,000 years. The presence of fish in archaeological deposits predating 7000 B.P., and from 3500 B.P. to historic times, demonstrates that fish were able to adjust to these changing conditions. The nature of those adjustments was undoubtedly complex, including changes in productivity that would have affected the overall abundance and distribution of fish across the basin. We also suggest, however, that different species of fish would have responded differently to habitat changes, owing to differences in their life history strategies, and it is to these issues that we turn next.

Evolutionary ecologists long have recognized wide variation in life history strategies among organisms, including growth rate and overall body size attained, age at first reproduction, number of offspring, and reproductive cycles (MacArthur and Wilson 1967; Pianka 1970; Ricklefs 1979). In recognition of these factors, researchers have suggested that in more stable environments, populations live at limits imposed by the resources (or carrying capacity, *K*). Conversely, in more fluctuating environments, where populations periodically crash because of catastrophic events, adaptations that increase intrinsic population growth *(r)* are advantageous. In a catastrophic event, organisms die without regard to their genotype; in environments subjected to periodic fluctuations in temperature or moisture, selection favors rapid growth, early age of maturation, and small body size. In short, *r*-selected traits are favored in unstable environments, and *K*-selected traits are favored in stable settings.

Smith (1981) has used this distinction in a study of Great Basin fish and suggests that life history traits were strongly correlated with *size* of aquatic habitat: the larger the creek, river, or lake, the larger the fish and the older the fish at first spawning. Smith argues that habitat size is a good predictor of life history characteristics because of the link between environmental stability and habitat size. If all other variables are equal, then the larger the habitat, the more stable it is. Smith also found a strong positive relationship between body size and size of aquatic habitat, which he thought resulted from larger habitats being more stable.

Comparative life history data for tui chub and other suckers in California and Nevada show that the chub is more an *r*-strategist and that suckers are more *K*-strategists. *Catostomus fumeiventris* has received little study but is generally thought to resemble *C. tahoensis* (Tahoe sucker) in life history traits (Moyle 2002). Tui chub mature at smaller sizes and younger ages than the suckers most like Owens sucker. Also, the maximum size attained by chub is usually smaller than that reached by suckers. Historically, chub have thrived in the fluctuating environments of the western Great Basin, being the most abundant species in the large, shallow Harney Lake of southeastern Oregon and Eagle Lake of northeastern California. The ability of chub to "take advantage" of temporary improvements in habitat was illustrated in the 1980s when exceptionally high water flows into the Carson Sink of northeastern Nevada created vast shallow lake and marsh habitats. This led to a tremendous population explosion of tui chub. Subsequent declines in water level resulted in the mass death of an estimated seven million fish (Rowe and Hoffman 1987). Tui chub is the dominant fish in archaeological deposits dating to the last 3,000 years in this area, suggesting chub's prominence in these settings for an extended period (Butler 1996). Historically, the primary sucker of the Lahontan system in the western Great Basin, the Tahoe sucker, is less abundant in aquatic systems, and this at least indirectly suggests that suckers are not as successful as chub in highly fluctuating environments.

Smith's (1981) notions and the life history observations summarized in the preceding paragraph provide a basis on which to predict how chub and sucker would respond to changes in aquatic habitat over the last several thousand years. We predict that sucker would thrive in expanded or stable habitats and that tui chub would be favored in more constricted or fluctuating habitats or if both conditions obtained. As well, we predict that fish body size would decline with the constriction of aquatic habitat owing to the decline in stability.

Testing of the first prediction cannot be rigorous because we lack sufficient temporal resolution. For example, the earliest archaeological period spans several thousand years before 7000 B.P., and thus the fish record for this time cannot be readily compared with the detailed environmental reconstructions. Nevertheless, in expanded aquatic habitats of the Late Pleistocene/Early Holocene we find evidence for large Owens sucker, as expected. Toward the end of the Holocene, when aquatic habitats were reduced relative to Late Pleistocene–Early Holocene conditions and were subject to alternating periods of wetter and drier conditions, we find a more balanced mix of chub and sucker of generally smaller body size.

We can test the second prediction more rigorously using historic data on fish size. If the late-prehistoric pattern for small size is environmentally controlled—fish were relatively small because of habitat constraints—then small size should continue into the historic period. Alternatively, if small size reflects cultural selection—large fish were in the water system but not targeted for capture—then large fish should be present in the historic period.

Snyder (1917) lists individual body lengths of sucker and tui chub obtained from the Owens River drainage in the 1910s. These fish apparently were collected near the town of Laws, about 5 km northeast of Bishop. Sample sizes were small (n = 10 for each taxon), but the results are consistent with the hypothesis that modern chub and sucker are small. Sucker body length averaged 154 ± 16 mm, and chub body length averaged 89 ± 8 mm.

More recent collections reported by Miller (1973) include over 1,600 individuals each of chub and sucker. Collection dates are listed for some fish and indicate that they were caught in the 1940s and 1950s. Fish were collected throughout Owens Valley—from the main river channel, springs, irrigation ditches, sloughs, and reservoirs constructed for water diversion. Miller lists the range in body size (standard length) for each collection of fish, not individual specimens, precluding the calculation of summary statistics. Tui chub were consistently small, with a maximum standard length of 180 mm, and most fish were considerably smaller than this (Figure 2.5). The body size of Owens sucker is extremely variable, with some fish attaining lengths of over 400 mm (Figure 2.6). Important to our purpose, the largest body sizes of Owens sucker are from fish that had access to a

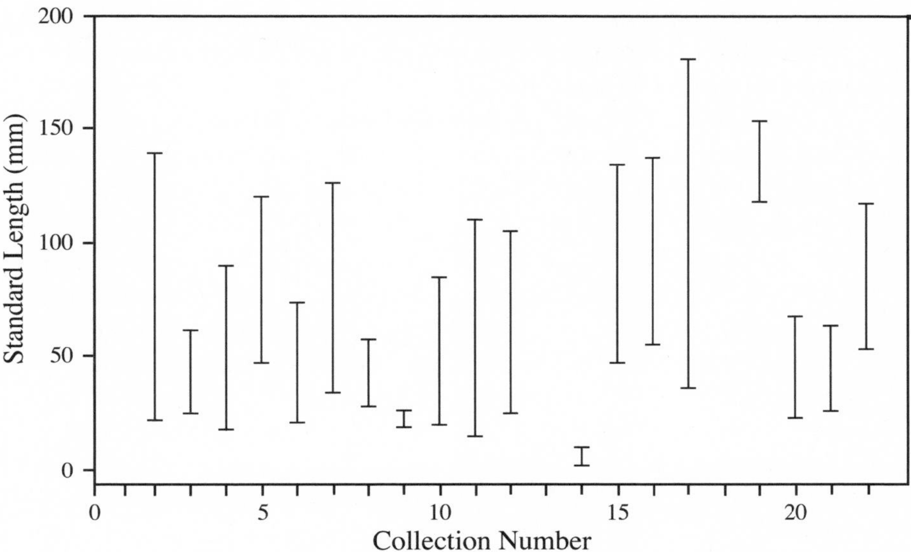

Figure 2.5. Standard length (mm) of tui chub *(Gila bicolor)* in 20th-century collections (N = 1,844 fish; bars are maximum–minimum size per collection).

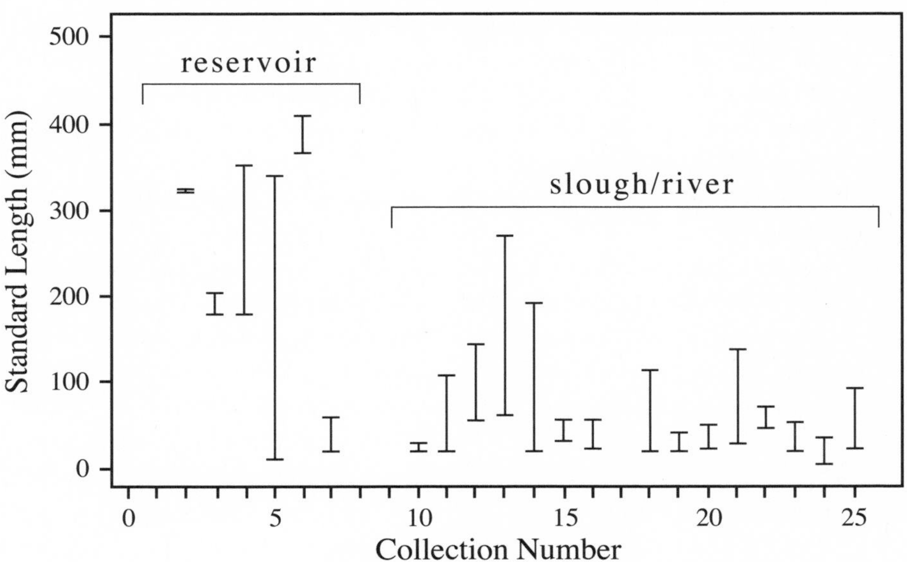

Figure 2.6. Standard length (mm) of Owens sucker *(Catostomus fumeiventris)* in 20th-century collections (N = 1,692 fish; bars are maximum–minimum size per collection).

large reservoir (Crowley Lake) during their yearly life cycle (Figure 2.6). The maximum size of sucker captured from sloughs and the Owens River itself is < 300 mm, and most fish are much smaller than this.

The large suckers found in association with reservoirs are the exceptions that prove the rule. Suckers attain relatively large sizes in modern times because they have access to reservoirs and thus are artifacts of 20th-century water projects. This supports our prediction that fish size (in historic and prehistoric times) has been constrained by the size of aquatic habitats. In turn, this result is consistent with the suggestion that the general trend toward smaller body size, from the early to the later periods (Figure 2.4), results from reduction in the size of aquatic habitat.

IMPLICATIONS FOR FISHERIES MANAGEMENT

Our results have two main implications for modern fishery issues in the Owens Valley. First, they may explain why Owens sucker, of all the native fish, is surviving relatively well in the valley today. Its success may be linked to the species' ability to thrive in artificially created lakes. Such lakes provide relatively large, stable habitats, which favor *K*-selected species such as Owens sucker. While not specifying the cause, Moyle recently commented on the relative success of the sucker in Owens Valley, noting that the fish "showed some capacity to adjust to the presence of nonnative fishes" (2002:195). Varying life histories may explain why certain fish are coping well with major changes wrought by modern water-use practices and fish introductions.

Second, our historical perspective allows us to isolate particular causes for modern declines in native fish. Biologists note two main causes for the declines: the significant loss of aquatic habitat associated with large-scale water-diversion projects and the introduction of alien species, mainly predaceous fish (U.S. Department of the Interior, Fish and Wildlife Service 1998). Paleoenvironmental records for Owens Valley clearly show, however, that aquatic habitats underwent major fluctuations over the last 15,000 years. Owens Lake has been desiccated or nearly so at least twice in the last 6,700 years; at other times conditions were much wetter, and the basin contained more wetlands than are known for the historic period. The zooarchaeological record demonstrates that fish inhabited the basin over this entire time and that they adjusted to these changes. That Owens Valley fish were able to cope with significant loss in habitat in ancient times (by finding refuge in available wetlands or reducing body size) suggests that these fish should have been capable of adjusting to habitat changes caused by 20th-century water-diversion projects. History did not, however, prepare native fish for introduced predators. Our study supports the position that nonnative predator fish are primarily responsible for modern declines in native fish. Unless more efforts are made to reduce or eliminate these alien fish from the critical habitat, the native species are probably doomed to extinction.

FUTURE STUDIES

Additional zooarchaeological samples from throughout the basin should be studied to develop a comprehensive record of fish distribution and abundance. The resulting data will allow us to track faunal changes that might be linked to environmental versus cultural changes. One archaeological site that merits particular attention is Fish Slough Cave, located next to Fish Slough, an extensive riparian habitat just north of the Owens River near Bishop (Figure 2.1). Archaeological projects carried out there in the early 1990s suggest that most cultural remains date between 1350 and 100 B.P. (Nelson 1999). Over 300 human coprolites were recovered, and faunal and floral preservation within them is excellent. Fish remains are common but have received little detailed analysis (Nelson 1999). The fish record here is important because it spans Stine's period of purportedly extreme drought (during the so-called medieval climatic anomaly). It should be possible in this context to obtain high-resolution radiocarbon dates of individual coprolites and to establish a precise record of fish response to what were likely significant changes in habitat.

If study of the Fish Slough Cave zooarchaeological collection (or others from the Owens Valley) produces results similar to those reported here, then ecologists will have strong evidence of baseline ichthyofaunal conditions. Such information can then be used to modify the existing recovery plan, and appropriate actions can be taken. By themselves, the data and analyses we have presented here indicate that management actions should minimally comprise significant reduction of alien predatory fish if a pre-19th-century ecosystem constitutes the desired baseline conditions. Our study also suggests that native fish taxa can withstand major fluctuations in local water levels, provided that they are not under additional stresses such as predation by alien species. In our view, this is an important bit of information for conservation biologists to have as modern Californians continue to divert water to their own uses.

Acknowledgments. Phil Pister, Steve Parmenter, Don Sada, Ray Temple, Rollie White, and Darrell Wong generously shared their knowledge of desert fish. Mark Scott's and Lee Lyman's editorial suggestions much improved the chapter. Betsy Reitz and others at the Georgia Museum of Natural History assisted Butler in various ways during the chapter's preparation. Doug Nelson and the Museum of Zoology, University of Michigan, loaned several comparative specimens used in this analysis. Liz Honeysett and Amy Gilreath facilitated the analysis of fish remains. We thank all of these people and any others we have inadvertently omitted.

3

Zooarchaeology and Wildlife Management in the Greater Yellowstone Ecosystem

Kenneth P. Cannon and Molly Boeka Cannon

When Yellowstone National Park (YNP) was created by an act of Congress in 1872 its boundaries were arbitrarily drawn in the hopes of including for protection all of the region's geothermal basins. From its infancy Yellowstone has been the focus of an ongoing debate regarding how its wildlife should be managed (Pritchard 1999). Initially the park was intended to provide various animal taxa with protection from poachers (Jacoby 2001). The debate has now evolved to include (1) the reestablishment of locally extirpated species, (2) the region's carrying capacity, and (3) future climatic change. In this chapter we explore how the zooarchaeological record has been applied to some of these issues and, more important, how the zooarchaeological record can become an integral part of management discourse.

DESCRIPTION OF THE ECOSYSTEM

The Greater Yellowstone Ecosystem (GYE) is an 18,000-mi^2 (4.6 million-ha) region in northwestern Wyoming, southwestern Montana, and northeastern Idaho. It includes two national parks and seven national forests (Figure 3.1). Ecosystem boundaries were first proposed in the 1970s and 1980s based on the range of local grizzly bears (*Ursus arctos* [Schullery 1997]). More recent definitions have expanded the size of the GYE and changed the focus from individual species to more general ecological principles (Keiter and Boyce 1991; Schullery 1997).

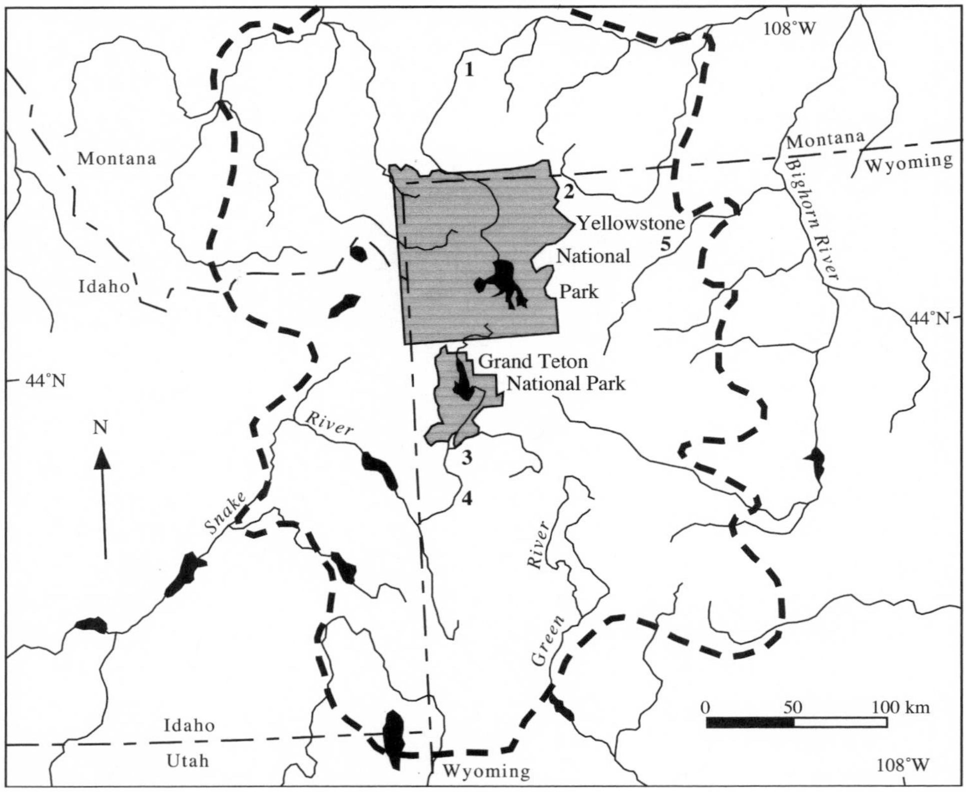

Figure 3.1. Greater Yellowstone Ecosystem (bold dashed line) and locations of zooarchaeological sites and places mentioned in the text—1: Myers-Hindman site; 2: Bugas-Holding site; 3: National Elk Refuge; 4: Hoback; 5: Horner site.

The high-elevation mountains and plateaus that characterize the GYE are the result of uplift associated with the Yellowstone hot spot. The southwestward migration of the North American plate over the hot spot has caused a northeastward migration of geothermal and tectonic activity for which the region is world famous (Pierce and Morgan 1992). During the mid-Quaternary (150,000–12,000 B.P.) the GYE experienced several episodes of glaciation. The 900-m-thick Pinedale glaciation was centered along a north–south axis through Yellowstone Lake, with ice flowing radially to the northeast, west, and southwest (Good and Pierce 1996; Pierce 1976). The annual temperature during full glaciation was probably 12°C colder than that at present. Regional biotic communities underwent significant changes, with species responding to environmental change based on their individual tolerances (FAUNMAP Working Group 1996; see also

Thompson et al. 1993; Whitlock 1993). Today 80 percent of the GYE is forested, although many vegetational communities are present (Despain 1990) and range from sagebrush grasslands at 1,370 m to alpine tundra at elevations over 3,900 m. Topographic relief provided by the uplift creates a mosaic of biotic communities within relatively small areas (Clark 1999).

Because species respond to environmental change based on their individual tolerances (Graham 1985; Whitlock et al. 1995), community composition is not stable over time. Shifts in climatic patterns have significant influences on local vegetation communities, depending on elevation, edaphic conditions, slope, aspect, and other factors. The community structure in the GYE today is geologically recent, though it is a product of its history. To understand how these communities develop we need to consult a record that spans thousands of years. The zooarchaeological record provides this time depth, and it also provides evidence of past variability that can be used to inform modern management decisions. To use the evidence in this way we must develop a management context that integrates modern ecological studies and prehistoric data (Committee on Ungulate Management in Yellowstone National Park [CUMYNP] 2002).

ZOOARCHAEOLOGY AND WILDLIFE MANAGEMENT

The Organic Act (16USC1–4) that created Yellowstone National Park (Haines 1977) calls for "the preservation, from injury or spoliation, of all timber, mineral deposits, natural curiosities, or wonders . . . and their retention in their natural condition." Congress also charged the secretary of the interior with preventing the "wanton destruction of the fish and game," as well as preventing the capture or killing of animals "for the purposes of merchandise or profit." The concept of a "natural condition" was implicit in the inception of Yellowstone (Pritchard 1999:5). Almost immediately it became apparent that greater protection of the region's large mammals from "market-hunting slaughter" was needed (Schullery et al. 1998). Lobbying by sportsmen and conservationists, led by *Forest and Stream* editor George Bird Grinnell, resulted in a secretarial order in 1883 that prohibited hunting in the park. The perception was that the park would serve not only as a game reserve but also as a game reservoir from which surrounding public hunting lands could be perpetually restocked by emigrating animals (Schullery et al. 1998). In 1894 public grassroots action resulted in passage of the Lacey Act, which provided legislative protection for large game animals within Yellowstone (Pritchard 1999).

Throughout much of the early to mid–20th century, management of large mammals was based on the emerging science of range management. Inherent in the Lacey Act was the perception that elk *(Cervus elaphus)* were overpopulating the northern range of Yellowstone and thus causing range deterioration and other problems (Schullery 1997). The act included provisions for the introduction of Plains bison *(Bison bison)* from private herds (Meagher 1973), periodic culling of elk and bison (Houston 1982), and the extirpation of predators (Schullery and Whittlesey 1999), particularly the wolf *(Canis lupus)*. The Leopold Report of 1963 (Leopold et al. 1963) provided the seeds for a new management paradigm that became known as "natural regulation." In 1967 this policy was enacted, but the culling of elk and bison was still a common practice. The "balance of nature" was being disturbed by such human actions, and the Leopold Report advocated active management to restore this balance (Pritchard 1999:208).

The public conception of the GYE was presented in the 1980s based largely on the migration patterns of local grizzly bears. The vision for management of the GYE incorporated such modern concepts of ecology as landscape-level change and the role of chance events within the context of island biogeography. It was during this period that wildlife biologists, both inside and outside the National Park Service, began consulting the archaeological record. Initially it was to argue for the role of First Americans in ecosystem management, but the zooarchaeological record was also searched for evidence of the presence (or absence) of particular species.

Wolf Reintroduction

One of the major goals of the natural regulation policy in the GYE is the establishment of the full suite of species that were present at the time of Yellowstone's creation. One of the first steps in this process was the reestablishment of wolves (Fischer 1995; Milstein 1995; U.S. Department of the Interior, Fish and Wildlife Service 1987). A review of the prehistoric record of wolves (Cannon 1992) prepared as part of a report for Congress bolstered the historical record (Schullery and Whittlesey 1992) and countered arguments by opposition groups. The latter claimed that wolves were recent immigrants that had been forced into this "marginal" environment by Euro-American settlement (Laundré 1992). Gray wolf remains have been found in 10 prehistoric deposits within the GYE and northern Rocky Mountains; these deposits span the last 12,000 years. The prehistoric evidence thus provides documentation of the continuous presence of wolves and important prey in several ecological zones since the Late Pleistocene.

And it legitimates the reintroduction of wolves because it indicates that wolves are what the National Park Service (1978) defines as a "native species."

In 1995, 14 wolves were released in YNP, and within the first year two litters were born, and four separate packs formed (Schullery 1997; U.S. Department of the Interior, Fish and Wildlife Service 1996). In 2002 there were approximately 160 individual wolves distributed in 14 packs in YNP, and there were several more packs in the GYE with ranges largely outside YNP (Smith et al. 2003). In the absence of modern human predation, the wolf seems to thrive in the GYE, much as it seems to have over the last 12,000 years. Most interestingly, from the perspective of conservation biology, the establishment of wolves in the ecosystem has had several notable influences on local ecology. Elk and moose *(Alces alces)* initially displayed no fear of wolves or their vocalizations or scents; now these ungulates are showing sensitivity to wolf vocalizations (Berger 2002). Predation by wolves has produced perhaps three times as much carrion as was available to scavengers prior to wolf reintroduction, supporting more ravens *(Corvus corax)*, magpies (*Pica* sp.), bald *(Haliaeetus leucocephalus)* and golden *(Aquila chrysaetos)* eagles, and bears (Ursidae), foxes, and coyotes *(Canis latrans)*. Finally, predation of elk by wolves seems to have prompted the former to alter its behaviors such that quaking aspen *(Populus tremuloides)*, a favored food of elk, is increasing in biomass (Ripple et al. 2001) and perhaps returning to pre-park abundances. This does not necessarily mean that the GYE will return to some sort of ecologically natural balance of predators, prey, and vegetation. This is so because eventually state agencies will take over wolf management from the federal government, and if these agencies determine that wolf populations outside of park boundaries should not be allowed to continue to grow, then only the parklands will have the opportunity to be somehow "natural" (see chap. 1). Here, public opinion may weigh more heavily on what eventually transpires than the structure of the ecosystem (Berger 2002). Our point, however, is that a combination of zooarchaeological and palynological research (Whitlock 1993) could provide predictions of such intertaxonomic ecological relationships.

Elk

The public and scientific interest in elk in the GYE is not new. During the 1890s Yellowstone's acting superintendent showed concern over the growing elk population and the impact that this large ungulate was having on the region (Schullery 1997). Human settlement of Jackson Hole south of Grand Teton National Park displaced elk from their prime winter range, and hard winters in the early years of the 20th century had a devastating impact on the elk population. Members of the local community, along with government representatives, raised money for the purchase of feed; despite their efforts, hundreds of elk died (Boyce 1989). With funding from public and private sources the National Elk Refuge (Figure 3.1) was established in 1912. Today concern has shifted again to whether elk numbers are inflated and to the effect elk may be having on vegetation, soils, and other animal species (Boyce 1989; Kay 1990). As Schullery has stated, "No single issue has so engaged Yellowstone's managers and constituencies as the 'elk problem,' and no other issue is more likely to shape future attempts to manage the park with concern for ecological processes" (1997: 149).

To understand the nature of precontact elk populations, researchers began in the 1980s to consider the zooarchaeological record. Archaeologist Gary Wright (1984) had recently presented two hypotheses concerning the paucity of elk in northwestern Wyoming archaeological sites. The first, based on accounts from the 19th century, suggested that elk were insufficiently abundant to provide a consistent and predictable resource for prehistoric humans. Although this may be true, we suggest that some elk would have been exploited, even if only opportunistically. Wright's second hypothesis was that the migration patterns of human groups and those of elk rarely overlapped and then only for short periods during the middle of the spring and late autumn. When humans were occupying the valley floor, elk were on their summer ranges in the higher elevations, and during the winter when elk were occupying the valley, human groups had abandoned the area. We do not yet have the data to test this hypothesis.

The authors of two important publications at the time—*Playing God in Yellowstone* (Chase 1987) and *Wildlife in Transition* (Despain et al. 1986)—were not archaeologists, but they consulted the zooarchaeological record during the course of their research. Chase (1987) basically follows Wright's (1984) earlier suggestions and concludes that elk had never been abundant in the GYE. Despain et al. (1986) hypothesize that elk used Yellowstone for winter range prior to the arrival of Euro-Americans. Data collected from the literature suggested that elk were present in the area in precontact times. The evidence was, however, limited to one archaeological site and a paleontological context in the north-central portion of YNP. The depositional context of the latter is not clear, but Despain et al. (1986:

TABLE 3.1. Abundance of Ungulate Remains per Settlement Unit at the Myers-Hindman Site.

Settlement Unit	Age (B.P.)	Number of Identified Specimens					
		Bison	Deer	Elk	Bighorn Sheep	Pronghorn	Total
1	9000	14 (37.84)	10 (27.03)	2 (5.40)	9 (24.32)	2 (5.40)	37
3	5500	30 (24.79)	8 (6.61)	7 (3.31)	62 (51.24)	17 (14.05)	124
4	3300	48 (28.57)	48 (28.57)	20 (11.90)	46 (27.38)	6 (3.57)	168
5	2300	33 (31.43)	28 (26.67)	13 (12.38)	24 (22.86)	7 (6.67)	105
6	1900	38 (56.72)	6 (8.95)	8 (11.94)	7 (10.45)	8 (11.94)	67
7	1450	23 (62.16)	3 (8.11)	7 (18.92)	3 (8.11)	1 (2.70)	37
8	800	22 (47.83)	2 (3.35)	16 (34.78)	8 (11.87)	1 (2.7)	49
Total		208	105	73	159	42	587

Note: After Lahren 1976. Values in parentheses are relative (percent) abundances per settlement unit.

118, n.6) feel that the remains are at least 250 years old. The elk bones from archaeological deposits are also of uncertain age. Houston (1982) had earlier argued for a long record of elk in the region based on the 9,000-year record at the Myers-Hindman site (Table 3.1, Figure 3.1).

Use of the zooarchaeological record became commonplace in the literature of the 1990s. One of the more prolific researchers to utilize the prehistoric record of elk in discussions of contemporary wildlife-management issues is Charles Kay. Two critical assumptions in his (1990, 1994, 2002) studies are that First Americans were hunting elk in proportion to elk abundance on the landscape and that the zooarchaeological record should reflect the abundance of elk killed. According to these assumptions, if elk populations today are as large as they were in the past, then elk should dominate the zooarchaeological record. Kay (1990, 1994) has probably compiled more zooarchaeological data for the western states than anyone else to date. He (1990:57) reviewed more than 500 archaeological reports on excavated sites in Idaho, Montana, Nevada, Oregon, Utah, Washington, and Wyoming. In trying to understand those data he has identified a number of biases that may have influenced them: (1) inconsistent recovery and reporting of faunal remains, (2) limited excavation, (3) poor preservation of faunal remains, and (4) archaeological research driven largely by cultural resource management projects and minimal problem-oriented research. By increasing the sample to include data from seven western states rather than, say, just YNP or the GYE, and by lumping all the data he compiled from those states, Kay (1990) believed that he could minimize such biases. He has concluded that

> archaeological evidence indicates that pre-Columbian ungulate populations were not resource limited. . . . Of nearly 60,000 ungulate bones unearthed at > 400 archaeological sites in the United States and Canadian Rockies, < 3% were elk, and only about 10% were bison. . . . Even in the Greater Yellowstone Ecosystem, where elk presently constitute around 80% of the total ungulate fauna, elk are rare to nonexistent in archaeological sites. (1990:487; see also 1994)

It may be, however, that Kay's data do "not get us back to the original population density, for too many unknowns are involved, the least of which may be due to sampling error. [Further,] elk remains, while never a dominant member of the faunal assemblage, are consistently present throughout the prehistoric record" (Cannon 1992:1–252). For example, in a study independent of Kay's, Barnosky (1996) notes that more than one-third of the 200 archaeological and paleontological sites she examined contained elk remains. Further, she has found that of "the late Holocene records of Wyoming, Montana, and Idaho, only four of 19 did not contain elk" (1996:161). She also observes that paleontological sites in the region were slightly more likely to contain elk remains than archaeological sites were, suggesting that there was either a cultural bias reducing the representation of elk or a bias in the reporting or identification of faunal remains from archaeological sites.

Kay's comparison of the zooarchaeological record with modern conditions is flawed for several reasons. His lumping of data from a seven-state area and more than 10,000 years of time into a single value may minimize various taphonomic and sampling biases just as he hopes, but this is unknown (CUMYNP 2002). More important, it masks what may be significant spatial and temporal variation in elk abundances. Temporal variation is masked when, for example, the number of identified specimens from seven temporally distinct settlement units defined by Lahren (1976) at the Myers-Hindman site are summed. The sum indicates that elk remains constitute about 12 percent of all ungulate remains. But if calculated for each individual settlement unit, elk abundance ranges from 5.40 percent of all ungulate remains to 32.65 percent (Table 3.1). Kay also masks spatial variation by data lumping. The 400-year-old Bugas-Holding site, occupied during a single winter (Rapson 1990), becomes comparable to the Myers-Hindman site, which was occupied intermittently between 9000 and 800 B.P. (Lahren 1976); the nearly 100 km that separate the two sites

(Figure 3.1) and attendant environmental differences are also masked (for additional evaluation of the archaeological data Kay reviews, see Lyman 2004a). Elk and other animals are not managed by one set of rules over the entire geographic area making up Kay's sampling universe, nor were they subjected to identical environmental and predation histories, but his lumping of all spatiotemporally distinct data presumes both. Similar problems attend other data that Kay (1990, 1994) uses (Yochim 2001). Our point is simple. We advocate the use of zooarchaeological data to help resolve wildlife-management and conservation problems, but like any other kind of data, they must be used wisely and with full recognition of their biases and weaknesses.

Bison

The management policies concerning the GYE have intimately involved bison. Expressions of this range from the public outcry over their slaughter in the late 19th century that produced the Lacey Act to the current outpouring of support on behalf of the Yellowstone bison slaughtered during winter 1996–1997 in the name of protecting the local cattle industry (Peacock 1997). Federal agencies in the GYE are currently developing management plans for the region's bison herds (Grand Teton National Park and National Elk Refuge [GRTE–NER] 1996; National Park Service 2000).

The Yellowstone bison herd is one of the few remaining free-ranging herds in North America, rescued from near extinction in the late 19th century by a combination of the aggressive protection of the native herd and the introduction of bison from private herds (Keiter 1997). During the early part of the 20th century the two herds were managed separately, but eventually they were allowed to interbreed. Over the next 50 years Yellowstone's bison were intensively managed, with culling a common practice (Schullery 1986; see also Meagher 1973; Schullery et al. 1998). Shortly after the Leopold Report (Leopold et al. 1963) was issued, the National Park Service took a noninterventionist approach to natural resource management, relying instead on natural processes to effect change and to control wildlife population numbers (Keiter 1997). Bison responded by increasing their numbers from 397 in 1967 to a high of 3,956 individuals in 1995 (National Park Service 1997:113–114; Figure 3.2).

The Jackson Hole Bison Management Plan notes that bison were absent from Jackson Hole between "at least 1840 and 1948" (GRTE–NER 1996: 5). The modern Jackson Hole bison herd was created in 1948 with the

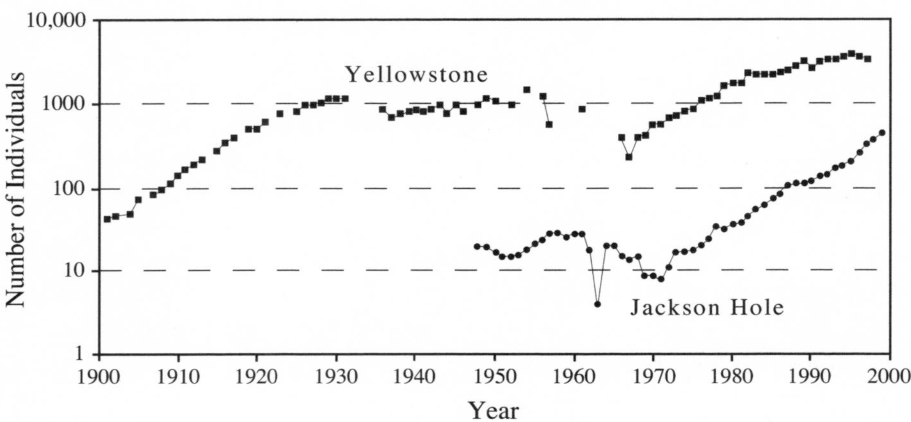

Figure 3.2. Winter bison counts for Yellowstone National Park (National Park Service 1997) and Jackson Hole (data provided by Steve Cain, Grand Teton National Park).

introduction of 20 individuals (3 bulls, 12 cows, and 5 calves) from YNP to the 1,500-acre (600-ha) Jackson Hole Wildlife Park near the eastern border of Grand Teton National Park (Figure 3.1). This private, nonprofit endeavor was sponsored by the New York Zoological Society, the Jackson Hole Preserve, Inc., and the Wyoming Game and Fish Commission. This population was maintained at between 15 and 30 individuals until 1963, when brucellosis *(Brucella abortus)* was detected in the herd, and the bison, with the exception of four vaccinated yearlings and five new calves, were destroyed (Cain et al. 1998; GRTE–NER 1996).

The herd was revitalized in 1964 with the introduction of 12 bison from Theodore Roosevelt National Park, bringing the herd size up to 21. In 1968 the herd was down to 11 adults and four or five calves, who later in the year escaped the confines of the wildlife park. The herd was eventually allowed to range freely in 1969, partially because of the Leopold Report, which called for the incorporation of ecological principles into the management of natural resources. The free-ranging herd soon established fairly well-defined movement patterns in GRTE, with summers in the Potholes/Signal Mountain/Snake River bottoms area and winters in the Snake River bottoms and further south. Since winter 1975–1976, with the exception of the 1976–1977 winter, the herd has wintered on the National Elk Refuge (GRTE–NER 1996:6). Herd size has grown substantially since it became free ranging. Growth in the 1970s was relatively slow, but in 1980 bison began feeding on supplemental winter feed intended for elk. Herd growth has been dramatic since 1980, probably in large part because of the supplemental feed and the subsequent decrease in winter mortality (GRTE–NER 1996:6).

Currently, managers in GYE are faced with the task of "maintain[ing] a wild, free-ranging population of bison" (National Park Service 2000:i), yet it is only recently that they have begun to study more than the last 100 years of bison history. For example, quite recently the following recommendation was made: "Yellowstone is a dynamic landscape, and we cannot determine whether management actions have forced components of the system beyond their historical range of variability unless we place recent dynamics in a longer time frame. Knowledge of prehistoric and historical environments is essential for creating a context for this evaluation" (CUMYNP 2002:32).

Schullery et al. are correct "that paleontological, archaeological, and historical research completed so far does not allow for reliable comparisons of the abundance of bison . . . at times past with abundance now" (1998:327). We believe, however, that a cross-disciplinary approach to the management of bison can go far beyond merely tallying numbers of specimens. New techniques such as stable isotope analysis, pollen and phytolith analysis, and DNA extraction can assist with reconstructing the biology and ecology of prehistoric bison. Application of these techniques will provide empirical data relevant to contemporary management issues such as "(1) how long bison have resided in the Greater Yellowstone Ecosystem, (2) the characteristics of the pre-park population, (3) the influence of prehistoric humans on bison, (4) how populations reacted to past climatic change, and (5) what management decisions can be made to ensure viable populations, in light of our current understanding of future climatic change" (Cannon 2001:147).

The prehistoric record of bison in the GYE extends back at least 10,000 years (Cannon 1992). Nineteenth-century observations suggest that bison ranged throughout low-elevation meadows, with probable summer migrations into the high alpine meadows (Meagher 1973). Today, bison are restricted to public lands in YNP and Jackson Hole. Migrations beyond these political boundaries result in either hazing or death (Peacock 1997). On the one hand, a general paucity of bison remains in the archaeological record, as well as low and fluctuating numbers of modern bison in Yellowstone and Jackson Hole, led Wright to conclude that "bison were always relatively rare in northwestern Wyoming, and that they would have been too unpredictable in numbers to provide a stable food source" for humans (1984:28). He believes that because populations were small, a single successful kill of adults would have reduced the reproductive potential of the herd to a level where it would no longer have been a significant part of the ecosystem. Meagher, on the other hand, suggests that "substantial numbers of bison inhabited the Yellowstone Plateau at all seasons, and long before the killing of the northern herd of Great Plains bison in the early 1880s" (1973:14). These opposing views make it clear that there are many details about the population history of bison left to learn.

Since the time when Wright and Meagher presented their views, new information has become available concerning both modern and prehistoric populations. Part of Wright's argument for low numbers of bison in the prehistoric record came from the extrapolation of the population dynamics of modern bison in both Yellowstone and Jackson Hole. Although bison in both areas received protection by the Department of the Interior, Wright failed to mention that bison were often removed from the herds based on various management decisions. Winter counts of bison in Jackson Hole indicate that since the mid 1960s bison numbers have increased to 438 in 1999 (Figure 3.2).

Although it is problematic to interpret similarities between prehistoric bison populations and modern managed herds, it is apparent that the region can support a sizable population. Given new zooarchaeological data, it is time to reevaluate the role of bison in the GYE. The known prehistoric record of the GYE provides a minimum of 66 strata in 30 archaeological and three paleontological sites that have produced bison remains (Cannon 2001). These represent 29 open archaeological sites, one archaeological cave site, and three paleontological sites but do not include the various drive sites in Paradise Valley north of YNP (Cannon 2001). George Arthur (1966) has estimated that at least 10 bison kill sites are present in Paradise Valley, including a large complex of drive lines and rock cairns known as the Emigrant Buffalo Jump.

Thirteen sites in Jackson Hole have produced bison remains. The earliest evidence of bison in the region is reported from south of Jackson Hole on the Snake River near Hoback (Figure 3.1). During excavation for development, "a layer of mixed *bison* bone and shell was exposed.... Several *bison* skulls were retrieved from this layer [and] were not of any *bison* larger than modern populations" (Love 1972:50). Mollusk shell collected from a "trench intersecting 2-ft shell bed at depth of 3 ft" by J. D. Love in 1959 and submitted to the U.S. Geological Survey produced an age of 11,940 ± 500 B.P. (W-1070; Ives et al. 1964:60), though this date should be viewed with some caution (Cannon 2001).

A well-dated archaeological assemblage of bison *(Bison antiquus)* remains was found at the Horner site (Frison and Todd 1987), located on the Shoshone River north of Cody, Wyoming, and east of YNP (Figure 3.1). Excavations produced the remains of about 300 individual bison that date to about 9,000 years ago. Given the age of these remains, it is not surprising that they are larger than homologous skeletal elements in modern bison (Todd and Hofman 1987), as this is the pattern documented throughout the continent (e.g., McDonald 1981). *Why* bison underwent diminution during the Late Pleistocene and Holocene is unclear, but suggestions concern forage quality and quantity, intensity of intraspecific competition, and predation-influenced demography. In the process of figuring out why bison got smaller, we may discover information valuable to ensuring the survival of existing bison herds.

Three sites in Yellowstone and several sites in Jackson Hole are either adjacent to modern migration routes or within modern seasonal ranges of bison (Cannon 2001). Archaeological investigations in areas currently used by bison could inform the development of a model of bison habitat use and selection under various climatic regimes. This information may be useful when managing herds in anticipation of future climatic change, as well as for managing modern winter range (National Park Service 2000). Understanding the relationship between past and future climatic change, and its implication for ecosystem management, is a high-priority research need for federal agencies (CUMYNP 2002; U.S. Department of the Interior, Fish and Wildlife Service 1999).

The zooarchaeological record by its nature provides empirical data on how humans and bison interacted. As others have argued, humans were probably the main predator of bison (Fisher and Roll 1998) and significantly influenced their behavior, distribution, evolution, and abundance. During the past 100 years, culling of herds was a common management practice. However, the practice rarely took into consideration the impact this had on herd structure and genetic diversity (Shull and Tipton 1987). A unique aspect of the zooarchaeological record is that it provides snapshots of different times that allow us to explore such issues as herd structure and genetic diversity.

With recent advances in the extraction of DNA from fossils, the archaeological record provides a unique opportunity for addressing not only issues of taxonomy but also the genetic variability of bison populations prior to the 19th-century bottleneck. The zooarchaeological record can also be used to study migration (e.g., chap. 9) and gene flow among populations (Chambers 1998). The management of the genetic diversity and integrity of threatened populations is an important issue in conservation biology (Meffe and Carroll 1997). In addition to long-term conservation goals of protecting the germ plasm, other conservation issues can be addressed using genetic analyses, such as understanding the effect of the hybridization of the native YNP bison with bison introduced in the early 20th century and the determination of minimal viable population size (e.g., Schnabel et al. 2000; Ward et al. 2001). DNA analysis of archaeological bison remains should provide guidance on these issues (Ward et al. 1999). Archaeological bison kill sites provide moment-in-time information on herd demography (age and sex ratios) as well as genetic diversity. These attributes can be compared with those of modern herds to assess how genetic diversity and demography have changed over time. Such comparisons could help biologists and managers identify populations that may be at risk for the various consequences of low genetic diversity or unusual demography.

DISCUSSION

Understanding the relationship between past and future climatic change and its implications for ecosystem management is recognized as a high-priority research need (CUMYNP 2002). Simulation models indicate that doubling the carbon dioxide concentration in the atmosphere will produce a combination of elevational and directional range adjustments by individual plant taxa (Bartlein et al. 1997). The range of high-elevation species will be reduced, and some species will become regionally extirpated. Resulting new vegetation communities have no modern analogues because they mix low-elevation montane species currently in the region with extralocal species from the northern and central Rockies and Pacific Northwest. These results are similar to those that the FAUNMAP Working Group (1996) found when analyzing the zooarchaeological record—mammalian species respond as individuals based on their particular tolerances and not as communities. Such responses call into question the adequacy of current management to anticipate the nature of future climatic change. As prehistorians we have the tools to provide insight into how populations in the past responded to change and to model how populations in the future may respond.

The zooarchaeological record has much to offer the management of wildlife in the Greater Yellowstone Ecosystem. In preparing the justification for the reintroduction of the wolf, the prehistoric record provided a much longer record of the presence of the wolf and its prey species than was evident in the historic record alone. But we also know that there are many critical taphonomic and sampling issues to contend with when one uses the zooarchaeological record to address wildlife issues (Cannon 1992; CUMYNP 2002; Lyman 1994c, 1996).

The zooarchaeological record provides information on the presence or absence of individual species as well as insights into ecology and the evolution of community structures. This is exemplified by the records of elk and bison. Simulation models indicate that future climatic change will produce communities that have no modern analogues because of species-level responses. By understanding how mammalian species responded to previous shifts in climatic regimes, we may be better prepared to make empirically based management decisions concerning populations in the face of modern and future changes (Cannon 2001; CUMYNP 2002).

Another task at hand is deciding how we transform what appears to be an arcane argument among academics into a viable role in the wildlife management discussion. At a meeting of the Department of the Interior's Bison Management Group held in 2000 we were presented with the rebuff that the archaeological evidence of bison, though interesting, was like counting angels on the head of a pin. Boyce had earlier expressed this sentiment much more simply: "Even if we could find 'proof' of substantial Indian predation on elk and other ungulates, we have no way of estimating the number of animals that should be culled to duplicate this source of mortality" (1991:196). We argue differently. Berger and Cunningham (1994) provide a comprehensive ecological and behavioral study of the bison herd at Badlands National Park in South Dakota. Data gathered from this study could supplement precontact data derived from paleontological and archaeological sites to produce a comprehensive model of precontact populations of bison in North America. As we envision it, this model would include information on behavior, ecology, and the cultural and natural causes of bison mortality.

Contrary to the naysayers, we believe that zooarchaeology *can* contribute directly to the resolution of various conservation issues identified by Berger and Cunningham (1994). Zooarchaeology can (1) reveal precontact herd demographic structures, (2) identify the presence or absence of precontact populations in particular areas, and (3) provide a temporal record at an evolutionary scale for the genetic conservation of modern populations. With respect to the first, bison kill sites typically reveal much about herd demography (see Stiner 1991). Such sites are especially valuable because they provide demographic information that is limited to a particular herd at a particular time. This information also allows the measurement of climatic and predation pressures and how herds respond demographically to such pressures. The presence of herds at some time in the past is demonstrated by kill sites, although the absence of a herd is not necessarily reflected by the absence of such sites (e.g., Lyman and Wolverton 2002).

Zooarchaeological research can also contribute to the debate about the existence of multiple geographically or genetically distinct bison populations in North America. Considering the penultimate distribution of bison in many different ecozones, multiple subspecies of bison are conceivable, though their existence is debated (e.g., Geist 1991; van Zyll de Jong 1986; van Zyll de Jong et al. 1995). Recent success in studying the genetic history of modern bison and the taxonomic status of proposed subspecies has been gained by studying their mitochondrial DNA (Polziehn et al. 1995; Polziehn et al. 1996). There is the potential that mtDNA can be extracted from prehistoric bison remains (e.g., Richards et al. 1993; Richards et al. 1995). The mtDNA of precontact bison specimens would reveal much about the evolutionary histories of extant populations and thus provide information critical to wise genetic conservation within modern populations.

We believe it better to attempt to count angels than to ignore potentially significant (paleo)ecological information. The cost of making the wrong management decision will more often than not outweigh the cost of a failed tallying effort. We have shown here some of the ways that prehistoric data can be used in the service of conservation biology as practiced in one of the best-known ecosystems in the world.

4

Where the Muskox Roamed: Biogeography of Tundra Muskox *(Ovibos moschatus)* in the Eastern Arctic

CHRISTYANN M. DARWENT AND JOHN DARWENT

Thirty years ago, wildlife biologist Peter Lent (1971) noted that marked fluctuations in Canadian populations of tundra muskox *(Ovibos moschatus)* occupying various islands of the Arctic, or Canadian, Archipelago were inexplicable, and he implied that knowledge of the cause of those fluctuations was critical to wise management of extant herds. A decade later, biologist Anne Gunn remarked that "one of the most severe restrictions on the management of muskoxen is the extremely high logistical cost of obtaining even basic data" (1982:1033). High costs attend data gathering and management because this large ungulate occurs in high northern latitudes where access is limited and the climate is harsh much of the year. In North America muskoxen currently inhabit tundra regions surrounding glaciers and permanent snowfields in both Greenland and the islands of the Canadian archipelago, as well as areas with analogous vegetation on the Canadian Arctic mainland (Figure 4.1). Gathering zooarchaeological data on muskoxen is no easier than gathering biological data on them, but the former data have largely been ignored in the context of managing this large ungulate.

Muskoxen are remnants of the Pleistocene that tend to thrive where other large ungulates cannot (Klein 1996). Muskox populations have literally come "back from the brink" (Barr 1991) with their extirpation from Alaska in the late 1800s (Lent 1999) and their extirpation in parts of Canada resulting from the European demand for muskox robes (Barr 1991; Burch 1977). Because of the decline in the metapopulation of musk-

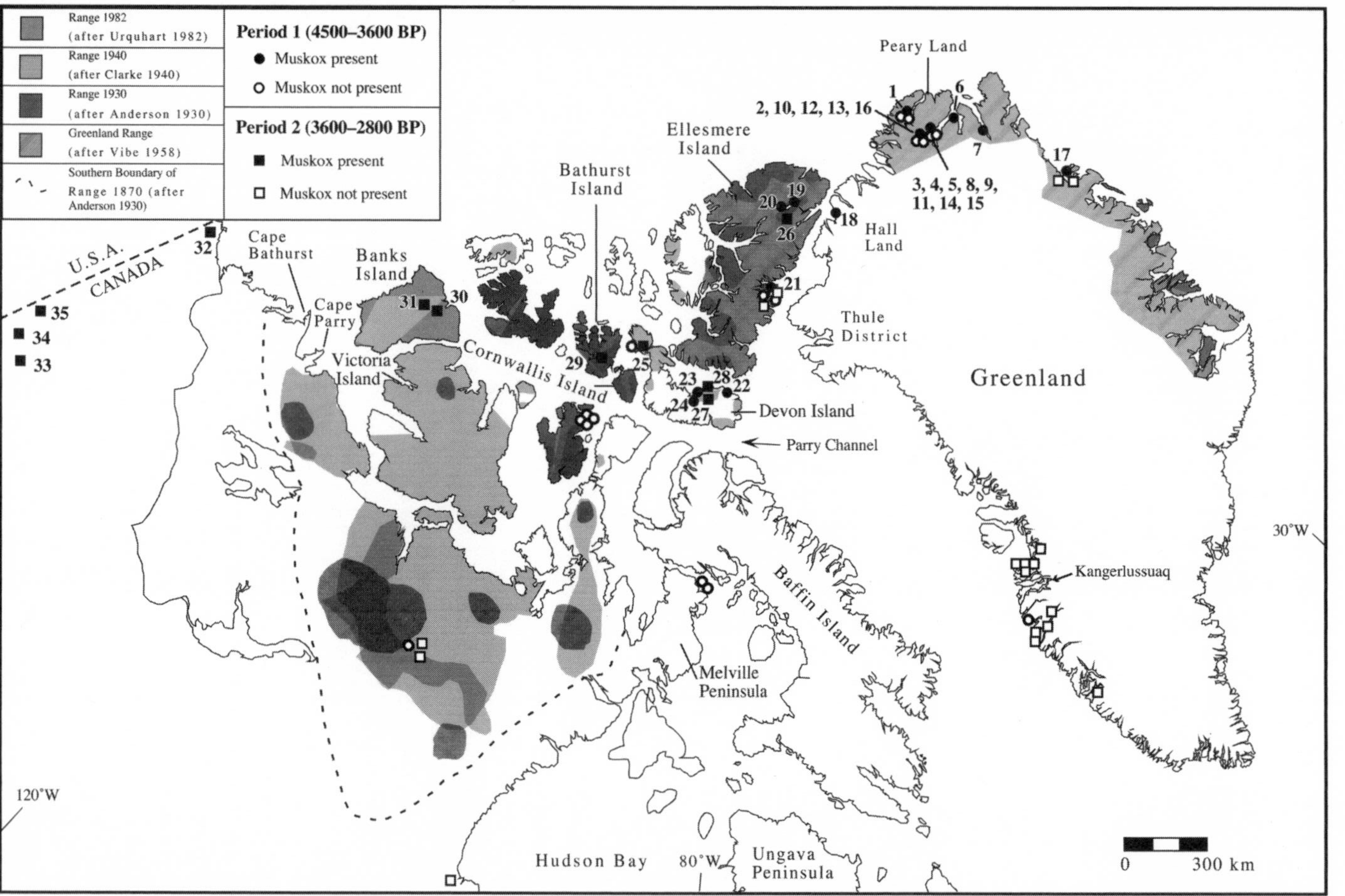

Figure 4.1. Locations of sites with identified mammalian remains and with muskox remains in the Canadian Arctic and Greenland for Period 1 (4500–3600 B.P.; n = 24) and Period 2 (3600–2800 B.P.; n = 11). Modern distributions of muskox shown for comparison.

oxen, the Canadian government banned hunting and placed the species under protection in 1917. In much of Canada muskox populations have increased steadily since this protection was enacted, and the species has recently been removed from endangered lists. Some populations on Arctic islands have, however, actually decreased in recent years (Miller 1988; Miller et al. 1977), forcing the government to revisit the status of muskoxen and to reconsider their protection in these remote island localities.

Following conservation biology definitions of a modern "natural" (see chap. 1) range, a group of muskoxen from northeastern Greenland was transplanted to Alaska in the 1930s; muskoxen from northeastern Greenland were introduced to western Greenland in the 1960s; and a captive herd was released in the Ungava region of northern Quebec during the 1970s and 1980s (Gray 1987; Gunn 1982; Klein 1996; Lent 1999). These transplant episodes were aimed at establishing herds that could be hunted either by sports hunters or for "traditional" subsistence purposes by Native Inuit (Eskimo) or that would add to the wilderness experience of tourists. These conservation efforts have, for the most part, been successful, although the herd transplanted to the Thule District of northwestern Greenland has declined, and Inughuit subsistence hunting is currently banned (Land et al. 2000). We suggest that the maintenance of such herds requires knowledge of the causes of fluctuations in herd size, and here we explore long-term zooarchaeological data as a little-tapped source of information on those causes.

The interaction of humans and muskoxen has long been a topic of interest both to archaeologists and to wildlife biologists. For archaeologists, muskoxen often have been the mystical animals that initially spurred people to leave Alaska, cross the Canadian Arctic, and settle in the muskox–laden utopian expanses of northern Greenland. For wildlife biologists, humans typically have been the primary culprits in a long-term decline in the distribution of muskoxen in the eastern Arctic and have thus heavily influenced "where the muskox roamed." Numerous investigators in both camps (Burch 1977; Knuth 1967; Lent 1999; Tener 1965; Wilkinson 1975) have discussed the potential importance of the muskox to early prehistoric occupants of the Canadian and Greenlandic Arctic and have proposed reasons for apparent decreases in muskox populations over time. Their conclusions suggest that muskoxen have experienced a dynamic biogeographic history over the past 4,500 years and that during that time humans have relied on, and thereby decimated, muskox populations in certain areas. The nature of the evidence on which these conclusions have been based is, however, generally anecdotal or, at best, unsystematic.

Lent (1999) demonstrates that understanding the prehistoric and historic distribution and use of muskoxen in Alaska is critical to the effective conservation and management of the species. Following his example, we here present two kinds of evidence. First, we document the biogeographic history of muskoxen in the eastern Arctic over the past 4,500 years using zooarchaeological and paleobiological evidence. Second, we examine the relative abundance of muskoxen over time in the eastern Arctic. Our findings indicate that muskoxen were established in their modern range by the Mid-Holocene, that this range was far more extensive than what was documented historically, that muskox abundance decreased over time until the period of historical European contact, and that concerns over the long-term survival of muskox populations may be misplaced.

DISTRIBUTION AND ECOLOGY

The only extant species of muskox is the tundra muskox, of which natural populations are found in the most northern parts of North America and Greenland. During the last glaciation, prior to 10,000 B.P., muskoxen ranged across northern Eurasia (Kahlke 1994), and in North America they ranged as far south as Iowa and Virginia (Graham and Lundelius 1994). The modern geographic range of the muskox (Figure 4.1) is climatically determined by the distribution and production of suitable forage plants (Klein 1996:52); these include "woody species, flowering plants, grasses, sedges, mosses, and fortuitously, lichens" (Tener 1965:45). Areas such as northern Greenland, eastern Ellesmere Island, Banks Island, and Melville Island that are rich in this kind of foliage tend to support large herds of muskoxen, with populations sometimes numbering several thousand individuals, though numbers can fluctuate widely (Barr 1991; Gunn et al. 1991; Miller 1988; Miller et al. 1977). Because of their dependence on a limited variety of plants, muskox populations have historically been reduced periodically by changes in climate, in particular by conditions that limit their access to consumable vegetation such as deep or dense layers of snow or warm conditions that result in freezing rain and ice crusts (Parker et al. 1975). Predation by humans, wolves *(Canis lupus)*, and polar bears *(Ursus maritimus)* also influences population sizes.

Compared with caribou *(Rangifer tarandus)*, muskoxen do not conduct long-range seasonal migrations; rather, they tend to move short distances (~75 km) between summer and winter feeding grounds (Banfield 1974). This may, in part, account for their susceptibility to the effects of foliage shortages and predation. Klein (1996) refers to caribou as having great locomotive efficiency and wide adaptability to substrates and habitats (see also Meldgaard 1986). In contrast, muskoxen are more limited in their morphological, physiological, and behavioral plasticity during times of stress (Klein 1996). Because of this inflexibility, muskoxen tend to be less successful than caribou in maintaining southern populations, but for reasons not fully understood, muskoxen are better able to maintain populations in the High Arctic and in areas with similar vegetation.

METHODS

To document changes in the Mid- to Late Holocene distribution of the muskox, we compared the location of archaeological and fossil (paleobiological) remains recovered from deposits ranging from 4,500 years ago with the modern, recorded distribution of the muskox. Prior to 4500 B.P., the record is particularly poor, as only six paleobiological muskox localities in the Canadian Arctic have been published (Morlan 1999a): LaVo-VP, in the Yukon Drainage (~20,000 B.P.); MgVo-3, Bluefish Cave in the Yukon (~14,000 B.P.); NjVi-VP, on Hershel Island, Yukon (~13,000 B.P.); OkRl-VP, Banks Island (~10,000 B.P.); and QjLj-VP and RaLl-VP, on Bathurst Island (~6500–6200 B.P.). These localities substantially predate deglaciation and the environmental conditions of the Middle–Late Holocene and are too few to provide a baseline of conditions prior to human colonization.

Our sample is derived from all published and unpublished reports known to us that discuss either the presence or the number of identified specimens (NISP) of mammals in Arctic Canada and Greenland. This information is supplemented by our identification and analysis of zooarchaeological material collected in the central High Arctic of Canada (Little Cornwallis Island and Lea Point on southern Ellesmere Island) and in the Peary Land and Hall Land regions of northern Greenland. Additional unpublished faunal localities in Greenland either with an associated radiocarbon date or assigned a general temporal range based on associated diagnostic artifacts were obtained from site archives at the Zoological Museum, University of Copenhagen. We compiled information for 292 temporally distinct assemblages of zooarchaeological remains from 272 sites, irrespective of whether they contained muskox remains or not. Although we recognize that the absence of evidence of muskoxen in an area does not necessarily constitute evidence for the prehistoric absence of muskoxen, we assume that multiple large samples of faunal remains that lack the bones and teeth of muskoxen can be taken as evidence for their absence.

Two additional assumptions underpin our study. One is that an animal bone found in an archaeological or paleobiological context is representative of an animal population in the local area. Prehistoric and historic human occupants of the Arctic were mobile hunter-gatherers, often characterized as opportunistic foragers; highly mobile foragers are unlikely to have transported bones long distances. Muskoxen meat was a source of food; hides were used for clothing; horn and bone were used for tool production; and bone was also used for fuel for fires (Darwent 2001a, 2001b). Given that horn and bone tools could have been carried considerable distances, we deleted all instances of horn and culturally modified bone from our tabulation of zooarchaeological assemblages to minimize the effects of human transport. We screened data for other taxa mentioned below using similar criteria, such as deleting fragments of walrus *(Odobenus rosmarus)* ivory and caribou antler typically representing tools. Our second assumption is that foragers in arctic environments take resources opportunistically, as they encounter them, because of the overall low biodiversity and wide dispersal of resource patches. Thus, the abundance of muskoxen remains in a zooarchaeological collection at least approximately reflects the abundance of muskoxen on the landscape (Gordon 1977).

We divided the last 4,500 years into six periods, each of which spans an average of 875 years (Table 4.1) and, with the exception of Saqqaq, corresponds with temporal boundaries for established archaeological cultural complexes (Appelt 1997; Elling 1996; Helmer 1994). The first four periods constitute the Paleoeskimo stage of eastern Arctic prehistory. Period 5 is the Neoeskimo stage, and assemblages from this period are from both Thule and Norse contexts. With the exception of a few items of European manufacture, the first significant impacts on native Inuit culture in this region began with Franklin's 1845–1848 ill-fated expedition (Maxwell 1985:310) and the subsequent 30 or more rescue ships that searched and wintered in the area the following decade. Therefore, we chose this time marker as the beginning of Period 6—the historical period.

The frequencies of the remains of all mammalian taxa were recorded and assigned to a temporally distinct period based on either associated radiocarbon dates or temporally diagnostic artifacts, with priority given to the former. If the average radiocarbon age for a particular assemblage fell on a period boundary, we used the archaeological cultural affiliation to assign the assemblage to a period. Most dates on marine bone collagen and driftwood were excluded (for further discussion, see Morlan 1999b), and if a date was considered acceptable but did not correspond with the cultural affiliation of the assemblage at two standard deviations, then that

TABLE 4.1. TEMPORAL FRAMEWORK FOR EASTERN ARCTIC SITES.

Period	Age (B.P.)	Archaeological Culture
6	150–the present	Historical
5	1000–150	Thule and Norse
4	2000–1000	Middle and Late Dorset
3	2800–2000	Transitional and Early Dorset (includes Independence II)
2	3600–2800	Middle and Late Pre-Dorset (includes Late Saqqaq)
1	4500–3600	Initial and Early Pre-Dorset (includes Independence I and Early Saqqaq)

Note: Modified from Helmer 1994.

date was given precedence. We corrected all radiocarbon dates for isotopic fractionation, but dates were not calibrated.

We use the historically recorded geographical boundaries of the muskox in Canada reported by Anderson (1930), Clarke (1940), and Urquhart (1982) and in Greenland by Vibe (1958) for comparative purposes (Figure 4.1). We do not include populations introduced recently to western Greenland and northern Quebec. The dashed line in Figure 4.1 indicates the southern boundary of muskox range circa 1870 (Anderson 1930)—20 years after the beginning of our historical period. Relative to the 20th-century distribution, this boundary demonstrates the marked range reduction that occurred in just 60 years; for the most part, it is believed that intensive indigenous use of muskoxen during the historical period, coupled with European fur-trading activities, particularly the introduction of rifles, severely reduced the species' population and thus its range (Barr 1991; Lent 1999). Several single sightings of muskoxen recorded along the margin of the southeastern boundary of the 1870 range—about 150 km inland from Hudson Bay—and as far west as Cape Bathurst and Cape Parry on the western mainland (Barr 1991; Urquhart 1982) suggest that environmental conditions would allow muskoxen to reoccupy the recently abandoned area were their population greater or were hunting pressure not so high.

RESULTS

Muskox bones occur in 43 percent (n = 116) of the archaeological sites (n = 272) and in 41 percent (n = 120) of the temporally distinct archaeological assemblages (n = 292); they also occur in nine paleobiological contexts (Table 4.2). All nine paleobiological occurrences have radiocarbon dates, and 78 of the 115 prehistoric zooarchaeological assemblages (68 percent) have radiocarbon dates. In the discussion below, we follow convention and use the term *High Arctic* to refer to regions north of Parry Channel; *Low Arctic* refers to regions to the south (Figure 4.1). To help ascertain where the muskox might not have occurred during particular times in the past, filled symbols in the figures denote the presence of muskox remains, whereas open symbols denote sites where faunal remains were recovered and identified but no muskox remains were identified.

Biogeography: Periods 1–2

Twenty-four localities dating to Period 1 (4500–3600 B.P.) have produced muskox remains and indicate that the species was well established within its modern range in the higher latitudes when the first human occupants appeared just over 4,000 years ago. Devon Island (Figure 4.1, nos. 22–24), Ellesmere Island (nos. 19–21), and northern Greenland (nos. 1–17) each have multiple sites with muskox bone, and, with one exception, all sites are within the taxon's historic range. The single exception is located in Hall Land in northwestern Greenland (no. 18); 19 percent of this mammalian assemblage is muskox. This site is 200 km southwest of Vibe's (1958) recorded distribution and suggests that the geographic range of the muskox was greater during this period than it has been historically. However, muskox range apparently did not extend down to the central western or southwestern coast during this period or, for that matter, during any of the periods reviewed. It is quite probable that their apparent absence from these areas is not a function of sampling, given the large size (50,000+ NISP) of some of the zooarchaeological collections from western Greenland.

Compared with those of later periods, few Period 1 sites have been recorded or investigated, particularly in the Low Arctic. It is therefore difficult to delineate muskox distribution in the lower islands of the Canadian Arctic Archipelago and along the mainland coast. Among those sites where mammal bone has been recovered—on Banks Island, on Igloolik Island just off Melville Peninsula, and in the Thelon River area of the interior mainland west of Hudson Bay—muskox has yet to be recorded.

Eleven localities dating to Period 2 (3600–2800 B.P.) have produced muskox remains. At the two sites on Banks Island (Figure 4.1) muskox bone constitutes the majority of the mammalian assemblage (69 percent at no. 30; 93 percent at no. 31). As with Period 1, the paucity of sites in the Low Arctic makes it difficult to assess muskox distribution in the lower latitudes. However, four sites (nos. 32–35) near the Canada–U.S. border strongly suggest that muskoxen had a much larger range in this area 3,600–2,800 years ago. Muskox bone has not been identified in localities in the eastern portion of the mainland—in the Thelon River and Hudson Bay regions.

During Period 2, muskoxen occurred on both Devon Island and Ellesmere Island. Also during this period the first evidence for the muskox on Bathurst Island is present at a paleobiological site in the Goodsir Inlet region (no. 29). There are no Period 2 records of muskoxen in northern Greenland. This lack is, however, probably the result of the paucity of known Period 2 sites in the area. This area was apparently abandoned by humans during Period 2, likely because of a severe decline in muskox resources resulting from climatic cooling, climatic instability, and possibly human predation (Darwent 2001a; see below).

Biogeography: Periods 3–4

Twenty-two localities dating to Period 3 (2800–2000 B.P.) have produced muskox remains (Figure 4.2). Most known High Arctic localities contain some muskox remains; Low Arctic sites with muskox are confined to the west. During this period in Greenland, there was heavy occupation of Peary Land, the northeast—> 400 ruins have been recorded on Île de France (Figure 4.2, no. 45)—and the west (Andreasen 1997). Most sites in Peary Land and northeastern Greenland have muskox remains, as do sites in the Lake Hazen area of Ellesmere Island. No Period 3 muskox bone has been identified on Devon Island; however, there is only one site recorded for this interval. There is evidence of muskoxen on Bathurst Island (no. 49), and the first evidence for muskoxen on tiny Kalvik Island, located between Cornwallis and Bathurst islands, is recorded at two sites (nos. 50–51).

With the exception of the western islands and mainland, there is meager evidence for Period 3 in the Low Arctic. Two localities on Banks Island (nos. 52, 54) and one site on the mainland at Cape Bathurst (no. 53) demonstrate that muskoxen were present within modern boundaries of their range in the western Low Arctic. No other remains are known for the rest of the region. Sites with mammalian remains on Victoria Island, Baffin Island, and the Ungava Peninsula have not yielded muskox bone, and no muskox remains have been recovered from western Greenland despite the excavation of numerous sites with large faunal assemblages.

TABLE 4.2. Sites in the Canadian Arctic and Greenland with Muskox Remains.

Site Name	Map Number	Locality	Period	Number of Identified Specimens: Muskox/ Mammal	Percent Muskox	Source(s)
Adam C. Knuth*	1	J. V. Jensen Land, Greenland	1	231/661	34.9	ZMK43/1986[a]
Bob	2	Peary Land, Greenland	1	50/89	56.2	ZMK107a/1974, 136/1978; Darwent 2001a
Deltaterrasserne I*	3	Peary Land, Greenland	1	74/328	22.6	ZMK112h/1950, 109a/1966; Darwent 2001a
Gammell Strand*	4	Peary Land, Greenland	1	25/33	75.8	ZMK109m/1966, 116v/1970, 107c,d/1974; Darwent 2001a
Hvalterrasserne	5	Peary Land, Greenland	1	—	—	ZMK112d/1950[b]
Kap Peter Henrik*	6	Peary Land, Greenland	1	164/274	59.9	ZMK112q/1950, 149/160, 109r/1966, 116n/1970; Darwent 2001a
Kap Holbæk*	7	Peary Land, Greenland	1	—	—	ZMK119/1956[b]
Kølterrasserne	8	Peary Land, Greenland	1	7/23	30.4	ZMK107g/1974; Darwent 2001a
Lagunhøj	9	Peary Land, Greenland	1	7/16	43.8	ZMK109n/1966; Darwent 2001a
Martin*	10	Peary Land, Greenland	1	2/2	100.0	ZMK116c/1970[a]
Midternæs*	11	Peary Land, Greenland	1	26/86	30.2	ZMK109f, 116t/1970; Darwent 2001a
Pearylandville*	12	Peary Land, Greenland	1	229/1,028	22.3	ZMK109p/1966, 116a/1970; Darwent 2001a
Portfjælt*	13	Peary Land, Greenland	1	1/10	10.0	ZMK109e/1966; Darwent 2001a
Vandfaldsnæs I*	14	Peary Land, Greenland	1	13/74	17.6	ZMK152/1960, 109e1966; Darwent 2001a
Vendenæs*	15	Peary Land, Greenland	1	6/27	22.2	ZMK109g/1966; Darwent 2001a
Walcott Delta	16	Peary Land, Greenland	1	1/9	11.1	ZMK116g/1970; Darwent 2001a

Sønderland Ø II*	17	Northeast Greenland	1	—	—	ZMK4/1991[c]; Andreasen 1996
Solbakken*	18	Hall Land, Greenland	1	12/63	19.0	ZMK111e/1966, 153/1960; Darwent 2001a
Daylight	19	Lake Hazen, Ellesmere Island	1	76/90	84.4	Balkwill n.d.; Sutherland 1996
Westwind	20	Lake Hazen, Ellesmere Island	1	76/121	62.8	Balkwill n.d.; Sutherland 1996
Bight (SgFm-16)*	21	Knud Peninsula, Ellesmere Island	1	127/2,637	4.8	Schledermann 1990
Ice Bay (QkHl-5)*	22	Cape Hardy, Devon Island	1	1/301	0.3	Helmer 1991; McCartney 1989
Hind (QkHn-38)*	23	Truelove Lowland, Devon Island	1	1/1,124	0.1	Helmer 1991; McCartney 1989
Icebreaker Beach (QkHn-13)*	24	Truelove Lowland, Devon Island	1	46/4,417	1.0	Helmer 1991; McCartney 1989
Gull Cliff (RbJu-1)*	25	Port Refuge, Devon Island	2	4/815	0.5	McGhee 1979
Rivendell (TjFd-10)*	26	Lake Hazen, Ellesmere Island	2	—	—	Sutherland 1996
Field School (QkHn-12)*	27	Truelove Lowland, Devon Island	2	5/476	1.1	Helmer 1991; McCartney 1989
Twin Ponds (QkHn-17)*	28	Truelove Lowland, Devon Island	2	4/526	0.8	Helmer 1991; McCartney 1989
QjLj-VP*†	29	Goodsir Inlet, Bathurst Island	2	—	—	Harington 1980
Shoran Lake	30	Shoran Lake, Banks Island	2	115/167	68.9	Taylor 1967
Umingmak (PjRa-2)*	31	Shoran Lake, Banks Island	2	24,963/26,716	93.4	Münzel 1983; Taylor 1967
Engigstciak (NiVk-1)*	32	Firth River, Yukon mainland	2	—	—	Morlan 1999a

TABLE 4.2. SITES IN THE CANADIAN ARCTIC AND GREENLAND WITH MUSKOX REMAINS *(CONTINUED)*.

Site Name	Map Number	Locality	Period	Number of Identified Specimens: Muskox/ Mammal	Percent Muskox	Source(s)
Pelly Farm (KfVd-2)*	33	Pelly River, Yukon mainland	2	—	—	MacNeish 1964; Wilmeth 1978
Brewer Creek (KhVj-VP)*†	34	Klondike, Yukon mainland	2	—	—	Harington 1980
Sixtymile (LaVo-VP-7)*†	35	Klondike, Yukon mainland	2	—	—	Harington 1980
Arnakke	36	Peary Land, Greenland	3	1/4	25.0	ZMK116x/1970; Darwent 2001
Deltaterrasserne II*	3	Peary Land, Greenland	3	23/51	45.1	ZMK112h/1950; Darwent 2001a
Engnæs*	37	Peary Land, Greenland	3	1/5	20.0	ZMK116a/1970; Darwent 2001a
Genbonæs	38	Peary Land, Greenland	3	2/20	10.0	ZMK116q/1970; Darwent 2001a
Juniskæret*	39	Peary Land, Greenland	3	—	—	ZMK151/1960[b]; Knuth 1967
Kap Holbæk (Gr. II)*	7	Peary Land, Greenland	3	—	—	ZMK119/1956[b]; Knuth 1967
Kap Ludovika*	40	Peary Land, Greenland	3	7/17	41.2	ZMK112p/1950, 116o/1970; Darwent 2001a
Kap Mylius-Erichsen*	41	Peary Land, Greenland	3	34/140	24.3	ZMK109h/1966, 126/1970; Darwent 2001a
Lolland Sø	42	Peary Land, Greenland	3	10/15	66.7	ZMK120/1956; Darwent 2001a
Vandfaldsnæs II*	14	Peary Land, Greenland	3	14/144	9.7	ZMK112g/1950, 109e/1966; Darwent 2001a
Bay (Amdrup 17)	43	Amdrup Land, Greenland	3	—	—	ZMK55/1993[c]; Andreasen 1996
Eigil Knuth (Holm 14)	44	Holm Land, northeast Greenland	3	—	—	ZMK54/1993[c]; Andreasen 1997
Frands, Sælsøen*	45	Dove Bugt, northeast Greenland	3	—	—	ZMK7/1991; Andreasen 1996

Mågefjeldet (Holm 13)	46	Holm Land, northeast Greenland	3	—	—	ZMK53/1993[c]; Andreasen 1996
Nørre Mellemland*	47	Northeast Greenland	3	—	—	ZMK6/1991; Andreasen 1996
Lonesome Cr. II (TjAo-8)*	48	Northeast Ellesmere Island	3	—	—	Knuth 1967
QiLf-4*	49	Markham Point, Bathurst Island	3	253/597	42.4	Helmer 1981
QjLd-21*	50	Kalivik (Karluk) Island	3	98/1,789	5.5	Helmer 1981
QjLd-22*	51	Kalivik (Karluk) Island	3	1/5	20.0	Helmer 1981
Lagoon (QjRl-3)*	52	South Coast, Banks Island	3	78/334	23.4	Arnold 1981
Crane (ObRu-1)*	53	Cape Bathurst, mainland	3	9/7,129	0.1	LeBlanc 1994a, 1994b
PfRa-VP*†	54	Banks Island	3	—	—	Harington, personal communication, in Morlan 1999a
Lauge Koch's Hus	55	Hall Land, Greenland	4	1/37	2.7	ZMK154/1960; Darwent 2001a
Qeqertaaraq (Structure 1)*	56	Inglefield Land, Greenland	4	224/2,342	9.6	Bendix 1998
Basil Noris (TkAp-1)	57	Northeast Ellesmere Island	4	—	—	Maxwell 1960
QiLf-25*	58	Markham Point, Bathurst Island	4	5/87	5.7	Helmer 1981
QjLd-17*	59	Kalivik (Karluk) Island	4	6/3,953	0.2	Helmer 1981
QjLd-25	60	Kalivik (Karluk) Island	4	42/5,210	0.8	Helmer 1981
Cove (SgFm-5)	61	Knud Peninsula, Ellesmere Island	4	7/510	1.4	Schledermann 1990
Longhouse (SgFm-3)	62	Knud Peninsula, Ellesmere Island	4	1/992	0.1	Schledermann 1990
Shelter (SgFm-17)	63	Knud Peninsula, Ellesmere Island	4	2/25	8.0	Schledermann 1990
Franklin Pierce (SiFi-4)*	64	Pierce Bay, Ellesmere Island	4	1/50	2.0	Schledermann 1990

TABLE 4.2. SITES IN THE CANADIAN ARCTIC AND GREENLAND WITH MUSKOX REMAINS *(CONTINUED)*.

Site Name	Map Number	Locality	Period	Number of Identified Specimens: Muskox/ Mammal	Percent Muskox	Source(s)
Lea Point (RcHh-1)	65	Lea Point, Ellesmere Island	4	12/776	1.5	Darwent 2001a
Arvik (QjJx-1)*	66a	Little Cornwallis Island	4	1/5,636	< 0.1	Darwent 2001a
Tasiarulik (QjJx-10)*	66b	Little Cornwallis Island	4	5/4,326	0.1	Darwent 1995, 2001a
Blanknæs*	67	Peary Land, Greenland	5	—	—	ZMK116f/1970[b]; Knuth 1981
Hans Tausen Iskappe*†	68	Peary Land, Greenland	5	—	—	ZMK42/1995[d]
Kølnæs*	69	Peary Land, Greenland	5	—	—	ZMK112i/1950[b]; Knuth 1981
Mellembygden*	70	Peary Land, Greenland	5	—	—	Knuth 1981
Oksejægerpynt	71	Peary Land, Greenland	5	—	—	ZMK112b/1950[b]; Knuth 1981
Qissivik	72	J. V. Jensen Land, Greenland	5	—	—	ZMK112c/1950[b]; Knuth 1983
Sommernæsset	73	Peary Land, Greenland	5	—	—	ZMK112m/1950[c]
Uranienborg*	74	Peary Land, Greenland	5	—	—	ZMK141/1976[a]; Knuth 1981
Eskimonesset	75	Northeast Greenland	5	—	—	ZMK48/1993[c]; Andreasen 1997
Henrik Krøyer Holme	76	Holm Land, northeast Greenland	5	—	—	ZMK49/1993[c]; Andreasen 1997
Holm Land 12	77	Holm Land, northeast Greenland	5	—	—	ZMK52/1993[c]
Sophus Müllers Næs	78	Northeast Greenland	5	—	—	ZMK50/1993[c]; Andreasen 1997
Nioghalvfjerdsbræ*†	79	Northeast Greenland	5	—	—	ZMK54/1996[d]
Renskæret	80	Dove Bugt, Greenland	5	—	—	ZMK13n/1909, 8/1921[e]; Thostrup 1911
Snenæs*	81	Dove Bugt, Greenland	5	—	—	ZKM13r/1909[e]
Hurry Inlet	82	Scoresbysund, Greenland	5	—	—	ZMK129/1964[f]

Harefjord	83	Scoresbysund, Greenland	5	—	—	ZMK124/1967[f]
Sydkap	84	Scoresbysund, Greenland	5	—	—	ZMK16/1987[g]
Dovemandsbugten	85	Clavering, Greenland	5	—	—	ZMK28/1932[h]; Vibe 1958
Lonesome (TjAq-1)	86	Northeast Ellesmere Island	5	—	—	Maxwell 1960
Maxwell (TlAt-8)*	87	Northeast Ellesmere Island	5	—	—	Sutherland 1989
Remus Creek (SlHq-3)*	88	Northeast Ellesmere Island	5	—	—	Sutherland 1993
Ruggles Outlet (TkAu-1)	89	Northeast Ellesmere Island	5	—	—	Maxwell 1960
Two House (TbHt-6)*	90	Northeast Ellesmere Island	5	—	—	Sutherland 1993
Eskimobyen (SgFm-4)*	91	Knud Peninsula, Ellesmere Island	5	66/3,184	2.1	McCullough 1989
Skræling Island (SfFk-4)*	92	Alexandra Fd., Ellesmere Island	5	81/12,151	0.7	McCullough 1989
Sverdup (SfFk-5)*	93	Alexandra Fd., Ellesmere Island	5	1/391	0.3	McCullough 1989
SjJh-VP*†	94	Axel Heiberg Island	5	—	—	Harington, personal communication, in Morlan 1999a
Buchanan Lake (SiHw-1)*	95	Axel Heiberg Island	5	—	—	Kalkreuth and Sutherland 1998
RbJr-1*	96	Porden Point, Devon Island	5	5/5,878	0.1	Park 1989
RbJr-4	97	Porden Point, Devon Island	5	4/4,229	0.1	Park 1989
RbJr-5	98	Porden Point, Devon Island	5	1/343	0.3	Park 1989
Resolute Bay	99	Cornwallis Island	5	—	—	Collins 1952
Brooman Point (QiLd-1)*	100	Brooman Point, Bathurst Island	5	—	—	McGhee 1984

TABLE 4.2. SITES IN THE CANADIAN ARCTIC AND GREENLAND WITH MUSKOX REMAINS *(CONTINUED)*.

Site Name	Map Number	Locality	Period	Number of Identified Specimens: Muskox/ Mammal	Percent Muskox	Source(s)
QkLh-VP*†	101	Goodsir River, Bathurst Island	5	—	—	Bowman et al. 1990
Gladman Point (NdLf-1)*	102	King William Island	5	—	—	Savelle 1987
Thom Bay 1/81-80 (OaJn-2)*	103	Thom Bay, Somerset Island	5	—	—	Savelle 1987
Cape Garry (PcJq-5)*	104	Creswell Bay, Somerset Island	5	9/2,845	3.2	Rick 1980
Learmouth (PeJr-1)*	105	Creswell Bay, Somerset Island	5	24/1,584	1.5	Rick 1980
Loon (PeJr-8)*	106	Creswell Bay, Somerset Island	5	—	—	Damkjar 1984; Damkjar, personal communication, in Morlan 1999a
PeJr-14*	107	Creswell Bay, Somerset Island	5	—	—	Damkjar 1984; Damkjar, personal communication, in Morlan 1999a
PaJa-13	108	Mt. Oliver, Somerset Island	5	2/8,766	< 0.1	Whitridge 1992
Crystal II	109	Frobisher Bay, Baffin Island	5	—	—	Collins 1950
Naujan	110	Repulse Bay, Melville Island	5	2/947	0.2	Mathiassen 1927
Silumiut (KkJg-1)*	111	Chesterfield Inlet, Hudson Bay	5	114/18,167	0.6	Staab 1979
Nelson River (OhRh-1)*	112	Southern coast, Banks Island	5	—	1.6	Arnold and McCullough 1990

Nichol Site (OhPo-6)	113	Minto Inlet, Victoria Island	5	—	—	McGhee 1972
Bloody Falls (MkPk-3)*	114	Coppermine River, mainland	5	15/365	4.0	McGhee 1972
Clachan (NaPi-2)*	115	Cape Hearne, mainland	5	6/40,599	< 0.1	Morrison 1983
Hornaday River 15 (NcRf-1)*	116	Hornaday River, mainland	5	—	—	Stevenson 1992
Iglulualuit (NlRu-1)*	117	Franklin Bay, mainland	5	3/3,421	0.1	Morrison 1990
Nadlock (MbNs-1)*	118	Burnside River, mainland	5	111/60,000	< 0.1	B. Gordon 1994
Bison Skull (OaRw-2)*†	119	Cape Bathurst, mainland	5	—	—	Harington, personal communication, in Morlan 1999a
Rita-Claire (OaRw-3)*	120	Cape Bathurst, mainland	5	6/3,343	0.2	Morrison 1997
Haogak (PhPo-3)	121	Prince of Wales Strait, Banks Island	6	880/911	96.6	Woolett 1991
Kuptana (PjRa-18)	122	Thomsen River, Banks Island	6	449/453	99.1	Woolett 1991
Nasogaluak (PgPw-3)	123	Thomsen River, Banks Island	6	605/607	99.7	Woolett 1991
Bison Skull (OaRw-2)	119	Cape Bathurst, mainland	6	4/717	0.6	Morrison 1997
Kunana (OdP3-1)	124	Prince Albert Sound, Victoria Island	6	—	1.0	McGhee 1972

Note: * denotes that the site has one or more radiocarbon dates; † denotes that the site is paleobiological (not archaeological); map number refers to designations used in Figures 4.1–4.3; ZMK designations refer to catalog numbers of collections stored at the Zoological Museum, University of Copenhagen.

[a]Identified by J. Møhl; collected by E. Knuth.

[b]Identified by U. Møhl; collected by E. Knuth.

[c]Identified by B. Bendix; collected by C. Andreasen.

[d]Identified and collected by N. Rech and H. H. Thomsen.

[e]Identified by H. Winge; collected by L. Mylius-Erichsen.

[f]Identified by U. Møhl; collected by C. Vibe.

[g]Collected by T. Møbjerg and H. Kapel.

[h]Identified by M. Degerbøl; collected by H. Larsen.

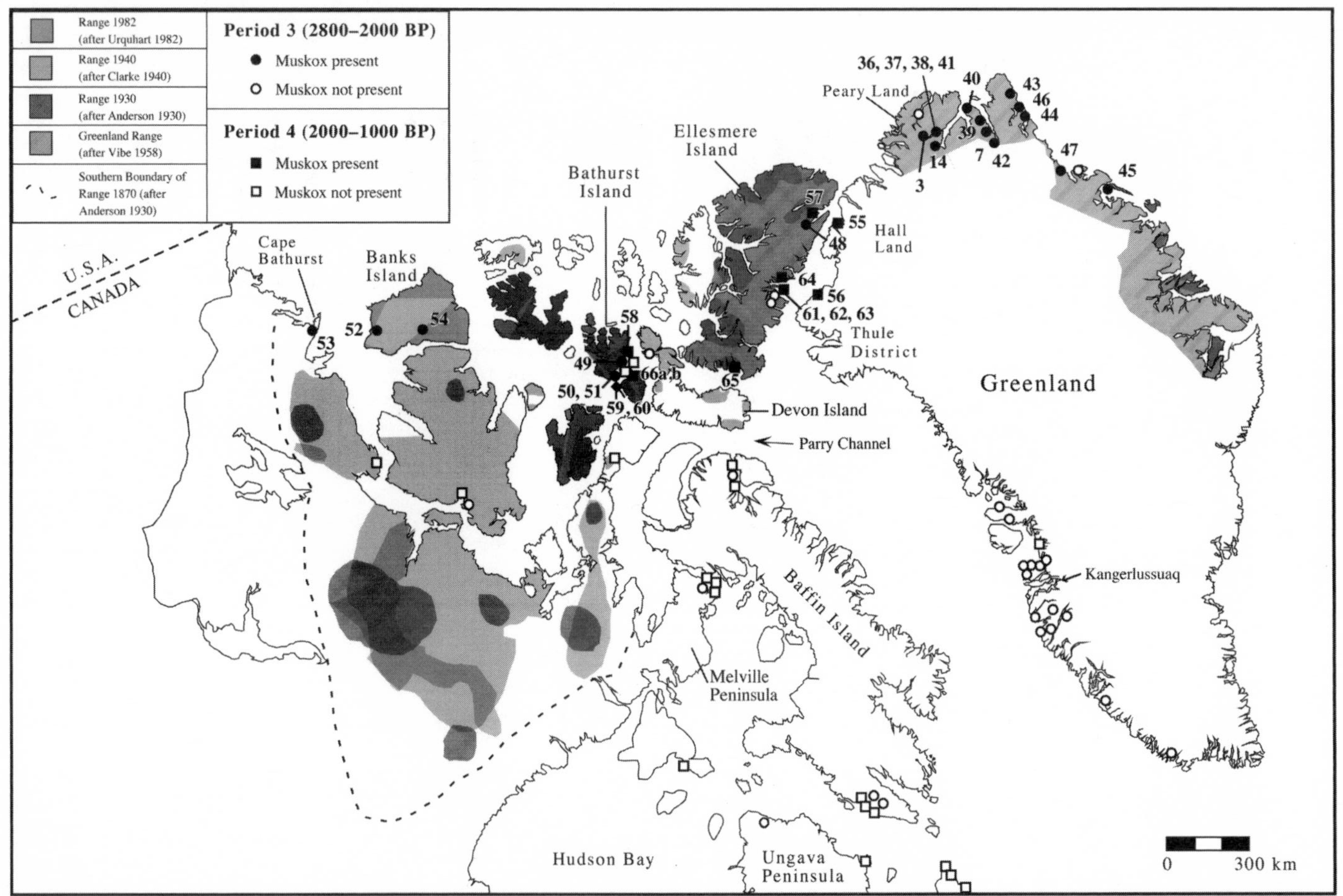

Figure 4.2. Locations of sites with identified mammalian remains and with muskox remains in the Canadian Arctic and Greenland for Period 3 (2800–2000 B.P.; n = 22) and Period 4 (2000–1000 B.P.; n = 13). Modern distributions of muskox shown for comparison.

Thirteen localities dating to Period 4 (2000–1000 B.P.) have produced remains of muskoxen, but no evidence for their presence in northeastern Greenland is available. All recorded sites for this period in Peary Land are paleobiological, apparently because humans largely abandoned the area during a period of climatic cooling and instability (Fitzhugh 1997). The area was reoccupied at the initiation of Period 5 when the climate warmed and Thule peoples immigrated from Alaska. None of the bone recovered from the Period 4 paleobiological sites is muskox. However, two sites in northwestern Greenland (nos. 55–56) indicate that muskoxen occurred in this region in Period 4, as in Period 1. There is evidence from both northern and southern Ellesmere Island of muskoxen, as well as on Bathurst (no. 58) and Kalvik islands (nos. 59–60). In addition, during this period the muskox is first documented on Little Cornwallis Island (nos. 66a–66b). No Period 4 sites with muskoxen have been recorded on Devon Island.

Although archaeological investigations have been carried out on Somerset Island, Victoria Island, mainland Cape Bathurst, Boothia Peninsula, Southampton Island, Baffin Island, Bylot Island, and northern Quebec, there is no evidence for muskoxen in the Low Arctic from any Period 4 assemblage. Likewise, the only Period 4 site in western Greenland known to us does not have muskox remains. There are no archaeological sites with identified faunal remains in the western regions of the Low Arctic (Banks Island) that date to Period 4.

Biogeography: Periods 5–6

Muskox remains dating to Period 5 (1000–150 B.P.) occur in 53 localities (Figure 4.3). In northern Greenland, sites with muskoxen are found throughout the modern range reported by Vibe (1958). No faunal assemblages are known for the northwestern part of the island, so we cannot determine if muskoxen continued to occupy the Thule District after Period 4. Muskox remains have been recovered from Period 5 sites on Ellesmere and eastern Bathurst islands, and muskox bone reappears on Devon Island at Porden Point (Figure 4.3, nos. 96–98). Although proximate to the modern range, muskox specimens are recorded for the first time on Axel Heiberg Island (nos. 94–95) and on Cornwallis Island (no. 99).

In the Low Arctic, muskoxen apparently had a larger range than that recorded during modern times. Two sites (nos. 110–111) with muskox remains are substantially east (150+ km) of the recorded modern range. One assemblage (no. 111) contains the remains of at least 13 individuals—a number indicating that the sample is not the product of a chance

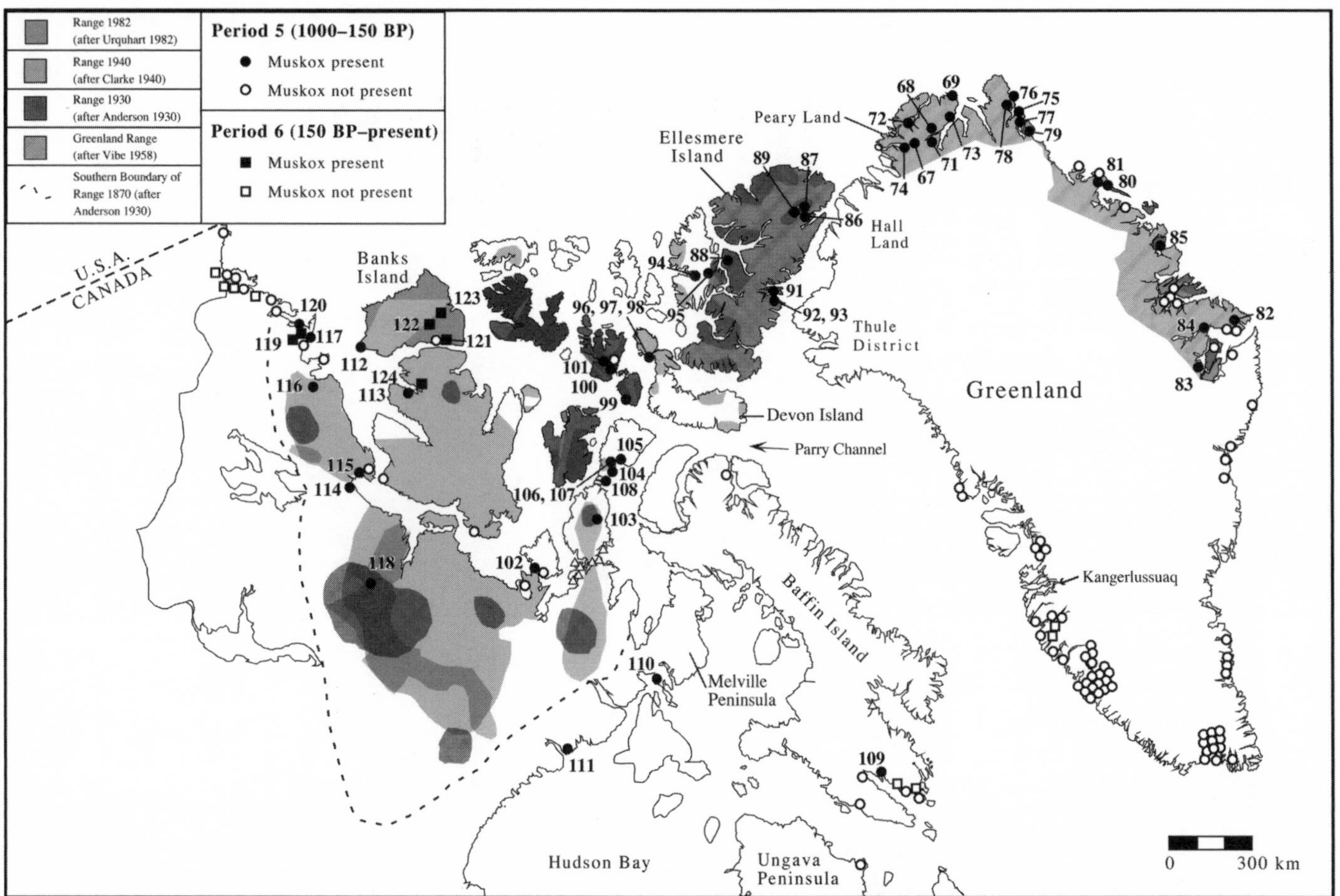

Figure 4.3. Locations of sites with identified mammalian remains and with muskox remains in the Canadian Arctic and Greenland for Period 5 (1000–150 B.P.; $n = 53$) and Period 6 (150–the present; $n = 6$). Modern distributions of muskox shown for comparison.

encounter with a lone wanderer but, rather, suggesting a more extensive geographic distribution of this species circa 200–800 years ago. These sites are also east of the 1870 range postulated by Anderson (1930).

Muskox remains have been recorded on King William Island at Gladman Point (no. 102), an area that muskoxen currently do not inhabit. Muskox bone has been identified from two sites on Cape Bathurst (nos. 119–120), 150 km west of the range recorded by Urquhart (1982) but within the southern boundary of the range in 1870. These localities suggest that muskox range extended from the western shore of Hudson Bay to just west of Cape Bathurst during Period 5. The western region has several mainland sites (nos. 114–116, 118) and sites on Banks and Victoria islands (nos. 112–113), all within the modern range. Muskox remains are also reported for the first time from Boothia Peninsula (no. 103) and Somerset Island (nos. 104–108).

Muskox bone has been recorded on southern Baffin Island (no. 109; see Taylor 1967). If it is authentic, then this record indicates the potential for a natural muskox population there. We hesitate to accept this record, however, because it is a field identification and therefore not verifiable, but we also note that there is one unverified muskox sighting in central Baffin Island (Jacobs 1989; Urquhart 1982). Because the archaeological record is anomalous, and because of its implications, we believe that other evidence is necessary to confirm a natural population of muskoxen on the island during Period 5 or during any other time in (pre)history.

Period 6 (A.D. 1850–the present) is represented by only five localities with muskox remains (Figure 4.3). At this time muskoxen apparently contracted their western limit eastward away from the Canada–U.S. border. The only site with muskox bone on the mainland that dates to the historical period (no. 119) is well within the 1870 range. No more than 1 percent of the mammalian faunal assemblage at this site, and of the assemblage on Victoria Island (no. 124), is composed of muskox. Of those sites that have muskox bone, only sites on Banks Island (nos. 121–123) have high relative frequencies (> 90 percent); these animals were used extensively by Copper Inuit populations in the 1800s (Will 1985).

Temporal Change in Relative Abundance

Ignoring for the moment the abundance of their remains, muskoxen occur in proportionately more Period 1 assemblages than in the assemblages of any other period (Figure 4.4). The proportion of sites containing muskox remains drops in Period 2, increases slightly in Period 3, and then levels off for Periods 4–6. There is no correlation between these abundances and the proportion of the total assemblages with identified mammal remains per period (Spearman's rho = 0.257, $p = 0.63$); sample size, measured as the total number of assemblages examined per period, is not driving the trend in abundance of sites with muskox remains. The decrease during Period 2 might be explained by the movement of Paleoeskimo populations out of northern Greenland to other areas of the eastern Arctic during a climatically cool and unstable period (Darwent 2001a). Paleoeskimo peoples may have moved to areas where muskoxen were not commonly encountered, such as (perhaps) the eastern Low Arctic and coastal areas where sea mammals dominate the local biota. Muskox populations in northern Greenland may have declined to such an extent that human emigration was prompted. Muskoxen were, however, taken in relatively high frequencies on Banks Island, suggesting that the populations there might not have been as impacted by climatic shifts as those in areas to the north and east.

Figure 4.5 plots the proportional abundance of muskox specimens relative to all mammalian remains (muskox NISP/mammal NISP) in collections against time, irrespective of the geographic location of remains. We omitted all samples with mammalian NISP < 25 (Table 4.2) to reduce the influences of sample size on our analysis. Remaining collections indicate a gradual decrease in the relative abundance of muskoxen over time (rho = –0.397, $p = 0.001$) when all sites and all periods are considered. This trend is strengthened when Period 6 sites are deleted (rho = –0.628, $p < 0.0001$). Only assemblages from Banks Island have relative frequencies of muskoxen greater than 90 percent; one dates to Period 2, and three date to Period 6 (Figure 4.5, Table 4.2). Banks Island was historically significant for Copper Inuit who hunted muskoxen there (Will 1985), and it continues to be a prime locality for indigenous subsistence hunters (M. Nagy, personal communication, 2001).

Regional differences are somewhat masked by Figure 4.5. For example, Period 1 sites in northern Greenland average more than 35 percent muskox, whereas all coastal sites in the Canadian Arctic produce many seal remains and average less than 2 percent muskox. Muskox remains in the few Period 2 sites range from 1 percent of all mammals on Devon Island to 69–93 percent on Banks Island. Northern Greenland assemblages are dominated by muskoxen in Period 3 but to a lesser extent than in Period 1. During Period 3, the muskox is more prevalent in the Canadian High Arctic than is documented for this region in prior or later periods. Muskox abundance plummets in Period 4 when it is reduced to an

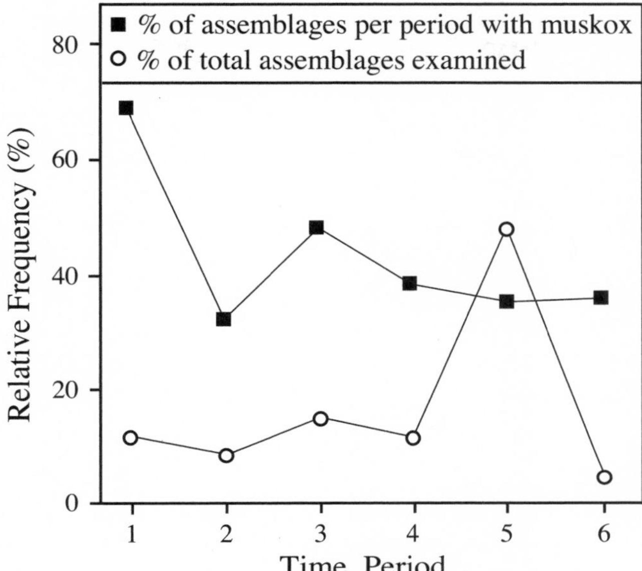

Figure 4.4. Relative (percent) frequency of eastern Arctic archaeological assemblages with muskox remains per time period (filled squares) and the relative frequency of all assemblages examined per time period (open circles). The total number of assemblages examined is 292—Period 1: $n = 35$; Period 2: $n = 25$; Period 3: $n = 44$; Period 4: $n = 34$; Period 5: $n = 140$; Period 6: $n = 14$. The two variables are not correlated (Spearman's rho = 0.257, p = 0.63), suggesting that the presence of muskoxen is not governed by sample size or the number of assemblages examined.

average of 3 percent. This decrease continues in Period 5, when the relative frequency of muskoxen is less than 1 percent on average.

The tendency toward a decrease in the relative frequency of muskoxen over time is not a function of sample size. The average relative frequency of muskox remains per assemblage per period and the number of zooarchaeological assemblages examined per period are inversely but insignificantly correlated (rho = –0.696, p = 0.124). Based on the large number of Period 5 sites investigated, we expect both the number of sites with muskox remains and the relative frequency of muskox remains to be high. Neither variable, however, displays a large value (Figures 4.4, 4.6). Our results support the archaeological hypothesis that there was a decline in the prehistoric use of terrestrial resources (Maxwell 1985), in this case muskoxen, over time. However, a caveat must be made with respect to the historical period. Of the 14 known zooarchaeological collections dating

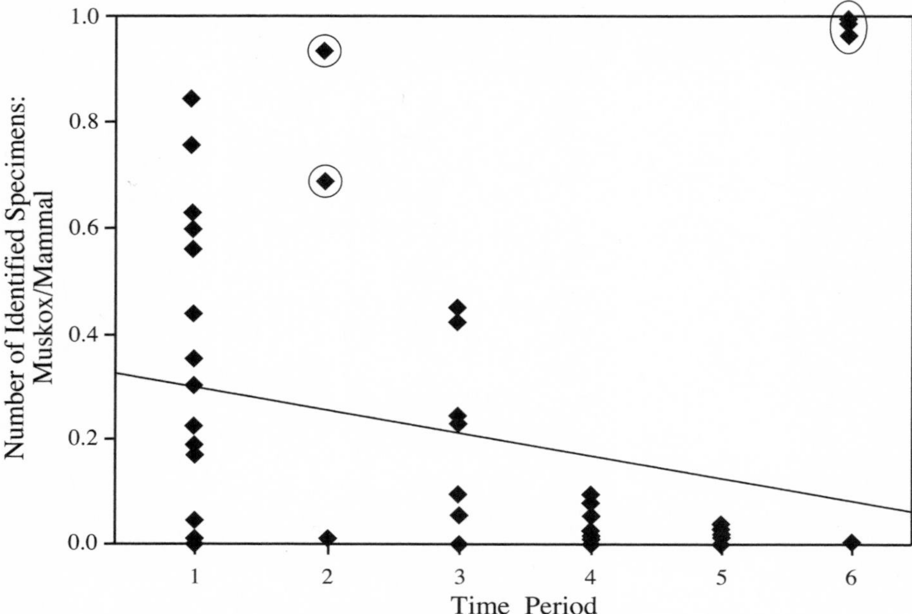

Figure 4.5. Number of identified specimens (NISP) of muskoxen divided by mammal NISP for each eastern Arctic assemblage per time period. Only assemblages with mammal NISP > 25 are plotted (from Table 4.2). Simple best-fit regression line is shown for reference; circled points represent assemblages from Banks Island. Frequencies are inversely correlated with age (Spearman's rho = –0.397, p = 0.001) and suggest a general trend of decreasing relative abundance of muskoxen over time.

to the historical period, only four have muskox remains; and of these four, only three have significant numbers of muskoxen. If there was extensive hunting of muskoxen coincident with European fur trading (Barr 1991), the available zooarchaeological data do not reflect it.

DISCUSSION

Some have suggested that High Arctic muskox populations could have been significantly larger and more stable during early Paleoeskimo times (Knuth 1967), citing the rapid increase in the size of muskox populations during the past three decades on Banks Island (Sutherland 1996:285)—an island with vegetation and topography similar to those of the High Arctic. However, this recent increase in muskoxen comes after a hunting ban was imposed. Therefore, we hesitate to use this historical event as an ana-

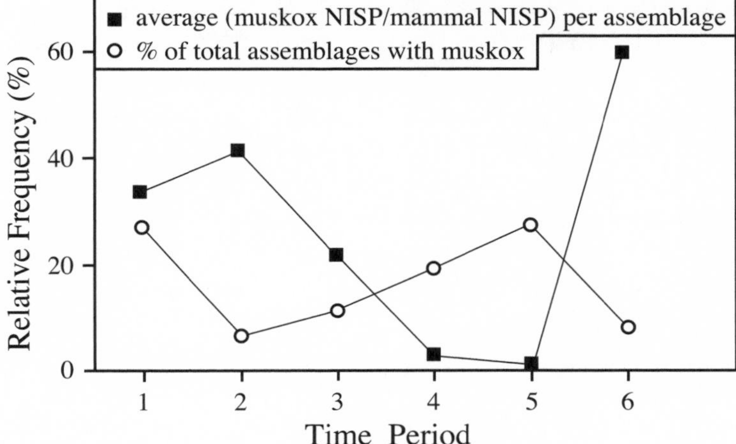

Figure 4.6. Average number of identified specimens (NISP) of muskoxen divided by mammal NISP for each eastern Arctic assemblage per time period (filled square) and the relative frequency of muskox assemblages examined per time period (open circle). Only assemblages with mammalian NISP > 25 are plotted (from Table 4.2). The two variables are inversely but insignificantly correlated (Spearman's rho = –0.696, p = 0.124), suggesting that the relative number of assemblages examined per time period is not governing the overall trend in muskox abundance relative to that of other mammals.

log to estimate the size and stability of High Arctic muskox populations 4,000 years ago because it arose under a different set of conditions.

Zooarchaeological and paleobiological occurrences of muskoxen demonstrate that the geographic range of this species was more extensive than has been historically documented. Sites that reflect a general shift south and west in muskox distribution date to circa 1000 B.P., coincident with warmer climatic conditions that may have increased the range and biomass of available forage. The expansion is also coincident with more limited hunting of muskoxen as Period 4 and Period 5 human populations were shifting to more stable, and apparently more predictable, marine resources. Large expanses of water, glaciers, and other environmental variables likely precluded the movement of ancient muskox populations into areas such as western Greenland, Baffin Island, and Ungava Quebec (Jacobs 1989).

Conditions affecting muskox forage, along with other factors such as introduced disease or hunting, might severely impact a population of muskoxen. Variation over time and across space in the abundance of muskox relative to other mammalian taxa suggests both local environmental changes and human movements. Banks Island has for the past 3,600 years been one of the places "where muskoxen roamed." The geographic range of the muskox was also far more extensive 3,600 years ago than it is today (Figure 4.1). By 1000 B.P. the western extent of the muskoxen was apparently within the 1870 boundary, although their eastern extent in the Low Arctic was considerably greater before the historical period (Figure 4.3). Prior to at least 1000 B.P., muskoxen also roamed northwestern Greenland (Figures 4.1–4.2).

IMPLICATIONS FOR WILDLIFE MANAGEMENT

In the 1960s, 27 subadult muskoxen were transplanted from northeastern Greenland to Kangerlussuaq (Søndre Strømfjord) along the west coast of Greenland (Figure 4.1). There is no evidence in our data that muskoxen ever occurred here or in nearby areas, so we wonder about the probability that the descendants of this translocated group will survive. According to Thing et al., and following Vibe (1958, 1967), "This transplant was promoted to secure at least *one* viable population in Greenland, should *all* the muskoxen in northeast Greenland perish with hunger during one or more winters with adverse climatic conditions" (1984:2, emphasis added). Our data presented here suggest that the latter possibility is remote. Although muskox populations probably varied greatly in size over time, they have persisted in northern and northeastern Greenland through at least 4,500 years of climatic variability as well as variation in the intensity of human predation, and, with the exception of those animals in northwestern Greenland, these populations did not perish. With respect to northwestern Greenland, muskox populations recently relocated to the Thule District are apparently in decline (Land et al. 2000), and although hunting by local Inughuit does not appear to be the primary reason for the decline, hunting is, as we noted earlier, presently on hold. Our zooarchaeological data suggest that muskoxen in this area were well established and that their numbers were stable for at least a millennium despite hunting by prehistoric humans. We need, however, to fill in the recent biogeographic history of this little-known region before the nature of past muskox extirpation (Vibe 1958, 1967) can be determined and the current decline can be explained.

It is well known that, as among other large mammals, small, isolated populations of muskoxen are "highly vulnerable to a variety of threats that can lead to local extinction" (Lent 1999:278). This is especially true for groups that are seasonally isolated on small islands and in geographically constrained regions such as northwestern Greenland. Even on larger islands, winter range may be limited relative to the number of resident muskoxen, and the resulting overcrowding and deterioration of winter range seem to be a catalyst for movement across fast (stable) sea ice (Lent 1999:169, 224). As Lent notes, "Such movements obviously are necessary for the [historically] documented natural recolonization of islands where populations were extirpated" (1988:5). These movements are also no doubt at least in part the cause of the prehistoric recolonization of various areas and the subsequent growth in various local populations. Such movements helped insure the long-term persistence of the species in the Arctic generally if not in all areas of the Arctic. It is for this reason that we believe conservation biologists should not be distressed about the loss of Greenland populations but, instead, should seek ways to insure that the "natural" ecology of the muskox is not disrupted to the point that they can no longer recolonize formerly occupied areas. The long-term nature of our zooarchaeological data provides clear guidance.

Acknowledgments. This research was funded by a doctoral fellowship from the Social Sciences and Humanities Research Council of Canada (#752–97–0659) awarded to Christyann Darwent. Travel to the Zoological Museum at the University of Copenhagen was funded by a travel scholarship from the University of Missouri Graduate School and by a grant from the Arctic Institute of North America. Our thanks go to Kim Aaris-Sørensen, Jeppe Møhl, and Knud Rosenlund for access to the Knuth faunal collections and the Greenland archives at the Zoological Museum; to Genny LeMoine and James Helmer for access to the Little Cornwallis Island and Lea Point, Ellesmere Island, faunal assemblages; to Richard Morlan for assistance with muskox material from the Canadian Archaeology Radiocarbon Database; and to R. Lee Lyman for his comments and encouragement to pursue this avenue of research.

5

The Potential of Zooarchaeological Data to Guide Pinniped Management Decisions in the Eastern North Pacific

MICHAEL A. ETNIER

Most pinniped populations in waters of the eastern North Pacific (ENP) adjacent to Washington, Oregon, and California (Figure 5.1) have increased dramatically over the past several decades (Table 5.1; see Cooper and Stewart 1983; DeLong and Antonelis 1991; Fleischer 1987; Gallo Reynoso 1994; Jeffries et al. 2003; Stewart 1997; Sydeman and Allen 1999). Exceptions are the Alaskan population of northern fur seals *(Callorhinus ursinus)* and the eastern stock of Steller sea lions *(Eumetopias jubatus)*, both of which have been stable or have grown only slightly over the past several decades (Table 5.1; see Loughlin and Miller 1989; Read and Wade 2000). Guadalupe fur seals *(Arctocephalus townsendi)* and the Alaskan stock of northern fur seals are included in the list of pinniped taxa under consideration (Table 5.1) because they migrate annually into waters of the ENP. The general pattern of increase is undoubtedly caused by the cessation of direct exploitation and bounty programs in the mid–20th century (Busch 1985; Hofman 1995). Commercial harvests of northern fur seals persisted into the 1980s (York 1987).

As pinniped populations in the ENP continue to increase, competition (either real or perceived) with humans will undoubtedly increase as well (Baraff and Loughlin 2000). Management decisions will have to distinguish between the reestablishment of old patterns of pinniped behavior and new patterns that have developed recently. Furthermore, management decisions will have to distinguish between patterns that are the result of

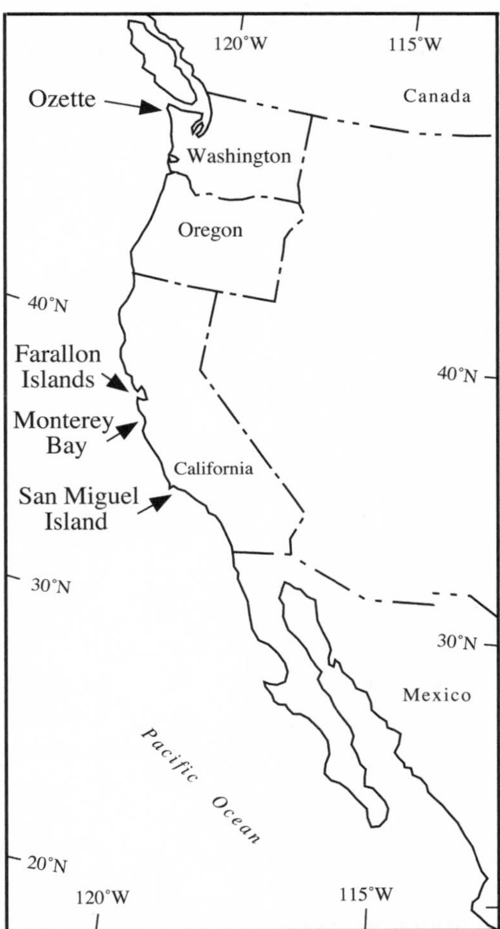

Figure 5.1. Coastline of the eastern North Pacific showing locations of places discussed in the text.

anthropogenic factors and those that are the result of natural events. Zooarchaeological data can help inform the decision-making process. In this chapter I present such data from the Ozette Village site in western Washington (Figure 5.1). These data show that three pinniped species generally considered to be well understood based on historical observations behaved quite differently prior to the early historical period. Any management plan based solely on historically documented patterns is therefore unlikely to accurately reflect long-term patterns of pinniped behavior in the ENP.

TABLE 5.1. Breeding Status and Population Trends of Pinniped Stocks in U.S. Waters of the Eastern North Pacific (ENP).

Scientific Name	Common Name	Stock	Breeding in ENP	Population Trend
Phoca vitulina	harbor seal	inland Washington	yes	increasing
		Oregon/Washington coast	yes	increasing
		California	yes	increasing
Mirounga angustirostris	northern elephant seal		yes	increasing
Arctocephalus townsendi	Guadalupe fur seal		no	increasing
Callorhinus ursinus	northern fur seal	Alaska	no	stable
		San Miguel, California	yes	increasing
Eumetopias jubatus	Steller sea lion	eastern stock	yes	stable or increasing
Zalophus californianus	California sea lion		yes	increasing

Note: Adapted from Read and Wade 2000.

LEGAL BACKGROUND

The specific goals of pinniped management plans have changed considerably over the past several decades (Gerber et al. 1999; Lavigne et al. 1999). Prior to 1972 pinnipeds were directly exploited, and management was aimed at maintaining populations at a level that would produce the maximum sustainable yield. With the 1972 passage of the Marine Mammal Protection Act (16USC1361–1421, Public Law 92–522), management aimed at maintaining an optimum sustainable population (OSP), and commercial harvesting of some species continued into the 1980s (Gerrodette and DeMaster 1990; Hofman 1995; Lavigne et al. 1999). Now that most direct threats to pinniped populations have been eliminated, the focus of management decisions has shifted to indirect threats such as bycatch in commercial fisheries and depletion of prey species (National Marine Fisheries Service 1995; Sinclair et al. 1994; Trites 1992).

Today, virtually all conservation efforts regarding pinnipeds in the ENP are driven by the Marine Mammal Protection Act (MMPA), the Endangered Species Act (ESA) of 1973 (16USC1531–1547, Public Law 93–205), and the Magnuson–Stevens Fishery Conservation and Management Act of 1976 (16USC1801–1882, Public Law 94–265). Management decisions have to carefully balance threats to marine mammal populations and threats to commerce (typically the fishing industry). Because of these potentially contradictory purposes, managers must anticipate the threat of lawsuits (Gerber et al. 1999), and all management decisions must be founded within a legally defensible framework. That framework is primarily based on the MMPA, which specifies that

marine mammal populations should be maintained at, or in some cases restored to, the level of the OSP;

stock-specific determinations of population status should be based on the best scientific evidence available; and

stock assessments should consider geographic range, *including seasonal or temporal variation.* (emphasis added)

Because of the vagaries of the specific management terms listed above, marine mammal scientists have operationalized the OSP as falling somewhere between carrying capacity *(K)* and the maximum net productivity level, which is usually assumed to be approximately *K*/2 (Gerrodette and DeMaster 1990; Wade 1998). In addition to the vagaries surrounding the operationalization of OSP, *K* has been notoriously difficult to measure. Technically speaking, *K* refers to an equilibrium population level prior to the impact of human hunting, where the last typically means commercial hunting. Because *K* is usually unknown, and perhaps unknowable, it is generally estimated via "back-calculation" based on historically documented population levels (Gerrodette and DeMaster 1990). Although the estimation of OSP can, theoretically, accommodate variability in *K*, the specific management action taken will depend on whether fluctuations in *K* are anthropogenic, such as when they are driven by indirect competition through fisheries (DeMaster et al. 2001; Sinclair et al. 1994), or natural, such as when they are driven by natural changes in primary productivity (Ebbesmeyer et al. 1991; Francis and Hare 1994; Mantua et al. 1997; Trites 1992).

Unfortunately, historical records of population levels and behavior patterns typically postdate massive reductions of marine mammal populations (Busch 1985). Zooarchaeological remains from the west coast indicate that pinniped migratory and breeding distributions, and presumably population levels, have changed significantly within the past 200–300 years (Burton and Koch 1999; Burton et al. 2001; Burton et al. 2002; Etnier 2002b; Gustafson 1968; Hildebrandt 1984; Lyman 1988b; Lyon 1937; Pyle and Long 2001; Walker and Craig 1979).

Despite arguments for ecosystem-level management (Fowler 1999; Mangel and Hofman 1999), most marine mammal management decisions are based on stock-specific evaluations of single species (Gerrodette and DeMaster 1990; Read and Wade 2000). Three types of zooarchaeological data contribute to stock-specific evaluations and can help managers maintain their legal defensibility. First, species-specific demographic patterns can be used to infer precommercial zoogeographic and migrational patterns. Second, the stable isotopic characterization of bone and teeth provides a proxy measure of variability in pinniped diet, migratory behavior, and variability in oceanographic conditions (which influence *K*). Finally, molecular (DNA) data can be used to evaluate the antiquity of stock distinctions and variability in population size. In this chapter I consider each kind of data as represented in faunal remains recovered from Ozette.

ZOOARCHAEOLOGICAL DATA

Ozette lies on Cape Alava, the western terminus of the Olympic Peninsula of Washington and the contiguous 48 states (Figure 5.1). Excavations have revealed that the site was occupied continuously for at least 2,000 years (Wessen 1990); historically, Makah Indians lived there until 1914 (Colson 1953). One section of the site, Area B70, consists of nine distinct strata dating from 800 years ago to the early 20th century (Table 5.2). Excavations in Area B70 yielded more than 64,000 pieces of identifiable mammal bone, 98 percent of which were from cetaceans or pinnipeds (Huelsbeck 1994a, 1994b). The data and analyses presented here are based on examination of more than 1,400 pinniped mandibles recovered from Area B70.

Distributional Data: Relative Abundance of Taxa

The dominance of northern fur seal remains in the Ozette assemblages (Table 5.2) is striking and has been well known for decades (Gustafson 1968). One hypothesis that explains the abundance of northern fur seals is the site's proximity to the historically documented migration route of animals from Alaska to midlatitude waters (Kajimura 1979; York 1995). This explanation is discussed at length below. The abundances of Guadalupe fur seals do not correspond to any historically documented patterns. Despite the fact that the historical range of Guadalupe fur seals in the ENP is thought to extend only as far north as northern California (Fleischer 1987; Hanni et al. 1997), mandibles of this species are present in low frequencies in five of nine Ozette strata (Table 5.2).

California sea lions *(Zalophus californianus)* have been documented in archaeological sites on the Oregon coast (Lyman 1988b) and are presently

TABLE 5.2. Frequencies (Number of Identified Specimens) of Mandibles of Pinniped Taxa at Ozette.

Stratum	Age	*Phoca vitulina*	*Mirounga angustirostris*	*Callorhinus ursinus*	*Arctocephalus townsendi*	*Eumetopias jubatus*	*Zalophus californianus*
I	A.D. 1850–1910	3	0	11	0	2	0
III	~A.D. 1780	2	0	2	0	0	0
IV	after A.D. 1719	0	0	145	7	1	0
House 2 and Unit VtV	A.D. 1650–1700	4	0	187	3	2	0
House 3 and Unit VtVI	?	7	0	174	2	2	0
House 5 and Unit VtVII	~A.D. 1500–1520	0	2	193	1	2	0
House 1 and Unit VXM	~A.D. 1500–1700	7	0	648	21	1	1
VI	?	0	0	8	0	0	0
VII	800 B.P.	0	0	6	0	0	0
Total		23	2	1,374	34	10	1
Percent of Total		1.6	0.1	95.3	2.4	0.7	0.1

abundant throughout the coastal waters of the Olympic Peninsula and Puget Sound (Gearin et al. 2001). This species is very rare at Ozette: only one of the 1,444 pinniped mandibles from the site has been identified as California sea lion (Table 5.2). It is doubtful that study of the complete collection of faunal remains from Area B70 would significantly change the relative abundance of California sea lion specimens because Huelsbeck (1994a) fails to identify this species in his study of nearly 53,000 non-cetacean mammalian specimens from the site. Although it cannot be determined if the relative abundance of California sea lions in the Ozette assemblage corresponds to their former relative abundance along the Washington coast, available data suggest that this is the case. One can imagine a culturally mediated avoidance of California sea lions (Sepez 2001), but this seems unlikely given the archaeological presence of every other species of pinniped extant in the ENP in the Ozette assemblage (Huelsbeck 1994a). Further, the remains of adult male and female Steller sea lions and the abundant remains of gray whales *(Eschrictius robustus)* in the assemblage (Huelsbeck 1994b) demonstrate the ability of the Makah to harvest the largest marine mammals. Thus, the single specimen of California sea lion suggests that this species was, unlike the case today, rarely found near Ozette during the late prehistoric period.

Distributional Data: Relative Abundance of Age Classes

Taxonomic abundance data (Table 5.2) suggest that Guadalupe fur seals and California sea lions may have had behavioral patterns in the ENP during the late prehistoric period that are different than those observed historically. The significance of the relative abundance data for both species of fur seals is emphasized by the ontogenic age distribution data (Gustafson 1968; Lyman 1988b). The latter data enable inferences regarding migration patterns and proximity to breeding colonies of both fur seal taxa.

Inferences regarding proximity to breeding colonies are based on the youngest age classes and hinge on the ability to distinguish between newborns deriving from local rookeries (Lyman 1988b) and pups that may have swum a considerable distance prior to being harvested. For northern fur seals, one approach has been to use four months as the threshold for identifying preweaned pups and, by extension, the presence of a local rookery (Burton et al. 2002). This threshold is based on age data for pups encountered historically along the Washington and Oregon coasts (Kajimura 1979; Kenyon and Wilke 1953; Scheffer 1950), as well as data on the average age of weaning and departure from rookeries (Gentry 1998; Ragen et al. 1995). There are, however, significant problems associated with using four months as a threshold for inferring the direct exploitation of fur seal rookeries. The age of pups encountered historically along the Oregon coast is based, at least in part, on surveys that predate the founding of the San Miguel Island, California, rookery (Figure 5.1; see Kajimura 1979; Kenyon and Wilke 1953). The presence of midlatitude northern fur seal rookeries that persisted into the early historic period, such as the one recently identified in the Farallon Islands, California (Figure 5.1; see Pyle and Long 2001), would be expected to dramatically influence the earliest age at which pups might be encountered along the mainland coast.

To evaluate the effects that these variables might have on the interpretation of archaeological fur seal remains, I analyzed stranding data for the California coast compiled by the Marine Mammal Stranding Network (U.S. Department of Commerce n.d.). The data consist of the date, location, and approximate age in 196 northern fur seal strandings for the years 1981–2000. Of these 196 strandings, 133 were identified as young of the year (YOYs; Table 5.3). Age at stranding was calculated using the long-term average birth date of June 24 for the San Miguel Island population (DeLong 1982). The age distribution of stranded YOYs plotted in one-month intervals (Figure 5.2) reveals the hazards of using a threshold of four months for identifying the local presence of a rookery. Although the modal stranding age is indeed four months (October), low frequencies of northern fur seals strand on the California coast between the ages of zero and three months (June–September). These strandings occur ≥ 45 km from San Miguel Island (Table 5.3).

The ontogenic ages of the Ozette northern fur seals were estimated based on the calibration of mandible measurements with growth curves generated from known-age YOYs (78 female, 100 male; see Etnier 2002a). In light of the California stranding data, the low proportion of animals zero–three months of age at Ozette (Figure 5.3) does not suggest immediate proximity to a rookery. Nor are the demographic data consistent with the hypothesis that these animals derive from the Alaska population. Although it is not possible to determine the proportion of Ozette YOYs that represent strandings, direct takes from a rookery, or animals intercepted in nearshore waters, the striking similarity between the Ozette data and the California stranding data (Figures 5.2–5.3) suggests that there was a rookery near Ozette, perhaps within 50–100 km. Stratigraphic analysis of the age distribution of the YOYs indicates that this demographic pattern

TABLE 5.3. FREQUENCIES OF NORTHERN FUR SEAL STRANDINGS ALONG THE CALIFORNIA COAST BY COUNTY.

County	Number of Strandings	Number of Young of the Year	Earliest Young of the Year Strandings	Inferred Age (Months)	Approximate Straight-Line Distance from San Miguel (km)
Del Norte	1	0	n.a.	n.a.	950
Humboldt	4	3	March[a]	8–9	740
Mendocino	1	0	n.a.	n.a.	600
Sonoma	0	0	n.a.	n.a.	530
Marin	12	7	October	3–4	465
Sacramento	1	1	December	5–6	460[b]
San Joaquin	1	1	November	4–5	460[b]
Contra Costa	1	1	October	3–4	460[b]
Alameda	3	2	October	3–4	460[b]
San Francisco	7	5	October	3–4	450
San Mateo	12	9	October	3–4	390
Santa Cruz	32	21	late September	3–4	360
Monterey	32	19	September	2–3	215
San Luis Obispo	54	40	September[a]	2–3	100
Santa Barbara	10	6	October	3–4	45
Ventura	8	6	September	2–3	95
Los Angeles	11	9	October	3–4	140
Orange	4	2	December	5–6	220
San Diego	2	1	November	4–5	270
Total	196	133			

Source: Data compiled from the Marine Mammal Stranding Network (U.S. Department of Commerce n.d.).

[a]This excludes pups born or aborted on the mainland (Stein et al. 1986).

[b]This is the distance between San Miguel and the mouth of San Francisco Bay.

persisted at least until A.D. 1719 (Etnier 2002a). There are no historical accounts of northern fur seal rookeries north of the Farallon Islands (Figure 5.1; see Scammon 1968; Swan 1870, 1883), although Lyman (1988b) infers the presence of two prehistoric rookeries along the Oregon coast on the basis of the archaeological remains of newborn northern fur seals.

The sample of known-age Guadalupe fur seals available for this study is quite small ($n = 3$), obviating the calibration of mandible measurements with growth curves. Direct comparison with known-age specimens indicates, however, that all of the 29 Guadalupe fur seal individuals from Ozette were between four and 12 months of age (Etnier 2002b). Canine teeth associated with the mandibles ($n = 15$) support this conclusion be-

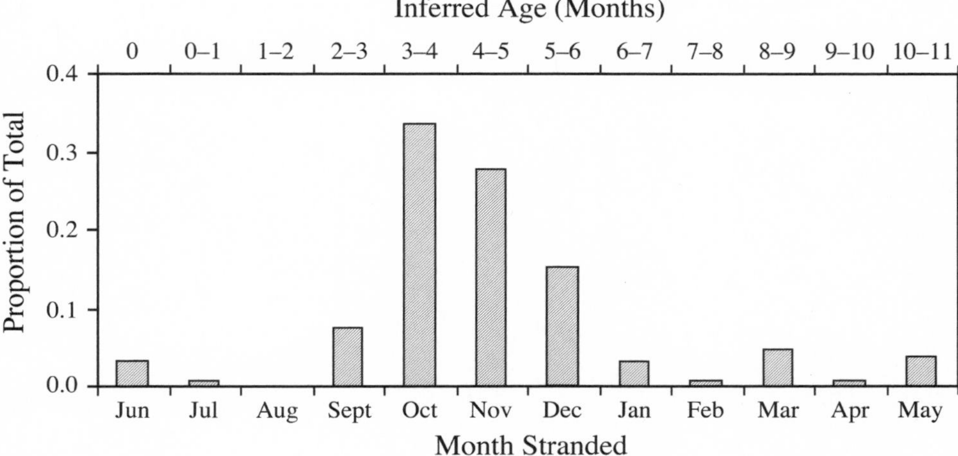

Figure 5.2. Age distribution of stranded young-of-the-year northern fur seals (n = 133), California coast (1981–2000). Data compiled from the Marine Mammal Stranding Network (U.S. Department of Commerce n.d.).

cause all lack the first annulus. Thus, rather than indicating a more extensive breeding distribution, the Ozette data indicate that YOY Guadalupe fur seals from southern latitudes occasionally strayed at least as far north as the Washington coast. This, too, contrasts strongly with what has been documented historically (Fleischer 1987; Hanni et al. 1997).

Stable Isotopic Characterizations

The analysis of stable isotopes of nitrogen and carbon in hair, soft tissues, and bone holds the potential to elucidate much regarding the diet and migratory behavior of pinnipeds. Of particular interest here are the facts that ^{13}C varies by latitude (Burton and Koch 1999; Burton et al. 2001; Burton et al. 2002) and ^{15}N varies with the trophic level at which pinnipeds forage (Hobson and Sease 1998; Hobson et al. 1997; Walker and Macko 1999) and, to a lesser extent, also varies by latitude (Burton and Koch 1999; Burton et al. 2001). It follows, then, that stable isotope analysis of archaeological pinniped bones and teeth provides a record of migration patterns and a long-term proxy of oceanographic conditions. Fur seal bones from archaeological deposits dating between 7000 and 600 B.P. in Monterey Bay, California, have ^{13}C ratios that are significantly different from those of modern Alaskan northern fur seals (Figure 5.4). Further-

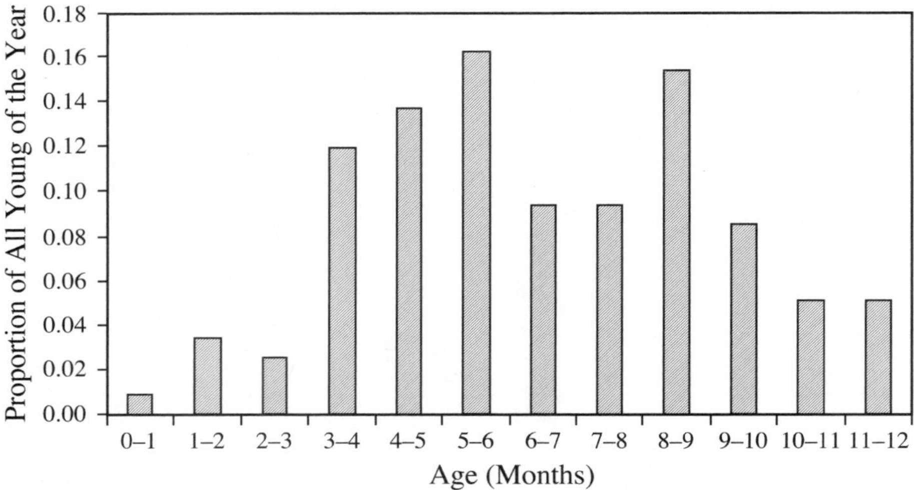

Figure 5.3. Age distribution of young-of-the-year northern fur seals from Ozette (n = 117), all stratigraphic levels combined.

more, the ^{13}C ratios of the Monterey Bay specimens are indicative of midlatitude foraging, suggesting that fur seals were year-round residents of California and Oregon prior to 600 B.P. (Burton et al. 2001; Burton et al. 2002).

The ^{15}N ratios indicate significant differences between the fur seals from Monterey Bay and samples from the modern fur seal population in Alaska. Burton et al. (2001) point out, however, that the midlatitude archaeological samples are statistically indistinguishable from samples derived from the modern fur seal populations on San Miguel Island. Thus, despite the fact that periods of climatic stress have been implicated in ecosystem-wide perturbations in the ENP (Glassow et al. 1994; Jones and Kennett 1999; Kennett and Kennett 2000; Pisias 1978), the preliminary results of the stable isotopic analysis of pinniped remains from archaeological sites in central and northern California suggest that these perturbations did not significantly affect pinniped populations (Burton and Koch 1999; Burton et al. 2001; Burton et al. 2002).

The Ozette demographic data for the YOY northern fur seals indicate that there was a breeding population on or near the Washington coast. To evaluate the hypothesis that some or all of the northern fur seals harvested at Ozette derived from the Alaska population, 50 adult female northern fur seal mandibles were submitted to the Earth Sciences Department, University of California, Santa Cruz, for isotopic analysis. Both the

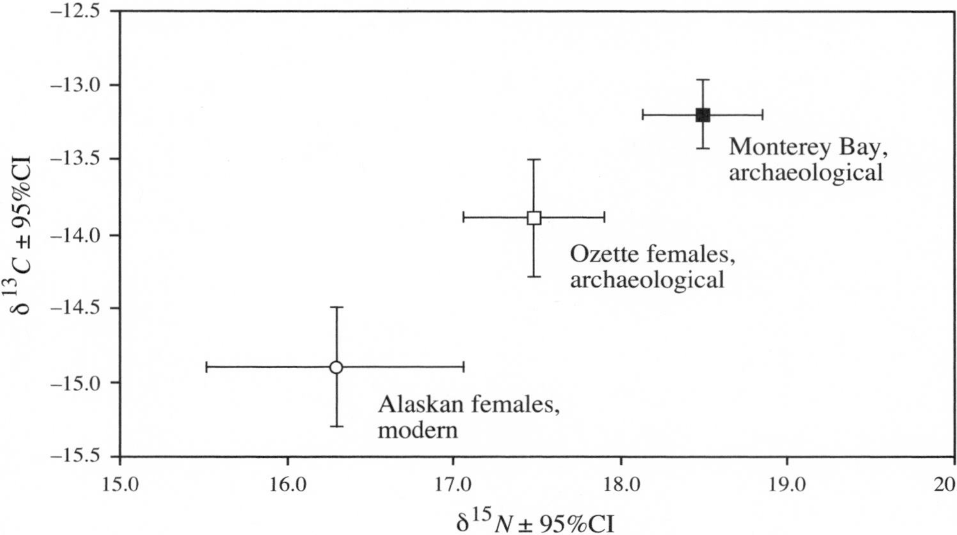

Figure 5.4. Comparison of the stable isotope composition of bone collagen from northern fur seals from archaeological sites (Monterey Bay, California, and Ozette, Washington) and northern fur seals from the modern Alaskan population. The California and Alaska data for a sample of both sexes and various ontogenic ages are from Burton et al. 2001; the Ozette data are from Etnier and Koch n.d.

^{13}C and the ^{15}N ratios of the Ozette samples are intermediate between the modern samples from Alaska and the archaeological samples from California (Figure 5.4; see Etnier and Koch n.d.). Although this may be viewed as evidence of a foraging pattern that is a mix of the California and Alaska patterns, the demographic data argue against this interpretation. The combination of evidence for a distinct breeding population and the unique isotopic signature suggests that the northern fur seals harvested at Ozette maintained a foraging pattern distinctly different than those of the California and Alaska populations.

Genetic Data

Given the heavy emphasis on stock-specific evaluations in pinniped management, the obvious questions to ask of the Ozette assemblage are: Did the population of northern fur seals exploited at Ozette make a significant contribution to the overall population level? And did the Ozette northern fur seals make up a stock distinct from other ENP populations? Analysis of ancient DNA from archaeological samples is a promising approach for determining population histories (Avise 1994; Pääbo 1993; Spong et al. 2000; Waples 1991) but to date has only been sporadically utilized in marine mammal studies (Weber et al. 2000). Although genetic analyses of the Ozette northern fur seals have not yet been conducted, a similar study completed for the Ozette sea otters *(Enhydra lutris)* provides a measure of the potential of this method.

Based on the analysis of genetic variation within four microsatellite markers and mitochondrial DNA, Ozette sea otters exhibit significantly more genetic variation than all extant sea otter populations combined (Larson et al. 2002). Microsatellite heterozygosity levels indicate that the effective breeding population from which the Ozette sea otters were harvested was significantly higher than that of any modern population. Further, the haplotype frequencies of the Ozette sea otters suggest that they were part of the northern sea otter subspecies *(E. l. kenyoni)* rather than the southern sea otter *(E. l. nereis)*.

Because the analysis of ancient DNA has the potential to track stock-specific variability in population size, genetic analyses might also track variability in *K* (Avise 1994; Spong et al. 2000; Waples 1991). Even if temporal variability in *K* cannot be tracked with sufficient resolution to maintain legal defensibility under the MMPA, the potential use of genetic analysis to determine the antiquity of stock distinctions in pinniped populations (Bickham et al. 1996; Ream 2002) would provide valuable information for guiding management decisions.

DISCUSSION

During the 19th and 20th centuries, many species of birds and mammals were driven to the brink of extinction. A species "whose population has been reduced to such a low level that it can no longer function as a significant part of its normal ecosystem . . . or to the point where there is considerable doubt whether the species remains extant" is said to have the status of "extation" (R. C. Banks, in LeBouef 1977:1). As pinniped populations throughout the eastern North Pacific recover from extation, we can expect to discover many examples of supposedly novel behavior. Consider northern fur seals. The migratory and behavioral patterns of the Alaskan population were believed for over 100 years to represent "the" pattern of fur seal behavior (Gentry 1998; Kajimura 1979; Scheffer 1958). The discovery of northern fur seals breeding in California in the late 1960s (Peterson et al. 1968) seemed unthinkable at the time. Archaeological data from California (Burton et al. 2001; Burton et al. 2002), Oregon (Lyman

1988b), and Washington (Crockford et al. 2002; Etnier 2002a) indicate, however, that the northern fur seals at San Miguel Island were merely reestablishing a pattern that had been in place for millennia prior to the onset of the commercial fur trade.

Turning to a more recent example, the National Marine Fisheries Service has expended considerable effort to mediate California sea lion predation on ESA-listed runs of steelhead trout (*Oncorhynchus mykiss;* see Gearin et al. 1988; Gearin et al. 2001; National Marine Fisheries Service 1997; Pfeifer 1987; Pfeifer et al. 1989). Although the need to protect endangered steelhead runs cannot be denied, the means used to accomplish this goal should take long-term patterns into consideration. If the current distribution of California sea lions represents expansion into *new* territory, rather than the restoration of an ancient pattern, then any management decisions concerning the control of California sea lion populations will need to take this into consideration.

Two points arise from this discussion. The first is the persistent, and probably fallacious, idea that if we leave things alone, they will go back to "normal." The second relates to the way in which we think of and define *normal* (or *natural;* see chap. 1). Because of the complexity of the ENP ecosystem, we cannot think of the included taxa as acting independently of each other. Rather, we should conceive of the taxa more as a closed array, with competition for resources a constant aspect of their interrelationships (Mangel and Hofman 1999). Viewed this way, a wide variety of so-called stable states is possible (Estes et al. 1998; Simenstad et al. 1978), such as the one recently hypothesized by Burton et al. (2001) for archaeofaunal pinniped assemblages from the central and northern coast of California. The possibility of multiple stable states underscores the problem of using uncritically the time period immediately prior to or shortly after the initiation of commercial exploitation as the baseline toward which management goals are driven (Jackson et al. 2001).

CONCLUSIONS

Data on the late-prehistoric remains of northern fur seals, Guadalupe fur seals, and California sea lions from the Ozette Village archaeological site indicate that as recently as 200 years ago these taxa were behaving much differently than has been documented historically. An increasing suite of zooarchaeological data indicates that the late-20th-century expansion of ranges and growth in the populations of some pinniped taxa represent the recolonization of prehistorically occupied areas and a release from human predation, respectively. Both range expansion and population growth constitute returns to prehistoric conditions, but even these seem to have fluctuated over time. One management issue must therefore involve a decision regarding the particular ecosystem conditions or ranges thereof that are legally defensible and biologically desirable.

I have shown here that management efforts directed toward restoring ENP pinniped populations to optimum sustainable population levels—if that is what is desired—cannot rely exclusively on historically documented levels (or back-calculations based on the same) as the proxy baseline for preharvest population levels. If they do, then the long-term population trends of some taxa will be significantly misrepresented. As pinniped populations throughout the eastern North Pacific continue to rebound from extation, human–pinniped interactions will undoubtedly increase. Responsible management decisions concerning these interactions require much more information than has typically been utilized. That information exists in the form of skeletal, chemical, and genetic data that can be gleaned from zooarchaeological remains. We just need to know how to look for it.

Acknowledgments. This research was funded through a generous fellowship administered through the Environmental Protection Agency. It could not have been completed without the extensive assistance of David Huelsbeck, Stephen Samuels, Paul Gleason, and the Makah Cultural and Research Center. I thank R. Lee Lyman and Ken Cannon for inviting me to participate in the Society for American Archaeology symposium at which this essay was first presented. The chapter was much improved based on comments received from Lyman and two anonymous reviewers.

6

Zooarchaeological Implications for Missouri's Elk *(Cervus elaphus)* Reintroduction Effort

Judith L. Harpole

North American elk *(Cervus elaphus)* were once found in the State of Missouri (Murie 1951:31), but as a result of Euro-American settlement and land-use practices, this large cervid (225–400 kg) became scarce in the state by 1830 and was effectively locally extirpated by the beginning of the 20th century (Schwartz and Schwartz 1981). In 1999 the Rocky Mountain Elk Foundation funded a Missouri Department of Conservation (MDC) study to determine the feasibility of reintroducing elk to the state. The study consists of two parts: a biological assessment of potential elk habitat and a survey to determine the attitudes of Missouri residents in counties likely to be affected by elk reintroduction (MDC 2000a). The two parts were integrated in an effort to identify suitable habitats for elk in areas with minimum potential for elk–human conflict. For example, suitable areas had to contain no four-lane highways and minimal agricultural activity. Interestingly, of some 5,500 state residents who responded to questionnaires regarding their thoughts on the possible reintroduction, about 88 percent felt that one benefit of the program would be the "restoration of native wildlife" (MDC 2000b). Other identified benefits were environmental education, elk viewing and tourism, and hunting.

The assessment identifies a ten-county area in the rugged Courtois Hills portion of the Ozark Highlands of southeastern Missouri (Figure 6.1) for detailed consideration as a potential release area. Two locations within the area are identified as suitable for supporting low densities of elk (about one individual per square mile). Peck Ranch is a large complex in Carter

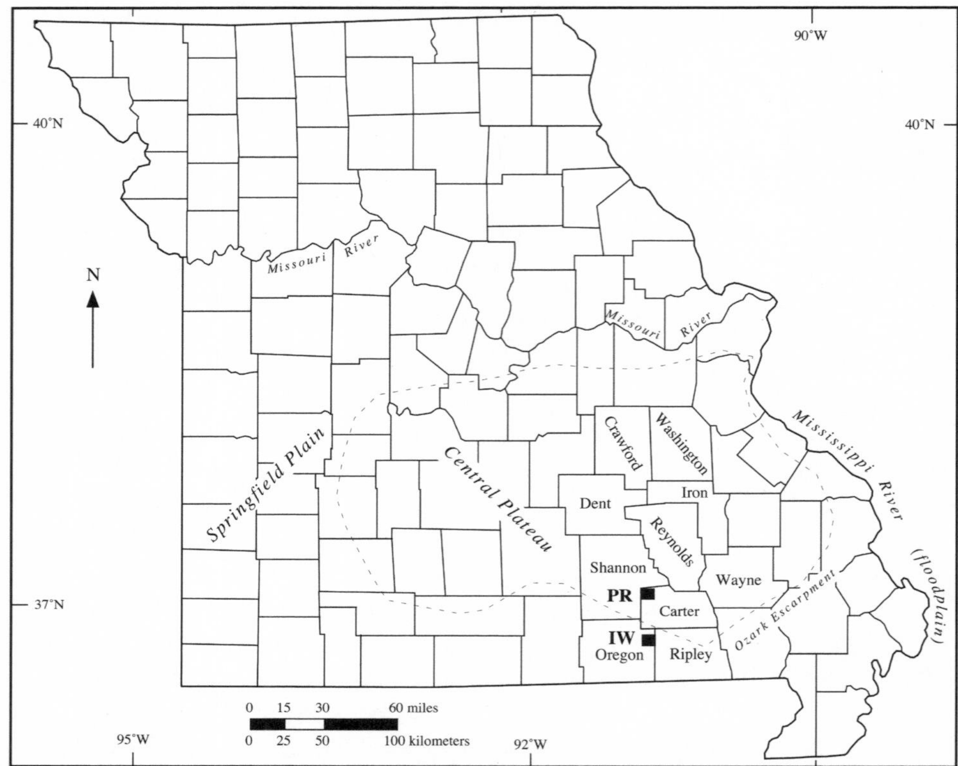

Figure 6.1. Map of Missouri and geographic places mentioned in the text. County lines are shown for reference; the dashed line outlines the Ozark Highlands. Counties with names are those considered for elk reintroduction; IW = Irish Wilderness; PR = Peck Ranch.

County owned by the MDC, and the Irish Wilderness in Oregon County is administered by the U.S. Department of Agriculture, Forest Service. These locations are proposed to serve as the first two in the state where transplanted elk would be released, though it is noted that a possible deficiency in these locations is the potential lack of a suitable habitat that would provide elk, primarily a grazer, with sufficient forage. A captive herd in St. Louis County had, during the 1950s, so heavily utilized its 2,400-acre range that it was exterminated (Murphy 1963). The feasibility study indicates that any reintroduction would need to be accompanied by intensive management of understory vegetation.

The feasibility study also mentions but does not explore the implications of the changes in Missouri forests and wildlife habitats that accompanied the urbanization of the state; nor does it identify the subspecies of elk native to Missouri. Rather, the study simply makes the following statement: "Unrestricted killing probably was responsible for the extirpation of elk throughout the eastern elk *[C. e. canadensis]* range although landscape changes that occurred with [Euro-American] settlement also may have had detrimental effects. The speed at which elk populations were decimated from yet unsettled landscapes in Missouri is somewhat remarkable" (MDC 2000a:5). There is no reference to the long-term biogeographic history of elk in Missouri; rather, it is concluded on the basis of scattered historical records (e.g., McKinley 1960) that elk were once found throughout the state.

In June 2001 the MDC decided against releasing elk in the state after the discovery of chronic wasting disease in western elk populations that were to serve as the source of the transplanted individuals (for an introduction to the presence of this disease among Yellowstone elk, see Keiter 1997; for a very readable discussion of the disease and its epidemiology, see Lott 2002:108–115). The MDC feared that the disease might spread to domestic livestock and the state's white-tailed deer *(Odocoileus virginianus)* population if the transplanting took place (Renken 2001). The possibility of transplanting may, however, be raised again in 2011 when western elk herds are projected to be free of the disease. I assume that the two previously chosen areas for elk release will be those used in the future.

In this chapter I use zooarchaeological data to show where elk occurred prehistorically in Missouri, and I consider how historic land-use activities have altered the landscapes where the MDC proposes to release transplanted elk. Both kinds of knowledge are important to implementing a successful reintroduction. If, for example, "unsettled landscapes in Missouri" were incapable of supporting elk in the 19th century, as the MDC study implies, then one has to wonder about the probability of a successful reintroduction, even in lightly populated areas. The same can be said for the greater proportion of anthropogenic landscape area relative to nonanthropogenic landscape area within state boundaries. Zooarchaeological data provide time depth and geographic breadth that may clarify the probability of success of a proposed reintroduction.

ELK ECOLOGY

Elk were once present throughout most of the 48 contiguous United States, with the exception of some parts of the Southeast (Bryant and Maser 1982; Van Gelder 1982). Limited only by their ability to withstand heat, elk occupied diverse regions throughout the nation. Presently, elk are found in the wild only along the Pacific coast and in the Rocky Mountains. Extirpation across much of their original range is widely believed to be the result of the overhunting and habitat modification that accompanied Euro-American settlement (Boyd 1978; Bryant and Maser 1982; Murie 1951).

Elk are browsers, feeding on grass, browse (twigs, bark, leaves), and forbs (Boyd 1978; Murie 1951; Nelson and Leege 1982). Grass seems to be the preferred food throughout spring, summer, and fall (May–November [Boyd 1978]), and browse is the dominant food consumed during winter and early spring (December–April). Forbs constitute a relatively minor part of the diet except during the mid-to-late summer months (July–August) when they may make up as much as 50 percent of the diet (Boyd 1978). These patterns are highly variable, and food preferences among elk are poorly understood, but it appears that grasses are generally the most important part of the diet.

Elk are social animals, and older cows, rather than bulls, are herd leaders (Boyd 1978). Males and females live separately, except during the fall mating season when bulls form harems of multiple cows. Elk divide into sexually segregated groups after the fall rut and migrate to their winter range. Many migrate from high-elevation summer ranges to low-elevation winter ranges, covering distances as great as 48 km (Boyd 1978).

PREHISTORIC AND HISTORIC ZOOGEOGRAPHY

Transplanting elk to Missouri is intended to re-create an earlier biological condition of the species being present within the geographic area identified by the state's borders. This phrasing prompts questions regarding specifics. In particular, did elk occur during some past time in the proposed release areas? And if so, did elk always occur there, or did they occur there at some times but not others? If the latter, then knowing why elk were sometimes absent would be critical to maintaining a newly introduced population. The beginnings of answers to these questions can be constructed by reference to zooarchaeological data and to historic records of elk sightings.

Zooarchaeological Data

In order to determine the prehistoric distribution of elk, various paleobiological data were examined. All sites in Missouri that have been radiometrically dated as of 1994 and which contain elk remains were extracted from FAUNMAP, a database organized around mammalian taxa found in archaeological and paleontological sites (Graham and Lundelius 1994). Original reports referenced in FAUNMAP were consulted to determine the exact location of sites, their age, and the nature of the elk remains they contained. In cases where the original report was unavailable, *The Prehistory of Missouri* (O'Brien and Wood 1998) was consulted for site location and age. These data were supplemented by examination of archaeological reports filed with the Missouri Department of Natural Resources Historic Preservation Program. Only reports that concerned sites within the ten counties designated for elk reintroduction were examined. Archaeological reports from Fort Leonard Wood were also consulted because this is one of the few areas in the state that features intense, ongoing archaeological research.

Sites with associated radiocarbon ages were preferred because I hoped to track elk distributions over time. When radiocarbon ages were unavailable, sites were assigned to temporal periods on the basis of associated, temporally diagnostic artifacts. Sites with poor chronological control or mixed stratigraphy were designated "age unknown" (Table 6.1). Sites containing only artificially modified elk bone and elk bone and elk antler artifacts were not included, as these items may have been transported or traded in from distant areas. Few historical archaeological sites in the Ozarks have faunal remains, and when faunal remains are present, they are usually small collections comprising less than 300 specimens. Eight Ozark sites dating to the early to mid–19th century have been excavated (Wettstaed 2003), and only two of these have faunal collections that have been analyzed; neither contained elk remains (Harcourt et al. 1997; Price 1985). Therefore, all sites discussed here date to the prehistoric period. The number of identified specimens of elk per site is small (Table 6.1), and this paucity of elk remains precludes quantitative analysis. I limit zooarchaeological analyses here to biogeography but note that deer remains greatly outnumber elk remains, raising the question of the appropriateness of reintroducing a species that may never have been common.

The geographic distribution of the 24 sites in Missouri that contain elk remains (Table 6.1) is interesting because only one of those sites is located within the proposed reintroduction area (Figure 6.2). Also of interest is the fact that the majority of the sites found south of the Missouri River are located on the Springfield Plain and the Central Plateau. These two regions are characterized by less relief than any other place within the Ozark High-

TABLE 6.1. Archaeological Sites in Missouri that Have Produced Elk Remains.

Site Name	County	Site Type	Occupation Period with Elk Remains	Associated Radiocarbon Ages	Number of Identified Specimens	Source(s)
Rodgers Shelter	Benton	Rock shelter	Dalton, Early Archaic	10,500–7500 B.P.	1	Wood and McMillan 1976
Hayti Bypass	Pemiscott	Open	Middle–Late Woodland, Mississippian	A.D. 1–600; A.D. 1000–1140	11	Conner 1995
Mellor	Cooper	Open	Middle Woodland	A.D. 328 ± 23	75	Kay 1980
Imhoff	Saline	Open	Middle Woodland		N/A	Kay 1980
Givens	Cooper	Open	Middle Woodland		N/A	Kay 1980
Renner	Platte	Open	Middle Woodland		14	Wedel 1943
Pigeon Roost Creek	Monroe	Open	Middle–Late Woodland		6	Bozell and Warren 1982
Burkemper	Lincoln	Open	Middle Woodland		5	Styles and Purdue 1996
Hoecake	Mississippi	Open	Late Woodland, Mississippian	A.D. 1185 ± 90; A.D. 640 ± 130	N/A	Williams 1974
Ross	Monroe	Open	Late Woodland		N/A	Graham and Lundelius 1994
Boschert	St. Charles	Open	Late Woodland		1	Purdue et al. 1989
Cooper	Monroe	Open	Late Woodland		3	Bozell and Warren 1982
Bryant Cave	St. Clair	Cave	Late Woodland		1	Warren 1983
Saltpeter Cave #3	Pulaski	Cave	Late Woodland		1	Ahler et al. 1998
Vista Shelter	St. Clair	Rock shelter	Mississippian	A.D. 860 ± 110; A.D. 1290 ± 80	1	Wood 1968

Snodgrass	Butler	Open	Middle Mississippian	A.D. 1200–1350	N/A	Smith 1974
Herrell Village	Jefferson	Open	Middle Mississippian		N/A	Adams 1949
Guthrey	Saline	Open	Oneota		9	Henning 1970; O'Brien and Wood 1998
Blackwell Cave	Hickory	Cave	Late Holocene		N/A	Graham and Lundelius 1994
Hidden Valley Shelter	Jefferson	Rock shelter	Unknown, mixed deposits		N/A	Adams 1949; Chapman 1975
Helmrich Shelter	Cooper	Shelter	Unknown, mixed deposits		N/A	Marino 1994
Tick Creek Cave	Phelps	Cave	Unknown, mixed deposits		285	Parmalee 1965; Reeder 1988
Lepold	Ripley	Open	Unknown, mixed deposits		N/A	C. Price, personal communication, 2001; Smith n.d.
Shallow Cave	Phelps	Cave	Unknown, mixed deposits		N/A	Wessel 1974
Arnold Research Cave	Calloway	Cave	Unknown, mixed deposits		38	Wolverton 2001

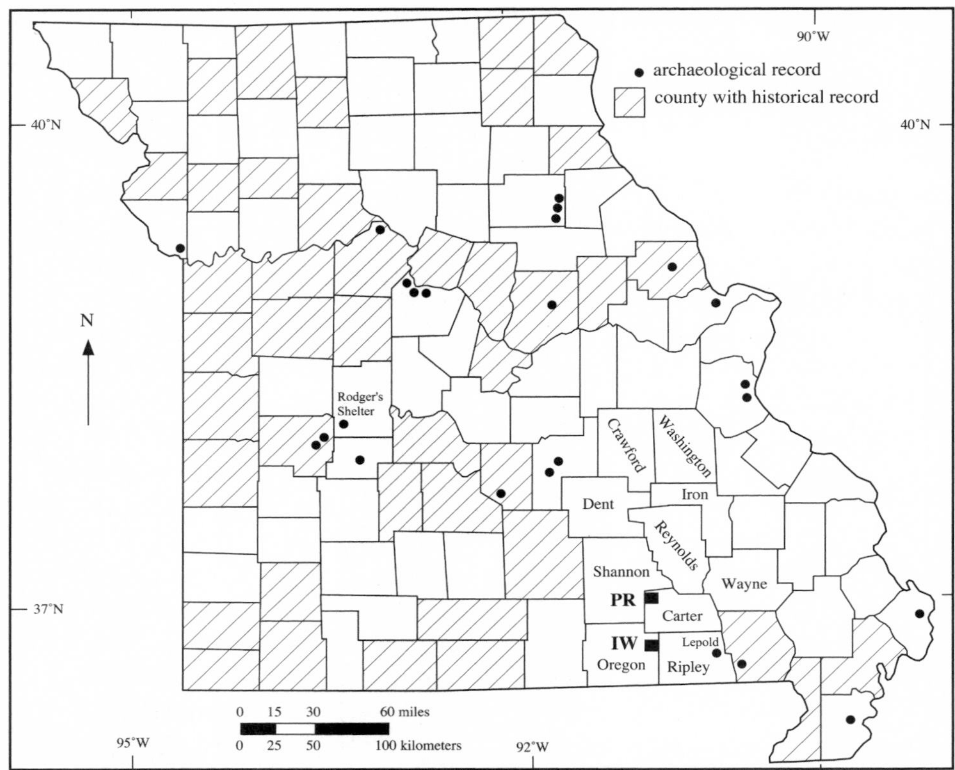

Figure 6.2. Distribution of Holocene archaeological sites (dots) in Missouri that have produced elk remains and counties (crosshatched) with historic records of elk. Named counties are those considered for elk reintroduction; IW = Irish Wilderness; PR = Peck Ranch.

lands, and they are covered with prairie vegetation (Rafferty 1980). Further, with one exception, all elk remains of known age date to the Middle Woodland period (250 B.C.–A.D. 450 [O'Brien and Wood 1998]) or later, even when the sites have faunal assemblages dating to earlier periods such as the Archaic (Table 6.1). Paleoclimatic studies note the beginning of a general decline in summer temperatures around 2000 B.P., coinciding with the beginning of the Middle Woodland period (Bryson and Bryson 1997). Although detailed studies of past climates across the state do not exist, it seems reasonable to propose that this decline in temperature may have induced elk to populate the area. Exemplifying this pattern is Rodger's Shelter, where elk remains are associated with the earliest period of occupation and coincide with a time when temperatures were cooler in the wake of the Wisconsin glaciation (R. B. McMillan, personal communication, 2001).

Historical Data

Using data gathered from historical journals and explorers' accounts, biologist Daniel McKinley (1960) has summarized instances of elk sightings across the state. Sightings are clustered in the southwestern portion of the state on the Springfield Plain and the Central Plateau (Figure 6.2). Although elk were present in many regions through the 1830s, a decline was noted as early as 1800, with the last documented elk kill taking place in 1886. Overall, elk seem to have been extirpated in most areas of the state during the first half of the 19th century, with a few "wily patriarchs" surviving into the late 1800s (McKinley 1960:364). McKinley found no mention of elk in counties in or near the proposed reintroduction area.

The same spatial pattern evident in the locations of the archaeological sites producing elk remains is also present in the historically documented distribution of elk (Figure 6.2). With the exception of the Lepold site, no elk remains have ever been found within the proposed reintroduction area. The Lepold site lies east of the Ozark Escarpment in the Mississippi River floodplain, a setting unlike the area proposed for elk reintroduction. Both archaeological data and historical accounts indicate that elk were never present within the proposed reintroduction area. This raises the question of the appropriateness of bringing elk to this part of the state if some sort of "natural" condition is what is sought by those advocating the transplanting.

WHICH TAXON?

Biologists generally recognize six subspecies of elk: Eastern elk *(C. e. canadensis),* Roosevelt elk *(C. e. roosevelti),* Merriam elk *(C. e. merriami),* Tule elk *(C. e. nannodes),* Manitoban elk *(C. e. manitobensis),* and Rocky Mountain elk (*C. e. nelsoni* [Bryant and Maser 1982]). These subspecies occupied different geographical ranges and are believed to have existed at the time of European contact. The degree of isolation of these taxa from one another and the degree of genetic differentiation among them prior to the 19th century are unknown and may be largely unknowable given the many transplanting events and subsequent hybridization between populations that took place in the 20th century (Polziehn et al. 1998). Eastern elk, the subspecies believed to have inhabited Missouri, is variously thought to now be extinct (Bryant and Maser 1982) or to be merely a geographically delimited population (Schonewald 1994). The MDC proposes to transplant Rocky Mountain elk to the Missouri Ozarks based on the premise that this subspecies is closely related to the Eastern subspecies.

Morphometric variation in the crania of elk subspecies does not coincide with subspecies designations (Schonewald 1994), so it is unclear if or how the Eastern subspecies differed osteologically from the others. Thus, it is unclear if the prehistoric remains of Eastern elk could be distinguished among elk remains recovered from archaeological sites in Missouri. There may, however, be a way to determine the degree of genetic relatedness of Rocky Mountain elk and Eastern elk prior to 20th-century transplanting and hybridization and, thus, to determine which, if either, of these subspecies was present prehistorically in Missouri. With the development of the polymerase chain reaction, it is now possible to amplify small amounts of DNA taken from archaeological samples and compare the genetic makeup of extinct populations with that of modern ones (Richards et al. 1993). This technique could be used to determine the degree of relatedness between the prehistoric elk that once inhabited Missouri and modern populations of Rocky Mountain elk. Such an analysis would aid in determining if, in fact, Rocky Mountain elk are the most appropriate subspecies to transplant to the area. Further, once the degrees of genetic similarity and difference among the extant subspecies (and populations) of elk are known, conservation biologists would be better equipped to determine an appropriate source population of elk for reintroduction to particular areas. However, even knowing this may be of little use if the history of the habitats where elk are to be reintroduced is not considered. Perhaps more important, the current ecological situation of the source population and its appropriateness, both genetic and ecological, for the release site(s) should be considered.

CHANGES IN MISSOURI FORESTS

After the retreat of the Laurentide ice sheet and the decline of its associated boreal forests, "silvic" systems in Missouri were dominated by oak (*Quercus* sp.), elm (*Ulmus* sp.), ash (*Fraximus* sp.), and other deciduous trees (U.S. Department of Agriculture, Forest Service 1999). This deciduous forest peaked at roughly 14,000 B.P. and lasted until the end of the Pleistocene ice age about 4,000 years later. The subsequent Holocene epoch began with relatively cool, moist climates, but these eventually changed. The Middle Holocene is characterized as a warmer, drier period termed the Hypsithermal (or Altithermal), which brought about an expansion of prairies and savannas in the state. As the climate subsequently changed to a wetter, cooler phase, Missouri forests changed from prairie-dominated landscapes to forest landscapes with inclusions of prairie. These forest landscapes have been dominated by pine (*Pinus* sp.) for about the last 4,000 years (U.S. Department of Agriculture, Forest Service 1999:9).

Early explorers and settlers described Missouri landscapes as open woodland forests with a grassy understory (Schoolcraft 1996). The arrival of large numbers of Euro-Americans had drastic impacts on Missouri's forests. Homesteaders worked to suppress wildfires, and as a result the once-open forests became choked with dense, brushy understories. Trees grew closer together and became more numerous. Fire-suppression policies resulted in a decline in biodiversity and more closed forests (U.S. Department of Agriculture, Forest Service 1999).

Fire suppression was not the only factor that changed the composition of Missouri forests. The arrival of railroad lines and the resultant ease of transporting goods to out-of-state markets spurred the timber industry to begin large-scale operations throughout the state (Rafferty 1980). Significant logging was done in Shannon, Oregon, Carter, Reynolds, Ripley, Wayne, and Butler (east of and adjacent to Carter and Ripley) counties. Logging operations covering areas ≥ 8,600 acres (3,480 ha) were not uncommon. One mill produced 220,000 board feet of lumber per day, a feat requiring 90 railroad cars per day to move the product. By the 1930s the majority of the Ozarks was deforested. Fire suppression began in earnest after logging companies moved out of the Ozarks and the federal government began acquiring the cutover lands (Rafferty 1980). Fire-suppression policies enacted by the government through the U.S. Department of Agriculture Forest Service allowed species with low tolerances for fire to take over areas once dominated by fire-resistant species.

The timber industry was not the only one with an interest in Missouri's forests. The mining industry relied primarily on wood products to fuel many of its furnaces. For example, the furnace at the Nova Scotia Ironworks in Dent County required that 10 acres (4 ha) of trees be cut each day to fire the furnace. This particular harvesting of timber for firewood continued for five years. The result of such widespread logging was a drastic change in the composition of the forests surrounding the mining center. General Land Office (GLO) survey notes from 1820 describe a forest of pine with an open understory in the area later occupied by Nova Scotia Ironworks. In 1999 the forest consisted mainly of black oak with a dense understory (Wettstaed and Harpole n.d.). Given the fact that elk consume grass as a preferred dietary item, these anthropogenically caused changes in vegetation should make one wonder if the artificial habitats of the eastern Ozarks are truly the best places to release transplanted elk.

DISCUSSION

The Missouri Department of Conservation may again consider reintroducing elk to the state in 2011. If so, the MDC should take the zooarchaeological and historical records into account. Those records show that elk occupied areas different than the proposed reintroduction area in the heart of the rugged Courtois Hills, a region marked by steep slopes covered with dense vegetation and deep, narrow valleys (Rafferty 1980). Zooarchaeological data show that elk occurred prehistorically in the open grasslands of the Springfield Plain and the Central Plateau. The only site located in the proposed reintroduction area lies not in the Ozarks but, rather, east of the Ozark Escarpment on the Mississippi River floodplain. Similarly, historical data fail to indicate that elk occurred in any of the ten counties considered as reintroduction areas. Reintroduction plans should consider the reasons for the differences between the prehistoric distribution of elk and the historic distribution of this taxon—are they climatic, anthropogenic, or some combination thereof?—and if those reasons require modification of the proposed reintroduction areas.

The zooarchaeological record also suggests that the prehistoric presence and also the abundance of elk in the state may well be the result of shifts in climate. If elk migrated into Missouri as a result of a drop in summer temperatures, then what effects would an increase in temperatures have on a reintroduced population? Pollen analysis and further zooarchaeological research may help determine if a decrease in temperature actually took place, allowing wildlife managers to plan accordingly.

The historical record indicates that many of Missouri's southern counties underwent significant change in vegetation and habitats during the 19th and early 20th centuries. Recall that Shannon, Carter, Ripley, Butler, Wayne, Oregon, and Reynolds counties were the sites of the most intense logging in the state. The proposed reintroduction lands lie in exactly this area (Figures 6.1–6.2). The composition of the forest surrounding the Nova Scotia Ironworks has changed radically since the 1820 GLO survey, and there is no reason to assume that other areas logged in a similar fashion were not equally affected. Any proposed reintroduction effort should take these changes into account; such alteration of habitats may decrease the probability that transplanted elk will survive, or not emigrate to another location, once they have been released.

Finally, recall that the two locations chosen as potential reintroduction sites were chosen in large part because they present a minimum potential for elk–human conflict. Yet more than 65 percent of the respondents to questionnaires indicated that the restoration of native wildlife, environmental education, elk viewing and tourism, and hunting would be the major benefits of the project. How can elk be viewed consistently if there are few highways in the area? This incongruity underscores one of the major hurdles of modern conservation biology: How are the different potential values suggesting a management action to be weighed? In the context of this book, it also highlights why zooarchaeological data may simply muddy the waters further. And if that is how these data are perceived by those in the position to make management decisions, then it would not be surprising if data such as those presented here are ignored. That would be a sad state of affairs indeed, especially if the restoration of "native" fauna were the alleged goal of a management activity.

Acknowledgments. I thank R. Lee Lyman and W. Raymond Wood for their assistance in locating references and their comments on an earlier draft. James R. Wettstaed kindly produced all figures.

7

Postcontact Changes in the Behavior and Distribution of Rocky Mountain Bighorn Sheep *(Ovis canadensis)* in Northwestern Wyoming

Susan S. Hughes

The Absaroka Mountains of northwestern Wyoming (Figure 7.1) today support one of the largest and most viable bighorn sheep *(Ovis canadensis)* populations in North America (Buechner 1960; Honess and Frost 1942; Hurley 1985). Hurley (1985) estimates the number of bighorn sheep to be 3,695, an increase since 1952 when populations reached an all-time low. The large sheep population in northwestern Wyoming is likely caused by the limited amount of human settlement in the area. Most of the area is managed by the U.S. Department of Agriculture Forest Service, with large portions designated as "wilderness." Most settlement is confined to the foothills and lower river valleys.

Although the bighorn population is large, wildlife biologists in northwestern Wyoming believe that 19th-century Euro-American colonization caused a substantial loss in bighorn numbers and changes in their migratory behavior and distribution. Bighorn sheep in the area today summer in high-elevation alpine meadows and winter in mountain valleys or the foothills bordering human settlement. Honess and Frost (1942) state that prior to Euro-American settlement, wintering bighorn sheep could be found at much lower elevations and occasionally migrated into the Bighorn Basin at the edge of the foothills. They and others also argue that the reduction in low-elevation winter range has forced sheep to winter at high elevations or to eliminate seasonal migrations altogether (Honess and Frost 1942; Packard 1946). A recent Yellowstone National Park (1997) northern range study recognizes that basic information has been lacking

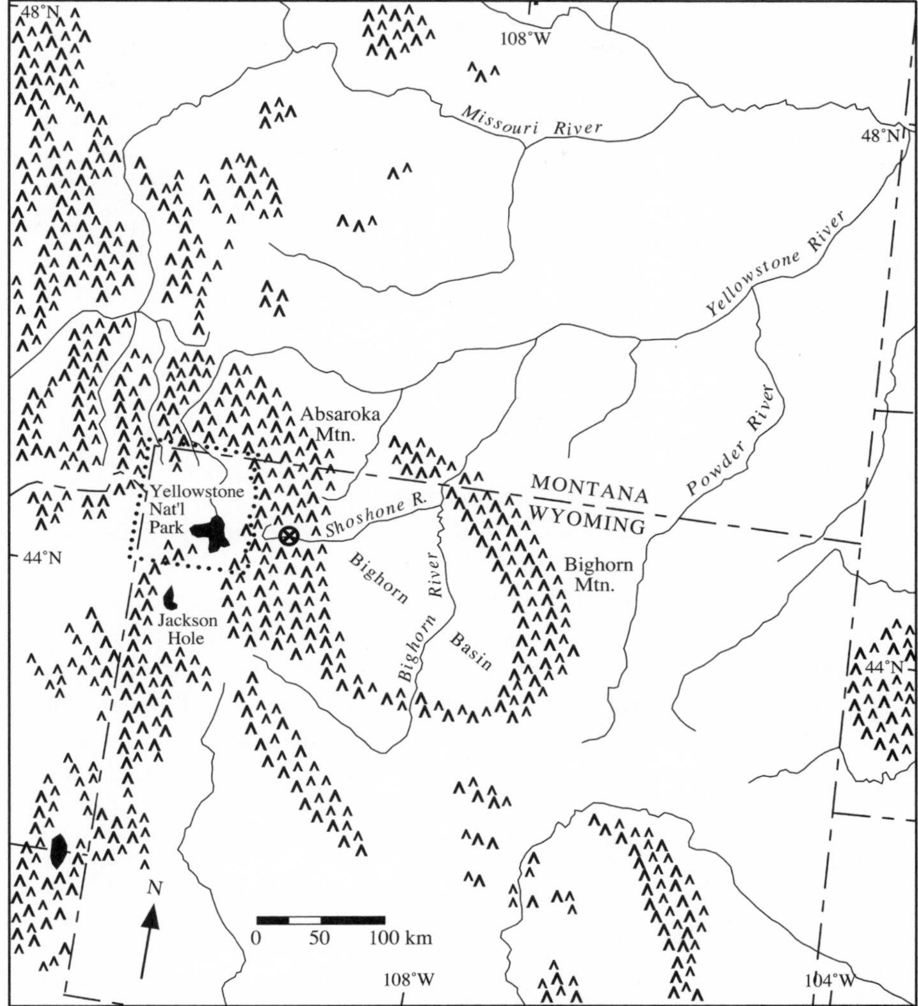

Figure 7.1. Map of northwestern Wyoming and the location of Mummy Cave (circled X). The site is just east of Yellowstone National Park and just west of the western edge of the Bighorn Basin.

on the seasonal movements, habitat use, and impacts of human development on bighorn sheep populations, but it confirms that a significant decrease in the bighorn population has occurred since the 19th century.

Zooarchaeological data are useful when examining these issues because they provide a historical perspective. In this chapter, bighorn habitat use and migratory behavior in northwestern Wyoming are examined using stable carbon and nitrogen isotope data derived from both archaeological and modern bighorn sheep bones from the area to gain insights into the impact of Euro-American colonization. As proxy measures of diet, stable carbon and nitrogen isotopes are useful tools in identifying animal habitat and range. Three questions are addressed here: Has there been a historic loss of low-elevation winter range? Has there been a historic loss of long-distance migration? Did high-elevation wintering behavior appear historically? Answers to these questions are of interest to wildlife managers who want to ensure the future viability of local bighorn sheep, as well as to anyone concerned with the impact of Euro-American colonization and anthropogenic effects on animal populations.

MUMMY CAVE

Prehistoric data are derived from bone recovered from Mummy Cave, a rockshelter in the mountains of northwestern Wyoming. With its 10,000-year record of bighorn sheep hunting, the site (Figure 7.1) is ideally suited for examining changes in bighorn sheep behavior through time. Thirty-eight occupational strata were identified, of which 27 produced faunal material. Radiocarbon dates on charcoal and bone securely date most strata (Table 7.1; see Hughes 2003; Husted and Edgar 2002). Although bighorn sheep dominate the assemblage, small numbers of deer (*Odocoileus* sp.), elk *(Cervus elaphus)*, other mammals, and birds are represented. Seasonal indicators point to winter and spring occupations, with strata 3, 6, 8, and 9 possibly representing multiple visits (Hughes 2003).

Physical Environment

Mummy Cave is situated on the eastern flank of the Absaroka Mountains within the North Fork River Valley, 27 km east of Yellowstone National Park (Figure 7.1). The Absarokas are a dissected volcanic plateau, 160 km long and 80 km wide, bounded on the east by the Bighorn Basin (Moss 2002). The North Fork of the Shoshone River, one of several rivers draining the Absaroka Mountains, originates near the Yellowstone National Park boundary west of Mummy Cave (Figure 7.1). Sometime in the Late Pleistocene, the river carved the rockshelter in a southwest-facing cliff of its upper canyon. At this point, the canyon bottom is 1,922 m in elevation and narrow, with steeply sloping walls rising to 2,700 m. Nearby peaks reach 3,600 m. The canyon begins to widen 18 km farther downstream in the Wapiti Valley, where sagebrush grasslands, more char-

TABLE 7.1. AGE, TOTAL NUMBER OF IDENTIFIED SPECIMENS (NISP), AND BIGHORN SHEEP NISP PER STRATUM AT MUMMY CAVE.

Stratum	Approximate Age (^{14}C Years)	Total NISP	Bighorn NISP	Percent Bighorn
1	370	13	13	100
3	1230	897	834	93
4	2050	59	45	76
5	2820	49	42	86
6/7	4420	1,448	1,365	94
8	4640	644	612	95
9	5390	319	287	90
10	5610	10	7	70
11	5800	34	23	68
11A		9	2	22
12	6400	104	73	70
12A	6780	30	19	63
13	7630	65	44	68
14		15	5	33
14A		9	2	22
15	7970	21	10	48
15A		3	3	100
16	8100	101	86	85
17	8135	75	73	97
18		107	99	93
19	8305	75	72	96
20	8465	52	43	83
21		3	0	0
22		35	3	9
22A		3	2	67
23	9250	17	2	12
24+[a]	10,890	26	3	12

[a]This is noncultural.

acteristic of the foothills environment, replace the coniferous forests of the Upper North Fork Valley.

Climate and Vegetational Zonation

Because of its high elevation and interior location, northwestern Wyoming is one of the coldest regions in the interior United States. Subzero temperatures are common in the winter, with scorching heat at lower elevations during the summer (Martner 1986). A correlation exists between temperature and elevation, with the adiabatic lapse rate of 9.8°C per 1,000 m of elevation (Davis et al. 1986; Knight 1994; Kutzbach and Guetter 1984;

Martner 1986). Greater precipitation usually in the form of snow occurs over the mountains—as much as 150 cm per year—with decreasing precipitation eastward toward the basin, where as little as 15 cm per year fall on the eastern edge (Knight 1994; Martner 1986). The relationships among precipitation, temperature, and elevation control the vegetational zonation in this area and the wildlife that depend on it.

Modern vegetation in northwestern Wyoming is characterized by a distinct altitudinal zonation (Figure 7.2; see Baker 1986; Daubenmire 1943; Gennett and Baker 1986; Waddington and Wright 1974). Grasslands and shrublands dominate the foothill zones where moisture stress can be severe (Tweit and Houston 1980). This habitat, especially the sagebrush browse (20 percent of ground cover), provides important winter range for big game in the Lower North Fork Valley (Tweit and Houston 1980). In areas of deep soils (alluvial fans, swales, and riparian zones), big sage *(Artemisia tridentata* ssp. *tridentata)* and other shrubs dominate (Tweit and Houston 1980).

The montane zone is a thick band of coniferous forest covering most of the steep mountain slopes. Grass is restricted to areas where annual precipitation is inadequate for tree growth, including steep south and west exposures, areas of poorly developed soils, and windswept loci (Tweit and Houston 1980). These areas occur as scattered, dry, "bald" patches of fescue grass *(Festuca idahoensis)*. No single patch is extensive, but their combined acreage makes this a significant winter habitat type for bighorn sheep, although of low productivity (Tweit and Houston 1980).

Above 2,900 m (the upper tree line), extreme temperature fluctuations, desiccating winds, and a short growing season prevent tree growth. The alpine tundra zone is a large expansive meadow of grass, forbs, and shrubland connecting rugged mountain peaks. This high-altitude forage sustains bighorn sheep throughout the summer and likely throughout the year because of heavy competition and overgrazing on winter ranges (Buechner 1960; Hurley 1985). Mummy Cave is situated in the ecotone between the sagebrush–grassland zone and the montane forest. Upstream from the cave, Douglas fir *(Pseudotsuga menziesii)* forest has invaded the valley bottom, and the montane "balds" are less frequent.

BIGHORN SHEEP ECOLOGY AND BEHAVIOR

Rocky Mountain bighorn sheep thrive in rugged, rocky terrain with high visibility, like the south-facing slopes and upland tundra of the Absarokas (Lawson and Johnson 1982). Sheep winter in the vicinity of Mummy Cave today and wintered there in the past (Dorn 1986; Honess and Frost 1942;

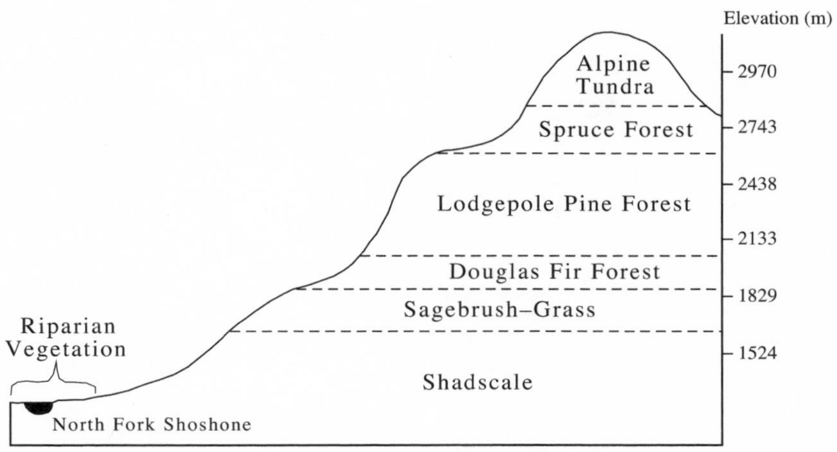

Figure 7.2. Vegetation zones in northwestern Wyoming (after Baker 1986). Mummy Cave is located at the ecotone between the Douglas fir forest and the sagebrush grassland.

Hughes 2003; Yellowstone National Park 1997). The sheep inhabiting the North Fork Valley today (the Trout Peak herd; Hurley 1985) are likely the descendants of sheep harvested prehistorically in the vicinity of Mummy Cave.

Individual adults weigh 50–140 kg, with males significantly larger than females (Wishart 1978). Rutting and birthing schedules are precisely defined because of the seasonal climate (Geist 1971; Hurley 1985). Sheep are gregarious and form small female and male groups. Eighty-six percent of the Trout Peak herd formed groups of less than 11 individuals. In winter, group size increased to 11–50 individuals as males joined females for the rut (Hurley 1985).

Most bighorn sheep near Mummy Cave today migrate seasonally (Hurley 1985) between low- and high-elevation ranges (Figure 7.3), likely because of a genetic predisposition to migrate in synchrony with external environmental factors (Geist 1971). Today, 25 percent of the Trout Peak herd remains on high-elevation ridges where strong winds remove the snow in winter (Hurley 1985). By April, when the snow at higher elevations begins to form icy crusts, about half of those that winter there drop down to join those wintering in the valley to take advantage of early spring "greenup." Thus, in April and May, 85–90 percent of all sheep are below 2,438 m, the majority occupying the mountain slopes and foothills on the north side of the North Fork River (Figure 7.3).

Young sheep learn home range patterns by following older rams and

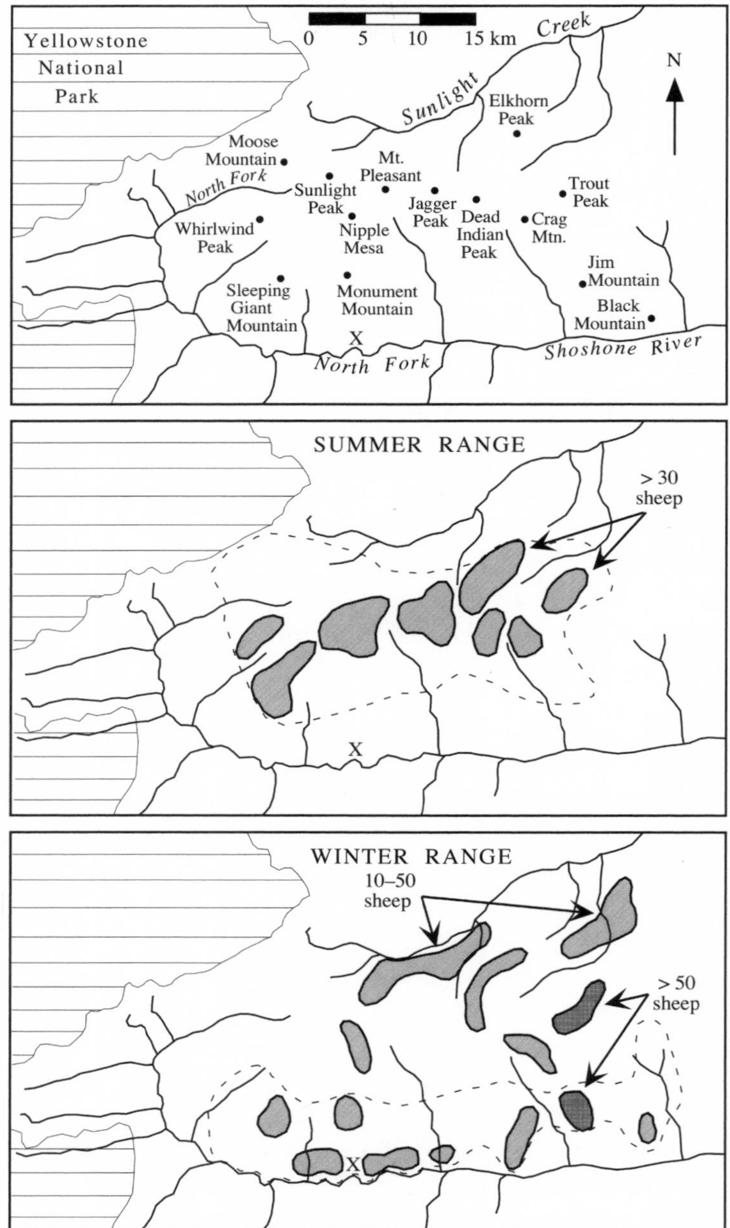

Figure 7.3. Geography and summer and winter ranges of bighorn sheep north of Mummy Cave (after Hurley 1985). Dashed lines indicate general ranges; crosshatched areas denote concentrations; X indicates the location of Mummy Cave.

ewes during the first three years of life. Because these relationships vary, sheep may adopt parts of several different home ranges. Females often remain in their mother's group, whereas males leave to join ram groups. By the age of four, individuals have established home ranges to which they are loyal throughout their lives unless deep snow or desiccated forage causes them to temporarily alter them (Geist 1971; Lawson and Johnson 1982).

In summer, sheep occupy the high alpine meadows (2,896–3,352 m) from Trout Peak in the east to the Yellowstone National Park boundary. Concentrations of sheep occur around Trout Peak, Crag Mountain, Dead Indian Peak, Jaggar Peak, Nipple Mesa, Sleeping Giant Mountain, and Whirlwind Peak (Figure 7.3), where they are widely dispersed on alpine plateaus and in cirque basins at drainage heads. Steep slopes are preferred over other slopes, and north and east exposures are avoided (Hurley 1985). Winter ranges are usually occupied from November through early June. Lambing takes place in late May–early June on protected rocky slopes and cliff faces.

As selective grazers, sheep avoid mixed conifer and montane meadow vegetation types, preferring alpine meadow communities and old-burn and sagebrush–grassland types. Alpine vegetation is typically higher in digestibility and nutrient content, providing the high-quality diet that sheep prefer (Hobbs et al. 1983; Knight 1994). Sheep use cushion plant *(Geum turf)* and dwarf willow *(Salix artica)* communities in early summer, shifting to forbs, grasses, and sedges later in summer as the latter are exposed by melting snowpack (Hurley 1985; Tweit and Houston 1980). On winter range, sheep prefer sagebrush grasslands, especially on southerly aspects where sunlight is absorbed and snow melts rapidly (Geist 1971; Hurley 1985).

ISOTOPE THEORY

Nitrogen

The nitrogen ratio is composed of the isotopes ^{14}N and ^{15}N. Nitrogen enters the ecosystem either from atmospheric N_2 or the decomposition of parent rock. Once in the ecosystem, nitrogen is taken up by plants and moves up through the food chain, enriching by 3–4% with each trophic level (Ambrose 1991; Faure 1986; Létolle 1980). The isotopic standard is atmospheric nitrogen with a value of 0%. The ratio is given as delta (δ) and calibrated to the atmospheric standard (Faure 1986; Högberg 1997).

Plants obtain nitrogen from three principle sources: bacterial N_2 fixation, the bacterial decomposition of organic matter (nitrification processes in the soil), and precipitation (Hobbie et al. 2000; Högberg 1997; Nadelhoffer et al. 1996). Nitrogen-fixing plants have isotopic values close to 0 because they obtain nitrogen directly from the atmosphere through symbiotic bacteria that convert N_2 to usable nitrate (Létolle 1980; Shearer and Kohl 1978, 1986; Virginia and Delwiche 1982). Because nitrogen-fixing plants are rare in northwestern Wyoming (Knight 1994), this source is not considered further.

Non–nitrogen fixers obtain usable nitrogen from water in the soil or through the processes of decomposition, and plant values are generally depleted (lower) by 3% relative to soil values (Faure 1986; Högberg 1997; Létolle 1980; Nadelhoffer and Fry 1994). Although tremendous variability exists in soil values, some generalizations can be made based on climatic conditions and soil types. The longer and more active the decomposition and recycling of soil nutrients, the greater the enrichment of soil values (Birkeland 1984; Jenny 1950). Grassland soils in tropical and temperate climates generally reflect enriched (higher) values because soils are older and more developed (Birkeland 1984; Rennie et al. 1976), but where temperature and precipitation extremes exist (nitrogen-limiting environments), nitrogen recycling is retarded, and isotopic values are depleted (Faure 1986; Jenny 1950; Ugolini et al. 1981). Eroded environments and young soils are also characterized by depleted values—values more closely approximating those of local precipitation, 1 to –6 per mil (parts per thousand relative to the atmospheric standard; see Vitousek et al. 1989; Wada et al. 1984). Forest soils are more depleted than grassland soils because their high acid content inhibits decomposition (Karamanos et al. 1981; Nadelhoffer and Fry 1988; Tieszen et al. 1984; Wada et al. 1981; Wada et al. 1984).

Based on these principles, predictions can be made concerning the nitrogen isotope signature of habitats in northwestern Wyoming. Alpine meadows characterized by extreme cold temperatures, steep slopes (balds) and exposed ridgetops, and conifer forests will provide the most negative values. River floodplains and terraces, montane meadows, and sagebrush grasslands in the foothills—areas with good soil development—will produce enriched values. High-elevation summer ranges will be depleted, whereas most low-elevation winter ranges will be enriched.

Carbon

The carbon ratio consists of the stable isotopes ^{12}C and ^{13}C (Farquhar et al. 1989; Faure 1986). Terrestrial plants incorporate atmospheric carbon

(CO_2) into their tissues along three different photosynthetic pathways: C_3, C_4, and CAM. C_3 plants include all trees, most shrubs and forbs, and temperate, cool-season grasses. C_4 plants include tropical and warm-season grasses and forbs (Pate 1994). CAM photosynthesis is restricted to arid-land succulents such as cacti, agave, and some euphorbias (Pate 1994), plants rarely consumed by sheep and thus not considered here. During photosynthesis, plants preferentially select the lighter isotope, and in the case of C_3 photosynthesis, the selection is considerably stronger. As a result, C_3 plants have markedly lower $\delta^{13}C$ values than C_4 plants (Ehleringer et al. 1991; Farquhar et al. 1989; O'Leary 1988; Teeri 1982), with values ranging from −20 to −35% with a mean of −27.1 ± 2.0% (Tieszen 1991). C_3 plant values range from −7 to −16% with a mean of −13.1 ± 1.2%. The carbon isotope ratio is expressed as delta (δ) and calibrated to the Peedee Formation belemnite ("PDB") standard (Faure 1986).

Carbon isotope ratio values will be a direct reflection of the proportion of C_3 or C_4 plants in sheep diet. Grazers consuming 100 percent C_3 plants will have values close to −21.0%, whereas those consuming 100 percent C_4 plants will have values of −6.8% (van der Merwe 1989). Although this ratio is a direct reflection of C_4/C_3 plant intake, it is influenced by climate (Fredlund and Tieszen 1997; Teeri and Stowe 1976; van der Merwe 1989). C_4 plants are abundant where summers are hot and light levels are high, such as open grasslands in tropical regions. C_3 plants are abundant where growing seasons are cool or cold (Bird et al. 1994; Ehleringer et al. 1991; Teeri and Stowe 1976). In tropical regions C_4 plants are not found above 3,000 m because of cool temperatures, and C_3 plants are not found below 2,000 m (Bird et al. 1994; Tieszen et al. 1979).

C_4 plants are abundant in the semiarid Bighorn Basin and foothills east of Mummy Cave (Bureau of Land Management n.d.; Teeri and Stowe 1976; Teeri et al. 1980), where summer temperatures frequently surpass 38°C. Blue bunch wheatgrass *(Agropyron spicatum)*, a C_3 grass, dominates the grasslands of the North Fork Valley (Tweit and Houston 1980), but blue grama *(Bouteloua gracilis)* and other C_4 grasses are present in small quantities. Bighorn sheep foraging in low-elevation sites in the Bighorn Basin and foothills will consume small quantities of C_4 plants.

Isotopic Expectations

Bighorn sheep isotopic values will be an average of the plants consumed along their seasonal migratory routes. Variation in isotopic values will reflect different routes. Because sheep are loyal to the routes, the routes should remain stable through time unless something causes sheep to change them. Vertical shifts in vegetation zones caused by climatic change, competition with domestic livestock, or disturbance by humans could cause such changes.

Variation in $\delta^{15}N$ will reflect the proportion of time spent grazing in nitrogen-limited environments relative to time spent in nitrogen-enriched environments during the year. Sheep that graze predominantly on alpine tundra or rocky south-facing escarpments will have lower $\delta^{15}N$ values than those that spend more time grazing in the basins and valley bottoms. Variation in $\delta^{13}C$ will reflect the amount of exposure to C_4 plants in lower valley foothills and basin environments (enriched values) relative to the time spent grazing on C_3 plants in colder environments (depleted values). C_4 plants are likely to be absent from the Upper North Fork because the narrow valley experiences cold air drainage resulting in a cool mesic climate throughout the year (Despain 1990; Wright 2002).

If Euro-American settlement in the foothills and Bighorn Basin eliminated parts of the bighorn sheep winter range and forced sheep to use more marginal environments, then modern sheep ratio values will be more depleted than those of prehistoric specimens, especially the maximum values, for these represent the low-elevation component of their habitat. Further, if Euro-American settlement caused a reduction in migration distance between high-elevation summer ranges and low-elevation winter ranges, then modern bighorn sheep will display less within-group variation than prehistoric sheep. Finally, if the reduction of winter ranges forced a subset of sheep to winter at high elevations, then a subset of carbon and nitrogen isotope values will be more depleted in modern sheep than in prehistoric sheep.

MATERIALS AND METHODS

Stable carbon and nitrogen isotope ratios were analyzed from the bone collagen of 56 Mummy Cave bighorn sheep bones in 13 strata and 12 modern bighorn (Table 7.2). Bone collagen remodels every five–ten years providing a long-term average of what an animal consumes (Pate 1994). The collagen yields of the bone specimens were calculated as a percent of dry bone weight and are in general high (Table 7.2), though yields decrease with increased age of the studied specimen (Kendall's tau $= -0.521$, $p < 0.001$). If the collagen yield of a specimen was < 5 percent,

TABLE 7.2. $\delta^{13}C$ AND $\delta^{15}N$ VALUES FOR MODERN AND PREHISTORIC BIGHORN SHEEP BONE FROM NORTHWEST WYOMING.

Sample	Stratum	$\delta^{13}C$	$\delta^{15}N$	Collagen Yield[a]
01A	modern	–21.35	0.84	23.3
02	modern	–21.42	0.64	18.8
03	modern	–21.60	0.60	22.4
04	modern	–21.18	0.60	19.8
06A	modern	–21.33	0.64	21.2
07	modern	–21.26	0.26	19.3
08	modern	–21.03	0.26	20.7
10	modern	–20.90	1.12	25.2
13AA	modern	–20.76	–0.99	25.8
14A	modern	–20.76	0.21	24.5
15A	modern	–20.94	0.88	6.7
16	modern	–20.82	0.96	21.9
30A	3	–20.74	1.82	20.2
32A	3	–20.26	0.15	23.7
33A	3	–18.88	1.11	28.7
34A	3	–19.76	1.09	29.3
35A	3	–18.00	–1.68	29.6
36A	3	–18.84	0.51	24.3
37A	3	–18.98	0.81	18.1
38A	3	–19.69	1.12	22.6
39A	3	–18.94	1.44	22.5
40A	3	–18.86	2.40	23.4
45A	4	–19.71	1.07	21.0
46A	4	–19.08	1.12	27.0
48A	6	–19.23	1.15	20.1
49A	6	–20.09	0.09	24.4
50A	6	–19.22	0.16	25.6
51A	6	–19.28	0.32	29.2
52A	6	–20.08	0.64	20.0
53A	6	–19.79	–0.14	21.9
54A	6	–20.20	–1.00	16.3
55A	6	–21.12	–0.42	10.0
56A	6	–20.23	–1.34	6.0
57A	6	–20.69	0.74	16.9
58A	6	–20.68	1.48	20.7
95A	8	–17.96	1.40	18.9
96A	8	–18.94	1.06	19.1
97A	8	–19.52	1.21	12.3
98B	8	–19.71	1.18	18.5
99B	8	–19.43	1.10	16.5
101B	8	–18.66	1.48	16.2
102B	8	–19.71	1.64	22.0

TABLE 7.2. $\delta^{13}C$ AND $\delta^{15}N$ VALUES FOR MODERN AND PREHISTORIC BIGHORN SHEEP BONE FROM NORTHWEST WYOMING *(CONTINUED)*.

Sample	Stratum	$\delta^{13}C$	$\delta^{15}N$	Collagen Yield[a]
103B	8	–19.24	0.40	16.0
104B	8	–18.80	1.03	19.1
59A	9	–19.47	2.03	11.7
60A	9	–18.87	1.52	5.7
62B	9	–20.21	2.28	11.4
64A	9	–19.66	1.34	9.3
65A	9	–19.28	1.70	12.7
66A	9	–20.46	3.88	13.7
67A	9	–20.34	2.89	7.4
63B	9	–21.00	0.92	10.7
90A	10	–19.00	0.68	11.7
91A	12	–19.62	1.02	18.5
70A	13	–19.39	0.43	9.3
74A	16	–18.78	0.42	16.6
75A	16	–18.64	0.14	15.4
76A	16	–19.02	0.66	12.7
80A	17	–19.12	1.44	15.0
83A	17	–19.73	0.89	6.4
84A	17	–19.09	2.00	12.5
78A	18	–18.74	1.74	19.5
86A	19	–20.40	0.16	9.2
87A	19	–19.74	1.38	12.3
88A	19	–19.51	1.50	9.5
89A	19	–18.91	1.46	14.2
72A	20	–19.02	1.88	10.3
73A	20	–19.60	0.66	11.9

[a]This is a percent of dry bone weight.

the sample was not analyzed. (For additional details on methods used to obtain isotope ratios and to control for diagenetic effects, see Hughes 2003.)

Sheep metapodials were used because they were abundant in the Mummy Cave assemblage and easy to acquire from modern bighorn sheep. It is probable that the Mummy Cave sheep represent a local population confined to the highlands north of the site and the North Fork River, but the modern specimens were collected throughout the Absaroka Mountains and, because of this, should display greater isotopic variability. The modern sample consisted of nine adult males harvested during the 1994,

1995, and 1996 fall hunting seasons. Three additional specimens were obtained from a small mixed-sex group trapped in a May 1995 snowstorm in the Dick Creek area.

ISOTOPE RESULTS

Nitrogen

The average $\delta^{15}N$ value for all sampled bighorn sheep is 0.91 ± 0.9%, and the range is 5.56 (Table 7.3). When the $\delta^{15}N$ values are plotted against time (Figure 7.4), the Late Holocene strata 3 and 6 and the modern sheep all reveal exceptionally low values (< 0), whereas the Early and Middle Holocene strata do not. It appears that a subset of Late Holocene sheep grazed in nitrogen-limiting environments, a pattern that has continued into the present. Today, 75 percent of the Trout Peak herd migrates to a low-elevation winter range, while the remaining 25 percent winter on high-elevation, windswept ridges (Hurley 1985). The latter may drop down into the North Fork Valley to take advantage of early spring greenup, but most of their nitrogen comes from depleted environments. Therefore, the sudden appearance of depleted values in stratum 6 may mark the beginning of high-altitude wintering.

The low minimum values are accompanied by notably high maximum values in strata 3 and 9. Taken as a group the Late Holocene (strata 3–9; 1230–5500 B.P.) values display greater isotopic variability than either the Early Holocene (strata 10–20; 5500–8500 B.P.) set or the larger and more environmentally diverse modern group. The maximum values of the modern group are much lower than the maximum values in most strata. Because the Middle Holocene samples are small, it is unclear when isotopic variation first increased, but the drop in values from stratum 9 to stratum 6 suggests that these strata represent a transitional period.

To examine temporal differences in variation, the ratios were divided into three groups: modern, Late Holocene, and Early Holocene. The differences in variance among these groups are not statistically significant ($p > 0.1$ in all); however, a greater difference exists between the modern and the Late Holocene groups (Levene's $F = 2.60$) than between the modern and Early Holocene groups ($F = 1.39$). These results suggest that modern sheep have experienced a reduction in range, especially in the more enriched component of their environment, the valley bottom. With a loss of valley bottom areas in the Lower North Fork Valley, modern sheep

TABLE 7.3. Means, Variances, and Ranges of Isotope Values for Groups of Bighorn Sheep Bones.

Group	Number	Mean	Variance	Range
Nitrogen				
Modern	12	0.50	0.30	2.11
Late Holocene	40	0.99	1.10	5.56
Early Holocene	16	1.03	0.37	1.86
Combined	68	0.91	0.81	5.56
Carbon				
Modern	12	–19.6	0.08	0.85
Late Holocene	40	–19.6	0.58	3.17
Early Holocene	16	–19.3	0.22	1.77
Combined	68	–19.5	0.42	3.17

may use more marginal sites such as the "balds" to avoid competition with other artiodactyls and interaction with humans.

Carbon

The modern bighorn sheep values were adjusted for the fossil fuel effect (Marino and McElroy 1991; van Klinken et al. 2000) and then plotted against time (Figure 7.5). A majority of the modern and prehistoric bighorn sheep consumed nearly 100 percent C_3 plants. A small proportion of C_4 plants may have contributed to the diets of those sheep with values greater than –19%, but at no time during the Holocene were C_4 plants abundant in the North Fork Valley.

The pattern of carbon isotope variation is similar to that observed for the nitrogen isotope. Variation increases from stratum 9 to stratum 3, and maximum and minimum values are less extreme in the modern sheep. Tests of differences in variance between the modern and Late Holocene sheep ($F = 8.48$, $p = 0.005$) and the Late and Early Holocene sheep ($F = 3.910$, $p = 0.053$) are both significant. This implies that a change took place in bighorn sheep distribution and migratory behavior around 5500 B.P. and that there has been a loss of range in the modern period.

Assuming that longer migrations result in greater isotopic variation, the decreased variance implies a loss in long-distance migration in the modern period, just as proposed by Honess and Frost (1942). Sheep from the Trout Peak herd today use three long-distance migration paths: (1) between the alpine summer range and the heavily used winter range in the foothills, an average of 32 km; (2) from the alpine summer range to the North

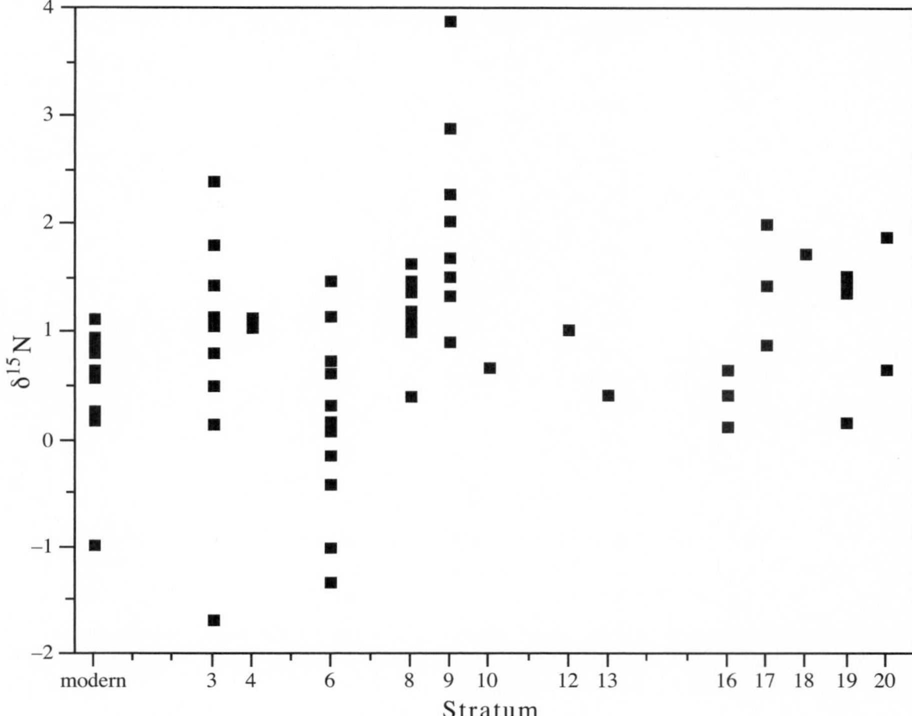

Figure 7.4. Bighorn sheep $\delta^{15}N$ values by Mummy Cave stratum (from Table 7.2).

Fork Valley, an average of 10 km; and (3) from the alpine summer range to the North Fork Valley with lateral movement along the valley bottom, an average of 26 km. Although these are substantial distances, in the past sheep may have migrated to the Lower North Fork Valley floor or into the Bighorn Basin, both heavily developed areas where sheep are absent today. Because sheep conform rigidly to their migration patterns, a loss of a specific pattern may represent a loss of the population(s) that followed that pattern.

Increase in isotopic variation in the Late Holocene is clearly revealed in a scatterplot of both isotopes (Figure 7.6). Although the Early Holocene values are slightly more enriched than modern values, both form tight clusters relative to the widely dispersed Late Holocene values. The Late Holocene is distinct for its widely varying combinations of both isotopes. This strongly suggests that Late Holocene sheep used a wider range of environments than either modern or Early Holocene sheep.

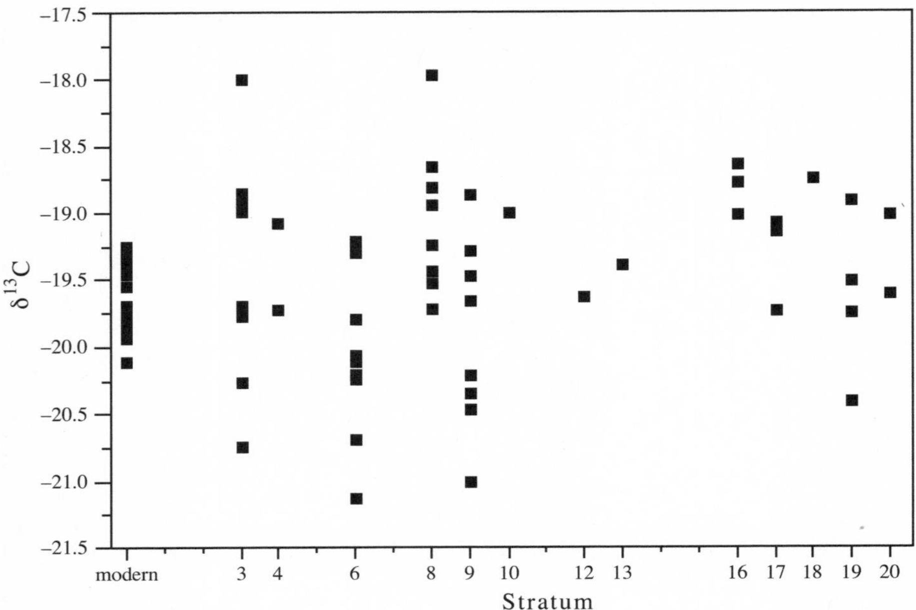

Figure 7.5. Bighorn sheep δ^{13}C values by Mummy Cave stratum. Because modern samples have been depleted by fossil fuels, they were adjusted by adding 1.5% to each value (from Table 7.2).

DISCUSSION

Both the carbon and the nitrogen isotope data reveal two major shifts in bighorn sheep distribution and migratory behavior in the Holocene—one circa 5500 B.P. and a second one prior to the modern era (Figure 7.6). Both shifts are characterized by changes in isotopic variability (Table 7.3). Modern bighorn are characterized by a loss in isotopic variability, a loss of enriched values, and a continuation of the depleted outliers observed in the Late Holocene. This suggests that during the historical period bighorn made more use of marginal soil environments and used foothills and basin habitats less. Both the scatterplot (Figure 7.6) and the statistical measures of variation (Table 7.3) indicate that use of habitats by bighorn was most diverse during the Late Holocene. The marked change from less variation during the Early Holocene to more variation during the Late Holocene indicates a change in sheep range and migratory behavior at about 5500 B.P.

The cause of the change in isotope variation seems to be a shift in climate resulting in a drop in the forest belt. Pollen data from lake cores in

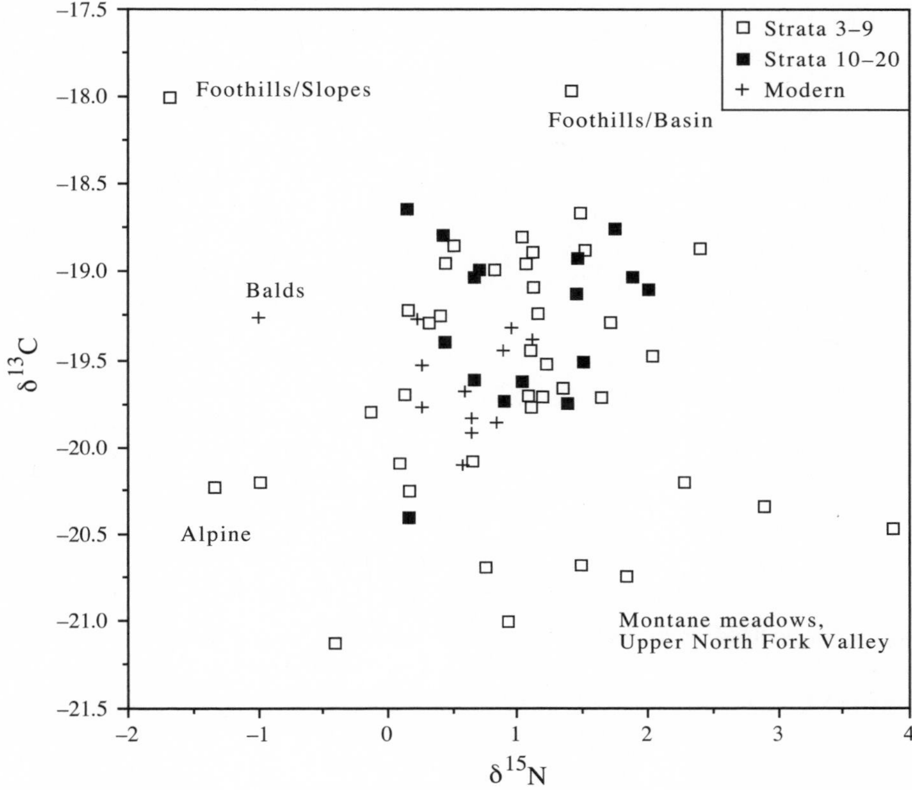

Figure 7.6. Covariate plot of $\delta^{15}N$ and $\delta^{13}C$ (from Table 7.2). Isotopic signatures of different habitats in the North Fork are indicated.

the greater Yellowstone area reveal a 200-m rise in the forest belt during the Early Holocene, with lowering to present levels around 5000 B.P. (Whitlock 1993; Whitlock and Bartlein 1993; Whitlock et al. 1995). Similar results have been recorded in the mountains of southeastern Idaho, Montana, and Alberta (Baker 1976; Barnosky et al. 1987; Beiswenger 1991; Davis et al. 1986; Kearney and Luckman 1983; Mehringer et al. 1977; Waddington and Wright 1974). The Mummy Cave $\delta^{15}N$ ratios may pin down these changes to 5500 B.P. in the North Fork Valley.

Whitlock and Bartlein (1993) attribute this phenomenon to a 10,000-year shift in the precession and tilt of the earth as it rotates around the sun. Ten thousand years ago, the earth's orbit brought the Northern Hemisphere to its closest proximity to the sun in summer. The greater tilt of the earth's rotational axis increased northern exposure, and summer droughts intensified. As the earth has moved farther from the sun in summer, temperatures have dropped.

A 200-m drop in upper timberline would have opened up much of the high-elevation grassland that presently exists in the Absaroka Mountains. North of Mummy Cave, this grassland extends approximately 37 km from Whirlwind Peak in the west to Black Mountain in the east (Figure 7.3). Because many of the higher peaks are separated by narrow ridges only slightly above timberline today, a small rise in timberline would effectively dissect this vast upland meadow into smaller segments, especially in the Upper North Fork area. As bighorn sheep avoid forests, this could change bighorn sheep distribution and migratory habits.

Today, all sheep move to the upland meadow in summer. With a range expansion 5,500 years ago, population numbers likely increased in the Upper North Fork area. Sheep wintering in a variety of locations around the mountain peripheries would have more opportunities for contact in the summer (Figure 7.3), thereby exposing young sheep to a greater variety of migratory behavior. The net effect in the Mummy Cave area would be greater numbers of sheep wintering there as well as greater variation in their isotopic signatures. The faunal record at Mummy Cave demonstrates that the abundance of bighorn sheep bone increased substantially after 5500 B.P. (Table 7.1). Bighorn remains constitute 72 percent of the identified specimens from strata 10–24 but 93 percent of the identified specimens from strata 3–9.

Migration patterns used today were likely established 5,500 years ago when the timberline dropped. With a larger upland meadow, migration distances may have increased, and certain upland locations may have become suitable for overwintering. Another change occurred in bighorn sheep distribution and migratory behavior just prior to the modern era. Because vegetation patterns remained essentially stable after 4500 B.P., the changes seen in the modern era are likely caused by anthropogenic effects on bighorn sheep habitat. Overall variability in sheep habitat declines. Because a loss in habitat can cause a decline in carrying capacity, sheep numbers will decline, especially among those populations competing with humans and their livestock. While some migration patterns disappear, some forms of long-distance migration and high-altitude wintering survive.

IMPLICATIONS FOR WILDLIFE MANAGEMENT

Lawson and Johnson have written that the "future of wild sheep depends on the preservation and improvement of critical native ranges," and they suggest that "curtailment of development" must be part of any conservation plan (1982:1051). Zooarchaeological data presented here provide insights into the Holocene range and the migratory behavior of bighorn sheep in northwestern Wyoming and also substantiate the claim made by Honess and Frost (1942) and others (Buechner 1960; Packard 1946) that modern development has impacted sheep populations. One of these impacts has been a reduction in bighorn sheep range, especially winter range. These data also suggest that modern migration patterns were established in the Middle Holocene possibly because of a drop in the tree line. Although some of the same migratory patterns have continued in modern populations (e.g., high-altitude wintering and long-distance migration), patterns that included the basin and lower valley floodplains have disappeared. A loss of range will cause a loss in carrying capacity, and population numbers will decline. Although summer range is critically important to sheep survival, these data underscore the importance of winter range in maintaining population numbers. To sustain sheep populations in the future, both ranges must be maintained.

Acknowledgments. This project was funded by National Science Foundation Dissertation Improvement Grant No. 9905628 and the Buffalo Bill Historical Center (BBHC) of Cody, Wyoming. I am deeply indebted to the BBHC for allowing me to study the Mummy Cave fauna, to the Wyoming Game and Fish Department and Tom Ball of the Worland Bureau of Land Management office for acquiring modern bighorn specimens for this analysis, and to Diana Greenlee for teaching me the Grootes method of collagen extraction. The insightful editorial work of Lee Lyman, Ken Cannon, and Paul Budd make this chapter what it is today. Finally, this research would not have happened without the support and encouragement of the University of Wyoming Anthropology Readers Guild, John Burns, and my family. All errors and omissions are my own.

8

Prehistoric Biogeography, Abundance, and Phenotypic Plasticity of Elk *(Cervus elaphus)* in Washington State

R. Lee Lyman

It has been estimated that the native range of elk *(Cervus elaphus)* in North America has been reduced by about 75 percent in post-Columbian times as a result of habitat loss and the fragmentation of the traditional ranges of various herds (Taber and Raedeke 1987). The State of Washington contains a large portion of the remaining range, but it also has the highest density of elk hunters of any state and a very high ratio of elk hunters to elk (Washington Department of Wildlife 1987). The U.S. Department of Energy's Arid Lands Ecology Reserve in south-central Washington and several national parks in the state provide refuges where elk are largely free of human harassment and completely free of human predation. Management of the several recognized herds in the state is today overseen by the Washington Department of Fish and Wildlife and is geared toward three general goals: (1) to produce a sustained yield; (2) to contribute to recreation, education, and aesthetic purposes including hunting, scientific research, wildlife observation and photography, and cultural use by First Americans; and (3) to preserve, protect, perpetuate, manage, and enhance healthy, productive elk populations (see various elk management plans for the state at http://wdfw.wa.gov/wlm/game/elk).

Management activities in the state include translocating elk from one herd to another to reduce or enhance a local herd within the state and in effect constitute artificial emigration and immigration. The state also artificially feeds some herds to prevent habitat damage and forage loss "where winter range has been eliminated" (Peek et al. 2002:620). Hunting seasons are structured so as to control populations for various ends (reduction, maintenance, increase). There is no critical management problem regarding the state's elk, but the potential is there for problems to develop with respect to the three general management goals. Even if problems do not develop, the attainment of those three goals would benefit from information on the long-term history of elk in the state. How, for example, have elk adapted to changes in climate and habitat over the last 10,000 years, and how have they adjusted to changes in human predation? With respect to the former, did they respond phenotypically, genetically, behaviorally, or in terms of population size? How did the shift from hunting virtually year-round with primitive technology to hunting for about ten days a year with firearms effect local populations? Did the creation of refuges where some populations are free from predation influence elk, and if so, how? In this chapter I discuss zooarchaeological data that bear on the attainment of the management goals and begin to answer several of the questions just posed.

In his classic study of elk across the North American continent, Olaus Murie (1951) makes two observations on Washington elk that seem to serve as the basis for many subsequent management activities in the state. Murie notes that historical documents indicate that "there must have been a gap in elk distribution between the Rocky Mountains and the Cascades" of Washington and that the "original ranges of *C. e. nelsoni* [Rocky Mountain elk] and *C. e. roosevelti* [Roosevelt elk] were separated by territory unoccupied by elk" (1951:40–41; see also Booth 1947; Figure 8.1). The Rocky Mountain subspecies occupied eastern Washington, whereas Roosevelt elk occupied the Pacific coast. Later commentators indicate that it was unclear which subspecies occupied the eastern slope of the Cascade Range—the crest of which basically splits the state into eastern and western halves—even though Murie implies that the identity of that subspecies is the Roosevelt elk (Bryant and Maser 1982). The identity of the eastern Cascade subspecies cannot be resolved by examination of modern elk there because in the early 20th century Rocky Mountain elk were transplanted to that location (Couch 1935; Mitchell and Lauckhart 1948). Zooarchaeological research may eventually reveal the subspecific identity of the pre-transplant elk.

The supposed gap in the statewide distribution of elk was closed in the 1980s and 1990s by zooarchaeological data indicating that this large ungulate had prehistorically been found throughout the state (Dixon and Lyman

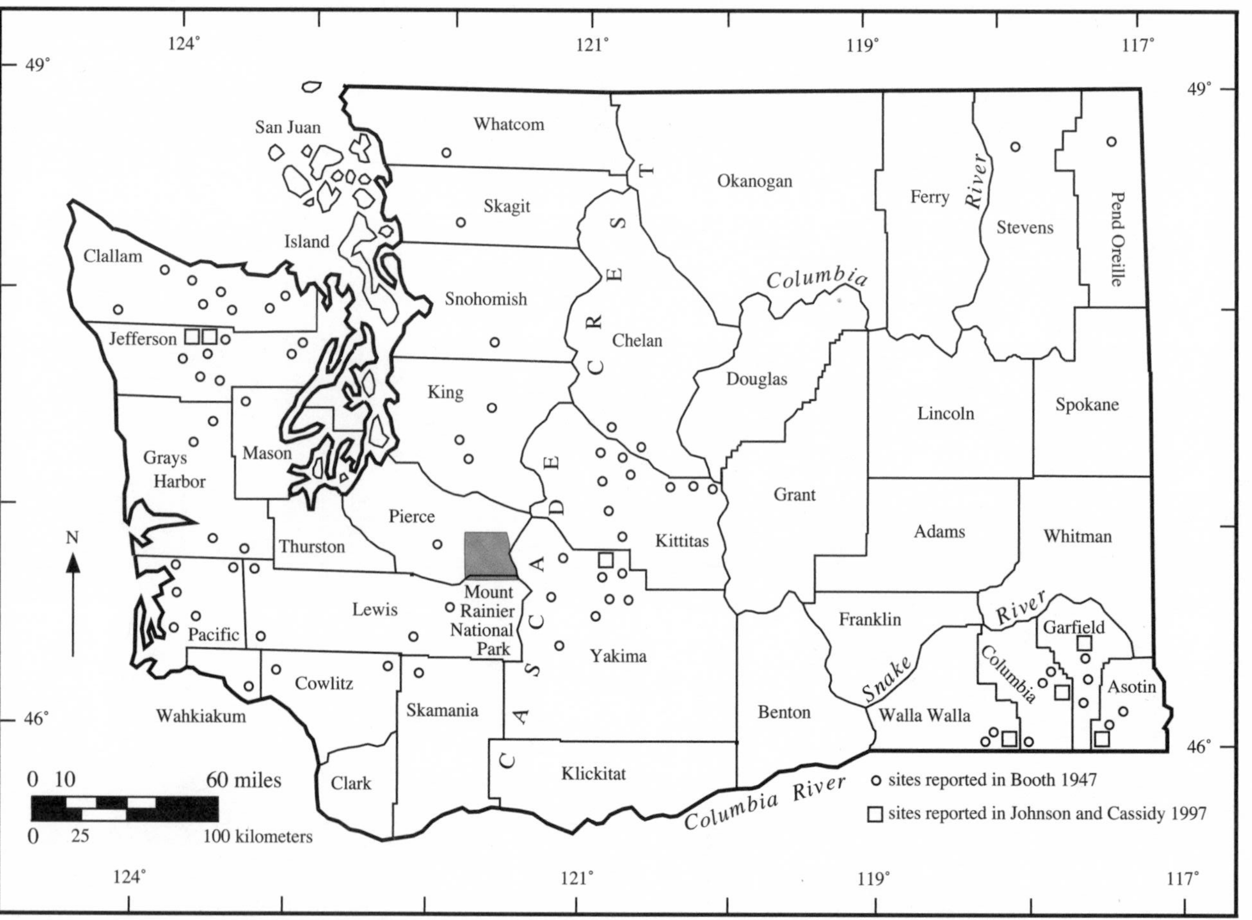

Figure 8.1. Locations of places and areas in Washington mentioned in the text and historic records of elk.

1996; Harpole and Lyman 1999; McCorquodale 1985). Nevertheless, statements continued to appear that elk had not occurred in various areas until early-20th-century transplants brought them to such areas as Mount Rainier National Park (Bradley and Driver 1981) and Yakima County (Hendrix 2000; see Figure 8.1). Twenty years ago, historical documents (Schullery 1984) and available zooarchaeological data (Gustafson 1983) failed to help answer questions regarding whether elk were in fact present in these areas. The historical record has not changed over the past two decades, but there are now available sufficient zooarchaeological data to allow a fairly detailed examination of the historical biogeography of elk. Those data are also sufficient to allow an evaluation of recent claims by biologists and paleoecologists that elk were not "abundant" in the eastern half of the state as a result of prehistoric human predation (Kay 1994; Martin and Szuter 1999a, 1999b). These are two of my goals here because precisely such claims influence management decisions.

The Roosevelt elk is often said by biologists to be somewhat larger than the Rocky Mountain subspecies (Bryant and Maser 1982; Murie 1936; Skinner 1936). The Roosevelt elk that today occupy the Olympic Peninsula of western Washington are some of the largest individuals of the species on the continent (Schonewald 1994; Schonewald-Cox et al. 1985). Perhaps, then, the prehistoric remains of elk can be distinguished as to subspecies based on their size. Some comparative data, however, indicate that this may not be possible because most standard biological measurements of historic elk of both subspecies suggest that Roosevelt elk are not larger than Rocky Mountain elk (Bryant and Maser 1982). Another goal here, then, is to provide a preliminary evaluation of whether or not the sizes of various bones of the two subspecies can be distinguished. If so, then the zooarchaeological record would allow the relatively inexpensive determination of which subspecies was present on the east slope of the Cascades prior to Euro-American settlement. If not, then the relatively more expensive alternative of studying ancient DNA may be the only viable means of determining which subspecies was in which locations and when.

The World Conservation Union (formerly the International Union for the Conservation of Nature and Natural Resources) recommends that supplementing or reestablishing animal populations should involve transplanting the closest genetic relatives of the natives (see chap. 1). This raises the question of which subspecies of elk to transplant to or allow in a particular area of Washington state. The question is typically answered on the basis of historical documents (Bradley and Driver 1981). Another goal, then, is to illustrate how zooarchaeological data can contribute to answering this question. I must, of course, be able to distinguish remains of the two subspecies on the basis of the size of their bones if I want to determine which subspecies occurred where on the basis of the size of prehistoric bones. My final goal is to examine selected aspects of the prehistory of elk in Washington to gain insights to how this large cervid should be managed so as to ensure its existence in perpetuity and to thereby attain the long-term goals of the Washington Department of Fish and Wildlife with respect to local elk herds.

MATERIALS AND METHODS

Many of the biogeographic data discussed here were compiled during the course of other projects (Dixon and Lyman 1996; Harpole and Lyman 1999). Additional data reported subsequent to the completion of those projects were compiled for the purposes of this overview. All available reports on the archaeology of Washington state were consulted. Those sites that produced elk remains were noted, and the ages of the remains, if known, were recorded. Identified elk remains that represented artifacts, such as antler digging-stick handles, were noted but not included in the analysis because such items may have been transported significant distances and curated for significant periods of time (Lyman 1994c). These artifacts could therefore potentially distort indications of historical biogeography and local abundances of elk.

Only elk remains dating to the last 2,000 (radiocarbon) years are included in the biogeographic analyses. The reasons for this are two. First, the zooarchaeological record becomes progressively more poorly known as age increases (Dixon and Lyman 1996; Harpole and Lyman 1999; Lyman 1992). The record is relatively well known, if imperfectly, only for the Late Holocene. Second, some commentators have suggested that elk were not abundant in the state as a result of prehistoric human predation (Kay 1994) and that this mechanism of population depression was exacerbated late in the prehistoric–early historic period with the introduction of horses and firearms (Martin and Szuter 1999a, 1999b). Focusing on the last 2,000 years may allow detection of the depression of elk populations if this reasoning is correct. However, it must also be shown that elk abundances did not fluctuate in like manner during earlier time periods if a late-prehistoric depression of their numbers is to be taken as evidence of more efficient hunting with firearms and horses, so greater time depths are examined when the concern is the history of elk abundance. With respect to that history, and with respect to the biogeographic history of elk, it is important to note several limitations of the available data.

Most archaeological research in that portion of Washington west of the crest of the Cascade Range (Figure 8.1) has been adjacent to saltwater coasts in response to cultural resource management mandate. Exacerbating this geographic bias is the fact that bones do not preserve well in the acidic sediments underlying the coniferous forests of western Washington (Harpole and Lyman 1999). Only those sites comprising shell midden deposits in western Washington tend to have good preservation of mammal remains, and such deposits tend to be found only in coastal locations. With respect to eastern Washington, most archaeological research has been adjacent to the Columbia and Snake rivers as a result of cultural resource management mandate (Lyman 2000, 2002; see below). Bone tends to preserve well in many sediments found in eastern Washington, but faunal remains have not often been identified here, and sometimes when they have been, their age has not been reported (Dixon and Lyman 1996). As a result of these factors, the data discussed below indicate only some of the locations where elk *were* during the prehistoric past; the available data should not be taken as good evidence of where elk did *not* occur during that time because a number of areas have not been zooarchaeologically sampled, and of those areas that have been sampled, sometimes faunal remains have not been recovered or, if recovered, described.

The absolute abundance(s) of elk on the prehistoric landscape will never be known. Instead, the *relative* abundance of elk can be estimated by study of the abundance of elk remains relative to the abundance of the remains of other taxa. This is basic paleozoological procedure (Grayson 1984; Lyman 1994b). Assuming that the abundance of elk remains relative to that of deer (*Odocoileus* spp.) remains is a good indicator of the relative abundance of elk on the landscape, then such abundances can be monitored to determine if elk abundances fluctuated in response to human predation, climatic change, and the like. This knowledge could assist modern managers concerned with establishing harvest quotas that will not influence sustainable yields or population sizes.

Published morphometric data recorded for modern elk by biologists tend to be taken from anatomically complete skulls. Because most zooarchaeological remains are made up of fragmented skulls and postcranial remains, comparative data for the postcranial remains of modern elk must be generated if prehistoric postcranial remains are to be identified to subspecies. Even then, however, such a taxonomic identification may not be possible. This is so because various postcranial remains of prehistoric elk from sites in the state have been reported to be larger than the bones of many modern elk, whether the prehistoric remains are ancient (Fryxell et al. 1968) or recent and whether they are from the eastern (Dixon and Lyman 1996) or western (Shaw 1977) portion of the state. Elk are ecophenotypically plastic (Hudson et al. 2002; Langvatn and Albon 1986), and thus, on the one hand, the size of their prehistoric bones may not be a reliable taxonomic signature. On the other hand, the sizes of those bones may be significant paleoenvironmental indicators, and they may grant insights to the ecophenotypic plasticity of elk and, thus, how they might adapt to altered climatic, habitat, or predation regimes. For example, if the size of elk bones fluctuates in concert with environmental change, this would be strong evidence that elk are capable of adapting to such change by altering their phenotype. To contend with the fact that the nature of the Holocene chronocline—temporal size gradient—of elk is unknown, analyses of elk size presented here are exploratory. In an effort to determine if the two subspecies can be distinguished on the basis of the size of their bones, morphometric data on mature elk skeletons representing both subspecies were compiled. The sample of measured skeletons is small, so results are tentative.

The phylogenetic relationships of the six recognized subspecies of North American elk have been undergoing detailed study over the past decade (Polziehn et al. 1998; Schonewald 1994). Similarly, study of the evolutionary relationship of European red deer and North American elk has resulted in fluctuations in taxonomic nomenclature (Lowe and Gardiner 1989; Schonewald 1994). The taxonomic nomenclature of Bryant and Maser (1982) is followed here. For comparative purposes, the historic records of elk in Washington as summarized in two biological studies—one accomplished in the 1940s (Booth 1947) and the other in the 1980s and 1990s (Johnson and Cassidy 1997)—are included. These data indicate where elk were found during the 20th century (Figure 8.1) and imply where elk might be expected to have been during the previous 2,000 or so years.

RESULTS

Historic Biogeography of Elk

Elk were widespread throughout much of the state of Washington during the last 2,000 years (Figure 8.2). The absence of elk remains from the

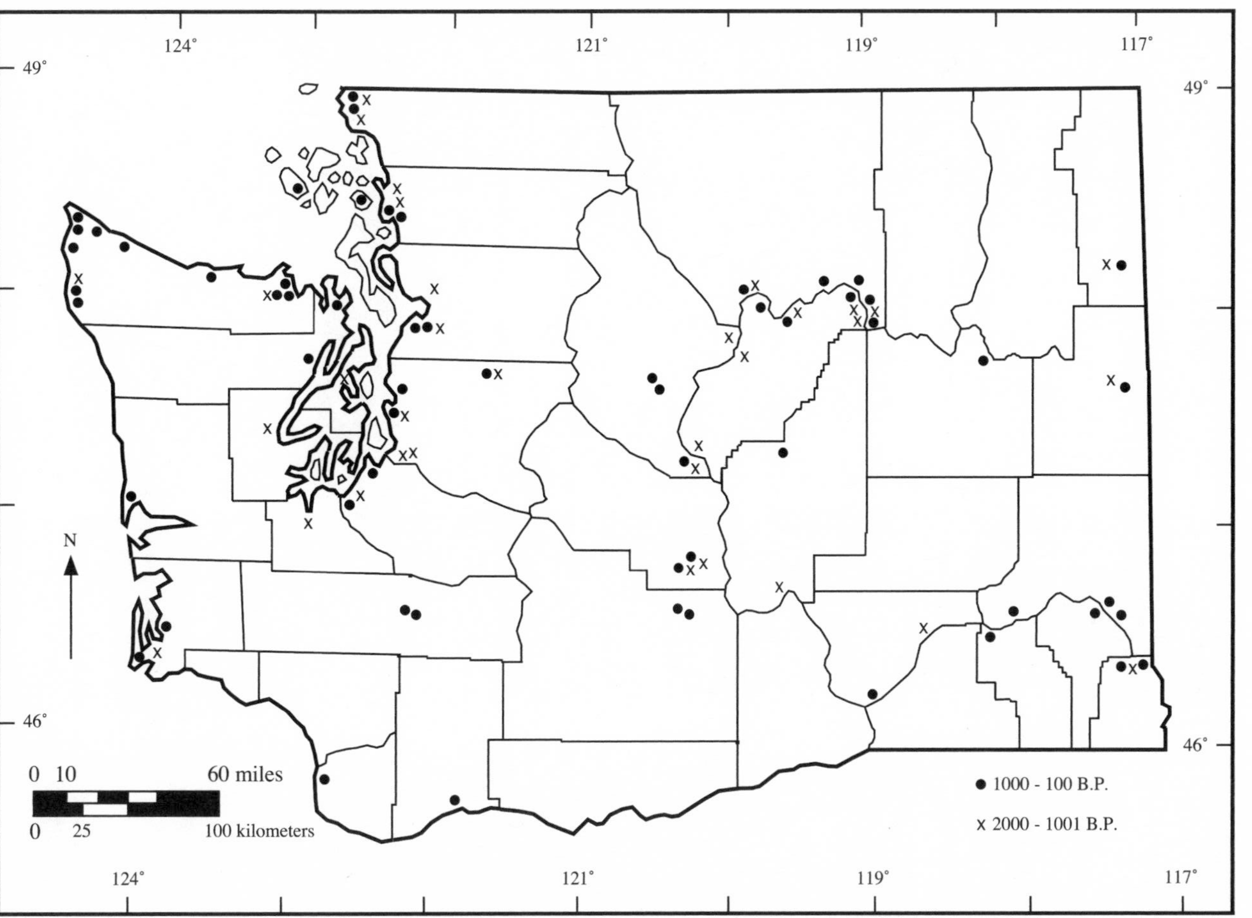

Figure 8.2. Locations of prehistoric sites in Washington that have produced elk remains dating to the last 2,000 years.

eastern and western slopes of the Cascade Range, from the interior of westernmost Washington (Clallam, Jefferson, Grays Harbor, and Mason counties), from the Blue Mountains of southeastern Washington, and from the Selkirk Range of northeastern Washington is unexpected *if* the modern distribution of elk (Figure 8.1) is an accurate indicator of where they should be found. However, these areas are also precisely those where minimal archaeological and virtually no zooarchaeological research has been done, underscoring the potential for misinterpretation if the quality of the zooarchaeological data are not evaluated in terms of geographic representativeness (Lyman 1995a). For example, consider that part of Washington east of the crest of the Cascade Range (Figure 8.1). The townships (generally 6 × 6 mi [9.7 × 9.7 km]) of eastern Washington can be used to assess how geographic space has been sampled. Figure 8.3 shows eastern Washington and indicates (1) townships in which sites have been tested and excavated, (2) townships in which archaeological faunal remains were recovered but not identified, (3) townships in which faunal remains from sampled sites have been identified, and (4) townships that have produced archaeological remains of elk irrespective of their age. This figure indicates clearly that the manner in which the zooarchaeological record has been sampled and studied must be considered if one wishes to make statements about the historic biogeography of elk.

Importantly, available data do indicate, contrary to Hendrix's (2000) claim, that elk *were* present prehistorically in Yakima County (Figure 8.2). The range they occupied within that county, however, is unclear as a result of the paucity of archaeological research there (Figure 8.3). Whether elk were present prehistorically in Mount Rainier National Park cannot be ascertained with any certainty because, although some archaeological research has been done within park boundaries and in areas adjacent to the park, seldom have faunal remains been recovered as a result of poor preservation (Burtchard 1998; Gustafson 1983). Elk remains have been found about 30 mi (48 km) southwest of the park (Figure 8.2), which suggests that they could have occupied what are today park lands at some time during the Holocene. In both of these cases, the known zooarchaeological record is at best an imprecise indicator of the late-prehistoric distribution of elk. The impression that that record gives, however, is that elk remains will be found in much of western Yakima County and eastern Pierce County once zooarchaeological research has been carried out in these areas. This information is critical to state management plans aimed at the "recovery" and maintenance of herds within their historic ranges, insofar as current

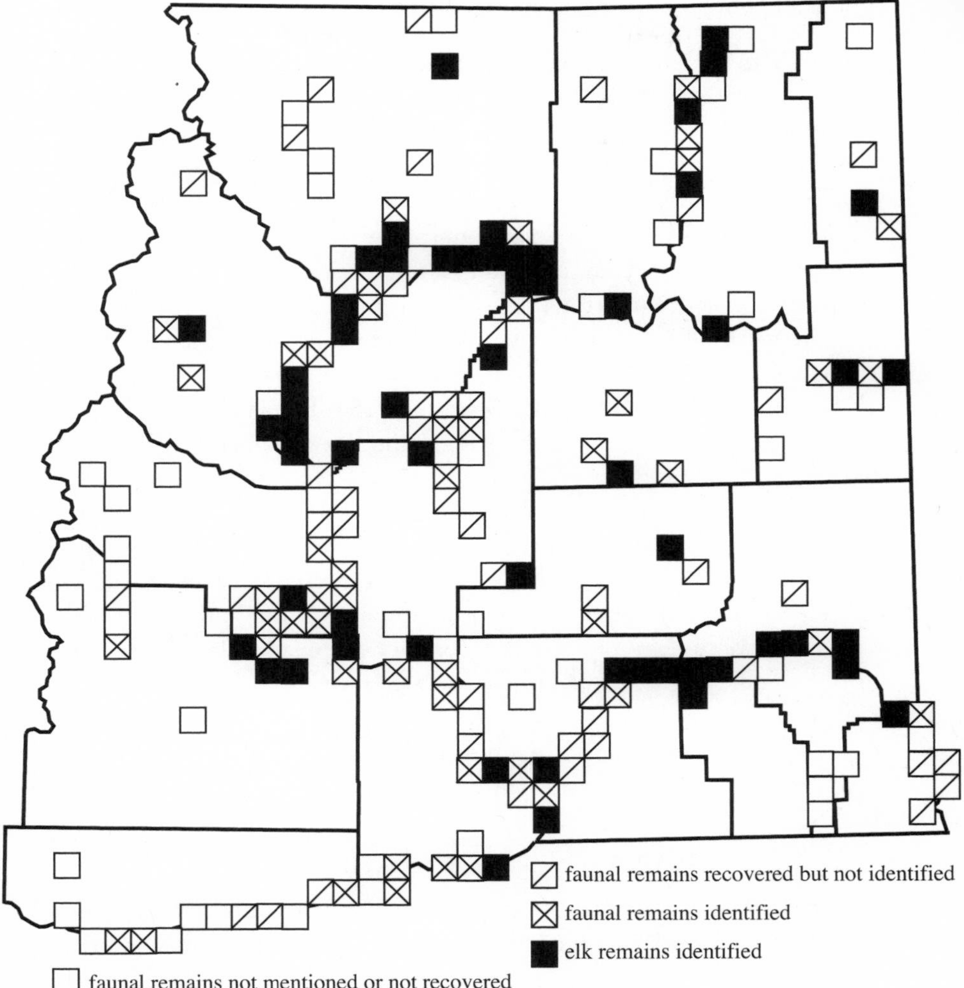

Figure 8.3. Townships (squares) in eastern Washington where archaeological excavations have taken place, where faunal remains have been recovered and identified, and where elk remains have been identified. All instances of elk remains, irrespective of age, are plotted. County lines are included for reference.

land use allows. Precisely such information is, for example, referred to in the state's various elk-management plans, though typically that information is not evaluated in terms of quality or studied for insights to how elk respond to various environmental perturbations.

bundance

le and Lyman (1999) argue that predation by Euro-American settlers during the 19th and early 20th centuries seems to have depressed the elk population in several areas of western Washington. They base their argument on the fact that elk remains dating to the last 1,000 years are abundant precisely in those areas that were the first colonized by white settlers (western Clallam County, Clark County, and western Whatcom, Skagit, Snohomish, and King counties) and that also basically lack historic records of elk. Lyman and Wolverton (2002) suggest that elk were never very abundant in Washington during the Holocene and also that elk abundance varied somewhat across geographic space.

As noted earlier, at best we can determine the abundance of elk relative to one or more other taxa. Given that (1) both elk and deer were exploited by prehistoric humans in Washington, (2) elk tend to graze more than browse whereas deer tend to browse more than graze, and (3) deer remains on average tend to be the most abundant ones zooarchaeologically representing an artiodactyl throughout the state and the Holocene, deer were chosen as the comparative taxon. To monitor variation in the abundance of elk relative to deer over space, taxonomic abundance data in the form of the number of identified specimens (NISP) for the sites plotted in Figure 8.2 were compiled. These data were limited to assemblages that dated to the last 2,000 years and that comprised $\geq$ 20 NISP. This resulted in 37 assemblages for the entire state. An "elk index" was calculated using the formula

$$\text{elk NISP} / (\text{elk NISP} + \text{deer NISP}) = \text{elk index}.$$

As elk abundance decreases relative to deer, the index value will decrease. If the index exceeds 0.5, then elk remains are more abundant than deer remains. Results are summarized in Table 8.1.

Index values were placed in one of three classes. Values $\leq$ 0.2 were classed as "rare"; values of 0.21–0.40 were classed as "medium rare"; and values $\geq$ 0.41 were classed as "medium." The three classes were then plotted on a map of Washington state (Figure 8.4). The mapping convention was to draw a circle with a 10-mi (16-km) diameter around each site. The map indicates that elk were abundant relative to deer in several locations. Interestingly, the locations designated by the circles where elk were of "medium rare" or "medium" abundance during the last 2,000 years tend to overlap, as do virtually all locations where the circles denote that elk were "rare." Overall, Figure 8.4 suggests that during the last 2,000 years elk were nearly as abundant as deer in areas of southeastern Washington,

TABLE 8.1. Abundances of Elk and Deer Remains (Number of Identified Specimens) in 37 Assemblages Dating to the Last 2,000 Years.

Site	Elk	Deer	Total	Elk Index[a]
45AS78	3	45	48	0.062
45AS80	2	76	78	0.026
45AS82	13	200	213	0.061
45CA204	2	32	34	0.059
45CA207	5	38	43	0.116
45CA21	149	158	307	0.485
45CA24	100	485	585	0.171
45CA426	69	49	118	0.585
45CH302	40	333	373	0.107
45CL1	441	399	840	0.525
45DO176	5	332	337	0.015
45DO326	5	86	91	0.055
45FR5	12	62	74	0.162
45GA61	260	284	544	0.478
45JE15	16	32	48	0.333
45JE16	11	9	20	0.550
45KI23	44	294	338	0.130
45KI59	5	97	102	0.049
45KP2	48	45	93	0.516
45KT979	21	30	51	0.410
45LE222	2	241	243	0.008
45LI6	15	16	31	0.484
45OK197	78	669	747	0.104
45OK2	4	1,206	1,210	0.003
45OK258	4	1,496	1,500	0.003
45OK58	5	45	50	0.100
45PI405	7	30	37	0.189
45SA11	387	1,519	1,906	0.203
45SJ1	14	47	61	0.230
45SK7	6	61	67	0.090
45SP238	29	33	62	0.468
45SP56	21	41	62	0.339
45WH11	11	18	29	0.379
45WH9	60	53	113	0.531
45WT134	1	43	44	0.023
45WT2	4	23	27	0.148
45WT41	7	21	28	0.250

[a]This is the number of elk divided by the total number of elk and deer.

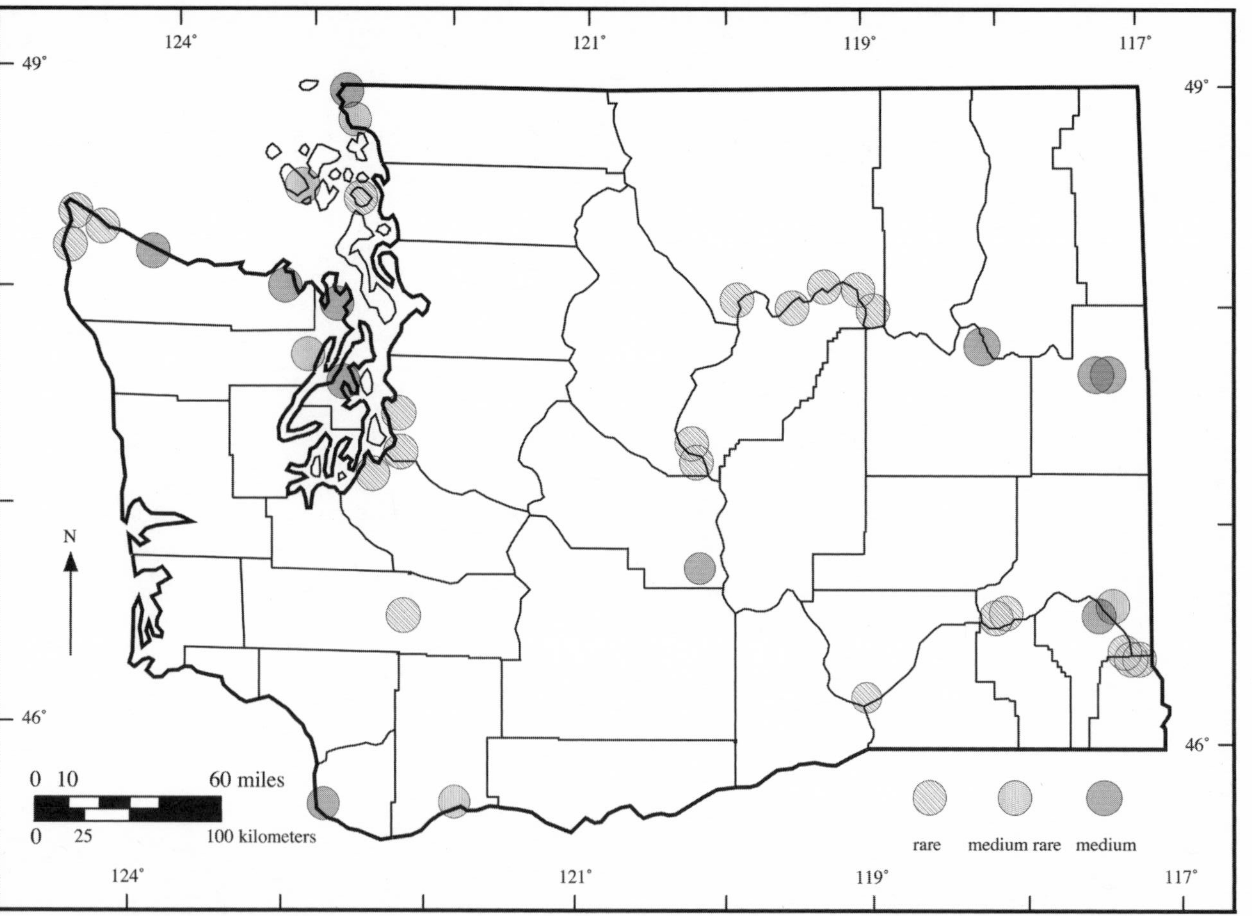

Figure 8.4. Geographic variation in Washington in the abundance of elk remains relative to the abundance of deer remains during the last 2,000 years.

east-central Washington, and south-central Washington (including, perhaps, Yakima County) and around Puget Sound and northwestern Washington. Suggestions that elk were rare to nonexistent in southern Washington (Martin and Szuter 1999a, 1999b) or rare in the eastern half of the state (Kay 1994) are contradicted by these data.

Lyman and Wolverton (2002) suggest that the abundance of artiodactyls relative to other mammals in the zooarchaeological record of eastern Washington fluctuated in concert with environmental change, particularly between 4000 and 2000 B.P. when grass—signifying relatively cool, moist conditions—increased relative to sagebrush—signifying relatively warm, dry conditions (see also Martin and Szuter 2002). The data they use are, however, rather coarse grained. In an effort to detect the possible effects of environmental change on elk abundances, the frequencies of deer and elk remains in 86 assemblages from eastern Washington were tallied. These assemblages span the last 9,000 years, a time when local climates and thus habitats fluctuated markedly (Chatters 1995, 1998). The elk index was calculated for each assemblage (Table 8.2). Plotted against age (Figure 8.5), the elk index values show no pattern of fluctuation. A simple best-fit regression line through the point scatter has no significant slope, suggesting that elk abundances neither changed in harmony with climatic fluctuation nor changed as a result of varying predation pressure (Lyman 2004a). However, this graph is space averaged. That is, it ignores spatial variation in elk abundances by lumping that potential cause of variation into one graph (Lyman 2003a, 2004a). If only the records from the Lower Snake River of southeastern Washington are considered, then elk are most abundant during the cool, moist climatic episode of 4000–2000 B.P. (elk index = 0.39) and the Little Ice Age of circa 700–200 B.P. (index = 0.38); elk are least abundant during the Middle Holocene warm, dry interval known as the Altithermal, dating between 8000 and 4000 B.P. (index = 0.28), and also during the warm, dry Medieval Climatic Optimum, dating between about 1100 and 700 B.P. (index = 0.11). Temporal resolution is not fine enough and insufficient samples are available to determine if elk abundances changed over the last 200 years in response to Euro-American influences.

Elk Size

Paleozoologist Carl Gustafson was the first to observe that the Late Pleistocene–Early Holocene elk remains recovered from the Marmes Rockshelter (45FR50) site in southeastern Washington "are larger than those

TABLE 8.2. Age and Abundances of Elk and Deer Remains (Number of Identified Specimens) and Elk Index for 86 Zooarchaeological Collections from Eastern Washington.

Site	Age (B.P.)	Elk	Deer	Total	Elk Index[a]
45KT979	100	2	10	12	0.17
45AS82	200	2	46	48	0.04
45OK2/2A	200	1	575	576	0.002
45KT285	300	0	68	68	0.00
45OK197	250	1	58	59	0.02
45DO285	350	1	7	8	0.125
45WT39	450	168	397	565	0.30
45LI6	500	15	16	31	0.48
45GA61	500	260	284	544	0.48
45OK258	500	4	1,496	1,500	0.003
45KT979	500	4	0	4	1.00
45DO211/214	600	1	169	170	0.006
45OK197	650	9	130	139	0.06
45CH212	700	0	20	20	0.00
45WT2	700	4	23	27	0.15
45FR5	700	12	62	74	0.16
45FR39	750	7	6	13	0.54
45OK287	800	0	128	128	0.00
45AS80	850	2	76	78	0.03
45DO326	900	5	86	91	0.05
45OK4	900	0	61	61	0.00
45OK2/2A	900	3	631	634	0.005
45OK197	950	3	136	139	0.02
45CH-RR	1000	20	6	26	0.77
45DO176	1000	5	332	337	0.01
45OK58	1000	5	45	50	0.10
45OK2/2A	1000	0	83	83	0.00
45SP56	1000	21	41	62	0.34
45SP238	1000	29	33	62	0.47
45WT134	1300	1	43	44	0.02
45OK197	1350	64	341	405	0.16
45AS78	1500	3	45	48	0.06
45AS82	1500	11	154	165	0.07
45CH-RR	1500	12	4	16	0.75
45CH302	1500	40	333	373	0.11
45FR40	1500	13	2	15	0.87
45WT41	1500	7	21	28	0.25
45DO242	1500	0	32	32	0.00
45KT979	1500	15	15	30	0.50
45OK287	1550	0	60	60	0.00
45OK197	1750	1	4	5	0.20
45KL5	1750	0	101	101	0.00
45OK250	1800	0	147	147	0.00
45KT980	1900	2	3	5	0.40

TABLE 8.2. Age and Abundances of Elk and Deer Remains (Number of Identified Specimens) and Elk Index for 86 Zooarchaeological Collections from Eastern Washington *(Continued)*.

Site	Age (B.P.)	Elk	Deer	Total	Elk Index[a]
45FR50	2000	2	26	28	0.07
45DO285	2000	1	3	4	0.25
45KT1003	2000	4	2	6	0.67
45KL5	2100	0	64	64	0.00
45DO285	2250	9	13	22	0.41
45FR36	2300	5	1	6	0.83
45GA17	2300	27	18	45	0.60
45GR445	2300	15	9	24	0.62
45CH-RR	2500	1	2	3	0.33
45OK4	2600	3	594	597	0.005
45DO372	2600	3	24	27	0.11
45DO189	3000	2	261	263	0.008
45-RM590	3000	2	100	102	0.02
45OK11	3000	24	232	256	0.09
45OK258	3000	10	1,844	1,854	0.005
45OK2/2A	3000	2	342	344	0.006
45DO211/214	3000	1	54	55	0.02
45OK250	3200	1	487	488	0.002
45DO285	3250	6	7	13	0.46
45FR39	3500	11	3	14	0.79
45DO242	3500	4	365	369	0.01
45OK2/2A	3500	1	473	474	0.002
45DO326	3750	0	5	5	0.00
45OK383	3900	29	30	59	0.49
45OK69	3950	4	51	55	0.07
45AS82	4000	10	31	41	0.24
45WT41	4000	8	82	90	0.09
45WT134	4000	3	31	34	0.09
45OK4	4100	1	58	59	0.02
45KT285	4100	0	364	364	0.00
45OK250	4400	0	104	104	0.00
45-RM590	4500	1	119	120	0.008
45DO326	4750	2	29	31	0.06
45FR50	5400	8	49	57	0.14
45OK11	5500	24	1,432	1,456	0.02
45OK287	5750	0	90	90	0.00
45AS82	6000	0	3	3	0.00
45FR50	7000	36	108	144	0.25
45WT2	7300	4	13	17	0.24
45WT41	7300	59	103	162	0.36
45GR97	8700	30	9	39	0.77
45FR50	9000	5	22	27	0.19

Note: Adapted from Lyman 2004a.

[a]This is the number of elk divided by the total number of elk and deer.

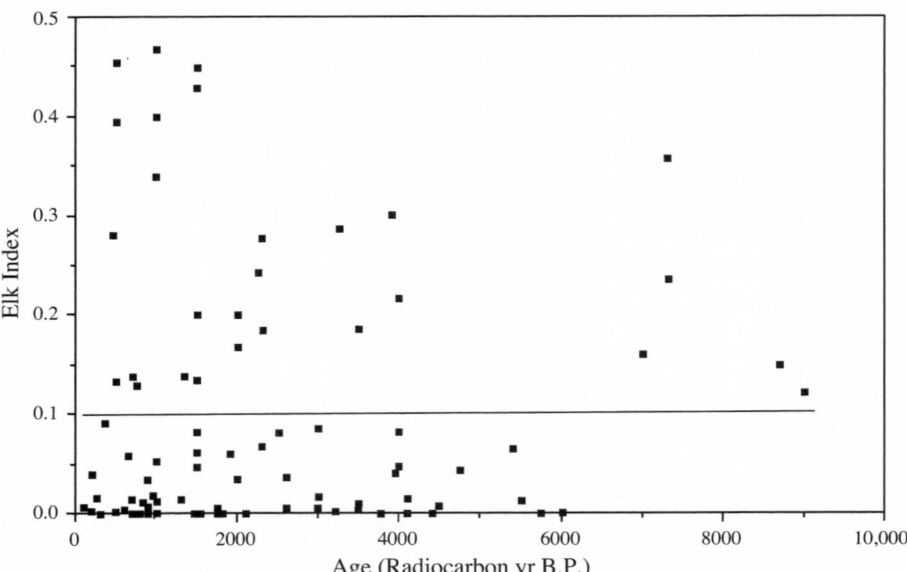

Figure 8.5. Abundance of elk remains relative to deer remains across time in 86 assemblages from eastern Washington (derived from Table 8.2).

of living representatives in the area today" (Fryxell et al. 1968:514). A decade later he indicated that elk long bones from 10,000-year-old sediments at Marmes Rockshelter "averaged some four to five percent greater in length and nearly eight percent greater in diameter" than "the largest modern specimen" (1983:24) of a male Rocky Mountain elk that Gustafson had examined. The comparative specimen referred to is accession number 65–68 in the Conner Biological Museum at Washington State University (WSU). After an examination of elk remains dating throughout the Holocene and from numerous sites in eastern Washington, Gustafson concluded that those remains did not represent a "Late Pleistocene species [even though] most wapiti bones and teeth from sites in eastern Washington [irrespective of their age] were larger than modern individuals east of the Cascades" (1983:24). Elk remains from western Washington dating to about 1400 B.P. were also noted to be from "abnormally large individuals" and to "presumedly" represent the Roosevelt elk (Shaw 1977:52). These elk remains were "significantly larger" than "a very old male of *[C. e. nelsoni]* which was near the upper size range for that subspecies" (Shaw 1977: 52). Again, the comparative specimen is WSU 65–68.

No modern comparative data and no measurements of prehistoric specimens have been reported by anyone who has commented on the size of prehistoric elk remains. Despite this, the suggestion that prehistoric elk in Washington were exceptionally large has become part of the received wisdom regarding the Holocene mammalian fauna of the state. For example, archaeologist James Chatters recently remarked that about 9,500 years ago "oversized elk still roamed the grasslands of the Columbia Basin" (2001:150). In the absence of data to support such statements, it is unclear (1) whether elk throughout the state were larger than their modern counterparts and, if so, how much larger they actually were; (2) what the shape of the elk chronocline might be through the Holocene and why it takes that shape; (3) whether that chronocline varies spatially; and (4) when resident prehistoric elk attained modern size.

To answer these questions, comparative metric data for modern Rocky Mountain and Roosevelt elk were collected (Table 8.3). Two measurements on astragali, two on distal metapodial condyles, and one on first phalanges were taken. The average and standard deviation of ten modern complete and partial skeletons of Roosevelt elk (5 females, 4 males, 1 of unknown sex) were calculated for each of the five dimensions measured. A summary of the comparative data is presented in Table 8.4. The same measurements were taken on 27 complete and partial skeletons of Rocky Mountain elk (13 females, 6 males, 8 unknown) and are summarized in Table 8.5. These data indicate that Roosevelt elk are on average significantly larger than Rocky Mountain elk in terms of the dimensions measured (Table 8.6). The differences may be found to be greater once the samples are increased to include more Roosevelt elk, but they suffice for my purpose here, which is to determine if the archaeological remains of the two subspecies might be distinguished on the basis of their size. My data (Tables 8.4–8.6) suggest that this may be possible. However, a bivariate scatterplot of the lateral length against the distal width of astragali of known sex and subspecies indicates that visual inspection of size (even when plotted in such a graph) will often be insufficient to identify the subspecies represented by an isolated prehistoric specimen (Figure 8.6). The graph indicates that male Roosevelt elk are largest, whereas female Rocky Mountain elk are smallest, but the marked overlap of the distributions of the four suggests that only quite small and quite large specimens can be assigned to subspecies. Can the size data be otherwise used?

Specimens from site 45CA426 in eastern Clallam County (Figure 8.1) where Roosevelt elk are found today date to the last 2,700 years and were treated as a single assemblage in a previous analysis (Lyman 1999, 2001). These specimens all fall within or exceed the size range of modern Roosevelt elk, and most exceed the size of modern Rocky Mountain elk. These

TABLE 8.3. Inventory of Elk Skeletons Measured.

Subspecies	Museum and Accession Number	Collection Site	Sex
Cervus elaphus roosevelti	Oregon State University, Anthropology, #115	Clatsop County, OR	F
	University of Washington, Burke Museum, #31685	Wahkiakum County, WA	M
	University of Washington, Burke Museum, #31684	Wahkiakum County, WA	F
	University of Washington, Burke Museum, #31683	Wahkiakum County, WA	F
	University of Washington, Burke Museum, #31681	Grays Harbor County, WA	F
	University of Victoria, Anthropology, #85-6	Vancouver Island, BC	?
	British Columbia Provincial Museum, #018556	Vancouver Island, BC	M
	British Columbia Provincial Museum, #6407	Vancouver Island, BC	M
	British Columbia Provincial Museum, #F81-10	Vancouver Island, BC	M
	British Columbia Provincial Museum, #6805	Nanaimo Lake, BC	F
Cervus elaphus nelsoni	University of Missouri, Lyman, #128	Columbia County, WA	?
	University of Missouri, Lyman, #112	Columbia County, WA	F
	University of Missouri, Anthropology, #781	Wyoming	?
	University of Missouri, Anthropology, #774	Wyoming	?
	University of Missouri, Anthropology, #769	Wyoming	?
	Washington State University, Connor Museum, #65–68	Montana	M
	Oregon State University, Anthropology, #88	Union County, OR	F
	Oregon State University, Anthropology, #59	Malheur County, OR	?
	Illinois State Museum, #687657	Wyoming	M
	Illinois State Museum, #687655	Wyoming	M
	Illinois State Museum, #687656	Wyoming	F
	University of Puget Sound, #26567	King County, WA	F
	British Columbia Provincial Museum, #9291	British Columbia	F
	British Columbia Provincial Museum, #9289	British Columbia	F
	Montana Department of Fish, Wildlife, Parks, #176439	Montana	?
	Montana Department of Fish, Wildlife, Parks, #175985	Montana	F
	Montana State University, Anthropology	Wyoming	F
	University of Wyoming, Anthropology, #9285B	Big Horn County, WY	M

TABLE 8.3. Inventory of Elk Skeletons Measured *(Continued)*.

Subspecies	Museum and Accession Number	Collection Site	Sex
	University of Wyoming, Anthropology, #8268B	Big Horn County, WY	F
	University of Wyoming, Anthropology, #8261	Big Horn County, WY	F
	University of Wyoming, Anthropology, #8441B	Jackson Hole, WY	F
	University of Wyoming, Anthropology, #8423B	Carbon County, WY	F
	University of Wyoming, Anthropology, #8862B	Albany County, WY	M
	University of Wyoming, Anthropology, #9072B	Teton County, WY	?
	University of Wyoming, Anthropology, #B0338	Washakie County, WY	F
	University of Wyoming, Anthropology, #8856B	Larimer County, CO	M
	University of Wyoming, Anthropology, #9286B	Larimer County, CO	?

Note: All skeletons are of mature individuals (with all epiphyses fused and all permanent teeth erupted).

TABLE 8.4. Summary of Comparative Data for Modern Roosevelt Elk.

Dimension of Skeletal Element	Number of Individuals Measured	Number of Specimens Measured	Average (mm)	Standard Deviation
First Phalanx				
Proximal width	8	53	26.60	1.28
Astragalus				
Distal width	8	15	43.75	1.55
Lateral length	8	15	70.25	2.04
Distal Metapodial				
Condyle width	9	63	24.70	1.15
Condyle length	9	63	36.38	1.61

remains seem, then, to represent the historically resident subspecies—the Roosevelt elk. But because this taxonomic assignment is based merely on bone size, we need to determine if elk size changed over time. In particular, did the 45CA426 elk change size over the last 2,700 years?

Following Simpson's (1941) lead, measurements of individual archaeological specimens with tight temporal control were chosen and converted

TABLE 8.5. Summary of Comparative Data for Modern Rocky Mountain Elk.

Dimension of Skeletal Element	Number of Individuals Measured	Number of Specimens Measured	Average (mm)	Standard Deviation
First Phalanx				
Proximal width	13	68	25.00	1.23
Astragalus				
Distal width	22	34	41.05	1.99
Lateral length	22	34	66.38	2.62
Distal Metapodial				
Condyle width	19	122	23.27	1.28
Condyle length	19	122	34.69	1.53

TABLE 8.6. Statistical Comparisons of Roosevelt and Rocky Mountain Elk.

Dimension of Skeletal Element	Student's t	Larger Subspecies
First Phalanx		
Proximal width	6.946	*Cervus elaphus roosevelti*
Astragalus		
Distal width	4.656	*C. e. roosevelti*
Lateral length	5.075	*C. e. roosevelti*
Distal Metapodial		
Condyle width	7.443	*C. e. roosevelti*
Condyle length	6.978	*C. e. roosevelti*

Note: One-tailed p for all = 0.0001.

to logs, and their difference from the log of the mean for each measurement evidenced by modern Roosevelt elk was determined. Simpson's graphic technique produces what he termed a "ratio diagram" meant to simultaneously display multiple measurements of numerous dimensions of multiple specimens relative to some standard. I modified his technique and plotted the difference between the log of the modern mean (set at 0.0) and the prehistoric specimen, irrespective of the dimension measured, against the age of the measured specimen.

Results are shown in Figure 8.7, where the log of the modern mean is signified by the vertical line near the middle of the point scatter. Points falling to the right of the zero line indicate prehistoric specimens that are larger than the average modern specimen; points to the left of the zero

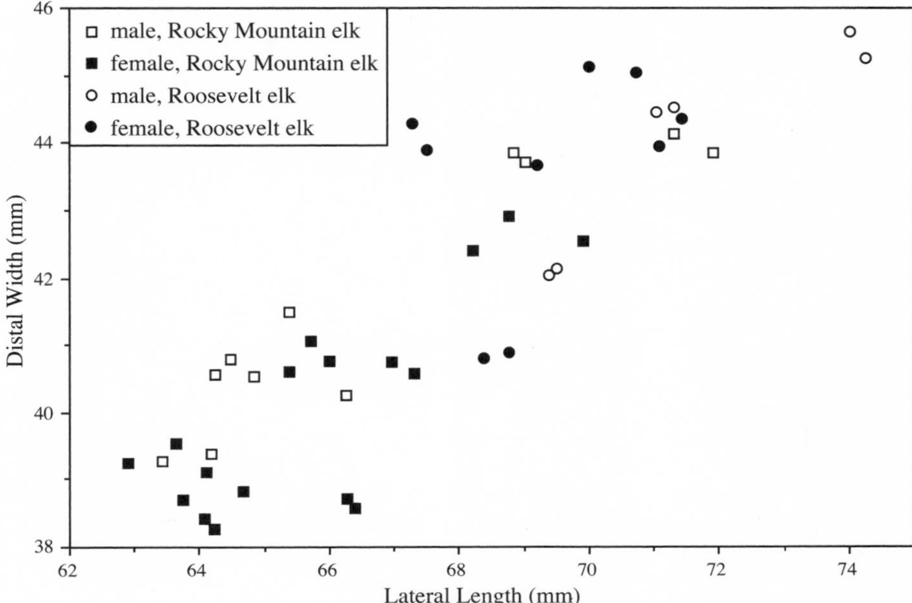

Figure 8.6. Bivariate scatterplot of the lateral length and distal width of astragali in modern specimens of male and female Rocky Mountain elk and Roosevelt elk.

line represent prehistoric specimens that are smaller than the average modern specimen. Figure 8.7 suggests that most elk exploited by the human occupants of 45CA426 were larger than modern elk, though some were smaller. A simple best-fit regression line calculated with age as the independent variable and the size value plotted in Figure 8.7 as the dependent variable suggests that elk were increasing in size between 2540 and 1330 B.P. Sample sizes per age are small, however, and not all measurement values are independent of one another. Further, what might be shown in Figure 8.7 is a change in the sex ratio of elk over time—adult male elk are larger than adult females (Figure 8.6). Too few of all the elk remains from the site could be sexed, so I cannot evaluate this possibility.

Given the preceding, it is obvious that more prehistoric data and more comparative data are required to ensure that Figure 8.7 represents a chronocline. Nevertheless, that graph is tantalizing for one simple reason. The red deer of Europe—placed by some in the same species as the North American elk—are demonstrably ecophenotypically plastic (Langvatn and Albon 1986). Their average size fluctuates with the quality and quantity of forage available during their growth. It seems that North American elk respond in similar fashion to variation in forage; small elk may be small

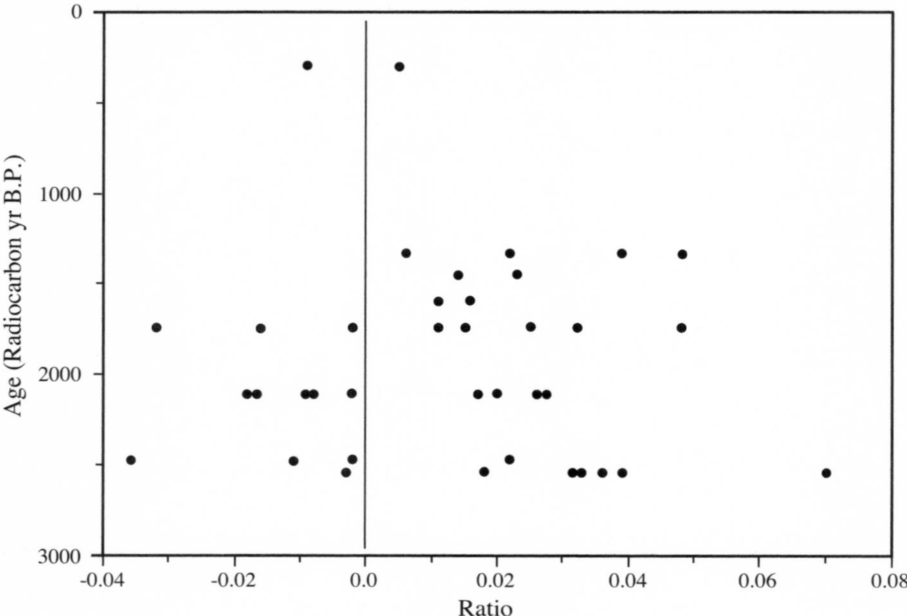

Figure 8.7. Temporal variation in the size of prehistoric elk remains from the Olympic Peninsula of western Washington. Points to the left of the vertical 0.0 line are smaller-than-average modern Roosevelt elk; points to the right of the 0.0 line are larger-than-average modern Roosevelt elk. The "ratio" is the difference between the log of the modern mean and the log of the prehistoric specimen.

as a result of relatively poor nourishment (Bubenik 1982; see also Guthrie 1984a). There has been some concern that Roosevelt elk on the Olympic Peninsula may not survive as a result of urbanization and the concomitant destruction of the winter range (Houston et al. 1990). Figure 8.7 suggests that they have survived the last 2,700 years—a period when climate and habitats were unstable (Hebda and Whitlock 1997)—with some change in size. If this is correct, and given the usually large size of Late Pleistocene elk in eastern Washington, then perhaps elk living in Washington are sufficiently ecophenotypically plastic to withstand, by further diminution, additional loss or degradation of habitat.

There is another factor that must be considered in efforts to explain any apparent chronocline in elk size. As much as one-third of the indigenous human population was lost to a smallpox epidemic in 1801; another 20 percent or so was lost 25 years later (Boyd 1998). The concomitant reduction in human predation that surely took place may have allowed elk populations to increase to such an extent that intraspecific competition within those populations resulted in smaller elk during the historic period. Perhaps as a result of this change in predation pressure over the last several hundred years, the average size of elk became smaller.

The preceding raises questions regarding the size of elk in other areas of the Pacific Northwest and of Washington state. Elk bones from the site of Cathlapotle (45CL1), located adjacent to the Columbia River in northwestern Clark County (Figure 8.1), are larger than the bones of modern elk. This is exemplified in a bivariate scatterplot of the maximum lateral length (proximo-distal) and maximum distal width of elk astragali (Figure 8.8). Given the size of the specimens and their geographic location, it is likely that they represent Roosevelt elk. However, what is difficult to explain at present is the larger-than-modern-elk size of many prehistoric specimens. Has modern human (firearm-assisted) predation reduced the size of individuals, perhaps by selective culling of large animals? Or is the large size of the Cathlapotle elk a result of their occurrence in a zone of relatively equable climate and a habitat rich in forage that has a relatively long growing season? This site is located in the Portland Basin, an area with over 200 frost-free days annually and rather equable seasonal variation in temperature. Future research will explore this issue by studying the size of deer remains from Cathlapotle. If deer from the site are also relatively large, then it is likely that habitat productivity has resulted in the local elk being large. If the deer are not relatively large, then genetic and predation causes must be explored.

DISCUSSION

There are reasons to suspect that if elk were as abundant as Kay (1994) and Martin and Szuter (1999a, 1999b) imply they were at some time in the past, and their populations were depressed by human predation, then a significant decrease in human population would result in a rebound of the elk population. The population of First Americans in the Pacific Northwest decreased by as much as one-half between about 1775 and 1850 (Campbell 1989; see also Boyd 1998). This decrease corresponds temporally with a rebound in various faunal taxa evidenced at archaeological sites across the Columbia River from Cathlapotle (Butler 2000b). Washington was designated a territory in 1853 and became the 42nd state in the Union on November 11, 1889. The Euro-American population in 1889 was just over 357,200 (Dryden 1968:201). In 1850 the Euro-American population of the Oregon Territory, comprising modern Oregon state, Washington, Idaho, and part of western Montana, was tallied at 13,300;

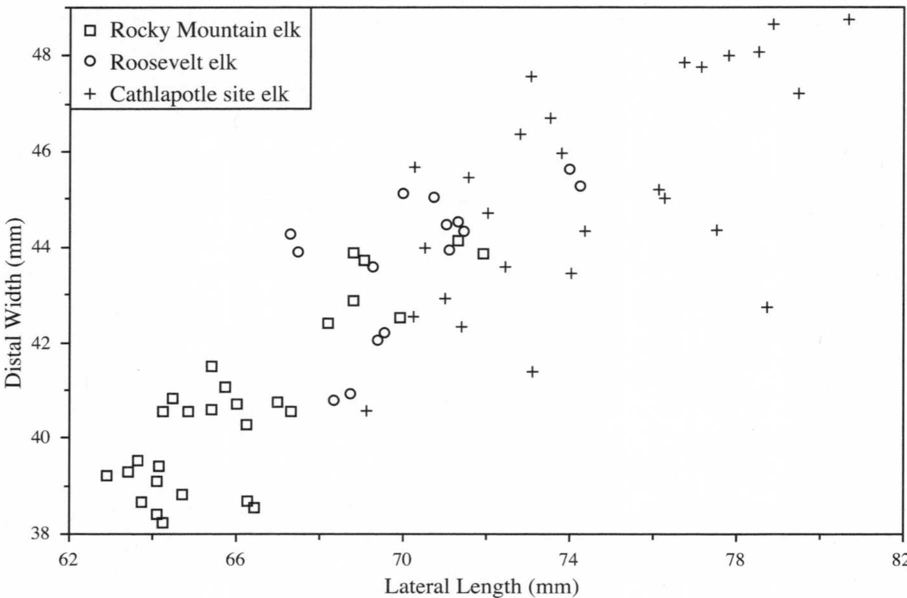

Figure 8.8. Bivariate scatterplot of the distal width and lateral length of elk astragali from modern elk and from the Cathlapotle site in Clark County.

just over 1,000 of these were said to live "north of the Columbia River" (Dryden 1968:110)—that is, in modern Washington state. A number of settlers had left the Oregon Territory in 1849 in an effort to strike it rich in the California gold fields, and what would become Washington state 40 years later was not densely populated by Euro-Americans during the middle of the 19th century. First American peoples were placed on reservations between about 1855 and 1870, at which time they subsisted largely on (insufficient) government-issued rations (Boyd 1998). Predation of large game such as elk was restricted to Euro-Americans who hunted for subsistence.

Given the preceding, if there was a rebound in Washington elk populations, it should have occurred sometime between 1800 and 1875 when the population of First Americans was in steep decline and the population of white settlers was relatively small and slowly growing. There are no zooarchaeological data with sufficient temporal control that can be brought to bear on this issue. It is thus perhaps worth noting that elk populations in British Columbia apparently declined during the 19th and early 20th centuries (Spalding 1992). Historic data for Washington suggest that the rebound of local elk populations occurred in the early 20th century subsequent to the implementation of restrictions on hunting, the removal of carnivorous predators, and the initiation of transplanting efforts. This rebound was prior to the implementation of modern habitat-management practices such as the suppression of natural fires and restricted timber harvesting (Christensen et al. 1999). It is thought that the last two factors may eventually result in reduced elk populations (Christensen et al. 1999). Archaeological data presented here (Table 8.2) suggest that it will be difficult to tease apart the influences of climatic fluctuations and human predation on local elk populations, but such must be attempted if the past is to shed light on the long-term influences of modern conservation biology practices.

CONCLUSION

Wildlife biologists have tended to be the ones who argue that elk were not abundant or were absent from various areas of Washington. They tend to focus on historic records (Bradley and Driver 1981; Rickard et al. 1977), and thus their temporal perspective is limited. Biologists occasionally consult zooarchaeological data, but when they do they tend to variously overlook numerous records (compare, for example, McCorquodale 1985 with Dixon and Lyman 1996) or to treat the evidence in a noncritical manner (Bradley and Driver 1981; Kay 1994). They cannot be faulted for the former oversight because many archaeological data produced after about 1970 are found only in the infamous "gray" literature of cultural resource management—literature that has limited publication and minimal circulation and distribution (Lyman 1997). With respect to the noncritical treatment of zooarchaeological data, an absence of identified elk remains is often taken to signify that elk were not present. This ignores what may be a complex taphonomic history and deficiencies of archaeological sampling. For example, Figure 8.2 not only indicates where elk remains have been found; it also indicates just as clearly where archaeological research has *not* been undertaken and where faunal remains were recovered but not identified (compare Figures 8.2 and 8.3). This is not to say that I think elk were ubiquitous in Washington during the last 2,000 years, but I would not hesitate to bet that many more points will be plotted on Figure 8.2 and many of the apparent gaps in the Late Holocene distribution of elk in the state will disappear once we have done the necessary zooarchaeological research.

The archaeofaunal record indicates that elk were indeed present in Yakima County prior to the 20th century and earlier. This means that it is false to say that elk are not "native" to this area; management decisions cannot rest on the claim that they are "exotic" to the county. Second, the zooarchaeological record indicates that elk were never abundant relative to deer during the last 2,000 years, save in a few spatially limited areas. There is no evidence that elk ever outnumbered deer or that they even approached the abundance of deer during the Middle and Late Holocene; the record for the terminal Pleistocene and Early Holocene (approximately 15,000–8000 B.P.) is inadequate to determine the relative abundances of deer and elk at these times. There is no clear evidence that prehistoric human predation depressed elk populations; the size of the metapopulation of elk in eastern Washington relative to that of deer seems to remain more or less stable over time. However, in some smaller-scale areas, elk were less abundant relative to deer during warm, dry climatic periods and more abundant during relatively cool, moist periods. This means that conservation biologists working toward the long-term management of resident elk must be cognizant of the potential that environmental change—whether natural or anthropogenic—may thwart their efforts. Finally, prehistoric elk in at least some areas were in many cases larger than their modern conspecifics, though the precise reasons for this are unclear. The zooarchaeological record suggests that elk can respond ecophenotypically in one or both of two ways to ecosystem change: they can change their size or their abundance. Learning more about the catalysts prompting these ecophenotypic responses could eventually aid in managing elk habitat, determining harvest rates, and the like.

The zooarchaeological record as it is presently known suggests that elk abundances and also perhaps elk sizes today are largely the result of human management actions, such as culling practices and early-20th-century transplanting. In combination with the removal of predators such as wolves, cougars, and grizzly bears and the effective removal of First American hunters, the 20th-century management of elk populations resulted in their expansion into areas not occupied during the late 19th and early 20th centuries (Rickard et al. 1977). The zooarchaeological record indicates that these animals are simply recolonizing portions of their former (pre-1800 A.D.) range. These observations raise the rather slippery issue of deciding on the baseline conditions that management efforts should seek to re-create (see chap. 1). Are many elk desired, or are large elk desired?

Acknowledgments. I thank Diane (Ledlin) McKeel for informing me about the discussions of elk in Yakima County, Susan Dixon and Judith Harpole for help with compiling data, and Ken Cannon and two anonymous reviewers for comments on an early draft. Access to modern elk skeletons was provided by Keith Aune and Neil Anderson (Montana Department of Fish, Wildlife, and Parks), Jeff Bradley and John Rozdilzky (Burke Museum, University of Washington), Jim Cosgrove and Lesley Kennes (British Columbia Provincial Museum), Jack Fisher and Tom Roll (Montana State University), Karen Lupo (Washington State University), Terrance Martin (Illinois State Museum), Danny Walker (University of Wyoming), and Rebecca Wigen (University of Victoria).

9

Archaeological Evidence of Pronghorn *(Antilocapra americana)* Migration in the Upper Green River Basin of Wyoming: Implications for Wildlife Management

Paul H. Sanders and Mark E. Miller

Wildlife managers are regularly faced with questions concerning the antiquity of animal behaviors observed today. When, for example, were migration routes in use today first used? Have those particular routes been used continuously since that initial use, and if not, why not, and what alternative routes were followed, and when? Has the seasonal timing of a population's migration movements been static? Have past migration events allowed gene flow between otherwise isolated conspecific populations? Answering such questions may be mandatory to the long-term survival of migratory populations of organisms because more and more barriers are being constructed across migration routes. Such barriers may be impassable, or they may merely restrict movements, but in either case a "natural" (see chap. 1) state of things has been anthropogenically altered. Although historical records may provide evidence of migration patterns, those records often lack sufficient geographic or temporal detail, especially compared with the resolution afforded by modern radio-collaring and satellite locational systems. Even when fine-scale resolution is provided, the questions listed above should be asked because Euro-American land-use practices may have altered migrational patterns for over 100 years in many areas. Are the migrational patterns observed today, then, a result of recent anthropogenic causes?

In this chapter we explore these and related questions using a set of zooarchaeological data collected from a site in southwestern Wyoming. We are specifically concerned here with the antiquity of the migration patterns of a population of pronghorn antelope *(Antilocapra americana)*. Data we describe indicate that migration corridors existed in the Trappers Point area for the last 6,000 years. These data have been used by conservationists in arguments for the preservation of modern migration corridors. The particular faunal collection we discuss also provides clear indications of the season of migration and suggests that the prehistoric population may have been somewhat genetically isolated, rather like the modern local pronghorn population may be.

TRAPPERS POINT SITE

The Trappers Point site (48SU1006) is located in the Upper Green River Basin of southwestern Wyoming (Figure 9.1). The site is situated on the upper leeward side of a sagebrush-covered ridge that links a large plateau to the south (known as The Mesa) with a series of hills (Cora Buttes) to the north and northwest (Figure 9.2). This area is west of Pinedale, Wyoming, just below the south flank of the Wind River Mountains. The site lies at an elevation of 2,226 m (7,300 ft) and is bordered by the Green River to the west and the wide meadows of the New Fork River to the east.

A block excavation of 129 m^2 yielded nearly 87,000 pieces of chipped stone debitage, almost 300 projectile points, 400 other stone tools, 86,000 faunal remains, and nine features (Miller et al. 1999). Evidence of three major human occupations, all attributable to the Early Archaic period, was found: stratum III (7880–6180 B.P.), stratum V (6010–5160 B.P.), and stratum VII (4690 B.P.). Pronghorn remains dominate each of the three strata but are most abundant in stratum V, where the remains of 27 mature and immature animals (based on left innominates) and eight fetuses (based on right humeri) were recovered (Table 9.1). Approximately 28 percent of this bone bed was excavated, indicating that the minimum number of individuals (or MNI) would be higher if more of the site were excavated. Materials in stratum V were deposited in mid-March through April based on pronghorn fetal development, stage of tooth eruption, and stage of tooth wear (Miller 1999; Miller and Sanders 2000). Based on the 25 right mandibles for which ontogenic age could be determined, most of the pronghorn were three years old or less (Figure 9.3), and, along with other evidence, these data suggest catastrophic mortality from a single event or several very closely spaced events.

No evidence of a corral or trap was noted, although either could have been constructed from the big sagebrush that surrounds the area, as is the case for similar ethnographic and archaeological examples (Arkrush 1986;

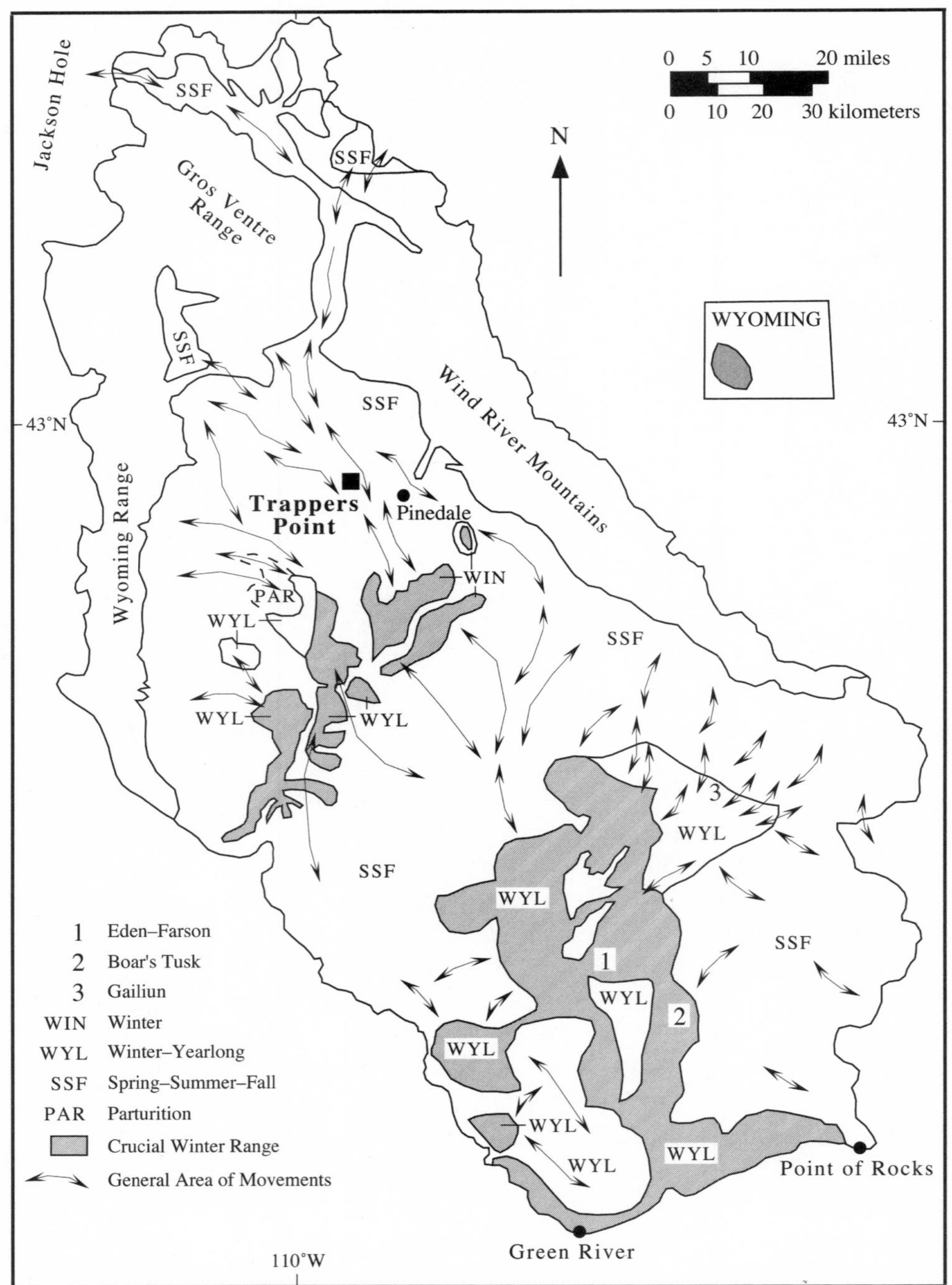

Figure 9.1. Map of Wyoming's Sublette pronghorn herd winter and summer ranges, general movements, and prehistoric pronghorn-processing/kill sites (adapted from Wyoming Game and Fish Department 1987).

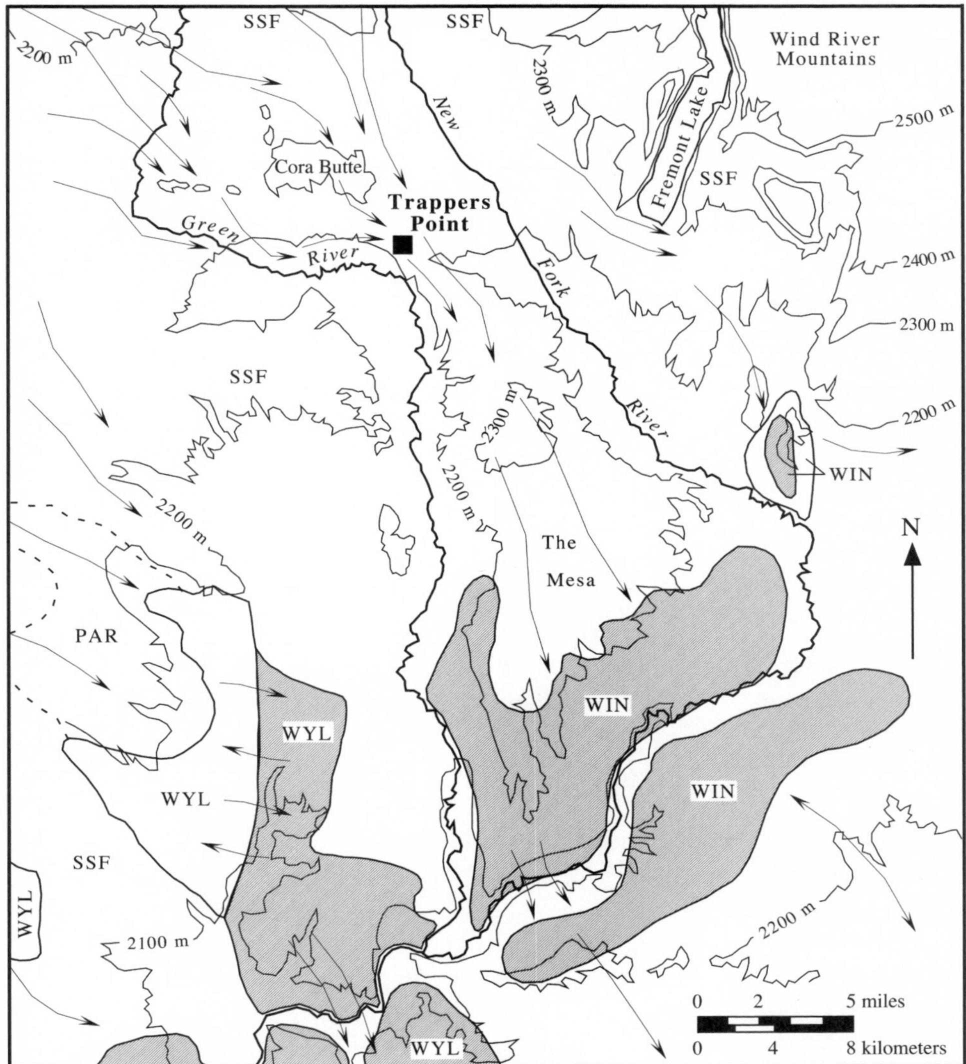

Figure 9.2. Location of general pronghorn herd movements and their winter and summer ranges within the vicinity of the Trappers Point site. Abbreviations as in Figure 9.1 (adapted from Wyoming Game and Fish Department 1987).

Egan 1917; Fowler 1989; Frison 1971, 1991; Steward 1941, 1943). The horizontally limited nature of the stratum V bone bed and the fact that all portions of the pronghorn, from head to toe, were recovered argue for some sort of trap. We believe that the site was utilized as a pronghorn-kill/

TABLE 9.1. Frequencies of Vertebrate Faunal Remains in Trappers Point Strata.

		Stratum III		Stratum V		Stratum VII	
Taxonomic Name	Common Name	NISP	MNI	NISP	MNI	NISP	MNI
Bison bison	bison	0	0	9	1	0	0
Cervus elaphus	elk	2	1	47	1	3	1
Odocoileus sp.	deer	0	0	2	1	0	0
Antilocapra americana	pronghorn	36	2	1,683	27	45	2
Sylvilagus sp.	cottontail	0	0	1	1	0	0
Spermophilus sp.	ground squirrel	19	4	42	6	1	1
Microtus sp.	vole	5	1	100	1	6	1
Centrocercus urophasianus	sage grouse	3	1	84	11	2	1
Branta canadensis	Canada goose	0	0	1	1	0	0
Cypriniformes	fish	0	0	1	1	0	0
Total		65	9	1,970	51	57	6

Note: NISP = number of identified specimens; MNI = minimum number of individuals. The remains of fetal pronghorn are excluded. Adapted from Eckles 1999.

butchering locale multiple times during the Early Archaic period (Miller and Sanders 2000; Miller et al. 1999).

PRONGHORN BIOLOGY AND BEHAVIOR

Pronghorn are an open plains–adapted species with keen eyesight and extraordinary speed but poor vertical-jumping abilities (Lubinski and Herren 2000). They are the smallest of the large game animals within the western United States, with body weights averaging approximately 50 kg (110 lbs) for does and 55 kg (120 lbs) for bucks (Hepworth and Blunt 1966). In Wyoming, shrubs (sagebrush [*Artemisia* sp.] and rabbitbrush [*Chrysothamnus* sp.]) account for 90–100 percent of their winter diet and 57 percent of their summer forage (Sundstrom et al. 1973).

Pronghorn are social animals that form mixed-sex herds that vary considerably in size and individual group membership (Fichter 1987; Gregg 1955; Kitchen and O'Gara 1982). For the Trappers Point area, 12 groups of pronghorn were recorded in early April 1994 that varied from 3 to 157 individuals and averaged about 27 per group (Doug McWhirter, personal communication, 1994). Their limited jumping ability, social herding behavior, and avoidance of fences and obstructions are characteristics that

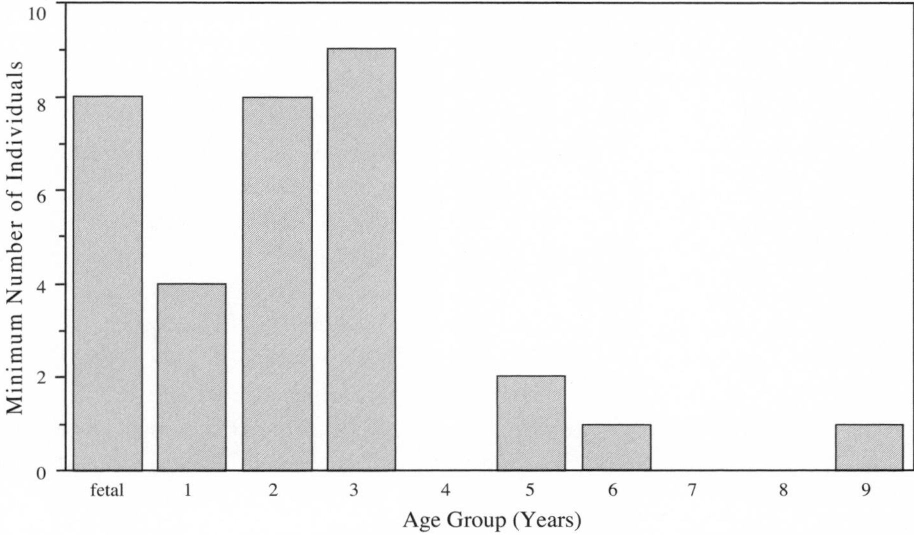

Figure 9.3. Trappers Point, stratum V, pronghorn age profile; age in years (using most frequent side from fetal bone and mandibular dentition).

favor hunting by prehistoric groups using various types of corrals and traps (Arkrush 1986; Frison 1971, 1991, 2000; Lubinski and Herren 2000).

Modern Migration Patterns

Many early naturalists and observers noted the seasonal migrations of pronghorn throughout various areas of the western United States (Burroughs 1961; Grinnell 1929; McLean 1944; Seton 1937; Skinner 1922). Pronghorn that cross the Trappers Point site are no different, except that their movements are better documented (Raper et al. 1989; Sawyer and Lindzey 1999, 2000). The Trappers Point site is within the modern range of the Sublette pronghorn herd unit as defined by the Wyoming Game and Fish Department. This herd has the distinction of following the longest annual pronghorn migration route in North America. The route extends from Jackson Hole in the north—occupied in the summer—as far as Green River and Point of Rocks 160–270 km (100–170 mi) to the south—occupied in winter (Harper 1985; Sawyer and Lindzey 1999, 2000; Segerstrom 1997; Seton 1937; see Figure 9.1). Doug McWhirter, a big game biologist with the Wyoming Game and Fish Department in Pinedale (personal communication, 1994), indicates that the Trappers Point site is located directly on a 1.6-km (1-mi)-wide migration bottleneck known as the Cora Y, through which pronghorn (and mule deer *[Odocoileus hemionus]*) move back and forth between their winter and summer ranges (Figure 9.2). The Cora Y is a natural bottleneck restricted on the southwest by the Green River riparian complex and on the northeast by the New Fork riparian complex (Sawyer and Lindzey 2000:20).

Direct observations and tracking with radio collars show that pronghorn typically cross the Cora Y bottleneck in late March–late April. Pronghorn follow the edge of snowmelt, moving as quickly as snow conditions allow (Sawyer and Lindzey 1999, 2000). Upward of 1,500–2,000 pronghorn and as many mule deer have crossed this bottleneck in recent years, providing an indication of the quantity of animals utilizing this corridor. As many as 600 pronghorn eventually make the trek across the Gros Ventre Range into the Gros Ventre River Valley and Jackson Hole, crossing through other bottlenecks, some as small as 100 m wide (Segerstrom 1997). These pronghorn typically move out of Jackson Hole in October–December, although their movements are more sporadic and less dependent on snow conditions. Sawyer and Lindzey describe some of the parameters of this migration and other biological characteristics of these pronghorn:

> Migration is an adaptive behavioral strategy that allows animals to avoid resource bottlenecks in temperate regions (Baker 1978) and find greater food resources prior to breeding (Sinclair 1983). Migrations between summer and winter ranges often follow traditional routes that are learned and passed on from mother to young (McCullough 1985). In the case of the GTNP [Grand Teton National Park] pronghorn it is possible the need to migrate an extremely long distance through difficult terrain has produced a separate population relative to other pronghorn in Wyoming. Anecdotal evidence suggests GTNP pronghorn give birth and mate at least 2 weeks late, which could result in genetic isolation and preclude reproductive success of pronghorn not native to GTNP (Segerstrom 1997). Additionally, fawn:doe ratios in GTNP are generally much lower than other areas, suggesting either 1) many GTNP females are barren or, 2) fawn mortality in GTNP is unusually high. (2000:2)

Wildlife studies of Sublette pronghorn (Harper 1985; Raper et al. 1989; Sawyer and Lindzey 1999, 2000; Segerstrom 1997) indicate that their movements follow seasonal patterns, especially when they travel to and from Jackson Hole. Although the severity of the climate, snowpack, and habitat condition can affect the actual timing of spring and winter migrations, these factors do not appear to result in a change of the route location

(Greenquist 1983; Sawyer and Lindzey 2000; Segerstrom 1997). Prehistoric peoples inhabiting the area would have needed to be quite familiar with pronghorn behavior, habitat, snowpack, and local weather conditions to predict the timing of the annual movements from winter to summer range as the animals crossed the Cora Y and other bottlenecks. The seasonal movement of pronghorn across the Cora Y/Trappers Point locale is a predictable annual event, usually occurring within a period of weeks. When food resources were predictable, and therefore reliable, they were likely to become a regular part of a prehistoric hunter-gatherer's diet and to influence settlement and subsistence, especially if the resource is high value, such as large game (Winterhalder and Smith 1981). The pronghorn remains at Trappers Point seem to verify this situation, at least during the Early Archaic period. The identification of three other bottlenecks along the pronghorn migration course into Jackson Hole (Sawyer and Lindzey 1999, 2000; Segerstrom 1997) provides the opportunity to search for other archaeological sites that may have coincided with the interception of these animals at different points along this route. If such sites are discovered and they contain well-preserved faunal remains, then additional details on the antiquity, continuity, and location of pronghorn migration will be available for study when considering management and conservation issues surrounding modern migrations.

Prehistoric Migration Patterns

Juxtaposition of the Trappers Point site with the Cora Y bottleneck begs a question: What is the relationship, if any, between modern pronghorn winter/summer ranges and other known prehistoric pronghorn-kill/processing sites? Sanders and Wedel (1999) have used three sites within the Sublette herd unit to answer this question. The sites are Boar's Tusk (48SW1373; see Fisher and Frison 2000), Eden-Farson (48SW304; see Frison 1971), and Gailiun (48SU1156; see Lubinski 1997; Figure 9.1). In contrast to Trappers Point, all three are late, ranging from the late prehistoric into the protohistoric period (ca. 1500–150 B.P.). All have fall–winter seasonality estimates (Lubinski 1997) and coincide with crucial pronghorn winter or yearlong ranges (Figure 9.1).

The correlation of these three sites with migration routes is less dramatic than that for Trappers Point. The former three are positioned where modern herds of pronghorn winter for several months and thus may not represent short-term locations used to intercept seasonally migrating pronghorn.

Prehistoric groups likely took advantage of the local terrain, habitats, and pronghorn behavior to facilitate hunting during all seasons because similar situations have been noted at the other prehistoric pronghorn-kill/processing and -trapping locales within southwestern Wyoming (Sanders and Wedel 1999). Wildlife-distribution maps produced in Wyoming and other western states by local wildlife agencies thus provide data to consider when interpreting prehistoric site locations in terms of function and land-use patterns. Conversely, wildlife agencies can utilize zooarchaeological data to establish the antiquity of the migration routes and ranges of specific wildlife taxa.

PRONGHORN SIZE REDUCTION

Fused pronghorn limb bones from Trappers Point were compared with samples from the late-prehistoric/protohistoric Eden-Farson site, the Late Pleistocene Natural Trap Cave in northern Wyoming, and three modern Wyoming samples (Adams et al. 1999). The modern samples included the University of Wyoming general comparative collection, a natural winter kill from Como Bluff in southeastern Wyoming, and hunter kills from the Green River Basin. The Como Bluff sample comprises 17 females and five males. Females range in age from 1.75 to 7.75 years (4.46 average), whereas males range from 2.75 to 6.75 years (4.55 average), indicating that the sample was derived from mature adults. The University of Wyoming sample was obtained primarily from eastern and central Wyoming and mostly consists of males; age data are unavailable. The modern Green River Basin sample was obtained by the Wyoming Game and Fish Department from hunters who stopped at game check stations within the Sublette herd unit. No age or sex characteristics are available, but the sample is thought to represent mature males and females.

Recall that the stratum V pronghorn are dominated by the one–three-year-old age classes (Figure 9.3). The fact that only a few male horn cores were present, along with the remains of eight fetuses, indicates a prevalence of female pronghorn. This suggests that the stratum V pronghorn are not overrepresented by large, old males. The modern samples providing bone-size data are believed to comprise a range of ages and sexes similar to the Trappers Point sample.

Pronghorn, unlike many other North American ungulates (Guthrie 1984a, 1984b), do not seem to have been represented by exceptionally large individuals during the Late Pleistocene, though some Natural Trap specimens are a bit larger than some modern specimens (Adams et al. 1999; Chorn et al. 1988). It is noteworthy, then, that the Trappers Point pronghorn calcanei are 3.2–4 percent larger than those from Natural Trap Cave. Interestingly, the Trappers Point bones are anywhere from 3.3 to 8.0 percent larger than specimens from the late-prehistoric/protohistoric Eden-Farson site, and they are anywhere from 3.4 to 8.5 percent larger than the modern comparative samples (Table 9.2). It is not known if this size difference is partially or wholly a function of variation in forage quality and quantity or exactly how forage was influenced by the xeric Early Archaic climate. Although reasons for the large size of the Trappers Point bones are unknown, available data suggest a possibility. The modern Sublette herd pronghorn as represented by the Green River Basin sample seem to have a slightly larger body size than pronghorn in southeastern Wyoming as represented by the Como Bluff sample; metatarsals of the former are closer in size to the Trappers Point specimens than are calcanei of the latter (Table 9.2). Perhaps the explanation for this difference also accounts for the large size of the prehistoric Trappers Point bones.

The possibility for genetic isolation is noted in Sawyer and Lindzey's (2000) statement quoted above indicating that the pronghorn migrating into Jackson Hole might be a separate biological or genetic population, given differences in breeding and birthing timing and rates. Radio-collar data indicate, however, that Jackson Hole pronghorn do not demonstrate a strong fidelity to return to the same summer range and instead intermingle with other Sublette herds (Sawyer and Lindzey 2000). Variation in fidelity to summer range does not support the suggestion that Jackson Hole pronghorn are genetically unique or isolated.

The Sublette and other herd units are biological populations with approximately 10 percent inflow–outflow of herd members in any given year (Doug McWhirter, personal communication, 1993), which precludes genetic uniqueness. Nonetheless, the larger body size of the Early Archaic Trappers Point pronghorn and the modern Sublette herd specimens suggests that some genetic or physiological differences have existed through time for the Sublette herd. A genetic study between Jackson Hole and other Sublette herd pronghorn was initiated in 1996 (Segerstrom 1997:24) but has not yet come to fruition (Hall Sawyer, personal communication, 2002). Our data suggest that a wider study including non-Sublette pronghorn is needed to understand apparent size differences between spatially and temporally isolated populations. This issue might be addressed using prehistoric genetic data derived from zooarchaeological collections (Richards

TABLE 9.2. Proportion by which Trappers Point Pronghorn Skeletal Elements Are Larger than Pronghorn Elements in Other Collections.

Measurement	University of Wyoming	Como Bluff	Green River Basin	Eden-Farson	Natural Trap Cave
Calcaneus GL	7.6	7.6		5.0	4.0
Calcaneus GF	7.3	7.4		5.0	3.2
Metatarsal AP			3.4	4.2	
Metatarsal ML			4.1	7.8	
Metacarpal AP				5.5	
Metacarpal ML				5.5	
Humerus AP				3.3	
Humerus ML	8.5			8.0	

Note: GL = greatest length; GF = greatest length to astragalar facet; AP = greatest anterior–posterior depth; ML = greatest medial–lateral breadth. Adapted from Adams et al. 1999.

et al. 1993), and this possibility further illustrates the relevance of zooarchaeological studies for strengthening analytical conclusions that can guide management decisions.

DISCUSSION

The simultaneous publication of the Trappers Point report (Miller et al. 1999), related popular articles in *Wyoming Wildlife* (Sanders 2000; Sawyer and McWhirter 2000), and pertinent wildlife studies (Sawyer and Lindzey 1999, 2000) has underscored the importance of understanding wildlife-migration corridors. Sawyer and McWhirter point out:

> It's fascinating that this antelope migration has survived for at least 6,000 years and troubling to think that, unless we take steps to protect the tradition, it could one day end. . . . The key will be to maintain as much open, unobstructed, undeveloped land as possible in the specific corridors. We can do this with land acquisitions or exchanges, and land use planning that allows for continued animal movements could be undertaken. In already developed areas, wildlife-friendly fencing could help ease the way for migration. . . . In all of these instances, public awareness of the vital nature of these migration corridors goes a long way toward ensuring their preservation. We've already learned much about these incredible big game migrations in western Wyoming. We hope this knowledge will help preserve these migrations well into the future. (2000:36, 41)

The Trappers Point data have enhanced public awareness of migration corridors. These data also illustrate the time depth of the pronghorn migration corridor through the Cora Y bottleneck, an area of "top management concern because of the current land-use practices and the sheer number of migratory animals that use the area" (Sawyer and Lindzey 1999:18). In response, conservation easements are being developed among land and wildlife agencies, private landholders, and the Nature Conservancy to help preserve migration corridors (Doug McWhirter and Hall Sawyer, personal communications, 2002). Similar preservation programs are being developed by the Wyoming Wildlife Federation (Wyoming Wildlife Federation 2003). As well, the Greater Yellowstone Coalition and Wyoming Outdoor Council have referred to the Trappers Point data in their comments regarding proposed oil and gas developments on nearby wildlife winter ranges (Bureau of Land Management 2000). Based on the historic and prehistoric evidence, they note the importance of preserving wildlife-migration corridors and bottlenecks. Such evidence is critical to developing management recommendations, and only interdisciplinary research is likely to produce the quality of data needed to support any decision. Although it can be argued that the issue of preserving migration corridors would have arisen without the discovery of the Trappers Point site, zooarchaeological data have definitely focused attention on the matter. One notable outcome was the recent, standing-room-only "Ancient Corridors Symposium: Understanding Western Wyoming's Human Impacts on Historic Migration Routes," held in Pinedale, Wyoming, in March 2003. This symposium brought together archaeologists, biologists, conservationists, ranchers, and others, many of whom gave formal presentations on the topic.

The correlation of the zooarchaeological evidence and migration route data suggests predictions of prehistoric site locations related to pronghorn procurement. The four modern bottleneck areas—Cora Y/Trappers Point, Upper Green River/Bridger Teton National Forest boundary, Upper Gros Ventre/Bacon Creek, and the Green River crossing (Sawyer and Lindzey 2000)—provide an opportunity to test the predictions and, once investigated, may reveal previously unsuspected details about stability or changes in the Holocene migration history of pronghorn.

Establishing the antiquity of pronghorn use of Jackson Hole as a summer range requires identifying archaeological sites with datable faunal remains in both Jackson Hole and the Gros Ventre River drainage. Knowing the migration route through the Gros Ventre Range (Segerstrom 1997) narrows the potential search locales that might also contain faunal remains. Intensive survey and test excavations in these bottlenecks are needed to determine whether they were used in a manner similar to Trappers Point. Examination of extant archaeofaunal assemblages from Jackson Hole could also be conducted to determine the presence of pronghorn remains, for they are often lumped into a general deer/sheep/pronghorn category.

Given the pronghorn's adaptation to open sagebrush/grassland habitats, the movement of these animals across the mountains into Jackson Hole seems anomalous. Miller and Sanders (2000) posit that the earliest use of the migration route by pronghorn into Jackson Hole coincided with Early Holocene warming conditions (ca. 9500–5000 B.P.) when tree lines retreated and meadows and grasslands expanded (Eckerle and Hobey 1999; Whitlock 1993). This hypothesis can be evaluated by the discovery of Late Pleistocene and Early Holocene archaeological or paleontological sites that contain pronghorn remains in Jackson Hole or the Gros Ventre River Valley.

Finally, genetic and physiological studies of the Sublette and other extant pronghorn herds should be conducted to establish the uniqueness of the Sublette herd and to help produce an explanation for the large pronghorn bones at Trappers Point. The Trappers Point data indicate that any such study should include non–Sublette herd pronghorn to fully document variation in pronghorn body size. DNA signatures can be sought from prehistoric skeletal assemblages and matched to data obtained from extant herds to establish a measure of genetic similarity.

CONCLUSIONS

The Trappers Point data indicate that the movement across the Cora Y is not a recent phenomenon and underscore the need to protect it, and other bottlenecks and wildlife-migration corridors in general, from recent incursions by residential, oil and gas, and other adverse developments. Wildlife managers and other environmental organizations have been able to use the Trappers Point data to help develop a conservation strategy for pronghorn that summer in the Jackson Hole area as well as for the preservation of wildlife corridors (Hall Sawyer, personal communication, 2002).

On the one hand, wildlife studies and distribution maps help model patterns of prehistoric site locations and functions. On the other hand, the identification and study of archaeological sites along animal-migration routes can reinforce the significance of observations made by wildlife managers and point to the antiquity and continuity of migration corridors.

This interdisciplinary dialogue has lately become much more important because many of these areas are already being impacted by the oil and gas industries, residential developers, and others. This mutually beneficial situation has forged new sets of relationships between archaeological investigators and wildlife managers, whose mutual interest involves understanding the diachronic relationship between human populations and big game species. In fact, it can be argued that interdisciplinary teams should collaborate in the development and review of management recommendations that derive from such research.

Acknowledgments. Excavations at the Trappers Point site were conducted by the Office of the Wyoming State Archaeologist with funding provided by the Wyoming Department of Transportation. The project was under the auspices of the Bureau of Land Management, Pinedale Resource Area. Wildlife scientists who contributed to this project include Hall Sawyer and Fred Lindzey of the Wyoming Cooperative Fish and Wildlife Research Unit at the University of Wyoming and Doug McWhirter, Reg Rothwell, and Dave Lockman of the Wyoming Game and Fish Department, Cheyenne and Pinedale offices. Numerous other individuals and organizations contributed to the original report on which this chapter is based; each of their contributions is appreciated.

10

Ecological Change in Western Utah: Comparisons between a Late Holocene Archaeological Fauna and Modern Small-Mammal Surveys

Dave N. Schmitt

A significant and persistent change in vegetation communities across much of western North America involves invasion by exotic annuals. One of the more prevalent exotic annuals in the Great Basin and other parts of western North America is cheatgrass or downy brome (*Bromus tectorum* [Humphrey and Schupp 2001; Whipple 2001]). Originating in Eurasia and first introduced to western North America in the late 1800s, cheatgrass is a hearty species that gained its modern distribution in western North America by about 1930 because it outcompeted many native plants (Mack 1981, 1984). A number of studies report the effects of this aggressive species on native desert grasses (Humphrey and Schupp 2001); other studies demonstrate how fire regimes have changed in areas that have become dominated by cheatgrass (Billings 1990; Knapp 1995).

On the one hand, there is little information on how *B. tectorum* invasion affects mammalian communities, especially small taxa that depend on native grasses and forbs for food. It is well known, on the other hand, that many variables affect small-mammal populations. Those variables include fire, shifts in precipitation patterns, and changes in plant food availability (Brown 1973; Brown and Harney 1993; Halford 1981; Price and Waser 1984; Whitford 1976). Studies have shown that small-mammal density and diversity decrease when annual grasses gain in dominance and vegetation communities become more homogeneous (Ports and Ports 1989; Sousa 1984). Further, dense grass cover can impede animal movements, which may affect breeding success and population size (Gano and Rickard 1982). These observations lead me to suspect that the invasion of cheatgrass has had significant influences on small-mammal faunas.

Here I compare zooarchaeological data with modern vegetation and small-mammal survey data to investigate recent changes in regional biotic communities. All data sets come from the U.S. Army Dugway Proving Ground in western Utah. The zooarchaeological data comprise a large sample of Late Holocene mammalian remains recovered from Camels Back Cave. These skeletal remains provide data on local small mammals in an environmental context analogous to modern conditions but represent a time prior to the Euro-American introduction of exotic annuals (Schmitt 1999). As such, the represented fauna provides a pre-Columbian baseline against which the modern fauna may be compared in order to assess the influence of recent anthropogenic habitat change on faunas. Data from small-mammal surveys conducted in Dugway Valley during the 1950s and 1990s are compared with the pre-Columbian small-mammal fauna. I focus specifically on the effects of expanding *B. tectorum* habitats on small-mammal species richness and diversity.

STUDY AREA

Dugway Proving Ground is a U.S. Department of Defense installation encompassing 2,100 km^2 across northern Juab County and southern Tooele County in western Utah. The installation lies entirely within the basin and range topography of the Bonneville Basin, and most local geomorphological features are the result of Pleistocene Lake Bonneville. Although various habitats occur in the area, most of Dugway comprises alkali playa flats and playa margin dunes. Modern vegetation in these areas consists largely of low desert scrub communities containing greasewood *(Sarcobatus vermiculatus),* horsebrush (*Tetradymia* sp.), saltbush (*Atriplex* sp.), and seepweed (*Suaeda* sp.); some low dunes contain big sagebrush *(Artemisia tridentata),* rabbitbrush (*Chrysothamnus* sp.), and Indian ricegrass *(Oryzopsis hymenoides).* Cheatgrass also occurs throughout the area and is especially abundant along dune margins and low alluvial fans in association with scattered greasewood and saltbush.

Camels Back Ridge is in the southeastern portion of Dugway Proving Ground in southern Tooele County. The ridge is an isolated desert island consisting of two north–south-trending fault-block mountain ridges composed of an Upper Cambrian limestone (Hintze 1980). The larger, northern ridge crests at 1,677 m, and the southern riser peaks at 1,517 m. Both ridges are surrounded by low dunes and vast alkali playa flats containing xerophytic shrubs (mostly greasewood) and a dense cheatgrass understory.

Camels Back Cave is a small wave-cut chamber situated at 1,380 m in the northern toe of the southern ridge (Figure 10.1). The ceiling and walls are coated in spots by tufa deposited during the Post-Provo regressive phase of Pleistocene Lake Bonneville approximately 13,000 years ago (Currey 1990; Oviatt et al. 1992). Archaeological excavations have encountered stratified deposits spanning most of the Holocene (7500 B.P.–ca. A.D. 1930). These deposits represent a series of short-term human occupations separated by periods of human absence (Schmitt and Madsen 2001; Schmitt et al. 1994; Schmitt et al. 2002). Partially digested small-mammal bones deposited in carnivore scat and egested raptor pellets occurred throughout the deposits and were particularly abundant in strata that contained no evidence of human occupation. The accumulated rodent remains afford a unique view of the local pre-Columbian mammalian fauna.

MATERIALS AND METHODS

An entryway trench excavated at the mouth of the cave encountered a stratigraphic layer lacking evidence of human occupation approximately 30 cm below the modern ground surface. Identified as Stratum XVIIIa, this unit contained thousands of small-animal remains, many of which were deposited in pellets cast by raptors roosting on the rock face above the cave's entrance (Schmitt 1999; Schmitt and Madsen 2001). Stratum XVIIIa overlies a horizon that contained ceramics and flaked-stone projectile points indicative of human occupation during the Fremont Period (A.D. 500–A.D. 1300). A radiocarbon assay of charcoal from a fire hearth on this underlying horizon returned a date of 790 ± 50 B.P. (Beta 94197). A second date of 470 ± 50 B.P. (Beta 94198) was extracted from a charcoal lens at the mouth of the cave overlying Stratum XVIIIa. These two dates bracket the deposition age of the Stratum XVIIIa small mammals.

Excavations in the entryway trench recovered approximately 3.5 m^2 of the Stratum XVIIIa deposits from a series of contiguous 50 × 50-cm units. All of the excavated matrix was passed through nested 0.64-cm (1/4-in) and 0.32-cm (1/8-in) mesh screens. The faunal remains from all 0.64 cm collections and two 0.32 cm units were examined as part of the archaeological investigations, and six additional 0.32 cm units were examined as part of an auxiliary study to increase the sample size, obtain rare species, and provide a more accurate portrait of the local small-mammal commu-

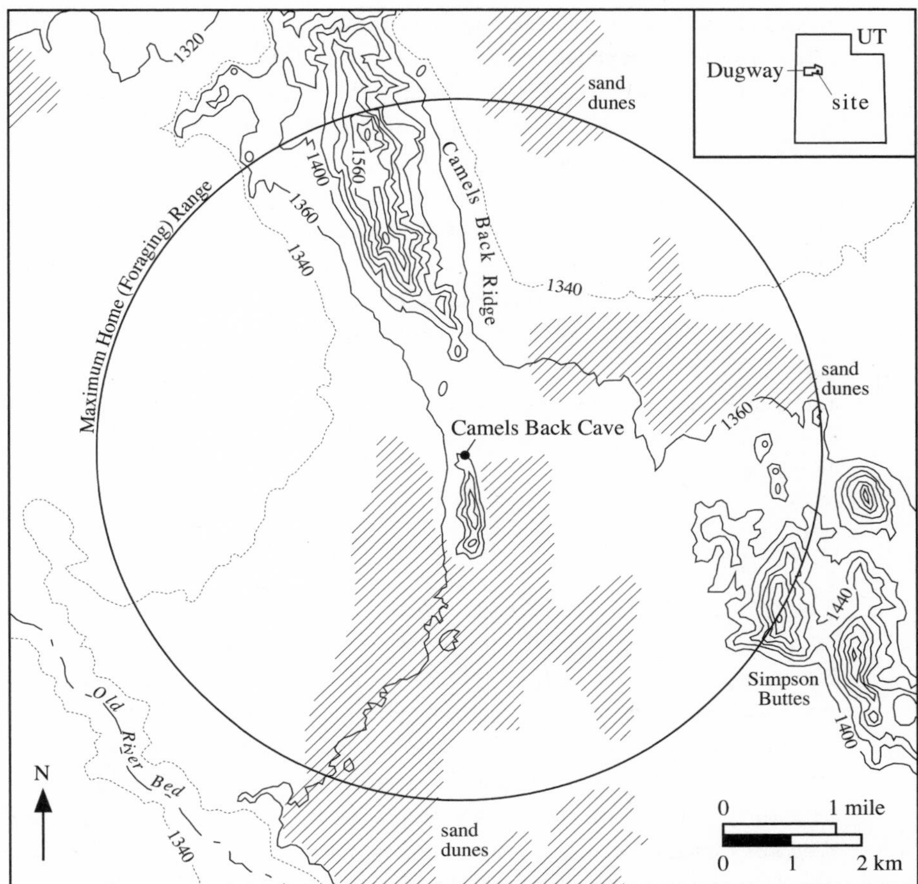

Figure 10.1. Location of Camels Back Cave on southern Camels Back Ridge, Tooele County, Utah, and the maximum home (foraging) range of local raptorial birds (*Aquila chrysaetos* [after Smith 1971]) centered on the cave. Contour interval is 40 m; supplemental contour is 20 m.

nity. Each 0.32 cm bone aggregate was split into two equal halves; one half was sorted and analyzed, and the other was bagged and labeled for museum curation. Animal remains were identified by comparison with osteological collections housed at the University of Utah Archaeological Center, Salt Lake City, and Conner Museum, Washington State University, Pullman (Schmitt 1999). The number of identified specimens (NISP) per taxon is used here to measure taxonomic abundance (Grayson 1984).

Two modern mammal surveys were conducted in the Woodbury Plots, each over a three-year period during the spring and summer months

(AGEISS Environmental, Inc. 1997, 1998; Carpenter and Arjo 1999; Vest 1962). Both surveys focused on trapping small mammals in a variety of plant communities. AGEISS Environmental, Inc.'s 1996–1998 survey involved replicating the methods and objectives of Vest's 1950s research and included relocating and trapping the same dune and greasewood communities investigated by Vest. Because the number of trap nights varied between 20 and eight, I follow AGEISS (1998) and use only the number of animals caught in trap nights one–eight to allow comparisons of taxonomic presences and abundances. Similarly, the number of vegetation communities sampled varied between eight (AGEISS 1997; Vest 1962) and three (AGEISS 1998), but I use only small-mammal data from surveys in the greasewood and stabilized dune plots here, for these communities dominated the Camels Back Cave vicinity throughout the Middle and Late Holocene.

THE CAMELS BACK CAVE SMALL MAMMALS

The Stratum XVIIIa faunal assemblage contains over 2,800 NISP (Table 10.1), representing at least 16 species of small mammals. A few bones represent coyote (*Canis latrans;* NISP = 1), kit fox (*Vulpes velox* [= *macrotis*]; NISP = 2), and mountain sheep (*Ovis canadensis;* NISP = 2). Auxiliary 0.32-cm mesh collections produced the remains of five species of rodents not found in the archaeological sample (*Tamias* cf. *minimus, Microdipodops megacephalus, Onychomys leucogaster, Reithrodontomys megalotis,* and Microtinae [for common names of small mammals, see Table 10.1]). These auxiliary samples also increased the proportions of *Ammospermophilus leucurus* and *Neotoma lepida.* Rank-order abundances of taxa in the archaeological and auxiliary samples from 0.32-cm mesh are correlated (Table 10.1; Spearman's rho = 0.85, p = 0.0001) and together provide a large and unique assemblage of the local small-mammal fauna dating to approximately 600 B.P.

Overall, the Late Holocene mammals from Camels Back Cave represent a "typical" low desert fauna characteristic of most modern alkali flat/dune habitats in the eastern Great Basin. The most abundant species include *Spermophilus mollis* (= *townsendii*), *Lepus* cf. *californicus,* and *Dipodomys* sp. The first two taxa are well adapted to open, arid environments (Best 1996; Hall 1946; Rickart 1987), and their abundance in the low-elevation, Late Holocene assemblage from Camels Back Cave is not surprising. Large numbers of *Dipodomys* (and additional heteromyids) were anticipated in the Stratum XVIIIa aggregate because these animals are

TABLE 10.1. Number of Identified Small-Mammal Specimens by Taxon Recovered from 0.64-cm and 0.32-cm Mesh Archaeological Samples (AS) and the Auxiliary Study, Stratum XVIIIa, Camels Back Cave, Utah.

Species	Common Name	AS 0.64 cm	AS 0.32 cm	Auxiliary Study (0.32 cm)	Total
Vespertilionidae					
Antrozous pallidus	pallid bat		1		1
Leporidae					
Sylvilagus sp.	cottontail	8	5	6	19
Lepus cf. *californicus*	black-tailed jackrabbit	318	48	96	462
Sciuridae					
Tamias cf. *minimus*	least chipmunk			2	2
Ammospermophilus leucurus	white-tailed antelope squirrel	1	1	7	9
Spermophilus sp.	ground squirrel	291	372	746	1,409
Spermophilus mollis	Townsend's ground squirrel	71	20	52	143
Geomyidae					
Thomomys sp.	pocket gopher	36	39	60	135
Thomomys bottae	Botta's pocket gopher	6		1	7
Heteromyidae					
Perognathus longimembris	little pocket mouse		4	9	13
Microdipodops megacephalus	dark kangaroo mouse			1	1
Dipodomys sp.	kangaroo rat	30	167	381	578
Dipodomys microps	chisel-toothed kangaroo rat	2	11	7	20
Muridae					
Peromyscus sp.	white-footed mouse		13	4	17
Peromyscus maniculatus	deer mouse		4	9	13
Onychomys leucogaster	northern grasshopper mouse			1	1
Neotoma lepida	desert woodrat	3	2	13	18
Reithrodontomys megalotis	western harvest mouse			1	1
Microtinae	vole			1	1
Mustelidae					
Mustela sp.	weasel		1		1
Mustela frenata	long-tailed weasel	1		3	4
Total		767	688	1,400	2,855

Note: See Schmitt and Lupo 2001.

common residents of arid contexts and typically represent a predominant species in North American deserts (Brown and Harney 1993; Grayson 2000b). Additional rodents include *Ammospermophilus leucurus, Thomomys bottae, Peromyscus maniculatus,* and *Neotoma lepida,* all of which are known to inhabit low-elevation contexts across most of the Bonneville Basin (Durrant 1952).

SMALL-MAMMAL SURVEY DATA

Small-mammal surveys conducted during the mid-1950s (Vest 1962) and in 1996–1998 (AGEISS 1998) provide quantitative data on modern faunas at Dugway. Table 10.2 presents the results of trap nights one–eight in local stabilized dune and greasewood communities. Vest (1962) reports nine species trapped in stabilized dune communities, whereas AGEISS's more recent survey reports ten. Except for the large numbers of *Tamias minimus* reported by Vest, both studies captured abundant *Dipodomys* and *Perognathus longimembris* and found *Onychomys leucogaster* and *Reithrodontomys megalotis* to be common. Rank-order abundances of the small mammals captured in these two dune surveys are correlated (rho = 0.52, p = 0.05), and Shannon Diversity indexes for the 1955–1957 study and the more recent survey reveal only a small decline in taxonomic diversity (AGEISS 1998). The most salient difference between the 1955–1957 small-mammal study in stabilized dunes and the 1996–1998 data is a marked decline in the number of individuals captured. Although species richness has changed only slightly, AGEISS's 1990s surveys in stabilized dunes captured less than one-third as many individuals as were caught in 1955–1957.

Comparison of taxonomic presences and abundances in greasewood communities discloses some substantial differences. Eight species were caught in the greasewood plots during the 1955–1957 survey, whereas AGEISS (1998) reports only six. Vest (1962) reports abundant *Ammospermophilus leucurus, Peromyscus maniculatus,* and *Perognathus longimembris;* AGEISS caught large numbers of *Reithrodontomys megalotis* and *P. maniculatus,* no *A. leucurus,* and only four *P. longimembris* (Table 10.2). Rank-order abundances of individuals captured per taxon are not correlated (rho = 0.08, p = 0.84), and the Shannon Diversity index for the earlier investigations is greater than that for the 1990s surveys and indicates an overall decline in species diversity over the past 40 years (Carpenter and Arjo 1999).

TABLE 10.2. Number of Individuals Captured in Stabilized Dune and Greasewood Communities during the 1955–1957 and 1996–1998 Small-Mammal Surveys at Dugway Proving Ground, Utah.

	1955–1957		1996–1998	
Species	Dune	Greasewood	Dune	Greasewood
Ammospermophilus leucurus	5	44	1	4
Tamias minimus	104	1	0	0
Spermophilus mollis	0	0	2	0
Perognathus longimembris	129	20	30	0
Microdipodops megacephalus	60	0	4	0
Dipodomys ordii	179	15	87	0
Dipodomys microps	181	1	24	7
Peromyscus maniculatus	57	42	18	27
Peromyscus truei	0	0	1	1
Onychomys leucogaster	11	0	19	0
Neotoma lepida	0	1	0	1
Reithrodontomys megalotis	14	3	41	50
Total	740	127	227	90
Shannon Diversity Index	2.66	2.13	2.53	1.53

Note: See AGEISS Environmental, Inc. 1998; Vest 1962.

DISCUSSION

20th-Century Changes

Annual precipitation affects the productivity of plants, which, in turn, influences the food supply available to small mammals (Brown 1973; Grayson 1998; Rosenzweig 1968). When rainfall is below average, germination and seed production by perennial and annual plants decline and eventually cause reductions in the abundance and diversity of small mammals that eat seeds (Whitford 1976). This is especially the case for heteromyids because these animals feed almost exclusively on the seeds of native desert grasses and forbs (Brown and Harney 1993). Interestingly, when compared with the relatively low annual precipitation that fell from 1954 through 1957, the 1990s decline in granivorous Heteromyidae (Table 10.2) corresponds with an increase in precipitation (Figure 10.2). Though heteromyids were caught in stabilized dune and greasewood communities during both small-mammal surveys at Dugway, the 1996–1998 survey shows a decline in their abundances. Small-mammal abundance and diver-

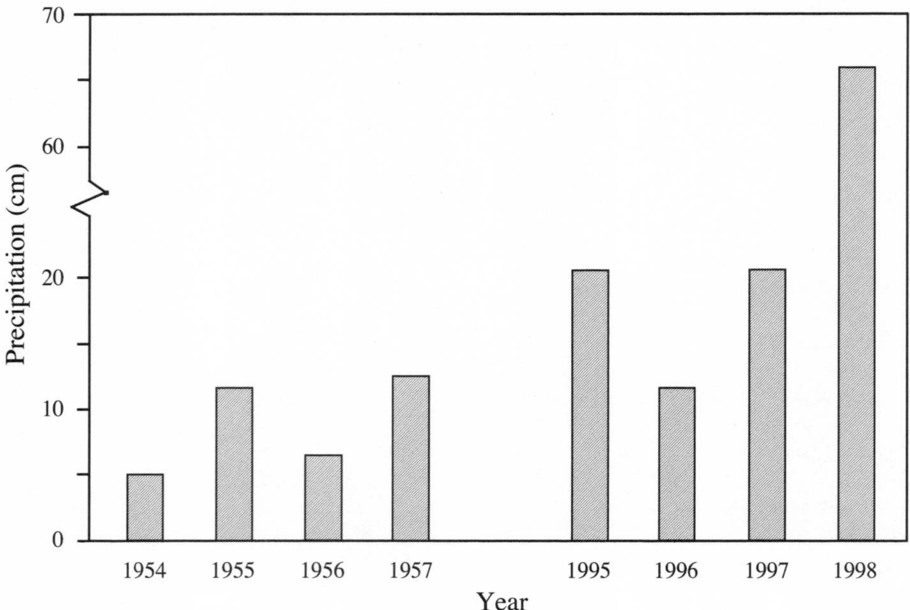

Figure 10.2. Precipitation (cm) from January through August 1954–1957 and 1995–1998 at Dugway Proving Ground, Utah (adopted from AGEISS 1998:6–7).

sity should have increased in response to increasing rainfall and productivity during the late 1990s.

Recent changes in the composition of small-mammal populations may have been caused by changes in local vegetation communities. One of the most significant changes in regional vegetation has been the historic introduction and continuing expansion of exotic annuals, notably *Bromus tectorum*. AGEISS (1997, 1998) observes that cheatgrass was the dominant exotic annual in all plots surveyed, that it was markedly abundant in greasewood communities where it dominated intershrub spaces, and that *B. tectorum* cover was significantly greater than that reported by Vest (1962). The overall decline in mammalian species diversity and abundance in Dugway greasewood plots during the late 1990s suggests that the expansion of exotic annuals is contributing to the deterioration of native flora and fauna (AGEISS 1998; Carpenter and Arjo 1999). For the northern Lakeside Mountains of western Utah, Grayson et al. (1996) report similarly low species richness and abundance in a xerophytic shrub community containing dense cheatgrass (June 1995; 21 individuals representing four taxa in 270 trap nights), and it appears that this same phenomenon is occurring elsewhere in the region.

The types and abundances of rodents captured in the 1996–1998 greasewood plot surveys also offer evidence for the recent expansion of cheatgrass. Most notable are the small numbers of heteromyids and *Ammospermophilus leucurus* and the large numbers of *Peromyscus maniculatus* and *Reithrodontomys megalotis* (Table 10.2). Several studies report that *P. maniculatus* and *R. megalotis* characteristically inhabit and often flourish in thick grass and exotic annual cover (Foster and Gaines 1991; Larrison and Johnson 1973), whereas heteromyids and *A. leucurus* prefer open habitats and are generally sparse in areas containing dense grass (Brown 1973; Larrison and Johnson 1973; Zeveloff and Collett 1988). In the 1996–1998 survey of stabilized dune plots, AGEISS notes that *B. tectorum* was present but that "dunes had the least amount of percent cover of *B. tectorum* and it was very patchy, unlike the other plots" (1998:24). In contrast to the case in the greasewood plots where diversity was low, mammalian diversity in the 1990s in stabilized dunes was highest, including a relatively rich and abundant heteromyid population (Table 10.2). This compares favorably with the stabilized dune species composition reported by Vest (1962).

Prehistoric–Historic Changes

Although species richness values are similar, there are some differences between the pre-Columbian fauna and the modern survey data in terms of the species represented and their abundances (Table 10.3). Rank-order abundances of small-mammal remains in Stratum XVIIIa are not correlated with the number of individuals reported by Vest (1962; rho = –0.03, p = 0.46), nor are they correlated with those reported by AGEISS (1998; rho = –0.15, p = 0.30). For example, *Reithrodontomys megalotis* are rare in the archaeological assemblage but are especially common in the 1990 surveys. As these mice prefer moist habitats (Hall 1946), the recent increase in *R. megalotis* may be in part caused by the large amount of precipitation that fell in the late 1990s. The most notable shift in taxonomic abundances involves the low frequency of *Spermophilus mollis* in the modern surveys and the large numbers of *S. mollis* in Stratum XVIIIa. In fact, *Spermophilus* represent 54 percent of the cave's identified small mammals (Table 10.1). Because modern trapping at Dugway was designed for nocturnal small mammals, the paucity of diurnal animals such as *Spermophilus* captured by Vest and AGEISS may represent a methodological

TABLE 10.3. Abundances (Number of Identified Specimens [NISP]) of Selected Small Mammals from Stratum XVIIIa in Camels Back Cave and the Number of Individuals (NIND) Captured in Greasewood and Stabilized Dune Communities (Combined) during the 1955–1957 and 1996–1998 Small-Mammal Surveys at Dugway Proving Ground, Utah.

	Stratum XVIIIa		1955–1957		1996–1998	
Species	NISP	Rank	NIND	Rank	NIND	Rank
Ammospermophilus leucurus	9	6	49	7	5	7
Tamias minimus	2	8	105	4	0	12.5
Spermophilus mollis	143	1	0	12	2	9.5
Thomomys bottae	7	7	0	12	0	12.5
Perognathus longimembris	13	4.5	149	3	30	5
Microdipodops megacephalus	1	10	60	6	4	8
Dipodomys ordii	0	12.5	194	1	87	2
Dipodomys microps	20	2	182	2	31	4
Peromyscus maniculatus	13	4.5	99	5	45	3
Peromyscus truei	0	12.5	0	12	2	9.5
Onychomys leucogaster	1	10	11	9	19	6
Neotoma lepida	18	3	1	10	1	11
Reithrodontomys megalotis	1	10	17	8	91	1
Total	228		867		317	

consequence rather than a decline in local populations. However, *Spermophilus* are characteristically active during the early morning hours (Rickart 1987), and it is surprising that so few individuals were captured, especially in the spring.

Additional differences between the archaeological fauna and modern survey records include variability in the presences and abundances of *Neotoma lepida* and *Dipodomys ordii*. Specimens of the former species are relatively abundant in the cave assemblage, but only two individuals are reported in the two surveys (Table 10.3). Although these data may reflect a local decline, *N. lepida* typically inhabit regional rock outcrops and caves for house construction and protection from predators (Hall 1946; Llewellyn 1981), thus the scarcity of *N. lepida* in the open greasewood and dune survey plots may be a result of recovery context. The lack of *D. ordii* in Stratum XVIIIa and the large numbers of this taxon reported by Vest (1962) and AGEISS (1998) also may be related to contextual differences. As shown in Table 10.2, most (95 percent) modern *D. ordii* were trapped in stabilized dune communities containing *Artemisia,* a habitat characteristically preferred by the species (Grayson 2000b). Stabilized dunes with *Artemisia* occur in the Camels Back Cave vicinity, but greasewood flats are dominant, and most of the surrounding dunes support *Sarcobatus vermiculatus* and *Atriplex canescens* with little or no *Artemisia*. As a result, the lack of *D. ordii* in Stratum XVIIIa is probably a reflection of local vegetation types.

Diminishing numbers of heteromyids (Figure 10.3) suggest that *Bromus tectorum* is replacing native grasses and forbs and that this replacement may be resulting in significant modification of the local small-mammal communities. As discussed above, heteromyids rely heavily on seeds produced by native desert grasses and forbs and prefer areas containing a relatively sparse grass understory. Figure 10.3 presents the proportion of Heteromyidae in Stratum XVIIIa and the two modern surveys, as well as late Fremont Period Stratum XVIIc at Camels Back Cave and Stratum XVII at Homestead Cave (ca. 950 B.P.) in the Lakeside Mountains (Grayson 2000a: table XV; Madsen 2000:39–40). The proportion of Heteromyidae for each is calculated as the total number of heteromyids divided by the total number of identified rodents; specimens identified to genera in the cave assemblages are included, and large sciurids are excluded from each assemblage because no diurnal trapping was conducted. Although the time-series analysis in Figure 10.3 has few data points, it suggests that the region supported a large and strikingly stable heteromyid population between A.D. 1000 and the late 1950s, and it illustrates a substantial decline in heteromyids over the past 40 years. This may be significant. Heteromyids are a keystone species of North American deserts and play important roles in the dispersal and germination of the seeds of native plants. The low numbers of heteromyids in the most recent surveys appear to be a consequence of increased cheatgrass, especially in local greasewood communities, and their status should be more fully investigated at Dugway (AGEISS 1998) and other Great Basin contexts containing abundant *B. tectorum*.

Future Changes

In a recent study, Reinhart et al. (2001) examine the affects of introduced flora and fauna on grizzly bears *(Ursus arctos horribilis)* in Yellowstone National Park and find that most exotic species are associated with detrimental impacts, including the loss of high-quality grizzly bear foods. In addition, they note that although these large carnivores have coexisted with exotic species for many years, the "potential negative impacts have only begun to unfold" (2001:286). It appears that similarly recent impacts are beginning to unfold in eastern Great Basin greasewood communities. The

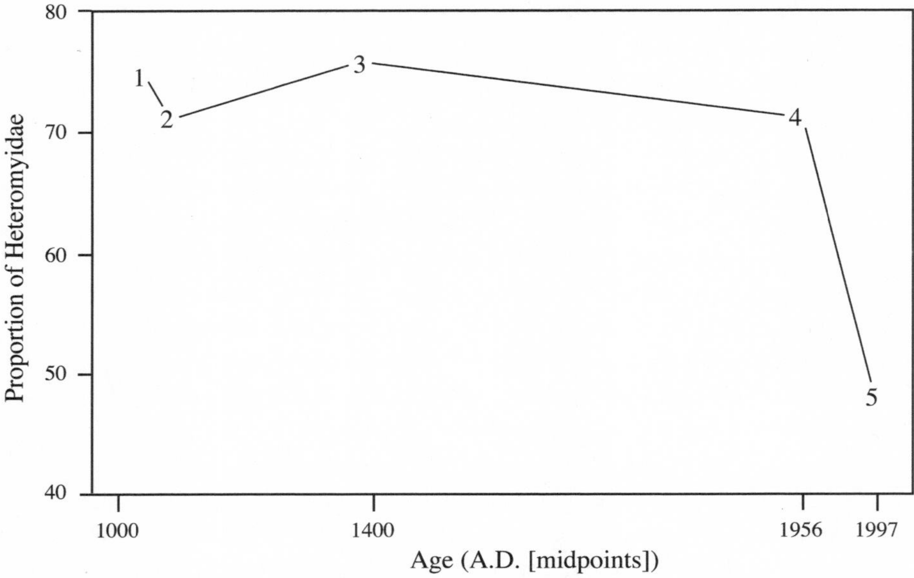

Figure 10.3. Relative proportions of the small-mammal fauna contributed by Heteromyidae in Late Holocene deposits in regional cave sites (percent of number of identified specimens of stratum rodent remains) and in the modern surveys (percent of captured rodents)—1: Stratum XVII, Homestead Cave (Grayson 2000a); 2: Stratum XVIIc, Camels Back Cave (Schmitt and Lupo 2001); 3: Stratum XVIIIa, Camels Back Cave (Table 10.1); 4: 1955–1957 survey (Vest 1962); 5: 1996–1998 survey (AGEISS Environmental, Inc. 1998). Large diurnal Sciuridae are not included.

results of the modern surveys at Dugway show decreases in small-mammal abundances and diversity that correspond with, and seem to be a result of, expanding *Bromus tectorum* habitats. The net result is a decrease in local biodiversity.

It is likely that the influences of *B. tectorum* will ultimately move up the food chain and that the local populations of terrestrial carnivores and raptorial birds that rely on small mammals for food will decline. Many canids and raptors are opportunistic foragers that pursue a wide variety of prey (MacCracken and Hansen 1987; Sherrod 1978; Smith et al. 1972), so as small-mammal density and diversity decline, so too will the food options available to these predators. For example, Woffinden and Murphy (1977) have investigated ferruginous hawk *(Buteo regalis)* population dynamics during a pronounced prey decline in nearby Cedar Valley, Utah. They observed marked declines in fledging success, at least one incident of death by starvation, and a steady decline in the number of nesting pairs (see also Murphy 1975). If *B. tectorum* expansion continues to diminish the types and abundances of native grasses and small mammals at Dugway, it is reasonable to assume that local mammalian and avian carnivore populations will ultimately wane, resulting in yet another kind of decrease in local biodiversity.

SUMMARY AND CONCLUSIONS

The small-mammal taxonomic richness in the Camels Back Cave fauna and in two modern surveys is similar. There are, however, a number of differences in the respective taxonomic compositions. *Spermophilus mollis* represent the most abundant taxon in the archaeological sample, so it is alarming that very few *Spermophilus* were captured in the modern surveys. Similarly, heteromyids display stable abundances until the 20th century, when they went into steep decline. The cause(s) of the declines in both taxa must be determined if recovery to pre-1950s conditions is desired. We must know if the cause was anthropogenic or natural because if it was the latter, then we are perhaps observing a natural cycle or chaotic event of nature, and thus no restoration efforts would be warranted (Landres 1992). The two 20th-century mammal surveys suggest that the change in the small-mammal fauna at Dugway is the result of a recent event—the invasion of cheatgrass—brought about by human causes. This suggestion receives strong support from the pre-Columbian zooarchaeological record at Camels Back Cave.

Local greasewood communities containing a dense *Bromus tectorum* understory witnessed a marked decrease in Heteromyidae, an overall decline in species diversity, and an increase only in *Bromus*-tolerant *Reithrodontomys megalotis*. The homogenization of local vegetation communities has been shown to often result in the homogenization of small-mammal communities; both constitute a form of decline in biodiversity (Germano and Lawhead 1986; Ports and Ports 1989). Because cheatgrass can outcompete a number of native grasses and forbs, it appears to be suppressing native floral diversity and, in turn, the small mammals that depend on native flora for food (Gano and Rickard 1982). Declines in small mammals will ultimately influence local terrestrial and avian predator populations that depend on small mammals for food, and it is possible that the overall ecological degradation may become severe.

Comparisons of the pre-Columbian faunal assemblage with modern survey data provide no definitive information regarding the influence of modern human activities on the local mammalian fauna. Regardless, it would be unreasonable to suppose that human activities have not affected mammalian communities at Dugway. Indeed, I assume that animals residing in a construction zone or military training area will witness detrimental (if not fatal) impacts, but most human activities are restricted to certain locations and occur in relatively confined spaces that encompass a very small portion of Dugway Proving Ground. Although various human activities have occurred and will continue to occur at Dugway, their overall impact on animal communities in most contexts seems negligible. The single notable exception appears to be the historic introduction of *Bromus tectorum* to Utah's west desert. The full biological impacts of that introduction are only now being learned (Carpenter and Arjo 1999), and I have shown here how that learning can be enhanced by study of the zooarchaeological record.

Acknowledgments. The Camels Back Cave excavations and analyses were supported by the Dugway Proving Ground Directorate of Environmental Programs and the Utah Geological Survey. Special thanks go to Wendy Arjo, Lance Carpenter, and Adam Kozlowski for conducting the small-mammal surveys and providing valuable insights and to Kathy Callister, Donald Grayson, Karen Lupo, Lee Lyman, David Madsen, Steven Plunkett, Rachel Quist, and David Rhode for useful comments and support. Portions of this chapter were presented (with Lupo and Madsen) at the Great Basin Anthropological Conference in Ogden, Utah, in October 2000.

11

Zooarchaeological Evidence of the Native Ichthyofauna of the Roanoke River in North Carolina and Virginia

THOMAS R. WHYTE

Efforts to conserve native species and their communities require knowledge of natural historical distributions. Ichthyologists have traditionally relied on modern sampling and sometimes questionable historical accounts to determine historical distributions of fish species. Knowledge of earlier distributions and the relationships among eastern North American drainages has thus occasionally been supplemented by paleontological evidence (Hocutt et al. 1986). More recently, researchers have recognized the value of zooarchaeological evidence to establish original Holocene distributions (Jenkins and Burkhead 1994). In prehistoric Holocene times, fish played an important role in the diets of Indians of the eastern United States. Fish bones have been found in both the earliest and the most recent prehistoric archaeological sites, both coastal and inland, in the region (McNett 1985; Whyte 1997). These remains permit documentation of not only prehistoric human subsistence and settlement but also prehistoric piscine geography (Dickinson 1982; Manzano and Dickinson 1991; VanDerwarker 2001; Whyte 1994). The latter can serve as an independent source of data on historical zoogeography extending farther into the past than written records as well as a test of the accuracy of such records. Such data are also potentially important to fish conservation and management. I illustrate this here by considering two issues.

Modern conservation efforts concerning fish on the Atlantic Slope of the eastern United States focus on diadromous species and the effects of dams on spawning migrations. Zooarchaeological records of preimpoundment distributions and spawning migration limits are now recognized as important considerations when relicensing dams because historic records of such may be variously incomplete, inaccurate, or unavailable. The first issue I address is that the native status of the largemouth bass *(Micropterus salmoides)* on the southern Atlantic Slope has been controversial because of the early historic stocking of this species (Jenkins and Burkhead 1994). Zooarchaeological data presented here resolve this controversy. The second issue addressed takes advantage of the fact that prehistoric data may reveal whether endangered taxa are threatened as a result of natural causes or anthropogenic ones (see chap. 2). The example I discuss concerns efforts to establish populations of Roanoke bass *(Ambloplites cavifrons)* in seemingly ideal habitats within its native river system. These efforts have, for unclear reasons, failed (Jenkins and Burkhead 1994). I propose that zooarchaeological data indicate that this taxon has a competitor in the form of an artificially introduced rival.

Archaeological investigations of prehistoric and early historic Native American village sites along the Roanoke River and its tributaries in Virginia and North Carolina have yielded many thousands of ichthyofaunal specimens representing nearly every family and most genera of fish known to have been native to the drainage in Holocene time (Whyte 1994, 1999). These data provide a baseline indication of pre-Euro-American-influenced ichthyofaunas of value to those who seek to restore such conditions.

MATERIALS AND METHODS

The Buzzard Rock site (44RN2) is located on the Roanoke River approximately 1.6 km upstream from Tinker Creek in the city of Roanoke (Figure 11.1). It is situated in the Blue Ridge physiographic province along a slow-flowing, meandering river section. Salvage excavations by the Virginia Research Center for Archaeology in 1977 revealed the remains of a prehistoric Siouan village site dating between 600 and 700 B.P. (Clark 1978; Gardner 1980).

Animal remains recovered from ten distinct archaeological deposits making up the Buzzard Rock site include 2,750 ichthyofaunal specimens and numerous remains of other classes of vertebrates and invertebrates. The fish remains were identified with reference to comparative collections of the Appalachian State University Department of Anthropology. These collections are representative of the contemporary ichthyofauna of the Roanoke River. No prehistoric specimens were unidentifiable because of the absence of particular species from the comparative collection. Speci-

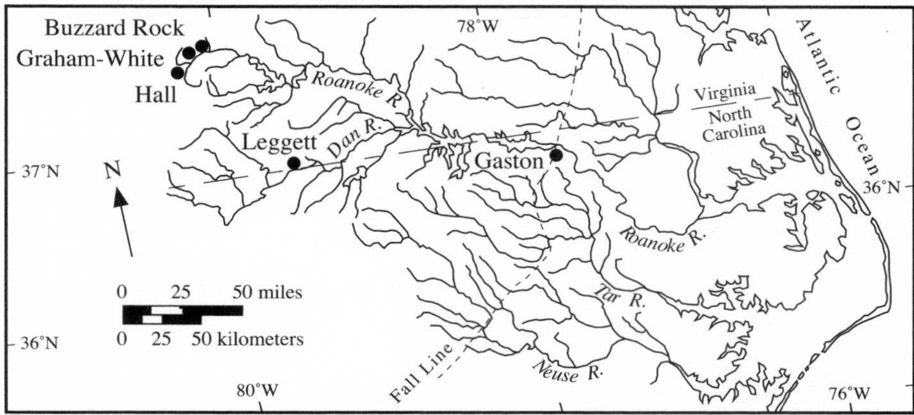

Figure 11.1. Location of the Buzzard Rock site in relation to other archaeological sites in the Roanoke drainage.

mens were identified as to skeletal element, side, and element portion and to the most specific taxon possible.

In most instances, no attempt was made to identify the species represented by postcranial bones (vertebrae, spines, pterygiophores, etc.). Certain fish, however, such as gar (Lepisosteidae) and eel (Anguillidae) were identified by their distinctive vertebrae, whereas catfishes (Ictaluridae) were frequently identified by their diagnostic dorsal and pectoral fin spines. The distinctive, large cycloid scales of suckers (Catostomidae) were well preserved and easily recognized.

The 2,750 specimens recovered include 395 (14 percent) identified to species, genus, or family, with the remainder identified only as bony fish. Although fragmentation caused by food processing, postdepositional processes, and recovery and handling accounts for many of the unidentified remains, most are relatively whole postcranial bones for which identification was not attempted. Both cranial and postcranial elements were present in proportions expected on the basis of a complete fish skeleton. Thirteen species and six families including gars, eels, minnows (Cyprinidae), suckers, catfishes, and sunfishes (Centrarchidae) are represented (Table 11.1).

THE BUZZARD ROCK FISH FAUNA

One vertebra and one scale of longnose gar *(Lepisosteus osseus)* were recovered. Gar probably were rare above the Piedmont of the Roanoke drainage in prehistoric times. However, the two specimens may have derived from downriver as part of a skin or parts of tools, weapons, or

TABLE 11.1. Ichthyofaunal Remains from the Buzzard Rock Site, Roanoke, Virginia.

Taxonomic Name	Common Name	Number of Identified Specimens
Lepisosteus osseus	longnose gar	2
Anguilla rostrata	American eel	12
Nocomis raneyi	bull chub	5
Nocomis sp.	chub	23
Semotilus atromaculatus	creek chub	3
Cyprinidae	minnow	10
Catostomus commersoni	white sucker	2
Hypentelium sp.	hog sucker	5
Moxostoma erythrurum	golden redhorse	2
Moxostoma sp.	redhorse	3
Catostomidae	sucker	78
Ameiurus natalis	yellow bullhead	2
Ameiurus nebulosus	brown bullhead	1
Ameiurus sp.	bullhead	2
Noturus insignis	margined madtom	49
Noturus sp.	madtom	87
Ictaluridae	catfish	2
Ambloplites cavifrons	Roanoke bass	34
Lepomis auritus	redbreast sunfish	24
Lepomis sp.	sunfish	20
Micropterus salmoides	largemouth bass	4
Centrarchidae	bass/sunfish	24
Osteichthyes	bony fish	2,356

ornaments. One gar scale was recovered from the prehistoric Mount Joy site on the Upper James River in Botetourt County, Virginia (Whyte 2000).

The American eel *(Anguilla rostrata)* is represented by 12 specimens. In preimpoundment time the American eel was abundant in Roanoke headwaters (Jenkins and Burkhead 1994). The individuals represented were of varying sizes and likely served as food.

At least two species of minnow are represented among the 41 specimens of Cyprinidae. These include the bull chub *(Nocomis raneyi)* and the creek chub *(Semotilus atromaculatus)*. Today minnows are abundant in the Upper Roanoke and include approximately 20 native species. The two species represented in the Buzzard Rock assemblage are some of the larger minnows and may have been sought as food. Smaller individuals may be poorly represented because of archaeological recovery bias. Indeed, several tiny pharyngeal arches identified only as Cyprinidae were recovered, indicating the capture of very small individuals by the site's inhabitants.

Suckers are represented by 90 specimens and three species: white sucker *(Catostomus commersoni)*, hog sucker *(Hypentelium nigricans* or *roanokense)*, and golden redhorse *(Moxostoma erythrurum)*. As 71 percent of the sucker remains identified are the distinctive large cycloid scales, their abundance in the assemblage is inflated relative to other families; scales were routinely used only in the identification of Catostomidae and Lepisosteidae. Species identifications were based on skull bones.

One hundred forty-three catfish remains were assigned to three species: yellow bullhead *(Ameiurus natalis)*, brown bullhead *(A. nebulosus)*, and margined madtom *(Noturus insignis)*. Represented by 49 specimens, the margined madtom probably accounts for the most individual fish in the assemblage. As only one other species of madtom *(N. gilberti)* is native to the Upper Roanoke and is osteologically distinct from *N. insignis*, it is probable that all specimens identified as *Noturus* sp. are actually *N. insignis*. The yellow bullhead was identified on the basis of an articulated right dentary and articular. These specimens were also compared with *A. nebulosus* and *A. catus*, which are native to the Roanoke. The identification of *A. natalis* in the assemblage supports the conclusion by Jenkins and Burkhead (1994) that its range extends upriver from lowland areas where it is abundant.

Three species were identified among the 106 centrarchid specimens: Roanoke bass *(Ambloplites cavifrons)*, redbreast sunfish *(Lepomis auritus)*, and largemouth bass *(Micropterus salmoides)*. The Roanoke bass was formerly widespread in the Roanoke drainage, but, perhaps because of competition with its introduced congener, *A. rupestris*, all populations within the city of Roanoke and upstream are apparently extirpated (Jenkins and Burkhead 1994). It is well represented in prehistoric archaeofaunal assemblages from other sites along the Upper Roanoke and Dan rivers (Whyte 1994). The redbreast sunfish is the most abundant species of *Lepomis* in upland streams. The pumpkinseed sunfish *(L. gibbosus)* is also native to the Upper Roanoke but is far less common (Jenkins and Burkhead 1994).

The four largemouth bass bones include a basioccipital and right ceratohyal from medium to large individuals and two right premaxillaries from juveniles. They were recovered from buried prehistoric contexts and do not represent recent intrusions affected by plowing or bioturbation. These specimens represent the first remains of *M. salmoides* identified from a prehistoric site along the Upper Roanoke. In an earlier study of smaller samples of archaeological fish remains from Buzzard Rock and three other sites on the Upper Roanoke and Dan rivers, I suggest that the largemouth bass "is probably not native to the Roanoke, Chowan, or drainages north of North Carolina" (1994:79). Ichthyologists are engaged in controversy over the northern native range of this species on the Atlantic Slope (Jenkins and Burkhead 1994:735). The Buzzard Rock specimens clearly establish the native status of *M. salmoides* for the Roanoke drainage.

No remains of *M. salmoides* were identified among the many fish bones recovered from sites upriver from Buzzard Rock or from the Leggett site on the Dan River in Halifax County, Virginia (Egloff et al. 1994; Whyte 1994). It is possible, however, that the depth, current, and substrate adjacent to these sites provided less-than-ideal conditions for the species. Numerous remains of *M. salmoides* were recently reported for the Gaston site on the Lower Roanoke in Halifax County, North Carolina (VanDerwarker 2001). The Buzzard Rock site thus may represent the upstream extent of the native distribution of this species, which prefers the deeper, slower waters of the Piedmont and Coastal Plain segments of the drainage.

DISCUSSION

It is now clear that the largemouth bass has occupied the Roanoke River system since at least 600 B.P. Its remains are abundant in late-prehistoric sites along the Lower Roanoke (VanDerwarker 2001) and are present in small amounts on sites along the Upper Roanoke (Whyte 1999). Furthermore, the distributions of other native species within the Roanoke, including *Lepisosteus osseus, Ameiurus natalis,* and *Ambloplites cavifrons,* are now better understood as a result of their identifications in archaeofaunal assemblages.

Another species whose status in the Roanoke is in question is the walleye *(Stizostedion vitreum).* Two dentaries from the Gaston site on the Roanoke River in Halifax County, North Carolina, have been identified as walleye by VanDerwarker (2001). Thus, the walleye may also be native to the Roanoke drainage; more specimens from other archaeological contexts would enhance any evaluation of this possibility. Multiple specimens of different ages and from different archaeological contexts would help ascertain the possibility that prehistoric humans moved live fish or their eggs between adjacent river systems. The largemouth bass, for example, may have been introduced to the Roanoke drainage from the Pee Dee by a transfer from the Yadkin to the Dan River in the North Carolina Piedmont.

The relevance of these discoveries to biological conservation and fish management lies in two arenas. On the one hand, data described here indicate that the introduction of individuals of *M. salmoides* and *S. vitreum* to the Roanoke drainage for the purpose of establishing a sport fish population can be undertaken in good conscience; they are, indeed, native species. On the other hand, Roanoke endemics such as *Ambloplites cavifrons,* a game fish now threatened because of competition with an introduced congener, *A. rupestris,* may eventually disappear unless measures are taken to preserve them. The zooarchaeological data described here indicate that *A. cavifrons* was, prior to that anthropogenic introduction, much more widespread than it is presently. Other influences of that introduction on the native species are unknown, but I predict that increased competition would reduce not only the reproduction rates and thus population sizes of the native species but also the maximum and average size of individual native fish. Interestingly, in 1997 the State of Virginia changed its size limits for *Ambloplites* (anglers often do not or cannot distinguish between the two species) in an effort to protect the Roanoke bass. The state of North Carolina, where the species occurs in the Tar and Neuse rivers, should perhaps do the same, but given the possibility of interspecific competition reducing the size of one or both taxa, this may not be a viable way to attain what conservation biologists hope to.

Another alternative is suggested by Jenkins and Burkhead, who note that "with the sport and food values, regional uniqueness, and decline of *A. cavifrons,* carefully planned attempts to establish new populations by stocking are merited" (1994:708). This solution, too, may not work well if the Roanoke bass must compete with its introduced congener. Further, the potential influence of hatchery fish, the likely source of the anticipated stocking, on the native gene pool is unclear. Clearly, more zooarchaeological work is called for in order to substantiate the management suggestions raised here, work like that described by Butler and Delacorte in chapter 2. Unlike the situation before the analyses reported here were performed, however, we currently know what that additional work must entail. The challenge now is to find the time and money to get that work done.

Acknowledgments. This research was made possible by the generosity of the Virginia Department of Historic Resources, Richmond. I am particularly indebted to certain of its staff, including Keith T. Egloff and Thomas Klatka. Amber VanDerwarker of the Research Laboratories of

Archaeology, University of North Carolina, Chapel Hill, was very kind to let me have a glance at the fish remains from the Gaston site. My biggest debt is to Robert E. Jenkins, Department of Biology, Roanoke College, and Wayne C. Starnes, North Carolina State Museum of Natural Sciences, for putting up with my questions.

References Cited

Adams, R., D. P. Davis, and M. E. Miller

1999 Osteometric Comparisons of Early Plains Archaic, Protohistoric, and Modern Pronghorn: A Case for Holocene Dwarfing. In *The Trappers Point Site (48SU1006): Early Archaic Adaptations in the Upper Green River Basin, Wyoming,* edited by M. E. Miller, P. H. Sanders, and J. E. Francis, pp. 279–289. Cultural Resource Series, 1. Office of the Wyoming State Archaeologist, Laramie.

Adams, R. M.

1949 Archaeological Investigations in Jefferson County, Missouri. *The Missouri Archaeologist* 11(3–4):1–72.

Adler, K.

1969 The Influence of Prehistoric Man on the Distribution of the Box Turtle. *Annals of the Carnegie Museum* 41:263–280.

AGEISS Environmental, Inc.

1997 Final Small Mammal Survey of Historic Woodbury Plots. Report on file, U.S. Army Dugway Proving Ground, Utah, and AGEISS Environmental, Inc., Denver.

1998 Small Mammal Survey of Historic Woodbury Plots, U.S. Army Dugway Proving Ground, Dugway, UT. Report on file, U.S. Army Dugway Proving Ground, Utah, and AGEISS Environmental, Inc., Denver.

Ahler, S. R., D. E. Harn, M. Neverett, M. B. Schroeder, B. W. Styles, R. E. Warren, K. White, and P. E. Albertson

1998 *Archaeological Assessment and Geotechnical Stabilization of Three Cave Sites at Fort Leonard Wood, Missouri.* Quaternary Studies Program, Technical Report, 98–1173–20. Illinois State Museum, Springfield.

Ambrose, S. H.
1991 Effects of Diet, Climate and Physiology on Nitrogen Isotope Abundances in Terrestrial Foodwebs. *Journal of Archaeological Science* 18: 293–317.
Amorosi, T., J. Woollett, S. Perdikaris, and T. McGovern
1996 Regional Zooarchaeology and Global Change: Problems and Potentials. *World Archaeology* 28:126–157.
Anderson, D. H., and B. D. Dugger
1998 A Conceptual Basis for Evaluating Restoration Success. *Transactions of the North American Wildlife and Natural Resources Conference* 63: 111–121.
Anderson, J. E.
1991 A Conceptual Framework for Evaluating and Quantifying Naturalness. *Conservation Biology* 5:347–352.
Anderson, K. M.
1996 Tending the Wilderness. *Restoration and Management Notes* 14: 154–166.
Anderson, R. M.
1930 Appendix B: Notes on the Musk-Ox and the Caribou. In *Conserving Canada's Musk-Oxen: Being an Account of an Investigation of the Thelon Game Sanctuary 1928–29,* edited by W. H. B. Hoare, pp. 29–53. King's Printer, Ottawa.
Andreasen, C.
1996 Survey of Paleo-Eskimo Sites in Northern East Greenland. In *The Paleo-Eskimo Cultures of Greenland,* edited by B. Grønnow, pp. 177–187. Danish Polar Center, Copenhagen.
1997 Independence II in North East Greenland: Some New Aspects. In *Fifty Years of Arctic Research: Anthropological Studies from Greenland to Siberia,* edited by R. Gilberg and H. C. Gulløv, pp. 23–32. Publications of the National Museum of Denmark, Ethnographical Series, 18. Copenhagen.
Angermeier, P. L.
1992 Does Biodiversity Include Artificial Diversity? *Conservation Biology* 8:600–602.
2000 The Natural Imperative for Biological Conservation. *Conservation Biology* 14:373–381.
Angermeier, P. L., and J. R. Karr
1994 Biological Integrity versus Biological Diversity as Policy Directives. *BioScience* 44:690–697.
Aplet, G. H., R. D. Laven, and P. L. Fiedler
1992 The Relevance of Conservation Biology to Natural Resource Management. *Conservation Biology* 6:298–300.
Appelt, M.
1997 Construction of an Archaeological "Culture": Similarities and Differences in Early Paleo-Eskimo Cultures of Greenland. In *Fifty Years of Arctic Research: Anthropological Studies from Greenland to Siberia,* edited by R. Gilberg and H. C. Gulløv, pp. 33–40. Publications of the National Museum of Denmark, Ethnographical Series, 18. Copenhagen.

Arkrush, B. S.
1986 Aboriginal Exploitation of Pronghorn in the Great Basin. *Journal of Ethnobiology* 6:239–255.
Arnold, C. D.
1981 *The Lagoon Site (OjRl-3): Implications for Paleoeskimo Interactions.* Mercury Series, Archaeological Survey of Canada Paper, 107. National Museum of Man, Ottawa.
Arnold, C. D., and K. M. McCullough
1990 Thule Pioneers in the Canadian Arctic. In *Canada's Missing Dimension: Science and History in the Canadian Arctic Islands,* edited by C. R. Harington, pp. 677–694. Canadian Museum of Nature, Ottawa.
Arthur, G. W.
1966 *An Archeological Survey of the Upper Yellowstone River Drainage, Montana.* Agricultural Economics Research Report, 26. Montana State University, Bozeman.
Avise, J. C.
1994 *Molecular Markers, Natural History and Evolution.* Chapman and Hall, New York.
Bailey, J. A.
1982 Implications of "Muddling Through" for Wildlife Management. *Wildlife Society Bulletin* 10:363–369.
Baker, R. G.
1976 *Late Quaternary Vegetation History of the Yellowstone Lake Basin, Wyoming.* U.S. Geological Survey Professional Paper, 729-E:E1–E48. Reston, Virginia.
1986 Sangamonian(?) and Wisconsinan Paleoenvironments in Yellowstone National Park. *Geological Society of America Bulletin* 97:717–736.
Baker, R. R.
1978 *The Evolutionary Ecology of Animal Migration.* Holmes and Meier, New York.
Balée, W. (editor)
1998 *Advances in Historical Ecology.* Columbia University Press, New York.
Balkwill, D.
n.d. Faunal Analysis of the Westwind and Daylight Sites, Northern Ellesmere Island. MS on file, Archaeological Survey of Canada, Canadian Museum of Civilization, Hull, Quebec.
Banfield, A. W. F.
1974 *The Mammals of Canada.* University of Toronto Press, Toronto.
Baraff, L. S., and T. R. Loughlin
2000 Trends and Potential Interactions between Pinnipeds and Fisheries of New England and the U.S. West Coast. *Marine Fisheries Review* 62: 1–39.
Barker, J. P.
1996 Archaeological Contributions to Ecosystem Management. *SAA Bulletin* 14(2):18–21.
Barnosky, A. D., E. A. Hadly, and C. J. Bell
2003 Mammalian Response to Global Warming on Varied Temporal Scales. *Journal of Mammalogy* 84:354–368.

Barnosky, C. W., E. C. Grimm, and H. E. Wright Jr.
1987 Towards a Postglacial History of the Northern Great Plains: A Review of the Paleoecologic Problems. *Annals of the Carnegie Museum* 56: 259–272.

Barnosky, E. H.
1996 Late Holocene Mammalian Fauna of Lamar Cave and Its Implications for Ecosystem Dynamics in Yellowstone National Park, Wyoming. In *Effects of Grazing by Wild Ungulates in Yellowstone National Park,* edited by F. Singer, pp. 154–163. Technical Report, NPS/NRYELL/NRTR/96–01. National Park Service, Yellowstone National Park, Wyoming.

Barr, W.
1991 *Back from the Brink: The Road to Muskox Conservation in the Northwest Territories.* Komatik Series, 3. Arctic Institute of North America of the University of Calgary, Calgary.

Bartlein, P. J., K. H. Anderson, P. M. Anderson, M. E. Edwards, C. J. Mock, R. S. Thompson, R. S. Webb, T. Webb III, and C. Whitlock
1998 Paleoclimate Simulations for North America over the Past 21,000 Years: Features of the Simulated Climate and Comparisons with Paleoenvironmental Data. *Quaternary Science Reviews* 17:549–585.

Bartlein, P. J., C. Whitlock, and S. L. Shafer
1997 Future Climate in the Yellowstone National Park Region and Its Potential Impact on Vegetation. *Conservation Biology* 11:782–792.

Basgall, M. E., and M. C. Hall
2001 Morphological and Temporal Variation in Bifurcate-Stemmed Dart Points of the Western Great Basin. *Journal of California and Great Basin Anthropology* 22:237–276.

Beever, E. A.
2002 Persistence of Pikas in Two Low-Elevation National Monuments in the Western United States. *Park Science* 21:23–29.

Beever, E. A., P. F. Brussard, and J. Berger
2003 Patterns of Apparent Extirpation among Isolated Populations of Pikas *(Ochotona princeps)* in the Great Basin. *Journal of Mammalogy* 84:37–54.

Beissinger, S. R.
1990 On the Limits and Directions of Conservation Biology. *BioScience* 40: 456–457.

Beiswenger, J. M.
1991 Late Quaternary Vegetational History of Grays Lake, Idaho. *Ecological Monographs* 6:165–182.

Bendix, B.
1998 Appendix 2: Quaternary Zoology, Preliminary Results from Analysis of Bones from Qeqertaaraq House 1, Midden Area. In *Man, Culture, and Environment in Ancient Greenland: Report on a Research Programme,* edited by J. Arneborg and H. C. Gøllov, pp. 188–190. Danish National Museum and Danish Polar Center, Copenhagen.

Bennett, D.
1994 The Unique Contribution of Wilderness to Values of Nature. *Natural Areas Journal* 14:203–208.

Benson, L. V., J. W. Burdett, M. Kashgarian, S. Lund, F. M. Phillips, and R. Rye
1996 Climatic and Hydrologic Oscillations in the Owens Lake Basin and Adjacent Sierra Nevada, California. *Science* 274:746–749.

Benson, L. V., J. W. Burdett, S. Lund, M. Kashgarian, and S. Mensing
1997 Nearly Synchronous Climate Change in the Northern Hemisphere during the Last Glacial Termination. *Nature* 388:263–265.

Berger, J.
2002 Wolves, Landscapes, and the Ecological Recovery of Yellowstone. *Wild Earth* 12(1):32–37.

Berger, J., and C. Cunningham
1994 *Bison: Mating and Conservation in Small Populations.* Columbia University Press, New York.

Best, T. L.
1996 *Lepus californicus. Mammalian Species* 530:1–10.

Bettinger, R. L.
1976 The Development of Pinyon Exploitation in Eastern California. *Journal of California Anthropology* 3:88–95.

Bickham, J. W., J. C. Patton, and T. R. Loughlin
1996 High Variability for Control-Region Sequences in a Marine Mammal: Implications for Conservation and Biogeography of Steller Sea Lions *(Eumetopias jubatus). Journal of Mammalogy* 77:95–108.

Billings, W. D.
1990 *Bromus tectorum,* a Biotic Cause of Ecosystem Impoverishment in the Great Basin. In *The Earth in Transition: Patterns and Processes of Biotic Impoverishment,* edited by G. M. Woodwell, pp. 301–322. Cambridge University Press, Cambridge.

Bird, M. I., S. G. Haberle, and A. R. Chivas
1994 Effect of Altitude on the Carbon-Isotope Composition of Forest and Grassland Soils from Papua, New Guinea. *Global Biogeochemical Cycles* 8:13–22.

Birkeland, P. W.
1984 *Soils and Geomorphology.* Oxford University Press, Oxford.

Bischoff, J. L., J. P. Fitts, and J. A. Fitzpatrick
1997 Responses of Sediment Chemistry to Climate Change in Owens Lake Sediment: An 800-k.y. Record of Saline/Fresh Cycles in Core OL-92. In *An 800,000-Year Paleoclimatic Record from Core OL-92, Owens Lake, Southeast California,* edited by G. I. Smith and J. L. Bischoff, pp. 37–47. Geological Society of America Special Paper, 317. Boulder.

Black, F. L.
1992 Why Did They Die? *Science* 258:1739–1740.

Boesch, D., E. Burreson, W. Dennison, E. Houde, M. Kemp, V. Kennedy, R. Newell, K. Paynter, R. Orth, and R. Ulanowicz
2001 Factors in the Decline of Coastal Ecosystems. *Science* 293:1589–1590.

Bonnicksen, T. M.
1989 Nature vs. Man(agement). *Journal of Forestry* 87(12):41–43.

Bonnicksen, T. M., and E. C. Stone
1985 Restoring Naturalness to National Parks. *Environmental Management* 9:479–486.

Booth, E. S.
1947 Systematic Review of the Land Mammals of Washington. Ph.D. dissertation, Department of Zoology, State College of Washington (Washington State University), Pullman.

Botkin, D. B.
2001 The Naturalness of Biological Invasions. *Western North American Naturalist* 61:261–266.

Bowden, M. J.
1992 The Invention of American Tradition. *Journal of Historical Geography* 18:3–26.

Bowman, S. G. E., J. C. Ambers, and M. N. Leese
1990 Re-Evaluation of British Museum Radiocarbon Dates Issued between 1980 and 1984. *Radiocarbon* 32:59–70.

Boyce, M. S.
1989 *The Jackson Hole Elk Herd: Intensive Management in North America.* Cambridge University Press, Cambridge.
1991 Natural Regulation or the Control of Nature? In *The Greater Yellowstone Ecosystem: Redefining America's Wilderness Heritage,* edited by R. B. Keiter and M. S. Boyce, pp. 183–208. Yale University Press, New Haven.

Boyd, R. J.
1978 American Elk. In *Big Game of North America: Ecology and Management,* edited by J. L. Schmidt and D. L. Gilbert, pp. 11–29. Stackpole Books, Harrisburg, Pennsylvania.

Boyd, R. S.
1998 Demographic History until 1990. In *Handbook of North American Indians, vol. 12: Plateau,* edited by D. E. Walker Jr., pp. 467–483. Smithsonian Institution Press, Washington, D.C.

Bozell, J. R., and R. E. Warren
1982 Analysis of Vertebrate Remains. In *The Cannon Reservoir Human Ecology Project: An Archaeological Study of Cultural Adaptations in the Southern Prairie Peninsula,* edited by M. J. O'Brien, R. E. Warren, and D. E. Lewarch, pp. 171–192. Academic Press, New York.

Bradley, W. P., and C. H. Driver
1981 *Elk Ecology and Management Perspectives at Mount Rainier National Park.* Cooperative Park Studies Unit, University of Washington Report, 81–2. Seattle.

Broughton, J. M
1994 Resource Intensification in Central California: Archaeological Vertebrate Evidence from the Sacramento Valley. *Journal of Archaeological Science* 21:501–514.
1999 *Resource Depression and Intensification during the Late Holocene, San Francisco Bay.* Anthropological Records, 32. University of California Press, Berkeley.

Brown, J. H.
1971 Mammals on Mountaintops: Nonequilibrium Insular Biogeography. *American Naturalist* 105:467–478.
1973 Species Diversity of Seed-Eating Desert Rodents in Sand Dune Habitats. *Ecology* 54:775–787.

1978 The Theory of Insular Biogeography and the Distribution of Boreal Mammals and Birds. In *Intermountain Biogeography: A Symposium,* edited by K. T. Harper and J. L. Reveal, pp. 209–228. Great Basin Naturalist Memoir, 2.

1986 Two Decades of Interaction between the MacArthur–Wilson Model and the Complexities of Mammalian Distributions. *Biological Journal of the Linnaean Society* 28:231–251.

Brown, J. H., and B. A. Harney

1993 Population and Community Ecology of Heteromyid Rodents in Temperate Habitats. In *Biology of the Heteromyidae,* edited by H. H. Genoways and J. H. Brown, pp. 163–180. American Society of Mammalogists, Provo, Utah.

Bryant, L. D., and C. Maser

1982 Classification and Distribution. In *Elk of North America: Ecology and Management,* edited by J. W. Thomas and D. E. Toweill, pp. 1–59. Stackpole Books, Harrisburg, Pennsylvania.

Bryson, R. A., and R. U. Bryson

1997 High Resolution Simulations of Regional Holocene Climate: North Africa and Near East. In *Third Millennium BC Climate Change and Old World Collapse,* edited by H. N. Dalfes, G. Kukla, and H. Weiss, pp. 565–593. Springer-Verlag, Berlin.

Bubenik, A. B.

1982 Physiology. In *Elk of North American: Ecology and Management,* edited by J. W. Thomas and D. E. Toweill, pp. 125–179. Stackpole Books, Harrisburg, Pennsylvania.

Buechner, H. K.

1960 *The Bighorn Sheep in the United States, Its Past, Present, and Future.* Wildlife Monographs, 4.

Buege, D. J.

1996 The Ecologically Noble Savage Revisited. *Environmental Ethics* 18: 71–88.

Bunnell, F. L., and L. A. Dupuis

1995 Conservation Biology's Literature Revisited: Wine or Vinaigrette? *Wildlife Society Bulletin* 23:56–62.

Burch, E. S.

1977 Muskox and Man in the Central Canadian Subarctic 1689–1974. *Arctic* 30:135–154.

Bureau of Land Management

2000 *Record of Decision Environmental Impact Statement for the Pinedale Anticline Oil and Gas Exploration and Development Project Sublette County, Wyoming [DEIS/FEIS-00–018].* U.S. Department of the Interior, Bureau of Land Management, Wyoming State Office, Cheyenne.

n.d. Worland District Plant List, April 1982. MS on file, Worland District Office, Worland, Wyoming.

Burney, D. A., D. W. Steadman, and P. S. Martin

2002 Evolution's Second Chance. *Wild Earth* 12(2):12–15.

Burnham, R. J.

2001 Is Conservation Biology a Paleontological Pursuit? *Palaios* 16:423–424.

Burroughs, R. D. (editor)
1961 *The Natural History of the Lewis and Clark Expedition.* Michigan State University Press, East Lansing.

Burtchard, G. C.
1998 Environment, Land-Use and Archaeology of Mount Rainier National Park, Washington. Report on file, U.S. Department of the Interior, National Park Service, Columbia Cascades System Support Office, Seattle.

Burton, R. K., D. Gifford-Gonzalez, and J. J. Snodgrass
2002 Isotopic Tracking of Prehistoric Pinniped Foraging and Distribution along the Central California Coast: Preliminary Results. *International Journal of Osteoarchaeology* 12:4–11.

Burton, R. K., and P. L. Koch
1999 Isotopic Tracking of Foraging and Long-Distance Migration in Northeastern Pacific Pinnipeds. *Oecologica* 119:578–585.

Burton, R. K., J. J. Snodgrass, D. Gifford-Gonzalez, T. Guilderson, T. Brown, and P. L. Koch
2001 Holocene Changes in the Ecology of Northern Fur Seals: Insights from Stable Isotopes and Archaeofauna. *Oecologia* 128:107–115.

Busch, B. C.
1985 *The War against the Seals: A History of the North American Seal Fishery.* McGill-Queens University Press, Kingston, Ontario.

Butler, V. L.
1996 Tui Chub Taphonomy and the Importance of Marsh Resources in the Western Great Basin of North America. *American Antiquity* 61: 699–717.
1999 Fish Remains from the Southern Owens Valley, Alabama Gates Project. In *The Changing Role of Riverine Environments in the Prehistory of the Central-Western Great Basin: Data Recovery Excavations at Six Prehistoric Sites in Owens Valley, California,* edited by M. G. Delacorte, pp. 317–338. Report to Caltrans, District 9. Far Western Anthropological Research Group, Davis, California.
2000a Fish Remains. In *By the Lake by the Mountains: Archaeological Investigations at CA-INY-4554 and CA-INY-1428,* edited by A. J. Gilreath and K. L. Holanda, pp. 59–67. Report to Caltrans, District 9. Far Western Anthropological Research Group, Davis, California.
2000b Resource Depression on the Northwest Coast of North America. *Antiquity* 74:649–661.

Cain, S. J., J. Berger, T. Roffe, C. Cunningham, and S. Patla
1998 Reproduction and Demography of Brucellosis Infected Bison in the Southern Greater Yellowstone Ecosystem. MS on file, National Park Service, Grand Teton National Park, Moose, Wyoming.

Callicott, J. B.
1989 American Indian Land Wisdom? Sorting Out the Issues. *Journal of Forest History* 33:35–42.
1995 A Critique of and an Alternative to the Wilderness Idea. *Wild Earth* 4:54–59.

Callicott, J. B., L. B. Crowder, and K. Mumford
1999 Current Normative Concepts in Conservation. *Conservation Biology* 13:22–35.
Callicott, J. B., and K. Mumford
1997 Ecological Sustainability as a Conservation Concept. *Conservation Biology* 11:32–40.
Campbell, S. K.
1989 PostColumbian Culture History in the Northern Columbia Plateau: A.D. 1500–1900. Ph.D. dissertation, Department of Anthropology, University of Washington, Seattle.
Cannon, K. P.
1992 A Review of the Archeological and Paleontological Evidence for the Prehistoric Presence of Wolf and Related Prey Species in the Northern and Central Rockies Physiographic Provinces. In *Wolves for Yellowstone? A Report to the United States Congress, vol. 4: Research and Analysis,* edited by J. D. Varley and W. G. Brewster, pp. 1–175–1–265. National Park Service, Yellowstone National Park, Wyoming.
2001 What the Past Can Provide: Contribution of Prehistoric Bison Studies to Modern Bison Management. *Great Plains Research* 11:145–174.
Carpenter, L. M., and W. M. Arjo
1999 Exotic Annuals and Changes in Small Mammal Communities. *Journal of the Colorado–Wyoming Academy of Science* 31:6.
Casteel, R. W.
1976 *Fish Remains in Archaeology.* Academic Press, New York.
Chambers, K. E.
1998 Using Genetic Data in the Management of Bison Herds. In *International Symposium on Bison Ecology and Management in North America,* edited by L. Irby and J. Knight, pp. 151–157. Montana State University, Bozeman.
Chapman, C. H.
1975 *The Archaeology of Missouri, I.* University of Missouri Press, Columbia.
Chase, A.
1987 *Playing God in Yellowstone: The Destruction of America's First National Park.* Harcourt Brace Jovanovich, New York.
Chatters, J. C.
1995 Population Growth, Climatic Cooling, and the Development of Collector Strategies on the Southern Plateau, Western North America. *Journal of World Prehistory* 9:341–400.
1998 Environment. In *Handbook of North American Indians, vol. 12: Plateau,* edited by D. E. Walker Jr., pp. 29–48. Smithsonian Institution Press, Washington, D.C.
2001 *Ancient Encounters: Kennewick Man and the First Americans.* Simon and Schuster, New York.
Chorn, J., B. A. Frase, and C. D. Frailey
1988 Late Pleistocene Pronghorn, *Antilocapra americana,* from Natural Trap Cave, Wyoming. *Transactions of the Nebraska Academy of Sciences* 16: 127–139.

Christensen, A. G., J. K. Lackey, and J. A. Rochelle
1999 Elk in Western Forests: Too Much Success? *Transactions of the North American Wildlife and Natural Resources Conference* 64:107–116.
Church, T.
1997 Ecosystem Management and CRM: Do We Have a Role? *SAA Bulletin* 15(2):25–26.
Chure, D.
2002 Paleontology as a New Tool for Conservation. *Park Science* 21:43–46.
Clark, T. W.
1999 *The Natural World of Jackson Hole: An Ecological Primer.* Grand Teton Natural History Association, Moose, Wyoming.
Clark, W. E.
1978 *A Preliminary Report on the 1977 Excavations of the Buzzard Rock Site, 44RN2.* Report to the Virginia Department of Transportation, Richmond.
Clarke, C. H. D.
1940 *A Biological Investigation of the Thelon Game Sanctuary.* National Museum of Canada Bulletin, 96, Biological Series, 25. Ottawa.
Collins, H. B.
1950 Excavations at Frobisher Bay, Baffin Island, N.W.T. *National Museum of Canada Bulletin* 123:49–63.
1952 Archaeological Excavations at Resolute, Cornwallis Island, N.W.T. *National Museum of Canada Bulletin* 126:48–63.
Colson, E.
1953 *The Makah Indians: A Study of an Indian Tribe in Modern American Society.* University of Minnesota Press, Minneapolis.
Committee on Ungulate Management in Yellowstone National Park
2002 *Ecological Dynamics on Yellowstone's Northern Range.* National Academy Press, Washington, D.C.
Conner, M. D. (editor)
1995 *Woodland and Mississippian Occupations at the Hayti Bypass Site, Pemiscott County, Missouri.* Southwest Missouri State University, Center for Archaeological Research, Special Publication, 1. Springfield.
Cooper, C. F., and B. S. Stewart
1983 Demography of Northern Elephant Seals, 1911–1982. *Science* 219:969–971.
Couch, L. K.
1935 Chronological Data on Elk Introduction into Oregon and Washington. *The Murrelet* 16:3–6, 42.
Crandall, K. A., O. R. P. Bininda-Emonds, G. M. Mace, and R. K. Wayne
2000 Considering Evolutionary Processes in Conservation Biology. *Trends in Ecology and Evolution* 15:290–295.
Crockford, S. J., S. G. Frederick, and R. J. Wigen
2002 The Cape Flattery Fur Seal: An Extinct Species of *Callorhinus* in the Eastern North Pacific? *Canadian Journal of Archaeology* 26:152–174.
Crumley, C. L.
1994a Historical Ecology: A Multidimensional Ecological Orientation. In *Historical Ecology: Cultural Knowledge and Changing Landscapes,*

edited by C. L. Crumley, pp. 1–16. School of American Research Press, Santa Fe.

Crumley, C. L. (editor)

1994b *Historical Ecology: Cultural Knowledge and Changing Landscapes.* School of American Research Press, Santa Fe.

Currey, D. R.

1990 Quaternary Palaeolakes in the Evolution of Semidesert Basins, with Special Emphasis on Lake Bonneville and the Great Basin, U.S.A. *Palaeogeography, Palaeoclimatology, Palaeoecology* 76:189–214.

Damkjar, E.

1984 Southeastern Somerset Island Paleoeskimo Project: 1984 Field Season. Report on file, Archaeological Survey of Canada, Canadian Museum of Civilization, Hull, Quebec.

Darwent, C. M.

1995 Late Dorset Faunal Remains from the Tasiarulik Site, Little Cornwallis Island, Central High Arctic, Canada. M.A. thesis, Department of Archaeology, Simon Fraser University, Burnaby, British Columbia.

2001a High Arctic Paleoeskimo Fauna: Temporal Changes and Regional Differences. Ph.D. dissertation, Department of Anthropology, University of Missouri, Columbia.

2001b Interpreting the Subsistence of the First High Arctic Occupants. In *On Being First: Cultural Innovation and Environmental Consequences of First Peopling,* edited by J. Gillespie, S. Tupakka, and C. de Mille, pp. 391–407. Archaeological Association of the University of Calgary, Calgary.

Daubenmire, R. F.

1943 Vegetational Zonation in the Rocky Mountains. *Botanical Review* 9: 325–393.

Davis, O. K., J. C. Sheppard, and S. Robertson

1986 Contrasting Climatic Histories for the Snake River Plain, Idaho, Resulting from Multiple Thermal Maxima. *Quaternary Research* 26:321–339.

Day, G. M.

1953 The Indian as an Ecological Factor in the Northeastern Forest. *Ecology* 34:329–346.

Delacorte, M. G.

1995 The Role of Structures. In *Prehistoric Use of a Marginal Environment: Continuity and Change in the Occupation of the Volcanic Tablelands, Mono and Inyo Counties, California,* edited by M. E. Basgall and M. A. Giambastiani, pp. 257–260. Number 12. Center for Archaeological Research, Davis, California.

Delacorte, M. G. (editor)

1999 *The Changing Role of Riverine Environments in the Prehistory of the Central-Western Great Basin: Data Recovery Excavations at Six Prehistoric Sites in Owens Valley, California.* Report to Caltrans, District 9. Far Western Anthropological Research Group, Davis, California.

DeLong, R. L.

1982 Population Biology of Northern Fur Seals at San Miguel Island, California. Ph.D. dissertation, University of California, Berkeley.

DeLong, R. L., and G. A. Antonelis
1991 Impact of the 1982–1983 El Niño on the Northern Fur Seal Population of San Miguel Island, California. In *Pinnipeds and El Niño: Responses to Environmental Stress,* edited by F. Trillmich and K. A. Ono, pp. 75–83. Springer-Verlag, Berlin.
DeMaster, D. P., C. W. Fowler, S. L. Perry, and M. F. Richlen
2001 Predation and Competition: The Impact of Fisheries on Marine-Mammal Populations over the Next One Hundred Years. *Journal of Mammalogy* 82:641–651.
Denevan, W. M.
1992 The Pristine Myth: The Landscape of the Americas in 1492. *Annals of the Association of American Geographers* 82:369–385.
Despain, D. G.
1990 *Yellowstone Vegetation: Consequences of Environment and History in a Natural Setting.* Roberts Rinehart, Boulder.
Despain, D. G., D. Houston, M. Meagher, and P. Schullery
1986 *Wildlife in Transition: Man and Nature on Yellowstone's Northern Range.* Roberts Rinehart, Boulder.
Diamond, J. M.
1986 The Environmentalist Myth. *Nature* 324:19–20.
Dickinson, W. C.
1982 Fish Remains from Cheek Bend Cave. In *The Paleontology of Cheek Bend Cave: Phase II Report to the Tennessee Valley Authority,* edited by W. E. Klippel and P. W. Parmalee, pp. 58–86. Report to the Tennessee Valley Authority, Norris.
Dickinson, W. R.
1995 The Times Are Always Changing: The Holocene Saga. *Geological Society of America Bulletin* 107:1–7.
Dixon, S. L., and R. L. Lyman
1996 On the Holocene History of Elk *(Cervus elaphus)* in Eastern Washington. *Northwest Science* 70:262–272.
Doak, D. F., and L. S. Mills
1994 A Useful Role for Theory in Conservation. *Ecology* 75:615–626.
Dobb, E.
1992 Cultivating Nature. *The Sciences* 32(1):44–50.
Dods, R. R.
2002 The Death of Smokey Bear: The Ecodisaster Myth and Forest Management Practices in Prehistoric North America. *World Archaeology* 33:475–487.
Dorn, R. D.
1986 *The Wyoming Landscape, 1805–1878.* Mountain West, Cheyenne, Wyoming.
Dryden, C.
1968 *Dryden's History of Washington.* Binfords and Mort, Portland, Oregon.
Durrant, S. D.
1952 *The Mammals of Utah: Taxonomy and Distributions.* University of Kansas, Museum of Natural History Publications, 6. Lawrence.

Ebbesmeyer, C. C., D. R. Cayan, D. R. McLain, F. H. Nichols, D. H. Peterson, and K. T. Redmond
1991 1976 Step in the Pacific Climate: Forty Environmental Changes between 1968–1975 and 1977–1984. In *Proceedings of the Seventh Annual Pacific Climate (PACLIM) Workshop, April 1990,* edited by J. L. Betancourt and V. L. Sharp, pp. 115–126. Technical Report, 26. California Department of Water Resources, Interagency Ecological Studies Program, for the Sacramento–San Joaquin Estuary, Sacramento.

Eckerle, W., and J. Hobey
1999 Paleoenvironmental Reconstruction and Prehistoric Lifeways. In *The Trappers Point Site (48SU1006): Early Archaic Adaptations in the Upper Green River Basin, Wyoming,* edited by M. E. Miller, P. H. Sanders, and J. E. Francis, pp. 452–475. Cultural Resource Series, 1. Office of the Wyoming State Archaeologist, Laramie.

Eckles, D. G.
1999 Taxonomic Identification, Bone Element Frequencies, and Bone Artifacts. In *The Trappers Point Site (48SU1006): Early Archaic Adaptations in the Upper Green River Basin, Wyoming,* edited by M. E. Miller, P. H. Sanders, and J. E. Francis, pp. 193–205. Cultural Resource Series, 1. Office of the Wyoming State Archaeologist, Laramie.

Edwards, T. C., Jr.
1989 The Wildlife Society and the Society for Conservation Biology: Strange but Unwilling Bedfellows. *Wildlife Society Bulletin* 17:340–343.

Egan, D., and E. A. Howell
2001 Introduction. In *The Historical Ecology Handbook: A Restorationist's Guide to Reference Ecosystems,* edited by D. Egan and E. A. Howell, pp. 1–23. Island Press, Washington, D.C.

Egan, H. R.
1917 *Pioneering the West, 1846 to 1878.* Edited by W. M. Egan. Skelton Publishing, Salt Lake City.

Egloff, K. T., M. B. Barber, C. Reed, and T. R. Whyte
1994 Leggett Site (44HA23, Halifax County): A Dan River Agricultural/Riverine Community. *Archaeological Society of Virginia Quarterly Bulletin* 49:89–120.

Ehleringer, J. R., R. F. Sage, L. B. Flanagan, and R. W. Pearcy
1991 Climate Change and the Evolution of C_4 Photosynthesis. *Trends in Ecology and Evolution* 6:95–99.

Elder, W. H.
1965 Primeval Deer Hunting Pressures Revealed by Remains from American Indian Middens. *Journal of Wildlife Management* 29:366–370.

Elling, H.
1996 The Independence I and Old Nuulliit Cultures in Relation to the Saqqaq Culture. In *The Paleo-Eskimo Cultures of Greenland,* edited by B. Grønnow, pp. 201–214. Danish Polar Center, Copenhagen.

Ellingson, T.
2001 *The Myth of the Noble Savage.* University of California Press, Berkeley.

Emslie, S. D.
1987 Age and Diet of Fossil California Condors in Grand Canyon, Arizona. *Science* 237:768–770.
Estes, J. A., M. T. Tinker, T. M. Williams, and D. F. Doak
1998 Killer Whale Predation on Sea Otters Linking Oceanic and Nearshore Ecosystems. *Science* 282:473–476.
Etnier, M. A.
2002a The Effects of Human Hunting on Northern Fur Seal *(Callorhinus ursinus)* Migration and Breeding Distributions in the Late Holocene. Ph.D. dissertation, Department of Anthropology, University of Washington, Seattle.
2002b Occurrences of Guadalupe Fur Seals *(Arctocephalus townsendi)* on the Washington Coast over the Past 500 Years. *Marine Mammal Science* 18:551–557.
Etnier, M. A., and P. Koch
n.d. Isotopic Characterization of Late Holocene Northern Fur Seals *(Callorhinus ursinus)* from the Washington Coast. MS in possession of the authors.
Falk, D.
1990 Discovering the Future, Creating the Past: Some Reflections on Restoration. *Restoration and Management Notes* 8:71–72.
Farquhar, G. D., J. R. Ehleringer, and K. T. Hubick
1989 Carbon Isotope Discrimination and Photosynthesis. *Annual Review of Plant Physiology and Plant Molecular Biology* 40:503–537.
FAUNMAP Working Group
1996 Spatial Response of Mammals to Late Quaternary Environmental Fluctuations. *Science* 272:1601–1606.
Faure, G.
1986 *Principles of Isotope Geology.* 2nd ed. Wiley, New York.
Fichter, E.
1987 Pronghorn Groups: On Social Organization. *Tebiwa* 23:11–22.
Fischer, H.
1995 *Wolf Wars: The Remarkable Inside Story of the Restoration of Wolves to Yellowstone.* Falcon Press, Helena, Montana.
Fisher, J. W., Jr., and G. C. Frison
2000 Site Structure at the Boar's Tusk Site, Wyoming. In *Pronghorn Past and Present: Archaeology, Ethnography, and Biology,* edited by J. V. Pastor and P. M. Lubinski, pp. 89–108. Plains Anthropologist Memoir, 32.
Fisher, J. W., Jr., and T. E. Roll
1998 Ecological Relationships between Bison and Native Americans during Late Prehistory and the Early Historic Period. In *International Symposium on Bison Ecology and Management in North America,* edited by L. Irby and J. Knight, pp. 283–302. Montana State University, Bozeman.
Fitzhugh, W. W.
1997 Biogeographical Archaeology in the Eastern North American Arctic. *Human Ecology* 25:385–418.

Flannery, T.
2001 *The Eternal Frontier.* Atlantic Monthly Press, New York.
Fleischer, L. A.
1987 Guadalupe Fur Seal, *Arctocephalus townsendi.* In *Status, Biology, and Ecology of Fur Seals: Proceedings of an International Symposium and Workshop,* edited by J. P. Croxall and R. L. Gentry, pp. 43–48. NOAA Technical Report NMFS, 51. National Oceanic and Atmospheric Administration, Cambridge, Massachusetts.
Flessa, K. W.
2002 Conservation Paleobiology. *American Paleontologist* 10:2–5.
Flores, D. L., and E. G. Bolen
1995 Animals and People in North American History. *Transactions of the North American Wildlife and Natural Resources Conference* 60: 517–520.
Foreman, D.
1995 Wilderness Areas Are Vital: A Response to Callicott. *Wild Earth* 4:64–68.
Foster, D. R.
2000 From Bobolinks to Bears: Interjecting Geographical History into Ecological Studies, Environmental Interpretation, and Conservation Planning. *Journal of Biogeography* 27:27–30.
Foster, J., and M. S. Gaines
1991 The Effects of a Successional Habitat Mosaic on a Small Mammal Community. *Ecology* 72:1358–1373.
Fowler, C. S. (editor)
1989 *Willard Z. Park's Ethnographic Notes on the Northern Paiute of Western Nevada, 1933–1944,* vol. 1. University of Utah Anthropological Papers, 114. Salt Lake City.
Fowler, C. W.
1999 Management of Multi-Species Fisheries: From Overfishing to Sustainability. *ICES Journal of Marine Science* 56:927–932.
Francis, R. C., and S. R. Hare
1994 Decadal-Scale Regime Shifts in the Large Marine Ecosystems of the Northeast Pacific: A Case for Historical Science. *Fisheries Oceanography* 3:279–291.
Fredlund, G. G., and L. L. Tieszen
1997 Phytolith and Carbon Isotope Evidence for Late Quaternary Vegetation and Climate Change in the Southern Black Hills, South Dakota. *Quaternary Research* 47:206–217.
Frison, G. C.
1971 Shoshonean Antelope Procurement in the Upper Green River Basin, Wyoming. *Plains Anthropologist* 16:258–284.
1991 *Prehistoric Hunters of the High Plains.* 2nd ed. Academic Press, San Diego.
2000 The Eden-Farson Pronghorn Kill 48SW304: Taphonomic Analysis and Animal Behavior. In *Pronghorn Past and Present: Archaeology, Ethnography, and Biology,* edited by J. V. Pastor and P. M. Lubinski, pp. 29–37. Plains Anthropologist Memoir, 32.

Frison, G. C., and L. C. Todd (editors)
1987 *The Horner Site: The Type Site of the Cody Cultural Complex*. Academic Press, Orlando.

Fryxell, R., T. Bielicki, R. D. Daugherty, C. E. Gustafson, H. T. Irwin, and B. C. Keel
1968 A Human Skeleton of Mid-Pinedale Age in Southeastern Washington. *American Antiquity* 33:511–515.

Gabler, K. I., L. T. Heady, and J. W. Laundré
2001 A Habitat Suitability Model for Pygmy Rabbits *(Brachylagus idahoensis)* in Southeastern Idaho. *Western North American Naturalist* 61: 480–489.

Gallo Reynoso, J. P.
1994 Factors Affecting the Population Status of Guadalupe Fur Seals, *Arctocephalus townsendi,* at Isla de Guadalupe, Baja California, Mexico. Ph.D. dissertation, University of California, Santa Cruz.

Gano, K. A., and W. H. Rickard
1982 Small Mammals of a Bitterbrush–Cheatgrass Community. *Northwest Science* 56:1–7.

Gardner, P. S.
1980 An Analysis of Dan River Ceramics from Virginia and North Carolina. M.A. thesis, Department of Anthropology, University of North Carolina, Chapel Hill.

Gavin, T. A.
1989 What's Wrong with the Questions We Ask in Wildlife Research? *Wildlife Society Bulletin* 17:345–350.

Gearin, P. J., S. J. Jeffries, R. L. DeLong, and M. E. Gosho
2001 Update on California Sea Lion Captures and Surveys in Puget Sound, Washington. MS on file, National Marine Mammal Laboratory, Seattle.

Gearin, P. J., R. Pfeifer, S. J. Jeffries, R. L. DeLong, and M. A. Johnson
1988 *Results of the 1986–87 California Sea Lion–Steelhead Trout Predation Control Program at the Hiram M. Chittenden Locks*. National Marine Fisheries Service NWAFSC Processed Report, 88–30. Seattle.

Geist, V.
1971 *Mountain Sheep: A Study in Behavior and Evolution*. University of Chicago Press, Chicago.
1991 Phantom Subspecies: The Wood Bison *Bison bison "athabascae"* Rhoads Is Not a Valid Taxon, but an Ecotype. *Arctic* 44:283–300.

Gennett, J. A., and R. G. Baker
1986 A Late Quaternary Pollen Sequence from Blacktail Pond, Yellowstone National Park, Wyoming, U.S.A. *Palynology* 10:61–71.

Gentry, R. L.
1998 *Behavior and Ecology of the Northern Fur Seal*. Princeton University Press, Princeton.

Gerber, L. R., W. S. Wooster, D. P. DeMaster, and G. R. VanBlaricom
1999 Marine Mammals: New Objectives in U.S. Fishery Management. *Reviews in Fisheries Science* 7:23–38.

Germano, D. J., and D. N. Lawhead
1986 Species Diversity and Habitat Complexity: Does Vegetation Organize

Vertebrate Communities in the Great Basin? *Great Basin Naturalist* 46:711–720.

Gerrodette, T., and D. P. DeMaster
1990 Quantitative Determination of Optimum Sustainable Population Level. *Marine Mammal Science* 6:1–16.

Gilbert, C. H.
1893 Report on the Fishes of the Death Valley Expedition Collected in Southern California and Nevada in 1891, with Descriptions of New Species. *North American Fauna* 7:229–234.

Gilmore, R. M.
1949 The Identification and Value of Mammal Bones from Archeologic Excavations. *Journal of Mammalogy* 30:163–169.

Gilreath, A. J., and K. L. Holanda (editors)
2000 *By the Lake by the Mountains: Archaeological Investigations at CA-INY-4554 and CA-INY-1428*. Report to Caltrans, District 9. Far Western Anthropological Research Group, Davis, California.

Glassow, M. A., D. J. Kennett, and L. R. Wilcoxon
1994 Confirmation of Middle Holocene Ocean Cooling Inferred from Stable Isotope Analysis of Prehistoric Shells from Santa Cruz Island, California. In *The Fourth California Islands Symposium: Update on the Status of Resources,* edited by W. L. Halvorson and G. J. Maender, pp. 223–232. Santa Barbara Museum of Natural History, Santa Barbara.

Glick, P., D. Inkley, and C. Tufts
2001 Climate Change and Wildlife: Integrating Global Climate Policy Implementation with Local Conservation Action. *Transactions of the North American Wildlife and Natural Resources Conference* 66:380–391.

Gómez-Pompa, A., and A. Kaus
1992 Taming the Wilderness Myth. *BioScience* 42:271–279.

Good, J. M., and K. L. Pierce
1996 *Interpreting the Landscape: Recent and Ongoing Geology of Grand Teton and Yellowstone National Parks.* Grand Teton Natural History Association, Moose, Wyoming.

Gordon, B. C.
1977 Muskox and Man in the Subarctic: An Archaeological View. *Arctic* 30:246.
1994 Nadlok and the Origin of the Copper Inuit. In *Threads of Arctic Prehistory: Papers in Honour of William E. Taylor, Jr.,* edited by D. Morrison and J.-L. Pilon, pp. 325–340. Mercury Series, Archaeological Survey of Canada Paper, 149. Canadian Museum of Civilization, Hull, Quebec.

Gordon, D. R.
1994 Translocation of Species into Conservation Areas: A Key for Natural Resource Managers. *Natural Areas Journal* 14:31–37.

Graham, R. W.
1985 Response of Mammalian Communities to Environmental Changes during the Late Quaternary. In *Community Ecology,* edited by J. Diamond and T. J. Case, pp. 300–313. Harper and Row, New York.

1988 The Role of Climatic Change in the Design of Biological Reserves: The Paleoecological Perspective for Conservation Biology. *Conservation Biology* 2:391–394.

1992 Late Pleistocene Changes as a Guide to Understanding Effects of Greenhouse Warming on the Mammalian Fauna of North America. In *Global Warming and Biological Diversity,* edited by R. L. Peters and T. E. Lovejoy, pp. 76–87. Yale University Press, New Haven.

Graham, R. W., and M. A. Graham

1994 Late Quaternary Distribution of *Martes* in North America. In *Martens, Sables, and Fishers: Biology and Conservation,* edited by S. W. Buskirk, A. S. Harestad, M. G. Raphael, and R. A. Powell, pp. 26–58. Cornell University Press, Ithaca.

Graham, R. W., and E. L. Lundelius Jr.

1994 *FAUNMAP: A Database Documenting Late Quaternary Distributions of Mammal Species in the United States.* Illinois State Museum Scientific Papers, 25. Springfield.

Grand Teton National Park and National Elk Refuge

1996 *Jackson Bison Herd: Long Term Management Plan and Environmental Assessment.* Grand Teton National Park and National Elk Refuge, Jackson, Wyoming.

Grande, S. M. A.

1999 Beyond the Ecologically Noble Savage: Deconstructing the White Man's Indian. *Environmental Ethics* 21:307–320.

Graumlich, L. J.

1993 A 1000-Year Record of Temperature and Precipitation in the Sierra Nevada. *Quaternary Research* 39:249–255.

Gray, D. R.

1987 *The Muskoxen of Polar Bear Pass.* Fitzhenry and Whiteside, Markham, Ontario.

Grayson, D. K.

1976 A Note on the Prehistoric Avifauna of the Lower Klamath Basin. *The Auk* 93:830–833.

1977 On the Holocene History of Some Northern Great Basin Lagomorphs. *Journal of Mammalogy* 58:507–513.

1981 A Mid-Holocene Record for the Heather Vole, *Phenacomys* cf. *intermedius,* in the Central Great Basin and Its Biogeographic Significance. *Journal of Mammalogy* 62:115–121.

1984 *Quantitative Zooarchaeology.* Academic Press, New York.

1987 The Biogeographic History of Small Mammals in the Great Basin: Observations on the Last 20,000 Years. *Journal of Mammalogy* 68:359–375.

1993 *The Desert's Past: A Natural Prehistory of the Great Basin.* Smithsonian Institution Press, Washington, D.C.

1998 Moisture History and Small Mammal Community Richness during the Latest Pleistocene and Holocene, Northern Bonneville Basin, Utah. *Quaternary Research* 49:330–334.

2000a The Homestead Cave Mammal Fauna. In *Late Quaternary Paleoecology in the Bonneville Basin,* by D. B. Madsen, pp. 67–89. Utah Geological Survey Bulletin, 130. Salt Lake City.

2000b Mammalian Responses to Middle Holocene Climatic Change in the Great Basin of the Western United States. *Journal of Biogeography* 27:181–192.

2001 The Archaeological Record of Human Impacts on Animal Populations. *Journal of World Prehistory* 15:1–68.

Grayson, D. K., S. D. Livingston, E. Rickart, and M. W. Shaver III

1996 Biogeographic Significance of Low-Elevation Records for *Neotoma cinerea* from the Northern Bonneville Basin, Utah. *Great Basin Naturalist* 56:191–196.

Green, J. S., and J. T. Flinders

1980a *Brachylagus idahoensis. Mammalian Species* 125:1–4.

1980b Habitat and Dietary Relationships of the Pygmy Rabbit. *Journal of Range Management* 33:136–142.

Greenquist, C. M.

1983 The American Pronghorn Antelope in Wyoming: A History of Human Influences and Management. Ph.D. dissertation, Department of Geography, University of Oregon, Eugene.

Gregg, P. A.

1955 *Summer Habits of Wyoming Antelope*. Ph.D. dissertation, Cornell University. University Microfilms, Ann Arbor.

Grieder, T.

1970 Ecology before Columbus. *The Americas* 22(5):21–28.

Grinnell, G. B.

1929 Pronghorn Antelope. *Journal of Mammalogy* 10:135–141.

Grove, R. H.

1992 Origins of Western Environmentalism. *Scientific American* 267(1): 42–47.

Gunn, A.

1982 Muskox: *Ovibos moschatus*. In *Wild Mammals of North America: Biology, Management, Economics*, edited by J. A. Chapman and G. A. Fledhamer, pp. 1021–1035. Johns Hopkins University Press, Baltimore.

Gunn, A., C. Shank, and B. Mclean

1991 The History, Status, and Management of Muskoxen on Banks Island. *Arctic* 44:188–195.

Gustafson, C. E.

1968 Prehistoric Use of Fur Seals: Evidence from the Olympic Coast of Washington. *Science* 161:49–51.

1983 Wapiti Populations in and Adjacent to Mount Rainier National Park: Archaeological and Ethnographic Evidence. MS on file, Mount Rainier National Park, Ashford, Washington.

Guthrie, D. A.

1971 Primitive Man's Relationship to Nature. *BioScience* 21:721–723.

Guthrie, R. D.

1984a Alaskan Megabucks, Megabulls, and Megagrams: The Issue of Pleistocene Gigantism. In *Contributions in Quaternary Vertebrate Paleontology: A Volume in Memorial to John E. Guilday*, edited by H. H. Genoways and M. R. Dawson, pp. 482–510. Carnegie Museum of Natural History Special Publication, 8. Pittsburgh.

1984b Mosaics, Allochemics, and Nutrients: An Ecological Theory of Late Pleistocene Megafaunal Extinctions. In *Quaternary Extinctions: A Prehistoric Revolution,* edited by P. S. Martin and R. G. Klein, pp. 259–298. University of Arizona Press, Tucson.

Haines, A. L.

1977 *The Yellowstone Story,* vol. 1. Yellowstone Museum and Library Association, Yellowstone National Park, Wyoming.

Haines, F.

1938a The Northward Spread of Horses among the Plains Indians. *American Anthropologist* 40:429–437.

1938b Where Did the Plains Indians Get Their Horses? *American Anthropologist* 40:112–117.

Halford, D. K.

1981 Repopulation and Food Habits of *Peromyscus maniculatus* on a Burned Sagebrush Desert in Southeastern Idaho. *Northwest Science* 55:44–49.

Hall, E. R.

1946 *Mammals of Nevada.* University of California Press, Berkeley.

Hall, L. S., P. R. Krausman, and M. L. Morrison

1997 The Habitat Concept and a Plea for Standard Terminology. *Wildlife Society Bulletin* 25:173–182.

Hamel, P. B., and E. R. Buckner

1998 How Far Could a Squirrel Travel in the Treetops? A Prehistory of the Southern Forest. *Transactions of the North American Wildlife and Natural Resources Conference* 63:309–315.

Hanni, K. D., D. J. Long, R. E. Jones, P. Pyle, and L. E. Morgan

1997 Sightings and Strandings of Guadalupe Fur Seals in Central and Northern California, 1988–1995. *Journal of Mammalogy* 78:684–690.

Harcourt, J. P., D. Austin, T. Porter, and D. Warren

1997 *Phase I Cultural Resources Survey of the Proposed Improvements to Route 63 and Phase II Testing and Evaluation of Sites 23TE146, 23TE147, 23TE 148, 23TE149, 23TE150, 23TE151, and 23TE152, Texas County, Missouri.* Missouri Department of Transportation, Jefferson City.

Harding, J. S., E. F. Benfield, P. V. Bolstad, G. S. Helfman, and E. B. D. Jones III

1998 Stream Biodiversity: The Ghost of Land Use Past. *Proceedings of the National Academy of Sciences* 95:14843–14847.

Harington, C. R.

1980 Radiocarbon Dates on Some Quaternary Mammals and Artifacts from Northern North America. *Arctic* 33:815–832.

Harper, H. A.

1985 A Review and Synthesis of Existing Information on the History, Migration Routes and Wintering Areas of Pronghorn that Summer in Grand Teton National Park. MS on file, Grand Teton National Park, Moose, Wyoming.

Harpole, J. L., and R. L. Lyman

1999 The Holocene Biogeographic History of Elk *(Cervus elaphus)* in Western Washington. *Northwest Science* 73:106–113.

Headland, T. N.
1997 Revisionism in Ecological Anthropology. *Current Anthropology* 38: 605–630.
Hebda, R. J., and C. Whitlock
1997 Environmental History. In *The Rain Forests of Home: Profile of a North American Bioregion,* edited by P. K. Schoonmaker, B. von Hagen, and E. C. Wolf, pp. 227–254. Island Press, Washington, D.C.
Heizer, R. F.
1955 Primitive Man as an Ecologic Factor. *Kroeber Anthropological Society Papers* 13:1–31.
Helmer, J. W.
1981 Climate Change and Dorset Culture Change in the Crozier Strait Region, N.W.T.: A Test of a Hypothesis. Ph.D. dissertation, Department of Archaeology, University of Calgary, Calgary.
1991 The Palaeo-Eskimo Prehistory of the North Devon Lowlands. *Arctic* 44:301–317.
1994 Resurrecting the Spirit(s) of Taylor's "Carlsberg Culture": Cultural Traditions and Cultural Horizons in Eastern Arctic Prehistory. In *Threads of Arctic Prehistory: Papers in Honour of William E. Taylor, Jr.,* edited by D. Morrison and J.-L. Pilon, pp. 15–34. Mercury Series, Archaeological Survey of Canada Paper, 149. Canadian Museum of Civilization, Hull, Quebec.
Hendrix, W. F.
2000 Elk in Yakima County. *Livestock Newsletter* (Washington State University, Cooperative Extension Office, Yakima), September:2–3.
Henning, D. R.
1970 Development and Interrelationships of Oneota Culture in the Lower Missouri River Valley. *The Missouri Archaeologist* 32.
Hepworth, W., and F. Blunt
1966 Research Findings on Wyoming Antelope. *Wyoming Wildlife* 30(6): 24–29.
Hester, F. E.
1991 The U.S. National Park Service Experience with Exotic Species. *Natural Areas Journal* 11:127–128.
Hewitt, G.
2000 The Genetic Legacy of the Quaternary Ice Ages. *Nature* 405:907–913.
Higg, E. S.
1997 What Is Good Ecological Restoration? *Conservation Biology* 11: 338–348.
Hildebrandt, W. R.
1984 Archaeological Presence of the Northern Fur Seal *(Callorhinus ursinus)* along the Coast of Northern California. *The Murrelet* 65:28–29.
Hildebrandt, W. R., and T. L. Jones
1992 Evolution of Marine Mammal Hunting: A View from the California and Oregon Coasts. *Journal of Anthropological Archaeology* 11: 360–401.
2002 Depletion of Prehistoric Pinniped Populations along the California and Oregon Coasts: Were Humans the Cause? In *Wilderness and Political*

Ecology: Aboriginal Influences and the Original State of Nature, edited by C. E. Kay and R. T. Simmons, pp. 72–110. University of Utah Press, Salt Lake City.

Hintze, L. F.
1980 *Geologic Map of Utah.* Utah Geological Survey, Salt Lake City.

Hobbie, E. A., S. A. Macko, and M. Williams
2000 Correlations between Foliar $d^{15}N$ and Nitrogen Concentrations May Indicate Plant–Mycorrhizal Interactions. *Oecologia* 122:273–283.

Hobbs, N. T., D. L. Baker, and R. B. Gill
1983 Comparative Nutritional Ecology of Montane Ungulates during Winter. *Journal of Wildlife Management* 47:1–16.

Hobson, K. A., and J. L. Sease
1998 Stable Isotope Analyses of Tooth Annuli Reveal Temporal Dietary Records: An Example Using Steller Sea Lions. *Marine Mammal Science* 14:116–129.

Hobson, K. A., J. L. Sease, R. L. Merrick, and J. F. Piatt
1997 Investigating Trophic Relationships of Pinnipeds in Alaska and Washington Using Stable Isotope Ratios of Nitrogen and Carbon. *Marine Mammal Science* 13:114–132.

Hocutt, C. H., R. E. Jenkins, and J. R. Stauffer Jr.
1986 Zoogeography of Fishes of the Central Appalachians and Central Atlantic Coastal Plain. In *The Zoogeography of North American Freshwater Fishes,* edited by C. H. Hocutt and E. O. Wiley, pp. 161–211. Wiley, New York.

Hoerr, W.
1993 The Concept of Naturalness in Environmental Discourse. *Natural Areas Journal* 13:29–32.

Hofman, R. J.
1995 The Changing Focus of Marine Mammal Conservation. *Trends in Ecology and Evolution* 10:462–465.

Högberg, P.
1997 Tansley Review No. 95: ^{15}N Natural Abundance in Soil–Plant Systems. *New Phytologist* 137:179–203.

Honess, R. F., and N. M. Frost
1942 *A Wyoming Bighorn Sheep Study.* Pittman-Robertson Project, Wyoming 13-R. Bulletin, 1. Wyoming Game and Fish Department, Cheyenne.

Houston, D. B.
1982 *The Northern Yellowstone Elk.* Macmillan, New York.

Houston, D. B., and E. G. Schreiner
1995 Alien Species in National Parks: Drawing Lines in Space and Time. *Conservation Biology* 9:204–209.

Houston, D. B., E. G. Schreiner, B. B. Moorhead, and K. A. Krueger
1990 Elk in Olympic National Park: Will They Persist Over Time? *Natural Areas Journal* 10:6–11.

Hubbs, C. L., and R. R. Miller
1948 The Zoological Evidence: Correlation between Fish Distribution and Hydrographic History in the Desert Basins of Western United States. *University of Utah Bulletin 38, Biological Series* 10(7):17–144.

Hudson, R. J., J. C. Haigh, and A. B. Bubenik

2002 Physical and Physiological Adaptations. In *North American Elk: Ecology and Management,* edited by D. E. Toweill and J. W. Thomas, pp. 199–257. Smithsonian Institution Press, Washington, D.C.

Huelsbeck, D. R.

1994a Mammals and Fish in the Subsistence Economy of Ozette. In *Ozette Archaeological Project Research Reports, vol. 2: Fauna,* edited by S. R. Samuels, pp. 17–91. Reports of Investigations, 66. Department of Anthropology, Washington State University, Pullman, and National Park Service, Pacific Northwest Regional Office, Seattle.

1994b The Utilization of Whales at Ozette. In *Ozette Archaeological Project Research Reports, vol. 2: Fauna,* edited by S. R. Samuels, pp. 265–303. Reports of Investigations, 66. Department of Anthropology, Washington State University, Pullman, and National Park Service, Pacific Northwest Regional Office, Seattle.

Huff, D. E.

1997 Defining Ecosystem Health in National Parks. *Transactions of the North American Wildlife and Natural Resources Conference* 62: 448–453.

Hughes, M. K., and L. J. Graumlich

1996 Multimillennial Dendroclimatic Studies from the Western United States. In *Climatic Variations and Forcing Mechanisms of the Last 2000 Years,* edited by P. D. Jones, R. S. Bradley, and J. Jouzel, pp. 109–124. NATO ASI Series, 141. Springer-Verlag, Berlin.

Hughes, S. S.

2003 Beyond the Altithermal: The Role of Climate Change in the Prehistoric Adaptations of Northwestern Wyoming. Ph.D. dissertation, Department of Anthropology, University of Washington, Seattle.

Hull, R. B., D. Richert, E. Seekamp, D. Robertson, and G. J. Buyhoff

2003 Understandings of Environmental Quality: Ambiguities and Values Held by Environmental Professionals. *Environmental Management* 31:1–13.

Humphrey, D. L., and E. W. Schupp

2001 Seed Banks of *Bromus tectorum*–Dominated Communities in the Great Basin. *Western North American Naturalist* 61:85–92.

Hunter, M. L., Jr.

1996 Benchmarks for Managing Ecosystems: Are Human Activties Natural? *Conservation Biology* 10:695–697.

Hunter, M. L., Jr., G. L. Jacobson Jr., and T. Webb III

1988 Paleoecology and the Coarse-Filter Approach to Maintaining Biological Diversity. *Conservation Biology* 2:375–385.

Hurley, K. P.

1985 The Trout Peak Bighorn Sheep Herd, Northwestern Wyoming. M.S. thesis, Department of Zoology and Physiology, University of Wyoming, Laramie.

Husted, W. M., and R. Edgar

2002 *The Archeology of Mummy Cave Wyoming: An Introduction to Shoshonean Prehistory.* U.S. Department of the Interior, National Park Service, Midwest Archeological Center, Lincoln.

Hutchins, M.
1995 Olympic Mountain Goat Controversy Continues. *Conservation Biology* 9:1324–1326.
International Union for the Conservation of Nature and Natural Resources Reintroduction Specialist Group
1992 Draft Guidelines for Reintroductions. *Newsletter of the IUCN Reintroduction Specialist Group* 4:2–3.
Ives, P. C., B. Levin, R. D. Robinson, and M. Rubin
1964 U.S. Geological Survey Radiocarbon Dates VII. *Radiocarbon* 6: 37–76.
Jackson, J. B. C., M. X. Kirby, W. H. Berger, K. A. Bjorndal, L. W. Botsford, B. J. Bourque, R. H. Bradbury, R. Cooke, J. Erlandson, J. A. Estes, T. P. Hughes, S. Kidwell, C. B. Lange, H. S. Lenihan, J. M. Pandolfi, C. H. Peterson, R. S. Steneck, M. J. Tegner, and R. R. Warner
2001 Historical Overfishing and the Recent Collapse of Coastal Ecosystems. *Science* 293:629–638.
Jacobs, J. D.
1989 Spatial Representativeness of Climatic Data from Baffin Island, N.W.T., with Implications for Muskoxen and Caribou Distribution. *Arctic* 42:50–56.
Jacoby, K.
2001 *Crimes against Nature: Squatters, Poachers, Thieves, and the Hidden History of American Conservation.* University of California Press, Berkeley.
Jeffries, S. J., H. Huber, J. Calambokidis, and J. Laake
2003 Trends and Status of Harbor Seals in Washington State: 1978–1999. *Journal of Wildlife Management* 67:207–218.
Jenkins, R. E., and N. M. Burkhead
1994 *Freshwater Fishes of Virginia.* American Fisheries Society, Bethesda.
Jenny, H.
1950 Causes of the High Nitrogen and Organic Matter Content of Certain Tropical Forest Soils. *Soil Science* 69:63–69.
Jensen, M. N., and P. R. Krausman
1993 Conservation Biology's Literature: New Wine or Just a New Bottle? *Wildlife Society Bulletin* 21:199–203.
Jepson, P., and S. Canney
2003 Values-Led Conservation. *Global Ecology and Biogeography* 12: 271–274.
Johnson, D. R., and D. H. Chance
1974 Presettlement Overharvest of Upper Columbia River Beaver Populations. *Canadian Journal of Zoology* 52:1519–1521.
Johnson, R. E., and K. M. Cassidy
1997 Terrestrial Mammals of Washington State: Location Data and Predicted Distributions. *Washington State Gap Analysis—Final Report,* vol. 3, edited by K. M. Cassidy, C. E. Grue, M. R. Smith, and K. M. Dvornich. Washington Cooperative Fish and Wildlife Research Unit, University of Washington, Seattle.

Jones, T. L., and W. R. Hildebrandt
1995 Reasserting a Prehistoric Tragedy of the Commons: Reply to Lyman. *Journal of Anthropological Archaeology* 14:78–98.
Jones, T. L., and D. J. Kennett
1999 Late Holocene Sea Temperatures along the Central California Coast. *Quaternary Research* 51:74–82.
Jordan, W. R., III
1999 Nature and Culture. *Ecological Restoration* 17:187–188.
Joyce, L. A., and A. Hansen
2001 Climate Change: Ecosystem Restructuring, Natural Disturbances and Land Use. *Transactions of the North American Wildlife and Natural Resources Conference* 66:327–343.
Kahlke, R.-D.
1994 Die Entstehungs-, Entwicklungs- und Verbreitungsgeschichte des Oberpleistozänen Mammuthus-Coelodonta-Faunenkomplexes in Eurasien (Großsäuger). *Abhandlungen der Senckenbergischen Naturforschenden Gesellschaft* 546:1–164.
Kahrl, W. L.
1982 *Water and Power.* University of California Press, Berkeley.
Kaiser, J.
2001a Bold Corridor Project Confronts Political Reality. *Science* 293: 2196–2199.
2001b An Experiment for All Seasons. *Science* 293:624–627.
Kajimura, H.
1979 Fur Seal Pup/Yearling Distribution in the Eastern North Pacific. In *Preliminary Analysis of Pelagic Fur Seal Data Collected by the United States and Canada during 1958–74,* edited by H. Kajimura, R. A. Lander, M. A. Perez, A. E. York, and M. A. Bigg, pp. 4–19. Report to the 22nd Annual Meeting of the Standing Scientific Committee, North Pacific Fur Seal Commission, 2–6 April 1979, Washington, D.C.
Kalkreuth, W., and P. D. Sutherland
1998 The Archaeology and Petrology of Coal Artifacts from a Thule Settlement on Axel Heiberg Island, Arctic Canada. *Arctic* 51:345–349.
Karamanos, R. E., R. P. Voroney, and D. A. Rennie
1981 Variation in Natural N-15 Abundance of Central Saskatchewan Soils. *Soil Science Society of America Journal* 45:826–828.
Kareiva, P. M.
2002 Applying Ecological Science to Recovery Planning. *Ecological Applications* 12:629.
Kay, C. E.
1990 Yellowstone's Northern Elk Herd: A Critical Evaluation of the "Natural Regulation" Paradigm. Ph.D. dissertation, Department of Wildlife Ecology, Utah State University, Logan.
1994 Aboriginal Overkill: The Role of Native Americans in Structuring Western Ecosystems. *Human Nature* 5:359–398.
2002 Are Ecosystems Structured from the Top-Down or Bottom-Up? In *Wilderness and Political Ecology: Aboriginal Influences and the*

Original State of Nature, edited by C. E. Kay and R. T. Simmons, pp. 215–237. University of Utah Press, Salt Lake City.

Kay, C. E., and R. T. Simmons

2002a Preface. In *Wilderness and Political Ecology: Aboriginal Influences and the Original State of Nature,* edited by C. E. Kay and R. T. Simmons, pp. xi–xix. University of Utah Press, Salt Lake City.

Kay, C. E., and R. T. Simmons (editors)

2002b *Wilderness and Political Ecology: Aboriginal Influences and the Original State of Nature.* University of Utah Press, Salt Lake City.

Kay, M.

1980 *The Central Missouri Hopewell Subsistence-Settlement System.* Missouri Archaeological Society Research Series, 15. Columbia.

Kearney, M. S., and B. H. Luckman

1983 Holocene Timberline Fluctuations in Jasper National Park, Alberta. *Science* 221:261–263.

Keiter, R. B.

1997 Greater Yellowstone's Bison: Unraveling of an Early American Wildlife Conservation Achievement. *Journal of Wildlife Management* 61:1–11.

Keiter, R. B., and M. S. Boyce (editors)

1991 *The Greater Yellowstone Ecosystem: Redefining America's Wilderness Heritage.* Yale University Press, New Haven.

Kennett, D. J., and J. P. Kennett

2000 Competitive and Cooperative Responses to Climatic Instability in Coastal Southern California. *American Antiquity* 65:379–395.

Kenyon, K. W., and F. Wilke

1953 Migration of the Northern Fur Seal, *Callorhinus ursinus. Journal of Mammalogy* 4:86–97.

Kitchen, D. W., and B. W. O'Gara

1982 Pronghorn. In *Wild Mammals of North America: Biology, Management, and Economics,* edited by J. A. Chapman and G. A. Feldhamer, pp. 960–971. Johns Hopkins University Press, Baltimore.

Klein, D. R.

1996 Arctic Ungulates at the Northern Edge of Terrestrial Life. *Rangifer* 16:51–56.

Knapp, P. A.

1995 Intermountain West Lightening-Caused Fires: Climatic Predictors of Area Burned. *Journal of Range Management* 48:85–91.

Knight, D. H.

1994 *Mountains and Plains: The Ecology of Wyoming Landscapes.* Yale University Press, New Haven.

Knight, R. L.

1996 Aldo Leopold, the Land Ethic, and Ecosystem Management. *Journal of Wildlife Management* 60:471–474.

Knuth, E.

1967 *Archaeology of the Musk-Ox Way.* Contributions du Centre D'Etudes Arctiques et Finno-Scandinaves, 5. Paris.

1981 Greenland News from between 81° and 83° North. *Folk* 23:91–111.

1983 The Northernmost Ruins of the Globe. *Folk* 25:5–21.

Korn, H.
1994 Genetic, Demographic, Spatial, Environmental and Catastrophic Effects on the Survival Probability of Small Populations of Mammals. In *Minimum Animal Populations,* edited by H. Remmert, pp. 33–49. Springer-Verlag, Berlin.
Krech, S., III
1999 *The Ecological Indian: Myth and History.* Norton, New York.
Kutzbach, J. E., and P. J. Guetter
1984 The Sensitivity of Monsoon Climates to Orbital Parameter Changes for 9000 Years B.P.: Experiments with the NCAR General Circulation Model. In *Milankovitch and Climate,* pt. 2, edited by A. L. Berger, J. Imbrie, J. Hayes, G. Kukla, and B. Salzman, pp. 801–820. D. Reidel, Dordrecht, the Netherlands.
Lahren, L. A.
1976 *The Myers-Hindman Site: An Exploratory Study of Human Occupation Patterns in the Upper Yellowstone Valley from 7000 B.C. to A.D. 1200.* Anthropologos Researches International, Inc., Livingston, Montana.
LaMarche,V. C.
1974 Paleoclimatic Inferences from Long Tree-Ring Records. *Science* 183:1043–1048.
Land, A., S. R. Jeremiassen, and R. Anderson
2000 *Rensdyr og Moskusokser i Inglefield Land, Nordvestgrønland.* Teknisk Rapport, 31. Pinngortitaleriffik, Grønland Natuinstitut, Nuuk, Greenland.
Landres, P. B.
1992 Temporal Scale Perspectives in Managing Biological Diversity. *Transactions of the North American Wildlife and Natural Resources Conference* 57:292–307.
Landres, P. B., M. W. Brunson, and L. Merigliano
2001 Naturalness and Wildness: The Dilemma and Irony of Ecological Restoration in Wilderness. *Wild Earth* 10(4):77–82.
Langvatn, R., and S. D. Albon
1986 Geographic Clines in Body Weight of Norwegian Red Deer: A Novel Explanation of Bergmann's Rule? *Holarctic Ecology* 9:285–293.
Larrison, E. J., and D. R. Johnson
1973 Density Changes in Habitat Affinities of Rodents of Shadscale and Sagebrush Associations. *Great Basin Naturalist* 33:205–254.
Larson, S., R. Jameson, M. A. Etnier, M. Fleming, and P. Bentzen
2002 Loss of Genetic Diversity in Sea Otters *(Enhydra lutris)* Associated with the Fur Trade of the 18th and 19th Centuries. *Molecular Ecology* 11:1899–1903.
Laundré, J. W.
1991 Mountain Goats in Yellowstone: The Horns of a Dilemma? *Park Science* 11(3):8–9.
1992 Are Wolves Native to Yellowstone National Park? In *Wolves for Yellowstone? A Report to the United States Congress, vol. 4: Research and Analysis,* edited by J. D. Varley and W. G. Brewster, pp. 1-266–1-274. National Park Service, Yellowstone National Park, Wyoming.

Lavigne, D. M., V. B. Scheffer, and S. R. Kellert

1999 The Evolution of North American Attitudes toward Marine Mammals. In *Conservation and Management of Marine Mammals,* edited by J. R. Twiss Jr. and R. R. Reeves, pp. 10–47. Smithsonian Institution Press, Washington, D.C.

Lawson, B., and R. Johnson

1982 Mountain Sheep. In *Wild Mammals of North America,* edited by J. A. Chapman and G. A. Feldhamer, pp. 1036–1055. Johns Hopkins University Press, Baltimore.

Lawton, J. H.

1997 The Science and Non-Science of Conservation Biology. *Oikos* 79:3–5.

LeBlanc, R. J.

1994a The Crane Site and the Lagoon Complex in the Western Canadian Arctic. In *Threads of Arctic Prehistory: Papers in Honour of William E. Taylor, Jr.,* edited by D. Morrison and J.-L. Pilon, pp. 87–102. Mercury Series, Archaeological Survey of Canada Paper, 149. Canadian Museum of Civilization, Hull, Quebec.

1994b *The Crane Site and the Palaeoeskimo Period in the Western Canadian Arctic.* Mercury Series, Archaeological Survey of Canada Paper, 148. Canadian Museum of Civilization, Hull, Quebec.

LeBoeuf, B. J.

1977 Back from Extation? *Pacific Discovery* 30(5):1–9.

Lélé, S., and R. Norgaard

1996 Sustainability and the Scientist's Burden. *Conservation Biology* 10: 354–365.

Lent, P. C.

1971 Muskox Management Controversies in North America. *Biological Conservation* 3:255–263.

1988 *Ovibos moschatus. Mammalian Species* 302:1–9.

1999 *Muskoxen and Their Hunters.* University of Oklahoma Press, Norman.

Leopold, A. S., S. A. Cain, C. M. Cottam, I. N. Gabrielson, and T. L. Kimball

1963 Wildlife Management in the National Parks. *Transactions of the North American Wildlife and Natural Resources Conference* 28:28–45.

Létolle, R.

1980 Nitrogen-15 in the Natural Environment. In *Handbook of Environmental Isotope Geochemistry,* vol. 1, edited by P. Fritz and J. C. Fontes, pp. 407–433. Elsevier, Oxford.

Livingston, S. D.

1987 Prehistoric Biogeography of White-Tailed Deer in Washington and Oregon. *Journal of Wildlife Management* 51:649–654.

1999 The Relevance of Ethnographic, Archaeological, and Paleontological Records to Models for Conservation Biology. In *Models for the Millennium: Great Basin Anthropology Today,* edited by C. Beck, pp. 152–160. University of Utah Press, Salt Lake City.

Llewellyn, J. B.

1981 Habitat Selection by the Desert Woodrat, *Neotoma lepida,* Inhabiting a Pinyon-Juniper Woodland in Western Nevada. *Southwestern Naturalist* 26:76–78.

Lodge, D. M.
1993 Biological Invasions: Lessons for Ecology. *Trends in Ecology and Evolution* 8:133–137.
Long Term Ecological Research Network
2001 Available at www.lternet.edu (accessed March 25 and June 5, 2002).
Lott, D. F.
2002 *American Bison*. University of California Press, Berkeley.
Loughlin, T. R., and R. V. Miller
1989 Growth of the Northern Fur Seal Colony on Bogoslof Island, Alaska. *Arctic* 42:368–372.
Love, C.
1972 An Archeological Survey of the Jackson Hole Region, Wyoming. M.A. thesis, Department of Anthropology, University of Wyoming, Laramie.
Low, B. S.
1996 Behavioral Ecology of Conservation in Traditional Societies. *Human Nature* 7:353–379.
Lowe, V. P. W., and A. S. Gardiner
1989 Are the New and Old World Wapiti *(Cervus canadensis)* Conspecific with Red Deer *(Cervus elaphus)? Journal of Zoology (London)* 218:51–58.
Lowenthal, D.
1964 Is Wilderness "Paradise Enow"? Images of Nature in America. *Columbia University Forum* 7(2):34–40.
Lubinski, P. M.
1997 Pronghorn Intensification in the Wyoming Basin: A Study of Mortality Patterns and Prehistoric Hunting Strategies. Ph.D. dissertation, Department of Anthropology, University of Wisconsin, Madison.
Lubinski, P. M., and V. Herren
2000 An Introduction to Pronghorn Biology, Ethnography, and Archaeology. In *Pronghorn Past and Present: Archaeology, Ethnography, and Biology,* edited by J. V. Pastor and P. M. Lubinski, pp. 3–11. Plains Anthropologist Memoir, 32.
Ludwig, D., R. Hilborn, and C. Walters
1993 Uncertainty, Resource Exploitation, and Conservation: Lessons from History. *Science* 260:17, 36.
Ludwig, D., M. Mangel, and B. Haddad
2001 Ecology, Conservation, and Public Policy. *Annual Review of Ecology and Systematics* 32:481–517.
Lyman, R. L.
1983 Prehistoric Extralimital Records for *Pappogeomys castanops* (Geomyidae) in Northwestern New Mexico. *Journal of Mammalogy* 64: 502–505.
1986 On the Holocene History of *Ursus* in Eastern Washington. *Northwest Science* 60:67–72.
1988a Significance for Wildlife Management of the Late Quaternary Biogeography of Mountain Goats *(Oreamnos americanus)* in the Pacific Northwest U.S.A. *Arctic and Alpine Research* 20:13–23.
1988b Zoogeography of Oregon Coast Marine Mammals: The Last 3000 Years. *Marine Mammal Science* 4:247–264.

1989 Seal and Sea Lion Hunting: A Zooarchaeological Study from the Southern Northwest Coast of North America. *Journal of Anthropological Archaeology* 8:68–99.

1991 Late Quaternary Biogeography of the Pygmy Rabbit *(Brachylagus idahoensis)* in Eastern Washington. *Journal of Mammalogy* 72:110–117.

1992 Influences of Mid-Holocene Altithermal Climates on Mammalian Faunas and Human Subsistence in Eastern Washington. *Journal of Ethnobiology* 12:37–62.

1994a The Olympic Mountain Goat Controversy: A Different Perspective. *Conservation Biology* 8:898–901.

1994b Quantitative Units and Terminology in Zooarchaeology. *American Antiquity* 59:36–71.

1994c *Vertebrate Taphonomy.* Cambridge University Press, Cambridge.

1995a Determining When Rare (Zoo)Archaeological Phenomena Are Truly Absent. *Journal of Archaeological Method and Theory* 2:369–424.

1995b Inaccurate Data and the Olympic National Park Mountain Goat Controversy. *Northwest Science* 69:234–238.

1995c On the Evolution of Marine Mammal Hunting on the West Coast of North America. *Journal of Anthropological Archaeology* 14:45–77.

1996 Applied Zooarchaeology: The Relevance of Faunal Analysis to Wildlife Management. *World Archaeology* 28:110–125.

1997 Impediments to Archaeology: Publishing and the (Growing) Translucency of Archaeological Research. *Northwest Anthropological Research Notes* 31:5–22.

1998 *White Goats, White Lies: The Misuse of Science in Olympic National Park.* University of Utah Press, Salt Lake City.

1999 Faunal Analysis: 45CA426 Component II. In *The SR-101 Sequim Bypass Archaeological Project: Mid- to Late-Holocene Occupations on the Northern Olympic Peninsula, Clallam County, Washington,* edited by V. E. Morgan, pp. 16.1–16.31. Eastern Washington University Reports in Archaeology and History, 100–108. Archaeological and Historical Services, Cheney.

2000 Building Cultural Chronology in Eastern Washington: The Influence of Geochronology, Index Fossils, and Radiocarbon Dating. *Geoarchaeology* 15:609–648.

2001 Vertebrate Faunal Remains from 45CA426, Component II. *Archaeology in Washington* 8:69–76.

2002 Cultural Resource Management–Driven Spatial Samples in Archaeology: An Example from Eastern Washington. *Journal of Northwest Anthropology* 36:51–67.

2003a The Influence of Time Averaging and Space Averaging on the Application of Foraging Theory in Zooarchaeology. *Journal of Archaeological Science* 30:595–610.

2003b Pinniped Behavior, Foraging Theory, and the Depression of Metapopulations and Nondepression of a Local Population on the Southern Northwest Coast of North America. *Journal of Anthropological Archaeology* 22:376–388.

2004a Aboriginal Overkill in the Intermountain West of North America: Zooarchaeological Tests and Implications. *Human Nature* 15:169–208.

2004b Biogeographic and Paleoenvironmental Implications of Late Quaternary Pygmy Rabbits *(Brachylagus idahoensis)* in Eastern Washington. *Western North American Naturalist* 64:1–6.

Lyman, R. L., and S. D. Livingston

1983 Late Quaternary Mammalian Zoogeography of Eastern Washington. *Quaternary Research* 20:360–373.

Lyman, R. L., and S. Wolverton

2002 The Late Prehistoric/Early Historic Game Sink in the Northwestern United States. *Conservation Biology* 16:73–85.

Lyon, G. M.

1937 Pinnipeds and a Sea Otter from the Point Mugu Shell Mound of California. *University of California Publications in Biological Sciences* 1:133–168.

MacArthur, R. H., and E. O. Wilson

1967 *The Theory of Island Biogeography.* Princeton University Press, Princeton.

MacCracken, J. G., and R. M. Hansen

1987 Coyote Feeding Strategies in Southeastern Idaho: Optimal Foraging by an Opportunistic Predator? *Journal of Wildlife Management* 51: 278–285.

Mack, R. N.

1981 Invasion of *Bromus tectorum L.* into Western North America: An Ecological Chronicle. *Agro-Ecosystems* 7:145–165.

1984 Invaders at Home on the Range. *Natural History* 93(2):40–47.

Macleod, W. C.

1936 Conservation among Primitive Hunting Peoples. *Scientific Monthly* 43:562–566.

MacNeish, R. S.

1964 Investigations in Southwest Yukon: Archaeological Excavations, Comparisons, and Speculations. *Papers of the Robert S. Peabody Foundation for Archaeology* 6:199–488.

Madsen, D. B.

2000 *Late Quaternary Paleoecology in the Bonneville Basin.* Utah Geological Survey Bulletin, 130. Salt Lake City.

Mangel, M., and R. J. Hofman

1999 Ecosystems: Patterns, Processes, and Paradigms. In *Conservation and Management of Marine Mammals,* edited by J. R. Twiss Jr. and R. R. Reeves, pp. 87–98. Smithsonian Institution Press, Washington, D.C.

Mann, C. C.

2002 1491. *The Atlantic Monthly* 289(3):41–53.

Mantua, N. J., S. R. Hare, Y. Zhang, J. M. Wallace, and R. C. Francis

1997 A Pacific Interdecadal Climate Oscillation with Impacts on Salmon Production. *Bulletin of the American Meteorological Society* 78: 1069–1079.

Manzano, B. L., and W. C. Dickinson
1991 Archaeological Occurrences of the Extinct Harelip Sucker, *Lagochila lacera Jordan* and *Brayton* (Pisces: Catostomidae). In *Beamers, Bobwhites, and Blue-Points: Tributes to the Career of Paul W. Parmalee,* edited by J. R. Purdue, W. E. Klippel, and B. W. Styles, pp. 163–176. Illinois State Museum Scientific Papers, 23. Springfield.
Margules, C. R., and R. L. Pressey
2000 Systematic Conservation Planning. *Nature* 405:243–253.
Marino, B. D., and M. B. McElroy
1991 Isotopic Composition of Atmospheric CO_2 Inferred from Carbon in C_4 Plant Cellulose. *Nature* 349:127–131.
Marino, E. A.
1994 An Examination of the Archaeofauna from 23CP40. *Missouri Archaeological Society Quarterly* 11(3):6–10.
Martin, C.
1981 The American as Miscast Ecologist. *The History Teacher* 14: 243–252.
Martin, P. S.
1970 Pleistocene Niches for Alien Animals. *BioScience* 20:218–221.
Martin, P. S., and D. A. Burney
1999 Bring Back the Elephants! *Wild Earth* 9(1):57–64.
Martin, P. S., and C. R. Szuter
1999a Megafauna of the Columbia Basin, 1800–1840: Lewis and Clark in a Game Sink. In *Northwest Lands, Northwest Peoples: Readings in Environmental History,* edited by D. D. Goble and P. W. Hirt, pp. 188–204. University of Washington Press, Seattle.
1999b War Zones and Game Sinks in Lewis and Clark's West. *Conservation Biology* 13:36–45.
2002 Game Parks before and after Lewis and Clark: Reply to Lyman and Wolverton. *Conservation Biology* 16:244–247.
Martner, B. E.
1986 *Wyoming Climate Atlas.* University of Nebraska Press, Lincoln.
Maser, C.
1990 On the "Naturalness" of Natural Areas: A Perspective for the Future. *Natural Areas Journal* 10:129–133.
Mathiassen, T.
1927 *Archaeology of the Central Eskimos: Report of the Fifth Thule Expedition, 1921–24,* vol. 4, pt. 1. Gyldendalske Boghandel, Nordisk Forlag, Copenhagen.
Maxwell, M. S.
1960 *An Archaeological Analysis of Eastern Grant Land, Ellesmere Island, Northwest Territories.* National Museum of Canada Bulletin, 170. Department of Northern Affairs and National Resources, Ottawa.
1985 *Eastern Arctic Prehistory.* Academic Press, Orlando.
McAllister, K. R.
1995 *Washington State Recovery Plan for the Pygmy Rabbit.* Washington Department of Fish and Wildlife, Olympia.

McAllister, K. R., and H. Allen
1993 *Status of the Pygmy Rabbit* (Brachylagus idahoensis) *in Washington.* Washington Department of Wildlife, Wildlife Management Division, Olympia.

McCartney, P. H.
1989 Paleoeskimo Subsistence and Settlement in the High Arctic. Ph.D. dissertation, Department of Archaeology, University of Calgary, Calgary.

McClelland, L. F.
1998 *Building the National Parks: Historic Landscape Design and Construction.* Johns Hopkins University Press, Baltimore.

McCorquodale, S. M.
1985 Archaeological Evidence of Elk in the Columbia Basin. *Northwest Science* 59:192–197.

McCullough, D. R.
1985 Long Range Movements of Large Terrestrial Animals. *Contributions in Marine Science Supplements* 27:444–465.

McCullough, K. M.
1989 *The Ruin Islanders: Thule Pioneers in the Eastern High Arctic.* Mercury Series, Archaeological Survey of Canada Paper, 141. Canadian Museum of Civilization, Hull, Quebec

McDonald, J. N.
1981 *North American Bison: Their Classification and Evolution.* University of California Press, Berkeley.

McGhee, R.
1972 *Copper Eskimo Prehistory.* National Museum of Man, Publications in Archaeology, 2. National Museums of Canada, Ottawa.
1979 *The Palaeoeskimo Occupations at Port Refuge, High Arctic Canada.* Mercury Series, Archaeological Survey of Canada Paper, 92. National Museum of Man, Ottawa.
1984 *The Thule Village at Brooman Point, High Arctic Canada.* Mercury Series, Archaeological Survey of Canada Paper, 105. National Museum of Man, Ottawa.

McKinley, D.
1960 The American Elk in Pioneer Missouri. *Missouri Historical Review* 54: 356–365.

McLean, D. D.
1944 The Prong-horned Antelope in California. *California Fish and Game* 30:221–241.

McNab, J.
1983 Wildlife Management as Scientific Experimentation. *Wildlife Society Bulletin* 11:397–401.

McNett, C. W., Jr.
1985 *Shawnee Minisink: A Stratified Paleoindian-Archaic Site in the Upper Delaware Valley of Pennsylvania.* Academic Press, Orlando.

Meagher, M.
1973 *The Bison of Yellowstone National Park.* National Park Service, Scientific Monograph, 1. Washington, D.C.

Meffe, G. K., and C. R. Carroll
1997 *Principles of Conservation Biology.* Sinauer, Sunderland, Massachusetts.
Meffe, G. K., and S. Viederman
1995 Combining Science and Policy in Conservation Biology. *Wildlife Society Bullètin* 23:327–332.
Mehringer, P. J., Jr., S. F. Arno, and K. L. Petersen
1977 Postglacial History of Lost Trail Pass Bog, Bitterroot Mountains, Montana. *Arctic and Alpine Research* 9:345–368.
Meine, C.
1999 It's about Time: Conservation Biology and History. *Conservation Biology* 13:1–3.
Meldgaard, M.
1986 The Greenland Caribou: Zoogeography, Taxonomy, and Population Dynamics. *Meddelelser om Grønland, Bioscience* 20:1–88.
Meltzer, D. J.
1992 How Columbus Sickened the New World. *New Scientist* 136:38–41.
Miller, F. L.
1988 *Peary Caribou and Muskoxen on Melville and Byam Martin Islands, Northwest Territories, July 1987.* Canadian Wildlife Service, Western and Northern Region, Technical Report Series, 37. Ottawa.
Miller, F. L., H. R. Russell, and A. Gunn
1977 *Peary Caribou and Muskoxen on Western Queen Elizabeth Islands, N.W.T., 1972–74.* Canadian Wildlife Service Report, 40. Ottawa.
Miller, M. E.
1999 Seasonality of the Early Archaic Trappers Point Pronghorn Bonebed. In *The Trappers Point Site (48SU1006): Early Archaic Adaptations in the Upper Green River Basin, Wyoming,* edited by M. E. Miller, P. H. Sanders, and J. E. Francis, pp. 206–241. Cultural Resource Series, 1. Office of the Wyoming State Archaeologist, Laramie.
Miller, M. E., and P. H. Sanders
2000 The Trappers Point Site (48SU1006): Early Archaic Adaptations and Pronghorn Procurement in the Upper Green River Basin, Wyoming. In *Pronghorn Past and Present: Archaeology, Ethnography, and Biology,* edited by J. V. Pastor and P. M. Lubinski, pp. 39–52. Plains Anthropologist Memoir, 32.
Miller, M. E., P. H. Sanders, and J. E. Francis (editors)
1999 *The Trappers Point Site (48SU1006): Early Archaic Adaptations in the Upper Green River Basin, Wyoming.* Cultural Resource Series, 1. Office of the Wyoming State Archaeologist, Laramie.
Miller, R. R.
1946 Correlation between Fish Distribution and Pleistocene Hydrography in Eastern California and Southwestern Nevada, with a Map of the Pleistocene Waters. *Journal of Geology* 54:43–53.
1973 Two New Fishes, *Gila bicolor snyderi* and *Catostomus fumeiventris,* from the Owens River Basin, California. *Occasional Papers of the Museum of Zoology, University of Michigan* 667:1–19.

Milstein, M.
1995 *Wolf: Return to Yellowstone.* The Billings Gazette, Billings, Montana.
Minckley, W. L., and J. E. Deacon (editors)
1991 *Battle against Extinction: Native Fish Management in the American West.* University of Arizona Press, Tucson.
Missouri Department of Conservation
2000a Missouri Elk Reintroduction Feasibility Study. Draft report on file, Missouri Department of Conservation, Columbia.
2000b Missouri Elk Reintroduction Feasibility Study. Summary statement on file, Missouri Department of Conservation, Columbia.
Mitchell, G. E., and J. B. Lauckhart
1948 Management of the Yakima Rocky Mountain Elk Herd. *Transactions of the North American Wildlife Conference* 13:401–409.
Mitchell, J. D.
1978 The American Indian: A Fire Ecologist. *American Indian Culture and Research Journal* 2(2):26–31.
Mooney, H. A., and E. E. Cleland
2001 The Evolutionary Impact of Invasive Species. *National Academy of Sciences, Proceedings* 98:5446–5451.
Moorhead, D. L., P. T. Doran, A. G. Fountain, W. B. Lyons, D. M. McKnight, J. C. Priscu, R. A. Virginia, and D. H. Wall
1999 Ecological Legacies: Impacts on Ecosystems of the McMurdo Dry Valleys. *BioScience* 49:1009–1019.
Moritz, C.
2002 Strategies to Protect Biological Diversity and the Evolutionary Processes That Sustain It. *Systematic Biology* 51:238–254.
Morlan, R. E.
1999a *Canadian Archaeological Radiocarbon Database.* Available at www.canadianarchaeology.com/radiocarbon/card/card.htm (accessed July 18, 2002).
1999b Canadian Archaeological Radiocarbon Database: Establishing Conventional Ages. *Canadian Journal of Archaeology* 23:3–10.
Morrison, D.
1983 *Thule Culture in Western Coronation Gulf, N.W.T.* Mercury Series, Archaeological Survey of Canada Paper, 116. National Museum of Man, Ottawa.
1990 *Iglulualumiut Prehistory: The Lost Inuit of Franklin Bay.* Mercury Series, Archaeological Survey of Canada Paper, 142. Canadian Museum of Civilization, Hull, Quebec.
1997 *Caribou Hunters in the Western Arctic: Zooarchaeology of the Rita-Claire and Bison Skull Sites.* Mercury Series, Archaeological Survey of Canada Paper, 157. Canadian Museum of Civilization, Hull, Quebec.
Moss, J. H.
2002 The Geology of Mummy Cave. In *The Archeology of Mummy Cave Wyoming: An Introduction to Shoshonean Prehistory,* by W. M. Husted and R. Edgar, pp. 7–12. U.S. Department of the Interior, National Park Service, Midwest Archeological Center, Lincoln.

Moyle, P. B.
2002 *Inland Fishes of California*. Rev. and expanded. University of California Press, Berkeley.

Münzel, S.
1983 Seasonal Activities at Umingmak a Muskox-Hunting Site on Banks Island, N.W.T., Canada, with Special Reference to Bird Remains. In *Animals in Archaeology 1: Hunters and Their Prey,* edited by J. Clutton-Brock and C. Grigson, pp. 249–257. British Archaeological Reports, International Series, 163.

Murie, O. J.
1936 The Roosevelt Elk. *American Forests* 42:163–164, 197–198.
1951 *The Elk of North America*. Stackpole Co., Harrisburg, Pennsylvania.

Murphy, D. A.
1963 A Captive Elk Herd in Missouri. *Journal of Wildlife Management* 27:411–414.

Murphy, J. R.
1975 Status of a Golden Eagle Population in Central Utah, 1967–1973. In *Status of Raptors,* edited by J. R. Murphy, C. M. White, and B. E. Harrel, pp. 91–96. Raptor Research Foundation Report, 3. Vermillion, South Dakota.

Murray, M. P.
1996 Natural Processes: Wilderness Management Unrealized. *Natural Areas Journal* 16:55–61.

Nadelhoffer, K. J., and B. Fry
1988 Controls on Natural Nitrogen-15 and Carbon-13 Abundances in Forest Soil Organic Matter. *Soil Science Society of America Journal* 52: 1633–1640.
1994 Nitrogen Isotope Studies in Forest Ecosystems. In *Stable Isotopes in Ecology and Environmental Science,* edited by K. Lajtha and R. H. Michener, pp. 22–44. Blackwell Scientific, Oxford.

Nadelhoffer, K. J., G. Shaver, B. Fry, A. Giblin, L. Johnson, and R. McKane
1996 ^{15}N Natural Abundances and N Use by Tundra Plants. *Oecologia* 107:386–394.

Nagorsen, D. W., and G. Keddie
2000 Late Pleistocene Mountain Goats *(Oreamnos americanus)* from Vancouver Island: Biogeographic Implications. *Journal of Mammalogy* 81: 666–675.

National Marine Fisheries Service
1995 *Status Review of Steller Sea Lions* (Eumetopias jubatus). National Marine Mammal Laboratory, Alaska Fisheries Science Center, National Marine Fisheries Service, National Oceanic and Atmospheric Administration, Seattle.
1997 *Investigation of Scientific Information on Impacts of California Sea Lions and Pacific Harbor Seals on Salmonids and the Coastal Ecosystems of Washington, Oregon and California.* NOAA Technical Memorandum, NMFS-NWFSC-28. National Marine Fisheries Service, Seattle.

National Park Service
1978 *Management Policies*. U.S. Department of the Interior, Washington, D.C.

1997 *Yellowstone's Northern Range: Complexity and Change in a Wildland Ecosystem.* National Park Service, Yellowstone National Park, Mammoth Hot Springs, Wyoming.

2000 *Bison Management for the State of Montana and Yellowstone National Park: Executive Summary.* U.S. Department of the Interior, National Park Service, Washington, D.C.

Nelson, J. R., and T. A. Leege

1982 Nutritional Requirements and Food Habits. In *Elk of North America: Ecology and Management,* edited by J. W. Thomas and D. E. Toweill, pp. 323–367. Stackpole Books, Harrisburg, Pennsylvania.

Nelson, W. J.

1999 A Paleodietary Approach to Late Prehistoric Hunter-Gatherer Settlement–Subsistence Change in Northern Owens Valley, Eastern California: The Fish Slough Cave Example. Ph.D dissertation, Department of Anthropology, University of California, Davis.

Noss, R. F.

1983 A Regional Landscape Approach to Maintain Diversity. *BioScience* 33: 700–706.

1990 Indicators for Monitoring Biodiversity: A Hierarchical Approach. *Conservation Biology* 4:355–364.

1995a Assessing Rigor and Objectivity in Conservation Science. *Wildlife Society Bulletin* 23:539–541.

1995b Wilderness—Now More than Ever: A Response to Callicott. *Wild Earth* 4:60–63.

1996 Conservation Biology, Values, and Advocacy. *Conservation Biology* 10:904.

1999 Is There a Special Conservation Biology? *Ecography* 22:113–122.

2001 Introduction: Why Restore Large Mammals? In *Large Mammal Restoration: Ecological and Sociological Challenges in the 21st Century,* edited by D. S. Maehr, R. F. Noss, and J. L. Larkin, pp. 1–21. Island Press, Washington, D.C.

O'Brien, M. J., and W. R. Wood

1998 *The Prehistory of Missouri.* University of Missouri Press, Columbia.

Ogden, A.

1933 Russian Sea Otter and Seal Hunting on the California Coast. *California Historical Society Quarterly* 12:29–51.

O'Leary, M. H.

1988 Carbon Isotopes in Photosynthesis. *BioScience* 38:328–335.

Oviatt, C. G., D. R. Currey, and D. Sack

1992 Radiocarbon Chronology of Lake Bonneville, Eastern Great Basin, U.S.A. *Palaeogeography, Palaeoclimatology, Palaeoecology* 99: 225–241.

Owen-Smith, N.

1989 Megafaunal Extinctions: The Conservation Message from 11,000 Years B.P. *Conservation Biology* 3:405–412.

Pääbo, S.

1993 Ancient DNA. *Scientific American* 269(5):86–92.

Packard, F. M.
1946 An Ecological Study of the Bighorn Sheep in Rocky Mountain National Park, Colorado. *Journal of Mammalogy* 27:3–28.
Palumbi, S. R.
2001 Humans as the World's Greatest Evolutionary Force. *Science* 293: 1786–1790.
Park, R.
1989 Porden Point, an Intrasite Approach to Settlement System Analysis. Ph.D. dissertation, Department of Anthropology, University of Alberta, Edmonton.
Parker, G. R., D. C. Thomas, E. Broughton, and D. R. Gray
1975 Crashes of Muskox and Peary Caribou Populations in 1973–74 on the Parry Islands, Arctic Canada. *Canadian Wildlife Service Program Notes* 56:1–10.
Parmalee, P. W.
1965 The Food Economy of Archaic and Woodland Peoples at the Tick Creek Cave Site, Missouri. *The Missouri Archaeologist* 27:1–34.
Parmalee, P. W., and W. E. Klippel
1984 The Naiad Fauna of the Tellico River, Monroe County, Tennessee. *American Malacological Bulletin* 3:41–44.
Parmalee, P. W., W. E. Klippel, and A. E. Bogan
1980 Notes on the Prehistoric and Present Status of the Naiad Fauna of the Middle Cumberland River, Smith County, Tennessee. *The Nautilus* 94:93–105.
1982 Aboriginal and Modern Freshwater Mussel Assemblages (Pelecypoda: Unionidae) from the Chickamauga Reservoir, Tennessee. *Brimleyana* 8:75–90.
Parsons, D. J., D. M. Graber, J. K. Agee, and J. W. van Wagtendonk
1986 Natural Fire Management in National Parks. *Environmental Management* 10:21–24.
Pate, F. D.
1994 Bone Chemistry and Paleodiet. *Journal of Archaeological Method and Theory* 1:161–209.
Peacock, D.
1997 The Yellowstone Massacre. *Audubon* 99:40–49, 102, 106–110.
Peek, J. M., D. G. Miquelle, and R. G. Wright
1987 Are Bison Exotic in the Wrangell–St. Elias National Park and Preserve? *Environmental Management* 11:149–153.
Peek, J. M., K. T. Schmidt, M. J. Dorrance, and B. L. Smith
2002 Supplemental Feeding and Farming of Elk. In *North American Elk: Ecology and Management,* edited by D. E. Toweill and J. W. Thomas, pp. 617–647. Smithsonian Institution Press, Washington, D.C.
Peterson, C., J. Jackson, M. Kirby, H. Lenihan, B. Bourque, R. Bradbury, R. Cooke, and S. Kidwell
2001 Factors in the Decline of Coastal Ecosystems. *Science* 293:1590–1591.
Peterson, R. S., B. J. LeBoeuf, and R. L. DeLong
1968 Fur Seals from the Bering Sea Breeding in California. *Nature* 219: 899–901.

Pfeifer, R.
1987 *Managing around Marine Mammal Predation on Winter Run Steelhead Returning to Lake Washington.* Washington Department of Fish and Wildlife, Fishery Management Division Report, 87–7. Olympia.
Pfeifer, R., P. J. Gearin, S. J. Jeffries, M. A. Johnson, and R. L. DeLong
1989 *Evaluation of the 1987–88 California Sea Lion Predation Control Program in the Lake Washington Estuary.* Washington Department of Fish and Wildlife, Fishery Management Report, 89–9. Olympia.
Pianka, E. R.
1970 On *r*- and *K*- Selection. *American Naturalist* 104:592–597.
Pierce, K. L.
1976 *History and Dynamics of Glaciation in the Northern Yellowstone National Park Area.* U.S. Geological Survey Professional Paper, 729-F. Reston, Virginia.
Pierce, K. L., and L. A. Morgan
1992 The Track of the Yellowstone Hot Spot: Volcanism, Faulting, and Uplift. In *Regional Geology of Eastern Idaho and Western Wyoming,* edited by P. Link, K. Kuntz, M. A. Kuntz, and L. B. Platt, pp. 1–53. Geological Society of America Memoir, 179. Boulder.
Pisias, N. G.
1978 Paleoceanography of the Santa Barbara Basin during the Last 8000 Years. *Quaternary Research* 10:366–384.
Polziehn, R. O., R. Beech, J. Sheraton, and C. Strobeck
1996 Genetic Relationships among North American Bison Populations. *Canadian Journal of Zoology* 74:738–749.
Polziehn, R. O., J. Hamr, F. F. Mallory, and C. Strobeck
1998 Phylogenetic Status of North American Wapiti *(Cervus elaphus)* Subspecies. *Canadian Journal of Zoology* 76:998–1010.
Polziehn, R. O., C. Strobeck, J. Sheraton, and R. Beech
1995 Bovine mtDNA Discovered in North American Bison Populations. *Conservation Biology* 9:1638–1643.
Ports, M. A., and L. K. Ports
1989 Associations of Small Mammals Occurring in a Pluvial Lake Basin, Ruby Lake, Nevada. *Great Basin Naturalist* 49:123–130.
Povilitis, T.
2002 What Is a Natural Area? *Natural Areas Journal* 21:70–74.
Presnall, C. C.
1943 Wildlife Conservation as Affected by American Indian and Caucasian Concepts. *Journal of Mammalogy* 24:458–464.
Price, C. R.
1985 Patterns of Cultural Behavior and Inter-Site Distributions of Faunal Remains at the Widow Harris Site. *Historical Archaeology* 19:40–56.
Price, M. V., and N. M. Waser
1984 On the Relative Abundance of Species: Postfire Changes in a Coastal Sage Scrub Rodent Community. *Ecology* 65:1161–1169.
Pritchard, J. A.
1999 *Preserving Yellowstone's Natural Conditions: Science and the Perception of Nature.* University of Nebraska Press, Lincoln.

Purdue, J. R., B. W. Styles, and M. C. Masulis
1989 Faunal Remains and White-tailed Deer Exploitation from a Late Woodland Upland Encampment: The Boschert Site (23SC609), St. Charles County, Missouri. *Midcontinental Journal of Archaeology* 14:146–163.
Pyle, P., and D. J. Long
2001 Historical and Recent Colonization of the South Farallon Islands, California, by Northern Fur Seals *(Callorhinus ursinus). Marine Mammal Science* 17:397–402.
Rafferty, M. D.
1980 *The Ozarks: Land and Life.* University of Oklahoma Press, Norman.
Ragen, T. J., G. A. Antonelis, and M. Kiyota
1995 Early Migration of Northern Fur Seal Pups from St. Paul Island, Alaska. *Journal of Mammalogy* 76:1137–1148.
Raper, E., T. Christiansen, and B. Petch
1989 Sublette Antelope Study: Final Report November 1985–February 1989. In *1988 Annual Big Game Herd Unit Report, District Four,* by Wyoming Game and Fish Department, pp. 124–179. Wyoming Game and Fish Department, Cheyenne.
Rapson, D. J.
1990 Pattern and Process in Intra-Site Spatial Analysis: Site Structural and Faunal Research at the Bugas-Holding Site. Ph.D. dissertation, Department of Anthropology, University of New Mexico, Albuquerque.
Read, A. J., and P. R. Wade
2000 Status of Marine Mammals in the United States. *Conservation Biology* 14:929–940.
Ream, R. R.
2002 Molecular Ecology of North Pacific Otariids: Genetic Assessment of Northern Fur Seal and Steller Sea Lion Distributions. Ph.D. dissertation, University of Washington, Seattle.
Redford, K. H.
1990 The Ecologically Noble Savage. *Orion* 9(3):25–29.
1991 The Ecologically Noble Savage. *Cultural Survival Quarterly* 15:46–48
Redman, C. L.
1999 *Human Impact on Ancient Environments.* University of Arizona Press, Tucson.
Reeder, R. L.
1988 Prehistory of the Gasconade River Basin. Ph.D. dissertation, Department of Anthropology, University of Missouri, Columbia.
Rees, P. A.
2001 Is There a Legal Obligation to Reintroduce Animal Species into Their Former Habitats? *Oryx* 35:216–223.
Reinhart, D. P., M. A. Haroldson, D. J. Mattson, and K. A. Gunther
2001 Effects of Exotic Species on Yellowstone's Grizzly Bears. *Western North American Naturalist* 61:277–288.
Renken, T.
2001 Conservation Commission Halts Elk-Restoration Program. *St. Louis Post-Dispatch,* June 30:D16.

Rennie, D. A., E. A. Paul, and L. E. Johns
1976 Natural Nitrogen-15 Abundance of Soil and Plant Samples. *Canadian Journal of Soil Science* 56:43–50.
Richards, M. B., K. Smalley, B. C. Sykes, and R. E. M. Hedges
1993 Archaeology and Genetics: Analysing DNA from Skeletal Remains. *World Archaeology* 25:18–28.
Richards, M. B., B. C. Sykes, and R. E. M. Hedges
1995 Authenticating DNA Extracted from Ancient Skeletal Remains. *Journal of Archaeological Science* 22:291–299.
Rick, A. M.
1980 Non-Cetacean Vertebrate Remains from Two Thule Winter Houses on Somerset Island, N.W.T. *Canadian Journal of Archaeology* 4:99–117.
Rickard, W. H., J. D. Hedlund, and R. E. Fitzner
1977 Elk in the Shrub-Steppe Region of Washington: An Authentic Record. *Science* 196:1009–1010.
Rickart, E. A.
1987 *Spermophilus townsendii. Mammalian Species* 268:1–6.
Ricklefs, R. E.
1979 *Ecology.* 2nd ed. Chiron Press, New York.
Ripple, W. J., E. J. Larsen, R. A. Renkin, and D. W. Smith
2001 Trophic Cascades among Wolves, Elk and Aspen on Yellowstone National Park's Northern Range. *Biological Conservation* 102: 227–234.
Rolston, H., III
2001 Natural and Unnatural: Wild and Cultural. *Western North American Naturalist* 61:267–276.
Rosenzweig, M. L.
1968 Net Primary Productivity of Terrestrial Native Communities: Habitat and Environmental Complexity. *American Midland Naturalist* 102:67–74.
Rowe, T. G., and R. J. Hoffman
1987 *Wildlife Kills in the Carson Sink, Western Nevada, Winter 1986–1987.* U.S. Geological Survey Water-Supply Paper, 2350. Reston, Virginia.
Russell, E.
2003 Evolutionary History: Prospectus for a New Field. *Environmental History* 8:204–228.
Rykiel, E. J., Jr.
2001 Scientific Objectivity, Value Systems, and Policymaking. *BioScience* 51: 433–436.
Sada, D. W., and G. L. Vinyard
2002 Anthropogenic Changes in Historical Biogeography of Great Basin Aquatic Biota. In *Great Basin Aquatic Systems History,* edited by R. Hershler, D. B. Madsen, and D. R. Currey, pp. 277–293. Smithsonian Contributions to the Earth Sciences, 33. Washington, D.C.
Sanders, P. H.
2000 Trappers Point. *Wyoming Wildlife* 64(5):30–35.
Sanders, P. H., and D. L. Wedel
1999 An Ethnographic and Prehistoric Summary of Pronghorn Procurement and Its Relation to Modern Habitat, Pronghorn Behavior, and Archaeo-

logical Site Locations in Southwestern Wyoming. In *The Trappers Point Site (48SU1006): Early Archaic Adaptations in the Upper Green River Basin, Wyoming,* edited by M. E. Miller, P. H. Sanders, and J. E. Francis, pp. 290–320. Cultural Resource Series, 1. Office of the Wyoming State Archaeologist, Laramie.

Sarkar, S.

1999 Wilderness Preservation and Biodiversity Conservation—Keeping Divergent Goals Distinct. *BioScience* 49:405–412.

Savelle, J. M.

1987 *Collectors and Foragers: Subsistence-Settlement System Change in the Central Canadian Arctic, A.D. 1000–1960.* British Archaeological Reports, International Series, 358.

Sawyer, H., and F. Lindzey

1999 *Jackson Hole Pronghorn Study: Annual Progress Report.* Report to Ultra Petroleum, Wyoming Game and Fish Department, U.S. Fish and Wildlife Service, U.S. Department of Agriculture Forest Service, Bureau of Land Management, Teton Science School, and Great Plains Wildlife Institute. On file, Wyoming Cooperative Fish and Wildlife Research Unit, Laramie.

2000 *Jackson Hole Pronghorn Study: Final Report.* Report to Ultra Petroleum, Wyoming Game and Fish Department, U.S. Fish and Wildlife Service, U.S. Department of Agriculture Forest Service, Bureau of Land Management, and Teton Science School. On file, Wyoming Cooperative Fish and Wildlife Research Unit, Laramie.

Sawyer, H., and D. McWhirter

2000 The Long Trail. *Wyoming Wildlife* 64(5):36–41.

Scammon, C. M.

1968 *The Marine Mammals of the North-Western Coast of North America, Described and Illustrated: Together with an Account of the American Whale-Fishery.* Dover Publications, New York.

Scheffer, V. B.

1950 Winter Injury to Young Fur Seals on the Northwest Coast. *California Fish and Game* 36:378–379.

1958 *Seals, Seal Lions, and Walruses: A Review of the Pinnipedia.* Stanford University Press, Stanford.

1976 The Future of Wildlife Management. *Wildlife Society Bulletin* 4:51–54.

1993 The Olympic Mountain Goat Controversy: A Perspective. *Conservation Biology* 7:916–919.

Scherer, D.

1994 Between Theory and Practice: Some Thoughts on Motivations behind Restoration. *Restoration and Management Notes* 12:184–188.

Schledermann, P.

1990 *Crossroads to Greenland: 3000 Years of Prehistory in the Eastern High Arctic.* Komatik Series, 2. Arctic Institute of North America of the University of Calgary, Calgary.

Schmitt, D. N.

1999 A Late Holocene Mammalian Fauna from Southern Camels Back Ridge and Vicinity, Dugway Proving Ground, Utah. Report on file,

Directorate of Environmental Programs, Dugway Proving Ground, Utah, and Utah Geological Survey, Salt Lake City.

Schmitt, D. N., and K. D. Lupo

2001 The Camels Back Cave Mammalian Fauna. In *The Archaeology of Camels Back Cave,* by D. N. Schmitt and D. B. Madsen, pp. 182–218. Report on file, Directorate of Environmental Programs, U.S. Army Dugway Proving Ground, Utah, and Utah Geological Survey, Salt Lake City.

Schmitt, D. N., and D. B. Madsen

2001 The Archaeology of Camels Back Cave. Report on file, Directorate of Environmental Programs, U.S. Army Dugway Proving Ground, Utah, and Utah Geological Survey, Salt Lake City.

Schmitt, D. N., D. B. Madsen, and K. D. Lupo

2002 Small-Mammal Data on Early and Middle Holocene Climates and Biotic Communities in the Bonneville Basin, U.S.A. *Quaternary Research* 58:255–260.

Schmitt, D. N., M. W. Shaver III, and J. M. Hunt

1994 From Here to Antiquity: Holocene Human Occupation on Camels Back Ridge, Tooele County, Utah. *Utah Archaeology* 7:35–50.

Schnabel, R. D., T. J. Ward, and J. N. Deer

2000 Validation of 15 Microsatellites for Parentage Testing in North American Bison *Bison bison* and Domestic Cattle. *Animal Genetics* 31:360–366.

Schonewald, C.

1994 *Cervus canadensis* and *C. elaphus:* North American Subspecies and Evaluation of Clinal Extremes. *Acta Theriologica* 39:431–452.

Schonewald-Cox, C. M., J. W. Bayless, and J. Schonewald

1985 Cranial Morphometry of Pacific Coast Elk *(Cervus elaphus). Journal of Mammalogy* 66:63–74.

Schoolcraft, H. R.

1996 *Rude Pursuits and Rugged Peaks: Schoolcraft's Ozark Journal 1818–1819.* University of Arkansas Press, Fayetteville.

Schullery, P.

1984 A History of Native Elk in Mount Rainier National Park. Report on file, Mount Rainier National Park, Ashford, Washington.

1986 Drawing the Lines in Yellowstone: The American Bison as Symbol and Scourge. *Orion Naturalist Quarterly* 5:33–45.

1997 *Searching for Yellowstone: Ecology and Wonder in the Last Wilderness.* Houghton Mifflin, New York.

2001 What Is Natural? Philosophical Analysis and Yellowstone Practice. *Western North American Naturalist* 61:255–256.

Schullery, P., W. Brewster, and J. Mack

1998 Bison in Yellowstone: A Historical Overview. In *International Symposium on Bison Ecology and Management in North America,* edited by L. Irby and J. Knight, pp. 326–336. Montana State University, Bozeman.

Schullery, P., and L. Whittlesey

1992 The Documentary Record of Wolves and Related Wildlife Species in the Yellowstone National Park Area Prior to 1882. In *Wolves for*

Yellowstone? A Report to the United States Congress, vol. 4: Research and Analysis, edited by J. D. Varley and W. G. Brewster, pp. 1-4–1-174. National Park Service, Yellowstone National Park, Wyoming.

1999 Greater Yellowstone Carnivores: A History of Changing Attitudes. In *Carnivores in Ecosystems: The Yellowstone Experience,* edited by T. W. Clark, A. P. Curlee, S. C. Minta, and P. M. Kareiva, pp. 11–49. Yale University Press, New Haven.

2001 Mountain Goats in the Greater Yellowstone Ecosystem: A Prehistoric and Historical Context. *Western North American Naturalist* 61:289–307.

Schwartz, C. W., and E. R. Schwartz

1981 *The Wild Mammals of Missouri.* Rev. ed. University of Missouri Press, Columbia.

Scott, D. W.

2002 "Untrammeled, Wilderness Character," and the Challenges of Wilderness Preservation. *Wild Earth* 11(3–4):72–79.

Segerstrom, T.

1997 *The History and Status of Pronghorn Antelope that Summer in Jackson Hole and the Upper Gros Ventre Drainage.* Great Plains Wildlife Institute, Jackson, Wyoming.

Sellars, R. W.

1997 *Preserving Nature in the National Parks: A History.* Yale University Press, New Haven.

Sepez, J.

2001 Political and Social Ecology of Contemporary Makah Subsistence Hunting, Fishing and Shellfish Collecting Practices. Ph.D. dissertation, Department of Anthropology, University of Washington, Seattle.

Sepkoski, J. J., Jr.

1997 Biodiversity: Past, Present, and Future. *Journal of Paleontology* 71: 533–539.

Seton, E. T.

1937 *Lives of Game Animals,* vol. 3. Literary Guild of America, New York.

Shafer, C. L.

2001 Conservation Biology Trailblazers: George Wright, Ben Thompson, and Joseph Dixon. *Conservation Biology* 15:332–344.

Shaw, R. D.

1977 *Report of Excavations: The Martin Site (45PC7), 1974.* Washington Archaeological Society Occasional Paper, 5. Seattle.

Shearer, G., and D. H. Kohl

1978 ^{15}N Abundance in N-Fixing and Non-N-Fixing Plants. In *Recent Developments in Mass Spectrometry in Biochemistry and Medicine,* vol. 1, edited by A. Frigerio, pp. 605–622. Plenum, New York.

1986 N_2-Fixation in Field Settings: Estimations Based on Natural ^{15}N Abundance. *Australian Journal of Plant Physiology* 13:699–756.

Sherrod, S. K.

1978 Diets of North American Falconiformes. *Raptor Research* 12:49–121.

Shrader-Frechette, K. S., and E. D. McCoy

1995 Natural Landscapes, Natural Communities, and Natural Ecosystems. *Forest and Conservation History* 39:138–142.

Shull, D. W., and A. R. Tipton
1987 Effective Population Size of Bison in the Wichita Mountains Wildlife Refuge. *Conservation Biology* 1:35–41.
Simenstad, C. A., J. A. Estes, and K. W. Kenyon
1978 Aleuts, Sea Otters, and Alternate Stable-State Communities. *Science* 200:403–411.
Simpson, G. G.
1941 Large Pleistocene Felines of North America. *American Museum Novitiates* 1136:1–27.
Sinclair, A. R. E.
1983 The Function of Distance Movements in Vertebrates. In *The Ecology of Animal Movement,* edited by I. R. Swingland and P. J. Greenwood, pp. 240–263. Clarendon Press, Oxford.
Sinclair, E., T. R. Loughlin, and W. Pearcy
1994 Prey Selection by Northern Fur Seals *(Callorhinus ursinus)* in the Eastern Bering Sea. *Fishery Bulletin* 92:144–156.
Sisk, T. D., and B. R. Noon
1995 Land Use History of North America—An Emerging Project of the National Biological Service. *SAA Bulletin* 13(3):21.
Skinner, M. P.
1922 The Prong-horn. *Journal of Mammalogy* 3:82–105.
1936 The Roosevelt Elk of the Olympic Peninsula. *The Murrelet* 17: 31–35.
Sloan, N. A.
2002 History and Application of the Wilderness Concept in Marine Conservation. *Conservation Biology* 16:294–305.
Smith, B. D.
1974 Middle Mississippi Exploitation of Animal Populations: A Predictive Model. *American Antiquity* 39:274–291.
n.d. Faunal List for the Lepold Site. Report on file with the author, Smithsonian Institution, Washington, D.C.
Smith, D. G.
1971 Population Dynamics, Habitat Selection, and Partitioning of Breeding Raptors in the Eastern Great Basin. Ph.D. dissertation, Brigham Young University, Provo, Utah.
Smith, D. G., C. R. Wilson, and H. H. Frost
1972 Seasonal Food Habits of Barn Owls in Utah. *Great Basin Naturalist* 32:229–234.
Smith, D. W., D. R. Stahler, and D. S. Guernsey
2003 *Yellowstone Wolf Project: Annual Report, 2002.* Yellowstone Center for Resources, YCR-NR-2003–04. National Park Service, Yellowstone National Park, Wyoming.
Smith, G. I., and J. L. Bischoff
1997 Core OL-92 from Owens Lake: Project Rationale, Geologic Setting, Drilling Procedures, and Summary. In *An 800,000-Year Paleoclimatic Record from Core OL-92, Owens Lake, Southeast California,* edited by G. I. Smith and J. L. Bischoff, pp. 1–8. Geological Society of America Special Paper, 317. Boulder.

Smith, G. R.
1981 Effects of Habitat Size on Species Richness and Adult Body Sizes of Desert Fishes. In *Fishes in North American Deserts,* edited by R. J. Naiman and D. L. Soltz, pp. 125–171. Wiley-Interscience, New York.
Smith, T. B., M. W. Bruford, and R. K. Wayne
1993 The Preservation of Process: The Missing Element of Conservation Programs. *Biodiversity Letters* 1:164–167.
Snyder, J. O.
1917 An Account of Some Fishes from Owens River, California. *Proceedings of the U.S. National Museum* 54:201–205.
Soulé, M. E.
1985 What Is Conservation Biology? *BioScience* 35:727–734.
Sousa, W. P.
1984 The Role of Disturbance in Natural Communities. *Annual Review of Ecology and Systematics* 15:353–391.
Spalding, D. J.
1992 *The History of Elk* (Cervus elaphus) *in British Columbia.* Contributions to Natural Sciences, 18. Royal British Columbia Museum, Victoria.
Speck, F. G.
1938 Aboriginal Conservators. *Bird Lore* 40:258–261.
Spong, G., M. Johansson, and M. Bjorklund
2000 High Genetic Variation in Leopards Indicates Large and Long-Term Stable Effective Population Size. *Molecular Ecology* 9:1773–1782.
Sprugel, Douglas G.
1991 Disturbance, Equilibrium, and Environmental Variability: What Is "Natural" Vegetation in a Changing Environment? *Biological Conservation* 58:1–18.
Srivastrava, D.
2002 The Role of Conservation in Expanding Biodiversity. *Oikos* 98: 351–360.
Staab, M. L.
1979 Analysis of the Faunal Material Recovered from a Thule Eskimo Site on the Island of Silumiut, N.W.T., Canada. In *Thule Eskimo Culture, an Anthropological Retrospective,* edited by A. P. McCartney, pp. 349–379. Mercury Series, Archaeological Survey of Canada Paper, 8. National Museum of Man, Ottawa.
Stahl, P. W.
1996 Holocene Biodiversity: An Archaeological Perspective from the Americas. *Annual Review of Anthropology* 25:105–126.
Stanturf, J. A., C. J. Schweitzer, S. H. Schoenholtz, J. P. Barrett, C. K. McMahon, and D. J. Tomczak
1998 Ecosystem Restoration: Fact or Fancy? *Transactions of the North American Wildlife and Natural Resources Conference* 63:376–383.
Steadman, D. W.
1995 Prehistoric Extinctions of Pacific Island Birds: Biodiversity Meets Zooarchaeology. *Science* 267:1123–1131.

Stein, J. L., M. Herder, and K. Miller
1986 Birth of a Northern Fur Seal on the Mainland California Coast. *California Fish and Game* 72:179–181.
Stephenson, R. O., S. C. Gerlach, R. D. Guthrie, C. R. Harington, R. O. Mills, and G. Hare
2001 Wood Bison in Late Holocene Alaska and Adjacent Canada: Paleontological, Archaeological and Historical Records. In *People and Wildlife in Northern North America: Essays in Honor of R. Dale Gutrie,* edited by S. C. Gerlach and M. S. Murray, pp. 124–158. British Archaeological Reports, International Series, 944.
Stevenson, M. G.
1992 Two Solitudes? South Amundsen Gulf History and Prehistory, N.W.T. MS on file, Archaeological Survey of Canada, Canadian Museum of Civilization, Hull, Quebec.
Steward, J. H.
1933 Ethnography of the Owens Valley Paiute. *University of California Publications in American Archaeology and Ethnology* 33:233–350.
1941 Culture Element Distributions XIII: Nevada Shoshone. *Anthropological Records* 4:209–359.
1943 Culture Element Distributions XXIII: Northern and Gosiute Shoshone. *Anthropological Records* 8:263–392.
Stewart, B. S.
1997 California Pinnipeds: Population Trends, Trans-Jurisdictional Migrations, and Ecological Function in Large Marine Ecosystems of the Eastern North Pacific Ocean. In *Pinniped Populations, Eastern North Pacific: Status, Trends, and Issues,* edited by G. Stone, J. Goebel, and S. Webster, pp. 13–21. American Fisheries Society, Monterey, California.
Stine, S.
1990 Late Holocene Fluctuations of Mono Lake, Eastern California. *Palaeogeography, Palaeoclimatology, Palaeoecology* 78:333–381.
1994a Extreme and Persistent Drought in California during Mediaeval Time. *Nature* 369:546–549.
1994b Late Holocene Fluctuations of Owens Lake, Inyo County, California, Appendix F. In *Archaeological Evaluations of Thirteen Sites for the Ash Creek Project, Inyo Co., California,* vol. 1, by A. J. Gilreath. Report to Caltrans, District 9, Contract No. 09H259. Far Western Anthropological Research Group, Davis, California.
1998 Medieval Climatic Anomaly in the Americas. In *Water, Environment and Society in Times of Climatic Change,* edited by A. S. Issar and N. Brown, pp. 43–67. Kluwer Academic, Boston.
Stiner, M. C. (editor)
1991 *Human Predators and Prey Mortality.* Westview Press, Boulder, Colorado.
Styles, B. W., and J. R. Purdue
1996 Animal Exploitation. In *Middle and Late Woodland Subsistence and Ceramic Technology in the Central Mississippi Rvier Valley,* by M. J. O'Brien, pp. 145–176. Illinois State Museum, Reports of Investigations, 52. Springfield.

Sundstrom, C., W. G. Hepworth, and K. L. Diem
1973 *Abundance, Distribution and Food Habits of the Pronghorn: A Partial Characterization of the Optimal Pronghorn Habitat.* Wyoming Game and Fish Commission Bulletin, 12. Cheyenne.
Sutherland, P. D.
1989 An Inventory and Assessment of the Prehistoric Archaeological Resources of the Ellesmere Island National Park Reserve. MS on file, Archaeological Survey of Canada, Canadian Museum of Civilization, Hull, Quebec.
1993 Prehistoric Adaptations to Changing Environments on Western Ellesmere Island and Eastern Axel Heiberg Island. MS on file, Archaeological Survey of Canada, Canadian Museum of Civilization, Hull, Quebec.
1996 Continuity and Change in the Paleo-Eskimo Prehistory of Northern Ellesmere Island. In *The Paleo-Eskimo Cultures of Greenland,* edited by B. Grønnow, pp. 271–294. Danish Polar Center, Copenhagen.
Swan, J. G.
1870 The Indians of Cape Flattery, at the Entrance of the Straight of Fuca, Washington Territory. *Smithsonian Contributions to Knowledge* 16(8):1–105.
1883 Report of Investigations at Neah Bay, Wash., Respecting the Habits of Fur Seals of That Vicinity, and to Arrange for Procuring Specimens of Skeletons of Cetacea. *Bulletin of the United States Fish Commission* 3:201–207.
Sydeman, W. J., and S. G. Allen
1999 Pinniped Population Dynamics in Central California: Correlations with Sea Surface Temperature and Upwelling Indices. *Marine Mammal Science* 15:446–461.
Taber, R. D., and K. D. Raedeke
1987 The Management of *Cervus* in North America. In *Biology and Management of the Cervidae,* edited by C. M. Wemmer, pp. 568–577. Smithsonian Institution Press, Washington, D.C.
Taylor, W.
1967 Summary of Archaeological Field Work on Banks and Victoria Islands, Arctic Canada, 1965. *Arctic Anthropology* 4:221–243.
Teer, J. G.
1988 Review of *Conservation Biology: The Science of Scarcity and Diversity* by M. E. Soulé. *Journal of Wildlife Management* 52:570–572.
Teeri, J. A.
1982 Carbon Isotopes and the Evolution of C_4 Photosynthesis and Crassulacean Acid Metabolism. In *Biochemical Aspects of Evolutionary Biology,* edited by M. H. Nitecki, pp. 93–130. University of Chicago Press, Chicago.
Teeri, J. A., and L. G. Stowe
1976 Climatic Patterns and the Distribution of C_4 Grasses in North America. *Oecologia* 23:1–12.
Teeri, J. A., L. G. Stowe, and D. A. Livingstone
1980 The Distribution of C_4 Species of the Cyperaceae in North America in Relation to Climate. *Oecologia* 47:307–310.

Temple, S. A.
1992 Conservation Biologists and Wildlife Managers Getting Together. *Conservation Biology* 6:4.
Temple, S. A., E. G. Bolen, M. E. Soulé, P. F. Brussard, H. Salwasser, and J. G. Teer
1988 What's So New about Conservation Biology? *Transactions of the North American Wildlife and Natural Resources Conference* 63:609–612.
Tener, J. S.
1965 *Muskoxen in Canada: A Biological and Taxonomic Review.* Queen's Printer, Ottawa.
Thing, H., P. Henrichsen, and P. Lassen
1984 Status of the Muskox in Greenland. In *Proceedings of the First International Muskox Symposium,* edited by D. R. Klein and R. G. White, pp. 1–6. Biological Papers of the University of Alaska Special Report, 4. Institute of Arctic Biology, University of Alaska, Fairbanks.
Thompson, R. S., C. Whitlock, P. J. Bartlein, S. P. Harrison, and W. G. Spaulding
1993 Climatic Changes in the Western United States since 18,000 Yr B.P. In *Global Climates since the Last Glacial Maximum,* edited by H. E. Wright Jr., J. E. Kutzbach, T. Webb III, W. F. Ruddiman, F. A. Street-Perrott, and P. J. Bartlein, pp. 468–513. University of Minnesota Press, Minneapolis.
Thornton, R.
1997 Aboriginal North American Population and Rates of Decline, ca. A.D. 1500–1900. *Current Anthropology* 38:310–315.
Thostrup, C. B.
1911 Ethnographic Description of the Eskimo Settlements and Stone Remains in North East Greenland. *Meddelelser om Grønland* 44:277–355.
Tieszen, H., R. E. Karamanos, J. W. B. Steward, and F. Selles
1984 Natural Nitrogen-15 Abundance as an Indicator of Soil Organic Matter Transformations in Native and Cultivated Soils. *Soil Science Society of America Journal* 48:312–315.
Tieszen, L. L.
1991 Natural Variations in the Carbon Isotope Values of Plants: Implications for Archaeology, Ecology, and Paleoecology. *Journal of Archaeological Science* 18:227–248.
Tieszen, L. L., M. M. Senyimba, S. K. Imbamba, and J. H. Troughton
1979 The Distribution of C_3 and C_4 Grasses and Carbon Isotope Discrimination along an Altitudinal and Moisture Gradient in Kenya. *Oecologia* 37:337–350.
Todd, L. C., and J. L. Hofman
1987 Bison Mandibles from the Horner and Finley Sites. In *The Horner Site: The Type Site of the Cody Cultural Context,* edited by G. C. Frison and L. C. Todd, pp. 493–539. Academic Press, Orlando.
Todd, M., and W. Elmore
1997 Historical Changes in Western Riparian Ecosystems. *Transactions of the North American Wildlife and Natural Resources Conference* 62:454–468.

Trites, A. W.

1992 Northern Fur Seals: Why Have They Declined? *Aquatic Mammals* 18:3–18.

Truett, J.

1996 Bison and Elk in the American Southwest: In Search of the Pristine. *Environmental Management* 20:195–206.

Tuohy, D. R., and T. N. Layton

1979 Toward the Establishment of a New Series of Great Basin Projectile Points. *Nevada Archaeological Survey Reports* 10:1–3.

Tweit, S. J., and K. E. Houston

1980 Grassland and Shrubland Habitat Types of the Shoshone National Forest. Report on file, Shoshone National Forest, U.S. Department of Agriculture, Forest Service, Cody, Wyoming.

Ugolini, F. C., R. E. Reanier, G. H. Rau, and J. I. Hedges

1981 Pedological, Isotopic, and Geochemical Investigations of the Soils at the Boreal Forest and Alpine Tundra Transition in Northern Alaska. *Soil Science* 131:359–374.

Urquhart, D. R.

1982 *Muskox: Life History and Current Status of Muskoxen in the N.W.T.* Renewable Resources, Government of the Northwest Territories, Yellowknife.

U.S. Department of Agriculture, Forest Service

1999 *Ozark–Ouachita Highlands Assessment: Terrestrial Vegetation and Wildlife.* U.S. Department of Agriculture, Forest Service, Southern Research Station, General Technical Report, SRS-35. Asheville, North Carolina.

U.S. Department of Commerce

n.d. *California Marine Mammal Stranding Network Database.* U.S. Department of Commerce, National Oceanic and Atmospheric Administration, National Marine Fisheries Service, Southwest Region, Long Beach.

U.S. Department of the Interior, Fish and Wildlife Service

1987 *Northern Rocky Mountain Wolf Recovery Plan.* U.S. Department of the Interior, Fish and Wildlife Service, Denver.

1996 *1995 Annual Report of the Rocky Mountain Interagency Wolf Recovery Program.* U.S. Department of the Interior, Fish and Wildlife Service, and Yellowstone National Park, Helena, Montana.

1998 *Owens Basin Wetland and Aquatic Species Recovery Plan, Inyo and Mono Counties, California.* U.S. Department of the Interior, Fish and Wildlife Service, Portland, Oregon.

1999 *Fulfilling the Promise: The National Wildlife Refuge System.* U.S. Department of the Interior, Fish and Wildlife Service, Washington, D.C.

Vale, T. R.

1998 The Myth of the Humanized Landscape: An Example from Yosemite National Park. *Natural Areas Journal* 18:231–236.

1999 The Myth of the Humanized Landscape: An Example from Yosemite National Park. *Wild Earth* 9(3):34–40.

van der Leeuw, S., and C. L. Redman

2002 Placing Archaeology at the Center of Socio-Natural Studies. *American Antiquity* 67:597–605.

van der Merwe, N. J.
1989 Natural Variation in ^{13}C Concentration and Its Effect on Environmental Reconstruction Using $^{13}C/^{12}C$ Ratios in Animal Bones. In *The Chemistry of Prehistoric Human Bone,* edited by T. D. Price, pp. 105–125. Cambridge University Press, Cambridge.
VanDerwarker, A.
2001 An Archaeological Study of Late Woodland Fauna in the Roanoke River Basin. *North Carolina Archaeology* 50:1–46.
Van Gelder, R. G.
1982 *Mammals of the National Parks.* Johns Hopkins University Press, Baltimore.
van Klinken, G. J., M. P. Richards, and R. E. M. Hedges
2000 An Overview of Causes for Stable Isotopic Variations in Past European Human Populations: Environmental, Ecophysiological, and Cultural Effects. In *Biogeochemical Approaches to Paleodietary Analysis,* edited by S. H. Ambrose and M. A. Katzenberg, pp. 39–63. Kluwer Academic/Plenum, New York.
van Zyll de Jong, C. G.
1986 *A Systematic Study of Recent Bison, with Particular Consideration of the Wood Bison* (Bison bison athabascae *Rhoads 1898*). National Museums of Canada, Publications in Natural Sciences, 6. Ottawa.
van Zyll de Jong, C. G., C. Gates, H. Reynolds, and W. Olson
1995 Phenotypic Variation in Remnant Populations of North American Bison. *Journal of Mammalogy* 76:391–405.
Varley, N. C., and J. D. Varley
1996 Introductions of Mountain Goats in the Greater Yellowstone Ecosystem: They're Here to Stay! or Are They? *Biennial Symposium of the Northern Wild Sheep and Goat Council* 10:113–117.
Vermeij, G. J.
1996 An Agenda for Invasion Biology. *Biological Conservation* 78:3–9.
Vest, D. E.
1962 The Plant Communities and Associated Fauna of Dugway Valley in Western Utah. Ph.D. dissertation, University of Utah, Salt Lake City.
Vibe, C.
1958 The Musk Ox in East Greenland. *Mammalia* 22:168–174.
1967 Arctic Animals in Relation to Climatic Fluctuations. *Meddelelser om Grønland* 170(5).
Virginia, R. A., and C. C. Delwiche
1982 Natural ^{15}N Abundance of Presumed N2-Fixing and Non-N_2-Fixing Plants from Selected Ecosystems. *Oecologia* 54:317–325.
Vitousek, P. M., H. A. Mooney, J. Lubchenco, and J. M. Melillo
1997 Human Domination of Earth's Ecosystems. *Science* 277:494–499.
Vitousek, P. M., G. Shearer, and D. H. Kohl
1989 Foliar ^{15}N Natural Abundance in Hawaiian Rain Forest: Patterns and Possible Mechanisms. *Oecologia* 78:383–388.
Wada, E., R. Imaizumi, and Y. Takai
1984 Natural Abundance of ^{15}N in Soil Organic Matter with Special

Reference to Paddy Soils in Japan: Biogeochemical Implications on the Nitrogen Cycle. *Geochemical Journal* 18:109–123.

Wada, E., R. Shibata, and T. Torii

1981 ^{15}N Abundance in Antarctica: Origin of Soil Nitrogen and Ecological Implications. *Nature* 292:327–329.

Waddington, J. C. B., and H. E. Wright Jr.

1974 Late Quaternary Vegetational Changes on the East Side of Yellowstone Park, Wyoming. *Quaternary Research* 4:175–184.

Wade, P. R.

1998 Calculating Limits to the Allowable Human-Caused Mortality of Cetaceans and Pinnipeds. *Marine Mammal Science* 14:1–37.

Wagner, F. H.

1989 American Wildlife Management at the Crossroads. *Wildlife Society Bulletin* 17:354–360.

1996 Ethics, Science, and Public Policy. *BioScience* 46:765–766.

Wagner, F. H., R. Forest, R. B. Gill, D. R. McCullough, M. R. Pelton, W. F. Porter, and H. Salwasser

1995 *Wildlife Policies in the U.S. National Parks.* Island Press, Washington, D.C.

Walker, J. L., and S. A. Macko

1999 Dietary Studies of Marine Mammals Using Stable Carbon and Nitrogen Isotopic Ratios of Teeth. *Marine Mammal Science* 15:314–334.

Walker, P. L., and S. Craig

1979 Archaeological Evidence Concerning the Prehistoric Occurrence of Sea Mammals at Point Bennett, San Miguel Island. *California Fish and Game* 65:50–54.

Waples, R. S.

1991 Genetic Methods for Estimating the Effective Size of Cetacean Populations. *International Whaling Commission Report* (special issue) 13:279–297.

Ward, T. J., J. P. Bielawski, S. K. Davis, J. W. Templeton, and J. N. Derr

1999 Identification of Domestic Cattle Hybrids in Wild Cattle and Bison Species: A General Approach Using mtDNA Markers and the Parametric Bootstrap. *Animal Conservation* 2:51–57.

Ward, T. J., L. C. Skow, D. S. Gallagher, R. D. Schnabel, C. A. Nall, C. E. Kolenda, S. K. Davis, J. F. Taylor, and J. N. Deer

2001 Differential Introgression of Uniparentally Inherited Markers in Bison Populations with Hybrid Ancestries. *Animal Genetics* 32:89–91.

Warren, R. E.

1983 Late-Holocene Archeofaunal Variation in Ozark Highland Caves and Rockshelters: Environmental Correlates and Foraging Behavior. Ph.D. dissertation, Department of Anthropology, University of Missouri, Columbia.

Washington Department of Wildlife

1987 *History of Elk in Washington.* Washington Department of Wildife, Olympia.

Weber, D. S., B. S. Stewart, J. C. Garza, and N. Lehman

2000 An Empirical Genetic Assessment of the Severity of the Northern Elephant Seal Population Bottleneck. *Current Biology* 10:1287–1290.

Wedel, W. R.
1943 *Archaeological Investigations in Platte and Clay Counties, Missouri.* U.S. National Museum Bulletin, 183.
Wessel, G.
1974 Recent Excavations at Shallow Cave (23PH148): A Preliminary Report. *Central States Archaeological Journal* 21:120–126.
Wessen, G.
1990 Prehistory of the Ocean Coast of Washington. In *Handbook of North American Indians, vol. 7: Northwest Coast,* edited by W. Suttles, pp. 412–421. Smithsonian Institution Press, Washington, D.C.
Westbrooks, R. G.
2001 Potential Impacts of Global Climate Changes on the Establishment and Spread of Invasive Species. *Transactions of the North American Wildlife and Natural Resources Conference* 66:344–370.
Wettstaed, J. R.
2003 Perspectives on the Early Nineteenth Century Frontier Occupations of the Missouri Ozarks. *Historical Archaeology* 37:97–114.
Wettstaed, J. R., and J. L. Harpole
n.d. A Victorian Ghost in the Ozark Pines: Archaeological Investigations at the Nova Scotia Ironworks, Dent County, Missouri. MS in authors' possession.
Whipple, J. J.
2001 Annotated Checklist of Exotic Vascular Plants in Yellowstone National Park. *Western North American Naturalist* 61:336–346.
Whitford, G. W.
1976 Temporal Fluctuations in Density and Diversity of Desert Rodent Populations. *Journal of Mammalogy* 57:351–369.
Whitlock, C.
1993 Postglacial Vegetation and Climate of Grand Teton and Southern Yellowstone National Parks. *Ecological Monographs* 63:173–198.
Whitlock, C., and P. J. Bartlein
1993 Spatial Variations of Holocene Climatic Change in the Yellowstone Region. *Quaternary Research* 39:231–238.
Whitlock, C., P. J. Bartlein, and K. J. Van Norman
1995 Stability of Holocene Climate Regimes in the Yellowstone Region. *Quaternary Research* 43:433–436.
Whitridge, P.
1992 Thule Subsistence and Optimal Diet: A Zooarchaeological Test of a Linear Programming Model. M.A. thesis, Department of Anthropology, McGill University, Montreal.
Whyte, T. R.
1994 Archaeological Records of the Roanoke Bass, *Ambloplites cavifrons Cope,* 1868 (Pisces, Centrarchidae). *Southeastern Archaeology* 13: 77–80.
1997 Vertebrate Archaeofaunal Remains from the Cactus Hill Site (44SX202), Sussex County, Virginia. In *Archaeological Investigations of Site 44SX202, Cactus Hill, Sussex County, Virginia,* edited by J. M. McAvoy and L. D. McAvoy, appendix E. Research Report Series, 8.

Commonwealth of Virginia, Department of Historic Resources, Richmond.
1999 *Ichthyofaunal Remains from the Buzzard Rock Site (44RN2), Roanoke, Virginia.* Report to the Virginia Department of Historic Resources, Richmond.
2000 *Archaeofaunal Remains from the Mount Joy Site (44BO2), Botetourt County, Virginia.* Report to the Virginia Department of Historic Resources, Richmond.

Wilcove, D. S., D. Rothstein, J. Dubow, A. Phillips, and E. Losos
1998 Quantifying Threats to Imperiled Species in the United States. *BioScience* 48:607–615.

Wilke, P. J., and H. W. Lawton (editors)
1976 *The Expedition of Capt. J. W. Davidson from Fort Tejon to the Owens Valley in 1859.* Ballena Press, Socorro, New Mexico.

Wilkinson, P. F.
1975 The Relevance of Musk Ox Exploitation to the Study of Prehistoric Animal Economies. In *Palaeoeconomy,* edited by E. S. Higgs and M. R. Jarman, pp. 9–53. Cambridge University Press, Cambridge.

Will, R. T.
1985 Nineteenth Century Copper Inuit Subsistence Practices on Banks Island, N.W.T. Ph.D. dissertation, Department of Anthropology, University of Alberta, Edmonton.

Willers, B.
2002 Pleistocene Biodiversity as a Biological "Baseline." *Conservation Biology* 16:564–565.

Williams, J. R.
1974 The Baytown Phases in the Cairo Lowland of Southeast Missouri. *The Missouri Archaeologist* 36.

Wilmeth, R. E.
1978 *Canadian Archaeological Radiocarbon Dates.* Rev. ed. Mercury Series, Archaeological Survey of Canada Paper, 77. National Museum of Man, Ottawa.

Wilson, E. W.
1949 The American Indian as a Conservationist. *Viriginia Wildlife* 10(8): 22–24.

Wilson, S. M.
1992 "That Unmanned Wild Countrey." *Natural History* 101(5):16–17.

Wintemberg, W. J.
1919 Archaeology as an Aid to Zoology. *Canadian Field Naturalist* 33:63–72.

Winterhalder, B.
1994 Concepts in Historical Ecology: The View from Evolutionary Ecology. In *Historical Ecology: Cultural Knowledge and Changing Landscapes,* edited by C. L. Crumley, pp. 17–41. School of American Research Press, Santa Fe.

Winterhalder, B., and E. A. Smith (editors)
1981 *Hunter-Gatherer Foraging Strategies: Ethnographic and Archeological Analyses.* University of Chicago Press, Chicago.

Wishart, W.
1978 Bighorn Sheep. In *Big Game of North America: Ecology and Management,* edited by J. L. Schmidt and D. L. Gilbert, pp. 161–171. Stackpole Books, Harrisburg, Pennsylvania.
Woffinden, N. D., and J. R. Murphy
1977 Population Dynamics of the Ferruginous Hawk during a Prey Decline. *Great Basin Naturalist* 37:411–425.
Wolverton, S.
2001 Environmental Implications of Zooarchaeological Measures of Resource Depression. Ph.D. dissertation, Department of Anthropology, University of Missouri, Columbia.
Wood, W. R.
1968 Mississippian Hunting and Butchering Patterns: Bone from the Vista Shelter, 23SR20, Missouri. *American Antiquity* 33:170–179.
Wood, W. R., and R. B. McMillan (editors)
1976 *Prehistoric Man and His Environments: A Case Study in the Ozark Highland.* Academic Press, New York.
Woolett, J. M.
1991 Cultural Perceptions of Man–Animal Relationships and Carcass Utilization. M.A. thesis, Department of Anthropology, University of Alberta, Edmonton.
Wright, G. A.
1984 *People of the High Country: Jackson Hole before the Settlers.* Peter Lang, New York.
Wright, H. E., Jr.
1974 Landscape Development, Forest Fires, and Wilderness Management. *Science* 186:487–495.
2002 Pollen Analyses at Mummy Cave and Nearby Areas, Northwestern Wyoming. In *The Archeology of Mummy Cave Wyoming: An Introduction to Shoshonean Prehistory,* by W. M. Husted and R. Edgar, pp. 13–18. U.S. Department of the Interior, National Park Service, Midwest Archeological Center, Lincoln.
Wyoming Game and Fish Department
1987 *Wildlife Distribution Overlays: Antelope—Sublette, District 4. Revised 3/87.* Wyoming Game and Fish Department, Biological Services, Cheyenne.
Wyoming Wildlife Federation
2003 What's Going On. *Wyoming Wildlife Pronghorn* 1:27.
Yellowstone National Park
1997 *Yellowstone's Northern Range: Complexity and Change in a Wildland Ecosystem.* U.S. Department of the Interior, National Park Service, Mammoth Hot Springs, Wyoming.
Yochim, M. J.
2001 Aboriginal Overkill Overstated: Errors in Charles Kay's Hypothesis. *Human Nature* 12:141–167.
York, A. E.
1987 Northern Fur Seal, *Callorhinus ursinus,* Eastern Pacific Population

(Pribilof Islands, Alaska, and San Miguel Island, California). In *Status, Biology, and Ecology of Fur Seals: Proceedings of an International Symposium and Workshop,* edited by J. P. Croxall and R. L. Gentry, pp. 9–21. NOAA Technical Report NMFS, 51. National Oceanic and Atmospheric Administration, Cambridge, Massachusetts.

1995 The Relationship of Several Environmental Indices to the Survival of Juvenile Male Northern Fur Seal *(Callorhinus ursinus)* from the Pribilof Islands. In *Climate Change and Northern Fish Populations,* edited by R. J. Beamish, pp. 317–327. Canadian Special Publication of Fisheries and Aquatic Sciences, 121.

Young, J. A.

2000 Range Research in the Far Western United States: The First Generation. *Journal of Range Management* 53:2–11.

Young, T. P.

2000 Restoration Ecology and Conservation Biology. *Biological Conservation* 92:73–83.

Yousef, N.

2001 Savage or Solitary: The Wild Child and Rousseau's Man of Nature. *Journal of the History of Ideas* 62:245–263.

Zeveloff, S. I., and F. R. Collett

1988 *Mammals of the Intermountain West.* University of Utah Press, Salt Lake City.

Zube, Ervin H.

1996 Management in National Parks: From Scenery to Science. In *Science and Ecosystem Management in the National Parks,* edited by W. L. Halvorson and G. E. Davis, pp. 11–22. University of Arizona Press, Tucson.

CONTRIBUTORS

Virginia L. Butler
Department of Anthropology
P.O. Box 751
Portland State University
Portland, OR 97207
butlerv @pdx.edu

Kenneth P. Cannon
Midwest Archaeological Center
100 Centennial Mall North
Federal Building, Room 474
Lincoln, NE 68508
ken_cannon@nps.gov

Molly Boeka Cannon
Midwest Archaeological Center
100 Centennial Mall North
Federal Building, Room 474
Lincoln, NE 68508
molly_cannon@nps.gov

Christyann M. Darwent
Department of Anthropology
330 Young Hall
One Shields Avenue
University of California
Davis, CA 95616-8522
cmdarwent@ucdavis.edu

John Darwent
Department of Anthropology
107 Swallow Hall
University of Missouri
Columbia, MO 65211-1440

Michael G. Delacorte
Department of Anthropology
California State University
Sacramento, CA 95819
delacorte@csus.edu

Michael A. Etnier
Department of Anthropology
Box 353100
University of Washington
Seattle, WA 98195
current address: National Marine Mammal Laboratory (F/AKC3)
7600 Sand Point Way Northeast
Seattle, WA 98115
Michael.Etnier@NOAA.gov

Judith L. Harpole
Department of Anthropology
107 Swallow Hall
University of Missouri
Columbia, MO 65211-1440

Susan S. Hughes
Department of Archaeology
University of Durham
South Road
Durham D41 3LE
United Kingdom
susan.hughes@durham.ac.uk

R. Lee Lyman
Department of Anthropology
107 Swallow Hall
University of Missouri
Columbia, MO 65211-1440
lymanr@missouri.edu

Mark E. Miller
Office of the Wyoming State Archaeologist
P.O. Box 3431

University of Wyoming
Laramie, WY 82071
mmiller@uwyo.edu

Paul H. Sanders
Office of the Wyoming State Archaeologist
P.O. Box 3431
University of Wyoming
Laramie, WY 82071
psande@state.wy.us

Dave N. Schmitt
Department of Anthropology
Washington State University
Pullman, WA 99164
taphos@gte.net

Thomas R. Whyte
Department of Anthropology
Appalachian State University
Boone, NC 28608-2016
whytetr@appstate.edu

Index